Witness and Memory

Witness and Memory

THE DISCOURSE OF TRAUMA

EDITED BY ANA DOUGLASS AND
THOMAS A. VOGLER

ROUTLEDGE
NEW YORK AND LONDON

Published in 2003 by
Routledge
29 West 35th Street
New York, NY 10001
www.routledge-ny.com

Published in Great Britain by
Routledge
11 New Fetter Lane
London EC4P 4EE
www.routledge.co.uk

10 9 8 7 6 5 4 3 2 1

Library of Congress Cataloging-in-Publication Data

Witness and memory : the discourse of trauma / edited by Ana Douglass and Thomas A.
Vogler.
    p. cm.
    Includes bibliographical references and index.
    ISBN 0-415-94454-6 — ISBN 0-415-94455-4 (pb.)
    1. Memory—Social aspects. 2. Memory—Political aspects. 3. Witnesses. 4. Psychic
trauma. 5. History—Psychological aspects. 6. Social perception. 7. Social psychology. I.
Douglass, Ana, 1966- II. Vogler, Thomas A., 1937-

BF378.S65.W58 2003
302'.12—dc21

2002036924

This book
is dedicated to
Hayden White
Historian
Theorist
Critic
Teacher
and
Friend
Non Pareil

Contents

Preface

This project got its start in two graduate seminars (Twentieth Century Poetry and Anthropological Approaches to Literature) at Rutgers University. The Rodney King video had thrust the country into a very public debate on racism and on our collective denial of the degree of institutionalized racism in America. In these two seminars, there were 20 students from various disciplines and interests, each preparing to start a dissertation, each teaching writing or some other entry level subject to a diverse student population at a large public university. It was not until we saw King's body being beaten, in a video that insisted we all bear witness to that beating, and then heard a mind-boggling verdict that dismissed entirely what we believed we had witnessed, that we had to consider—not necessarily reject—but simply consider our training, our personal and professional ethics, our place in a public discussion of such an astonishing cycle of events. How did we reconcile our theoretical models with the daily occurrence of violence and trauma in the world? The Los Angeles uprising was the daily backdrop to our discussions. In two otherwise distinct seminars, we argued with one another over the same issues: the role of the witness in our respective disciplines, the act of bearing witness in a poststructuralist age that seemingly (but only seemingly) forgets the body in favor of a fascination with language, the significance of "truth" and "lies" and the facile interchanging of them.

It would be some years later, after some more highly traumatic and equally public events—the O.J. Simpson trial, the bombings of the World Trade Center and the Federal Building in Oklahoma City, Waco, and on an international front, the Rwandan and Balkan genocides, the Gulf War and the endless violence in the Middle East, 9/11—that we were able to assemble the essays included in this collection.

Acknowledgments

Harriet Davidson and Marc Manganaro deserve special thanks for initiating the discussion of witness in their seminars and for believing in this project from its inception. We owe an enormous debt to James Clifford, Berel Lang, Murray Baumgarten, and Hayden White, each of whom provided invaluable feedback during the various stages of the project, and to John Lynch, Michael Warren, Harry Berger, Jr., Margaret Brose, Nate Mackey, David Hoy, and other colleagues whose humanizing presence made the academic workplace more bearable. We would also like to thank each of the contributors for believing in and for embracing the interdisciplinary nature of this project, and Priti Gress, Salwa Jabado, Ben McCanna and Paul Foster Johnson at Routledge, for their invaluable support in its production. The anonymous readers of the manuscript went far beyond routine duty, and their suggestions and meticulous critiques were as welcome as their praise. Thanks too to Rita Kerestezi, whose help with Hungarian was invaluable at a crucial point and, finally, to those near and dear ones who make life worth living: Mary-Kay, Josie, Steve, Liz, Bill, Emma [RIP], Foxy, and Blanco.

Introduction

Even a God needs a witness.
                        —Maurice Blanchot, *Le Dernier Homme*

Our primary goal as editors of this collection of essays is to suggest a wider range for the notion of witness studies than that found in more specialized approaches, and to explore by means of a set of previously unpublished essays some of its more salient aspects. Our hope is that by including fields as diverse as Holocaust studies, the Latin American *testimonio,* and atomic bomb survivor studies together with approaches ranging from the historical and anthropological to the literary and philosophical, and considering a range of genres and media, we might indicate the richness and diversity of the current attention being devoted to the topic of witness—broadly conceived, yet still from a primarily North American perspective. James Young has suggested that "historical inquiry" should be "the combined study of both *what happened* and *how it is passed down* to us" (this volume, 283). To that we add the study of *what we are doing with it now,* which is the nature of our concern here under the rubric of witness discourse in general and, more specifically, trauma discourse. We use the term "discourse" in the material sense of institutional practice, where the signs of a discourse include texts ascribed to it, conferences and symposia dedicated to it, theorists and critics who claim to practice it, academic curricula that study it, museums devoted to it, and cultural productions of all kinds that invoke it as referent or exploit its semiotic potential. According to Foucault, to study "the overall 'discursive fact' " is "to account for the fact that it is spoken about, to discover who does the speaking, the position and viewpoints from which they speak, the institutions which prompt people to speak about it and which store and distribute the things that are said" (1978a: 11). We cannot attempt so ambitious a project here, but we do want to offer an introductory map of some current positions in witness/trauma discourse. The sheer quantity of critical attention and cultural resources devoted to the Holocaust in the U.S. make it a useful paradigm for the discourse on witness in general and on trauma discourse more specifically. Hence we will draw heavily on Holocaust studies for examples, but with an emphasis on typicality rather than uniqueness. And since there is still a widespread claim for the uniqueness of the Holocaust as historical event, we will be somewhat critical of this historical/theoretical position.

In courts of law, where the referent of narrative is supposed to reign supreme, competing narrative discourses struggle in adversarial combat to produce "the facts," or the story of "what really happened." What is allowed to enter the discourse is based not solely on what happened but also on the rules of "evidence" that determine what the jury is allowed to hear. It is not only the narrative referent that counts but the proper construction and presentation of stories. Things are different in witness/trauma discourse, where each conceptual point on the map is a contested site, even though some points are frequently taken by commentators as transparently given in one sense or another. "Memory," for example, may be the same as "history" for one writer, and completely different for another. "Collective memory" or "public memory" may be employed as self-evident, unproblematic categories by some and denied by others, who limit memory to the individual consciousness. Recovery of "repressed memory" may be seen as a foundation for experiential reality, or the product of a fiction-making faculty.

In a century of atrocities and a world increasingly marked by traumatic shocks to human bodies and minds, we are faced with an extreme challenge to understand both the causes and the motives that lead humans to perpetuate violence on other human beings, and the nature of the effects of that violence on human subjects and on their ability to function meaningfully as witnesses. To speak of a "crisis of witness" in this context is redundant, since trauma witness inevitably occurs in a crisis zone. It is in the nature of a physical *trauma* ("wound" in Greek) to violate and impair the normal functioning of the body; and it is by definition in the nature of a mental, trauma to exceed and violate our normal mental processing ability and frames of reference. The more massive the traumatic impact, the more it will affect our ability to register it. In a psychological version of the Heisenberg uncertainty principle, human subjectivity is implicated in and essential to that which we seek to understand—both part of the problem and our means to finding an answer.

There is a stage where discourses begin to become self-conscious, aware

that they have not in fact finally achieved theoretical certainty and an ultimate unmasking of the Truth, but are only the embodiment of particular
perspectives at a particular moment in history. There are increasing signs
that we are reaching such a stage in what can broadly be conceived as a discourse of witness, with an increasing production of books and articles that
locate themselves *outside* of the "Holocaust industry" or "*Shoah* business,"
and try to discuss witness as a cultural and intellectual phenomenon. Concerns about the politics of discourse and its regulation by the academic
marketplace, about a possible displacement of Judaic Studies by Holocaust
Studies, and about academic opportunism and exploitation are emerging.[1]
In the 1990s a note of criticism and self-questioning began to appear in the
academic enthusiasm for Latin American *testimonio*, identified by Enrico
M. Santi as "Latinamericanism" (by analogy with Edward Said's "Orientalism") as yet another mode of colonial domination, where "implicit sympathy for the material plight of the people in whose country they do research
provides the moral justification of their work," and as yet another "attempt
to position the European in a superior relation to a non-European people
and culture" (94). Santi calls for the kind of epistemological self-questioning that has entered the discipline of cultural anthropology largely through
the work of James Clifford. The growth and refinements in the field of
comparative genocide studies have strongly challenged claims for the
Holocaust's uniqueness, and have begun to implicate other countries than
Germany in the perpetration of atrocities. Studies of Hiroshima, and of
"atomic bomb literature" are increasing Western awareness of the Japanese
holocaust, its consequences, and literature.[2]

We do not maintain that there is an Archimedean point "outside" the
discourse of witness from which one can survey the whole field in a
metadiscourse of theoretical certainty. But we do think that it is possible
and desirable to engage in the discourse with a more self-conscious understanding of what we are doing and its relationship to what others are doing.
As part of this effort towards self-conscious understanding, we preface this
collection with a quick historical sketch of the recent past of our intellectual history, during which we have seen the "linguistic turn" in academic
theory give way to a "narrative turn" and a "return of the represented" as
well as an "ethical turn," with analogous developments in all forms of cultural production. As a collateral development, we note an increasing recognition that many sub-discourses can be understood as special instances of
larger issues and concerns—that we are in fact wrestling with a few key
conceptual and cultural issues that manifest themselves in a wide variety of
forms. We will argue, for example, that there is a chronotopic relationship
between events like the opening of the Yale Video Archive, the release of the
film *Blade Runner*, and the publication of *I, Rigoberta Menchú*, all in the

same year, and between these events and the establishment in Japan at the same time of the Kataru Kai association and the Assembly of Witnessing (*Shogen no Tsudoi*), both emphasizing the identity of their members as *survivors* who had *active* roles as witnesses, in a strong reaction against the collective and reductive identity imposed on the survivors of the atomic bomb as passive victims.

We will also point out some key similarities in problems related to acts of witness: how to deal with trauma and atrocity, how to "remember" or "memorialize" it when all live witnesses are dead, how to move from the individual voice to a collective one, from an era of active witness to history, problems of forgetting and forgiving, of reparations and punishment and finally, inevitably, how to deal with the opportunistic vultures of commercialism, trivialization, vulgarization, self-deception, and downright fraud. Our hope is that these observations can point towards a more self-conscious sense of the temporal dimension in which our timeless Truths always turn out to have been discovered. There is increasing evidence that we are approaching what promises to be a comparative interdisciplinary discourse on trauma and witness, where the different aspects of a complex subject may be brought together in a reciprocally enlightening way. It is possible that what we are participating in is an epicycle in a larger historical movement, or a familiar swing of the pendulum in the eternal Western metaphysical opposition between the two poles of human existence and intellectual activity. It is not as spectacular as Marx's presumed inversion of the Hegelian dialectic, a teleological shift from Geist to materiality, but it is a similar move nonetheless. It may be more on the order of an "adjustment" comparable to that earlier in the twentieth century, when extremes of modernist experimentation combined with socio-economic crises to provoke something like "Social Realism" in the USSR, what the Germans called the *Neue Sachlichkeit*, the documentary movement in England, and in the U.S. a combination of all of these.[3]

The last two decades have seen the emergence of a new object of study in the human sciences, one that seemingly reconciles the opposition between the poststructuralist emphasis on the text, with the real understood as an effect of representation, and "the real" understood as an event marked by trauma. In the 1970s Derrida's famous battle cry "nothing outside the text" resonated with Barthes' insistence that the human sciences, needing a new object all their own rather than borrowing from an already-established discipline, should adopt "the text" as its special object (1972: 1–5). Foucault pointed out that the textual paradigm and a structuralist model for analysis combined to form "the most systematic effort to evacuate the concept of the event, not only from ethnology, but from a whole series of other sciences and in the extreme case from history." In that context, "The event is what always escapes our rational grasp, the domain of 'absolute contingency'; we are thinkers who analyze structures, history is no concern of ours, what could we be expected to say about it" (1980: 114, 80). Driven underground in the poststructuralist moment, the "real" has returned to mainstream discourse like the Freudian repressed, this time as the traumatic event. "History is what hurts," Fredric Jameson wrote in 1982, and the traumatic event, now the paradigm for the historical event, is what hurts by definition. The traumatic event bears a striking similarity to the always absent signified or referent of the poststructuralist discourse, an object that can by definition only be constructed retroactively, never observed directly. Even so, this elusive object now serves as paradigm for the indexically signified real of much of our historical and ethical commentary. Baudrillard was fond of reminding us that, under the old model for the real event, "the very definition of the real becomes: *that of which it is possible to give an equivalent reproduction.* . . . The real is not only what can be reproduced, but *that which is always already reproduced*" (1983: 146). Insofar as the real was that which met and satisfied our anticipations, it was always perceived under *a priori* expectations in a mode of mental "reproduction." By contrast the traumatic event, as that which violates expectations and traumatizes the perceiving subject, is that which cannot be anticipated or reproduced. It thus allows a return to the real without the discredited notions of transparent referentiality often found in traditional modes of historical discourse. This combination of the simultaneous undeniable reality of the traumatic event with its unapproachability offers the possibility for a seeming reconciliation between the undecidable text and the ontological status of the traumatic event as an absolute signified.

I. Memory and Trauma

> It is because we have disappeared *today* . . . that we want to prove we died between 1940 and 1945, at Auschwitz or Hiroshima—that, at least, was real history [*une histoire forte*].
>
> —Jean Baudrillard,
> *La transparence du mal: essai sur les phénomènes extrêmes*

The early 1980s saw the beginning of an academic boom in memory studies, stimulated in part by two books that valorized memory as a primitive or sacred form of experiential knowledge and opposed it to modern historical consciousness. In *Zakhor: Jewish History and Jewish Memory*, Yosef Yerushalmi argued that modern Jewish historiography can never replace an eroded group memory. Pierre Nora, in "Entre mémoire et histoire," asserted that archaic modes of being associated with memory were destroyed by intellectual abstractions, and observed that we talk about memory so much because there is so little of it left. These works were extremely popular and the end of the decade, as Kerwin Klein points out, saw "the crystallization of a self-conscious memory discourse" (127) with the founding of the *History and Memory* journal and the translation of Nora's essay into English for a special issue of *Representations* on "Memory and Counter-Memory" (Spring 1989). Meanwhile scholars in fields like literature and anthropology and art began invoking memory as a way to critique the totalizing mode of conventional historical discourse, and to venture more boldly into historicism. During the 1980s the average age of the survivors of the Holocaust and of the Hiroshima/Nagasaki bombings reached the sixties. That same period saw a rising concern in the U.S. and Japan for the imminent loss of a generation that would take with it all the unrecorded memories that comprised its witnessing of history, and in particular its experience of the holocaustal events of the mid-century. In the U.S., Alzheimer's became the most dreaded disease of middle-class Americans in their sixties, and by some fascinating quirk, the affliction of the president who occupied the White House for most of the 1980s.

Starting in the early 1980s in Japan, survivors of the atomic bomb began much more actively taking on the role of *hibakusha* as active witnesses or storytellers.[4] Lisa Yoneyama identifies 1982 as a year in which the media in Japan paid unprecedented attention to Hiroshima and Nagasaki, and notes that statistics on the rate of publications devoted to "8.6" (*Hachu roku*, August 6), went from 400 per year to over 1000 per year and continued at that rate for the next decade. The following year, a fifteen-volume *Atomic-Bomb Literature in Japan* collection was published, its goal to guarantee that fiction chronicling the nuclear holocaust not be forgotten. This important reference work amounts to what John Treat calls "the de facto canon of Japanese atomic criticism" (357). In January of 1982 the most widely hailed example of the Latin American *testimonio* genre came into being, as Rigoberta Menchú narrated her version of revolutionary struggle and atrocities in Guatemala to Elisabeth Burgos-Debray, a Venezuelan anthropologist, in Paris. Another significant event of 1982 was the opening of the Yale Video Archive, one of a rapidly growing number of such collections, part of what Henry Greenspan called "a modern crusade" to collect and distribute survivor testimony in the greatest possible quantity (59). By common consent the most important moment in the entry of the Holocaust into general American consciousness had occurred a few years before in April 1978, with the NBC presentation of the miniseries *Holocaust*. Close to 100 million Americans watched all or most of the four-part, 9½-hour program. While this introduced many to the existence of the Holocaust for the first time, it brought home to others an urgent need to document the realities of

Holocaust experience lest they be replaced by such unsatisfactory versions. Geoffrey Hartman attributes the Holocaust documentary archive movement directly to the series, but in a negative way. It struck the survivors as "a sanitized and distorted version of what they had suffered," prompting them to a sense of urgency in leaving their testimony. "So many lost their lives, will their life story too be taken away? was the complaint. Any survivor could tell a history more true and terrible in its detail, more authentic in its depiction" (1996: 21, 143).

It is not surprising that cultural productions meant for wide consumption should echo such concerns. The 1980s in particular saw frequent artistic expressions of a sadness at the inevitable decay of human memory, among them none more aggressively poignant than the final image of the "replicant" Roy Baty, in *Blade Runner* (1982), dying after only four years of life. In cyborg and android films the non-humans often display more emotions than the humans, and this postmodern classic is no exception. Like all the replicants in the film, Roy began his life not with the blank memory slate of a human consciousness, but with a rich store of memories constituting a past that was not "his," a synthesized construct designed to give him the realistic effect of a human identity. After four years Roy has presumably acquired memories that are truly his, and he may be on the brink of an identity transformation; but it is "time to die," and he can only lament the utter dissolution of his precious treasures:

> I've seen things you people wouldn't believe. Attack ships on fire off the shores of Orion. I watched sea beams glitter in the dark near the Tannhaüser Gate. All those moments will be lost in time like tears in rain. Time to die.

Roy's is a fate destined for all humans, but in its historical context it takes on a number of conflicting allegorical dimensions. Ridley Scott based his film on Philip K. Dick's 1968 novel, *Do Androids Dream of Electric Sheep?*, in which the author imagines a complete loss of terrestrial reality, as mechanical simulacra replace all "natural" objects and threaten to replace all humans left on the earth. Scott includes strong hints that even Deckard may be a replicant without knowing it, and by extension that the replicant status is the norm for human existence. If memory is the core of our unique personal identity, then when we die the precious moments of our existence will be lost. The pathos of this vision may blind us—as it seemed to blind Roy—to the ways in which his individuality is *already* lost. If he lives, there is no way he can keep those memories that are uniquely his separate from those programmed into him, because they all feel equally real. If the replicants of the 1980s were those with "false memory syndrome," then they were presumably a small number, but their status as replicants was "real." And to the degree that each individual memory is—or may be—socially constructed, every individul has the uncanny potential for being a replicant without knowing it.[5] The shudder that we feel on realizing that Deckard may be a replicant is a shudder about our own precious memory-based identity, that also may already be lost—like tears in rain.

Extension of these considerations to survivors of traumatic events, and to Holocaust survivors and "8.6" survivors, raises the same issues. The precious individuality of each survivor will be lost on death, but is already compromised unknowingly by information and impressions acquired after the "original" experience. We might also consider the sad case of Benjamin Wilkomirski, whose vivid account of childhood Holocaust trauma in the "autobiographical" *Bruchstücke* (*Fragments*) has recently been exposed as fake, showing how difficult such determinations can be.[6] Lacking anything he could feel as a "real" identity, the self-named Wilkomirski apparently faked it, or "remembered" it, and wrote down the memories he insists are really real and really his. A genuine replicant, he is living with identity-forming memories that are not "his" in the conventional sense. Unlike Jerzy Kosinski, who was probably a deliberate fraud, and Araki Yasusada (the celebrated *hibakusha* poet) who was a good-humored hoax, Wilkomirski may be truly self-deceived. If we ask how such a book could be taken as an authentic embodiment of Holocaust memory, even a "model" of that memory, the answer is simple. He made himself a replicant by following the models, recycling and imitating the discourse. Like Helen in the second book of Goethe's *Faust*, who was recognized as the real thing because she looked just like her pictures, Wilkomirski's book was pre-inscribed in the discourse.

Roy's elegiac mood is shared by another cultural monument of the 1980s, William Gibson's *Neuromancer* trilogy. The second volume of this "cyberpunk" opus, *Count Zero*, appropriates the idea of the Cornell box to generate both its quest motif (Andrea's search for the maker of the boxes) and its climax of recognition.[7] Early in the work Andrea, an art gallery employee, encounters representations of seven of the boxes and asks herself: "How could anyone have arranged these bits, this garbage, in such a way that it caught at the heart, snagged in the soul like a fishhook?" At the end she confronts the maker of the boxes not as a human, but as a "process" in which the manipulators of an electronic robot pick through the swirl of things that they also cause, "grasping and rejecting, the rejected objects whirling away, striking others, drifting into new alignments . . . gently, slowly, perpetually." Andrea addresses the robot in a penultimate moment of recognition: "You are someone else's collage. . . . Someone brought the machine here, welded it to the dome, and wired it to the traces of memory.

And spilled, somehow, all the worn sad evidence of a family's humanity, and left it all to be stirred, to be sorted by a poet. To be sealed away in boxes. I know of no more extraordinary work than this" (227). This is a good example of the pervasive association of memory with what Kerwin Klein calls a "picturesque body of objects" designed to represent the decaying contents of memory: "Ideally, the memory will be a dramatically imperfect piece of material culture, and such fragments are best if imbued with pathos. Such memorial tropes have emerged as one of the common features of our new cultural history where in monograph after monograph, readers confront the abject object; photographs are torn, mementos faded, toys broken" (135–36).

A) Traumatized Bodies and Minds

As if in an anthology of Greek fables from the House of Atreus, our present is shadowed by the past that we carry with us in our bodies and our psyches, in the form of repressed memories of childhood abuse, combat trauma, or Holocaust trauma. Almost anyone, it seems, may be vulnerable to retrieved information, perhaps insignificant in the past but now fraught with deferred consequence. Seemingly decent fathers find themselves contending with daughters and wives over who controls the story of their family's past, consulting the False Memory Syndrome Foundation to counteract the therapists and cognitive psychologists and the effects of sodium amytal. The psychological notion of a "return of the repressed" is matched in our time by a growing awareness of physical counterparts in the form of exposure to toxic substances, the belated effects of chemical ingestion, silicone implants, solar exposure, first- and second-hand tobacco smoke, HIV or Hepatitis C that can remain dormant for years before making a devastating strike, or severe postpolio sequelae that threaten the two million epidemic survivors decades later. The atomic bombs dropped on Hiroshima and Nagasaki produced instant death for hundreds of thousands, but their radioactive script continues to be inscribed in a genetic legacy for a second and third generation. As we were preparing this volume for publication, the horror we now call 9/11 was added to 8.6. Like 8.6 the events of 9/11 seemed to transpire in an amazingly brief moment of time, and like 8.6 the full consequences will take their toll over decades. Unlike 8.6, the full effects of which were kept in secrecy by the U. S. for many years, the inaugural events of 9/11 were made dramatically visible to hundreds of millions of viewers, producing a plenitude of mediatized witnesses, with the effect of secondary trauma in unknowable numbers. A less spectacular but equally hideous counterpart of modern warfare is the legacy of landmines left behind armed conflicts as a form of Western largesse to the Third World.[8]

Keats said of Shakespeare that he lived a life of allegory and that his works were comments on that life. As the discourse of witness continues to develop we can see that the life of the witness is an allegorical site, with a range of possible meanings already mapped out. The relationship between an event and its witnesses is symbiotic and circular. Acts of witness are required to establish an event as worthy of witnessing. The "event" that interpellates its witnesses must be an atrocity, inflicting on them a trauma that makes them members of that category. Since Freud's inaugural investigations of "shell-shock" in World War I, the study of psychological trauma as a cultural phenomenon and the discourse on trauma in medical ethnography have grown to a stage in the United States that can appropriately be called the "trauma industry."[9]

The standard dynamic of trauma makes the traumatized subject the passive recipient of the traumatic event, in categories that have moved beyond victim/survivor to include "onlooker trauma" (the effect of witnessing a traumatic event) and "secondary PTSD" (the post-traumatic stress disorder a therapist may get from treating a traumatized patient) to "transgenerational trauma" (descendants of trauma victims, ranging from Holocaust survivors and those of colonial regimes, slavery, apartheid, and "ethnic cleansing" to persons "living with AIDS"). As this range of traumata suggests, there is no special kind of event that provokes a traumatized reaction; nor is there a universal sensitivity to stress that produces uniform reactions to similar events. Just as the experience of physical pain may manifest differently in different subjects, the pathogenic traumatic experience of one person is an interpretive construct that may not be shared by another, even in identical situations. Mark Micale points out that it is not the physical injury *per se*, or even the emotional shock, but "rather the mental experiencing of it, the affective and ideational processing of the event, that constitutes the psychological trauma" (1995: 7). The process of witness depends heavily on cultural values and meanings, and changes in the cultural context have contributed significantly to changes in the discourse of witness in recent years.

Most commentators rely on some notion of traumatic impact on the witness/survivor, but these notions are often unexamined assumptions based on general conceptions of human nature and memory. Experts who have studied post-traumatic stress have come up with three general areas of agreement. First, trauma can indeed exert its effects long after its first impact, producing symptoms that are often disguised or symbolic in their manifestations, and that can also be somatic. The effects frequently include what therapists call "dissociation," a disorientation of the thinking process and panic at being possessed by what seems to be unthinkable, along with a loss of the ability to trust in any grounds for conventional reality. Second, post-traumatic stress carries what Herman calls "vicarious traumatization" (140–47) that functions like a contagion, capable of arousing symptoms in therapists and others exposed to the witness/survivor. Third, Freud's insistence, in *Beyond the Pleasure Principle*—that there need be no direct connection between trauma and an originating event, that where many subjects experience the same event, only some may develop a trauma linked to it, and that trauma can be experienced when the event did not happen—must be kept in mind when considering a specific case. Meanwhile, there continues to be much controversy over the reality and mechanism of "repressed memory." In *The Myth of Repressed Memory*, Loftus and Ketcham critique the 1980s enthusiasm for traumatic amnesia, challenging the truth of recovered memories, demonstrating that patients can learn to exhibit symptoms that conform to their therapists' expectations. They are part of a more general reaction to the PTSD enthusiasm and share a psychological perspective that does not think memory works in the simplistic mechanical fashion so often assumed in cases of recovered memory.[10]

Potential confusion is increased by the fact that there are two distinctive theoretical paradigms for psychic trauma. In *Trauma: A Genealogy*, Ruth Leys identifies these as the "mimetic" and the "anti-mimetic." Although overly reductive, the distinction is suggestive in useful ways. In the mimetic version, the traumatic experience results in an ongoing process of imitation, where the victim is compelled to imitate or even act out the painful event. The most common view here is that "the repetitive reliving of the traumatic experience must represent a spontaneous, unsuccessful attempt at healing" (Herman 44). Such theories lead to questions about the reliability of any acts of witness by such victims, because they are in a perpetual state of suggestibility and highly susceptible to influence from a therapist. For the anti-mimetic theories, trauma may severely damage a subject's psyche, but it does not necessarily interfere with the ability to remember the event or with the reliability and accuracy of recovering the actual past experience. These paradigms appear in two recognizable forms for witness discourse. On the one hand, there is a widespread view that witness/survivors are by definition traumatized by their experience, and that they exhibit the effects of trauma in the broken, incoherent nature of their acts of witness, which functions as authenticating sign for their testimony. This is prevalent in the Anglo-European community of trauma discourse. On the other hand, the assumption of a coherent ego and the reliability of language and the narrative trope are more prevalent in the Latin American *testimonio* and the Japanese *hibakusha* narratives.[11]

The notion that authority and authenticity are grounded in traumatic stories has become so pervasive that all of Western culture can now be seen as a post-traumatic narrative: "The genesis stories make history itself post-traumatic: an original injury endlessly re-experienced, so that all being is stained by that originary guilt and dread, and rescued through divine grace" (Farrell 44). Trauma offers itself everywhere as an antidote to the "triviality of daily life in late capitalism" and the answer to Fredric Jameson's problem, "how to project the illusion that things still happen, that events exist, that there are still stories to tell, in a situation in which the uniqueness and the irrevocability of private destinies and of individuality itself seem to have evaporated? This impossibility of realism—and more generally, the impossibility of a living culture which might speak to a unified public about shared experience—determines the metageneric solutions with which we began" (1992: 87). While individual trauma confers individual identity, the function of trauma as a "social glue" holds groups together on the basis of ethnicity, gender, race, sexual orientation, disease, or handicap. Hilene Flanzbaum has pointed out the increasing tendency in identity politics to assume "that learning about one's heritage automatically entails the glorification of suffering, as if without proving the persistence of persecution you cannot legitimate your claim to minority, or ethnic, status" (14). Trauma has been so successful in this function, as both individual and group identities are increasingly based on historical instances of victimization, that we may eventually need a new psychoanalytic term, "trauma envy," to describe those left behind.

Although most of trauma discourse is concerned with the psychological consequences of trauma, it is anchored in the conviction that special truths can manifest themselves in traumatized bodies. The force of the violated body as witness to the exercise of power is carried over to the violated psyche, with its analogous but invisible scars. As Hal Foster notes, "The insistence on the factuality of the body as against the fantasy of transcendence in spectacle, virtual reality, cyberspace, and the like" is "very different from the postmodern delight in the image world where it was often assumed that the real had succumbed to the simulacral" (1996a: 114). Traditionally in the West the human body has represented "the ultimate visual compendium, the comprehensive method of methods, the organizing structure of structures. As a visible natural whole made up of invisible dissimilar parts, it was the organic paradigm or architectonic standard for all complex unions. Whether ideal or caricatured, perfect or monstrous, it formed the model for proper or improper man-made assemblies and artificial compositions" (Stafford 12). As Peter Brown argues in *The Body and Society*, it was possible to ground most of the West's dualistic theological, legal, medical, and aesthetic notions on the supposition of the body's integrity and rectitude. Trauma discourse continues the practice of grounding concepts and reality in the body, but now it is the body as the primary site of what Julia Kristeva has called the "abject."

The traumatized body is part of a context in which there was a turn towards interest in and evocation of "the body as referent" (David Harvey's phrase), as a category with a material basis for anchoring important aspects of "the truth" of human existence and identity. The status and our understanding of "the body" became central to theoretical debate in a number of areas, as questions of gender, sexuality, the symbolic order and psychoanalysis, collective identities of all kinds, repositioned the body as subject to debate, and as both object and subject of discussion. As David Lowe observed:

> There still remains one referent apart from all the other destabilized referents, whose presence cannot be denied, and that is the body referent, our very own lived body. This body referent is in fact the referent of all referents, in the sense that ultimately all signifieds, values, or meanings refer to the delineation and satisfaction of the needs of the body. Precisely because all other referents are now destabilized, the body referent, our own body, has emerged as a problem. (14)

The "body" proved to be a fruitful site not only for theoretical debate, challenging the tyranny of scientific, social, political, economic, sexual, and biological abstractions, but for resistance and emancipatory politics as well. It promised a new and more authentic "grounding" of our epistemological and ontological intellectual activities and of our very Being. It energized new directions in the arts, and as the visible—or representable—site of trauma it proved an increasingly important signifier in all areas of the discourse of witness. The body can signify even in, or by, its absence, like the infamous "disappearing" signifier in Latin American regimes, or the even more spectacular non-body count of the 1991 non-war with Iraq.[12]

As the tendency to redefine individual and collective and historical experience in terms of trauma engaged artistic and theoretical culture, it swept through popular culture as well. Inevitably it proved the occasion for academic opportunism and excess, and the opportunity for trivialization in the wider world of cultural production. Starting in the late 1980s, the Anglo-American world of fashion advertising and fashion pictorials saw the entry of ads that featured a raw unstudied look in the photography and a dislocated and distressed look for the models. Steven Meisel (especially for Calvin Klein) populated his commercial work with ravaged faces and bodies that seem to be trying to escape from his seamless white backdrops. Juergen Teller (German-born, London-based) featured depressed figures in depressed surroundings. Corinne Day took the British youth-oriented markets by storm, earning a reputation as the photographer of grunge. A good example of this spread can be found in the Benetton ads of the early 1990s. They were opportunistically and successfully designed to push the trauma-as-style fashion to its limits, recycling stark news photographs for commercial purposes. One of the most controversial examples featured an AIDS victim (*not* a "survivor" or a PWA) and his weeping family, using a photograph first published in *Life* magazine, guaranteeing a base in the "real" by combining subject matter and photojournalistic technique. Vicki Goldberg's verdict on the practice seems just: "Benetton has given us what we should have expected and probably deserve: images of catastrophe as corporate ballyhoo" (33). In 1991 Cindy Sherman, whose work in the 1980s was based largely on imitations of fashion models, fairy tale illustrations, and art history portraits, reflected a similar shift. She began creating disaster images, scenes suffused with menstrual blood and sexual discharge, vomit and excrement, decay and death, joining what Hal Foster has called "the shit movement in contemporary art" (1996a: 118). Another growth industry in the last two decades is "Corpse Art," involving the photography of corpses, with artists like Rosamond Purcell, Jeffrey Silverthorne, Joel-Peter Witkin, Rudolf Schäfer, Gwen Akin and Allan Ludwig among the notable practitioners.[13] A comparison could also be made here with conspicuous changes in "stock photography," a commodity used since the 1920s to provide cheap marketing clichés that are instantly recognizable for magazines, advertising, and publications like annual reports and industrial brochures. FPG International, one of the largest photography houses, released a new stock photo catalogue in the mid-1990s called *Real Life*, that claims to be informed by the current atmosphere of "social upheaval, shifting values, and an environment on the brink of collapse." Instead of images of the happy consumer utopia of the 1950s–1980s, the cliché experts are pushing a form of "social realism" that features staged violence, street people, drug abuse, abundant sex. As Andrea Codrington points out "the 'real life' to which the title refers is the reality of market research, fed back to the consumer via ersatz commercial experience" (101).

B) But Is It Memory?

Nothing is more important for trauma discourse than the faculty of memory, yet nothing is so confused and confusing as the concepts of memory and their deployment that are at play in the discourse at this time. Perhaps nowhere are there more unexamined assumptions and unargued assertions than in the memory business, and few issues are as ideologically charged.[14] Among the terms one can find used as if they were in no way problematic are:

> memory, counter-memory, common memory, deep memory, post-memory, anti-memory, individual memory, repressed memory, so-

cial memory, socially constructed memory, public memory, collective memory, cultural memory, memorial practice, memorial consciousness, real memory, mythic memory, memory talk, memory industry, politics of memory.

Each of these conceptual terms marks at least one site of contestation, yet they are constantly deployed as if they had fixed, agreed on meanings and referred to aspects of experience that were unproblematic. Even though we still do not fully understand how individuals recall past events, or have a foolproof way to distinguish false memories from authentic ones, many simply assume that clinical vocabularies developed for the individual psyche can be applied to the collective level, and that we can speak meaningfully about the memory of an ethnic, religious, or other group.

Whether the focus of a given commentator is on personal memory, collective memory, or history, some form of binary opposition will be part of the discourse. Even the individual, personal history is divided by difference. For some, it is the difference between remembering something and knowing about it, or between the retrieval of stored information and experience and the active putting together of a claim about the past by means of a shared cultural knowledge and understanding. There is the context in which the memory traces were presumably laid down, and the later context in which memories are "recovered" or narrated. The trauma survivor's memory can be seen as a battleground between what Saul Friedlander calls "common memory" (that tends towards restoration of coherence, closure, redemptive posture) and "deep memory" (inarticulate, without meaning, unrepresentable), where the persistent return of "deep memory" undermines the possibility of a coherent self founded on "common memory." The difference between individual or personal memory and group/collective memory can be an even more powerful point of ideological and philosophical difference, and the opposition between memory and history an equally divisive point in the discourse.

Although there are still those who use "memory" and "history" interchangeably, they are more often linked in opposition, but to two quite different ends. On the one hand, "memory" can be valorized as a mode of authentic knowledge based on direct experience, that can only be valid at the individual level, opposed to a notion of history as a collective discursive project, always mediated and inferior to authentic memory. This view became very fashionable in the 1980s, with "memory" functioning almost as an antonym for "history." On the other hand, the fact that "history" is distanced from the vagaries of an immediate experience tainted by subjective inflections means for some that "history" can be more objective and scientific than memory, a better source of knowledge than that provided by any particular memory source. One of the very few areas of general agreement is the belief that trauma provides a criterion of authenticity for the "real," and that memories not somehow defined and authenticated by trauma cannot be trusted. It is history only if it hurts. For many the Holocaust is the ultimate traumatic decentering of history and subjectivity, giving it a privileged and paradigmatic place in twentieth-century memory.

The politics of memory and history are not limited to academic discourse. There used to be a Soviet saying, "The past is even less predictable than the future." Orwell forcefully reminded us in *1984* that whoever controls records and memories controls the past. Perhaps Orwell did not anticipate the full extent to which a modern state can control the media technologies that *produce* events before they are recorded in individual memories and unofficial records. He certainly didn't anticipate the tumultuous current "memory industry" with contests that range from the museum trade to legal battles over repressed memory and into the academic book market. "Experience is at once always already an interpretation and is in need of interpretation. What counts as experience is neither self-evident nor straightforward; it is always contested, always therefore political" (Scott 797). Over against the notion of memory as factual raw data, we now understand memory as mediated on various levels and always "managed," both at the level of the individual psychic economy and the institutionalized circulation of discourse.

Before the recent expansionist moves in conceptions of memory, the most common notion of memory on the personal level was that of a conscious recurrence of some aspect of past experience, a continuous living available version of a past event. In the modern era memory emerged as the core of the psychological self, the key to personal identity. Like the Cartesian *cogito*, memory seemed to be the self-identifying existential activity of the individual mind, the essential mental condition: *memini ergo sum*. It was strongly reinforced by Greek, Judaic, Christian, and Enlightenment traditions that considered the individual subject to be the atom of society, and the fully conscious individual mind to be the ground of all knowledge and moral action and of human existence itself—a primary source of value in the form of unique individual identity and action that does not follow conventions or copy models. The fact was generally acknowledged that it can be increasingly difficult over time to distinguish between what one has actually experienced and what one has read, heard, or imagined about what happened in the past, yet without seeming to endanger the equation between memory and identity.

C) Collective Memory

Collective memory is at the same time more elusively metaphysical than personal memory, and more concretely embodied. In the past collective memory was constructed over time and stored in ritual forms of repetition such as prayers and memorial ceremonies, common stories or myths, and thus given what Pierre Nora calls a "memory-place" (*lieu de mémoire*) and a set of observances. What is "collectively" remembered is not in this sense the sum of isolated personal experiences but something that was an intensely *shared* communal experience, the sum of a collection of separate but similar individual experiences. If indeed this was the case, then it would presumably take time before memory could be selected and collectivized into such ritual modes. Now, on the other hand, we have a much more immediately materialized history, one that can even be fabricated and recorded on the spot by the modern media—making history come *before* collective memory rather than after. Advances in technology do not guarantee greater accuracy for collective memory, since those technologies can readily be manipulated by those in power. As Mark Osiel observes, "If collective memory can be created deliberately, perhaps it can be done only dishonestly, that is, by concealing this very deliberateness from the intended audience" (467). The controlled productions of the media during the 1991 Gulf War are a good example of this process, short-circuiting the more conventional sense of a gradual process of the "transformation of memory into history" (Vidal-Nacquet 1992: 57).

The use of "memory" for both ends of this process may be only a metaphoric bridge that tries to link two completely different things: the memory of an individual and the memory of a group or community of individuals. Amos Funkenstein warns that we must use the term "collective memory" carefully, since "only individuals are capable of remembering," but he also points out that all remembering occurs within social contexts. He uses an analogy with Saussurean linguistics to suggest that "collective memory" functions as *langue* while individual memory is like *parole*. Like language, memory "can be characterized as a system of signs, symbols, and practices: memorial dates, names of places, monuments and victory arches, museums and texts, customs and manners, stereotype images," and the act of remembering that takes place at the level of the individual subject is "the instantiation of these symbols, analogous to 'speech' " (6). This is an interesting theoretical reconciliation of the opposition between personal and collective memory but, like Saussurean structural linguistics, its synchronic formulation does not explain how things come to be in *langue*, or how they can change after finding a place there, and it would seem to eliminate altogether the notion of personal memory in its ordinary "originary" sense. Michael Schudson points out that it is common to consider memory as "a property of individual minds," but he argues that memory is "essentially social," that it is located in "rules, laws, standardized procedures, and records . . . books, holidays, statues, souvenirs." As Kerwin Klein observes, in this view "Memory is not a property of individual minds, but a diverse and shifting collection of material artifacts and social practices" (51).[15]

One can't go far in the various expositions of collective memory without encountering one of the most basic conflicts of self-identity in Western history and culture: the individual subject as monad vs. the group. Here the autonomous individual consciousness taken as the basic site of identity, meaning, and value, is opposed by the communitarians who praise and mourn their visions of lost communality, exhibiting what Christopher Lasch called *Gemeinschaftschmerz*, and criticizing contemporary individualism as a "culture of Narcissism" (Lasch again) or "liquid modernity" (Bauman). In a Marxist version of this position, Fredric Jameson has urged the existence of a "collective subjectivity" that can be found in "certain forms of storytelling . . . in testimonial literature" as opposed to the old "bourgeois ego" and the "schizophrenic subject" of contemporary society (Stephanson 21).

D) Memory and History

As collective memory and its values are opposed to the claims of individual memory on one side, on the other they are also frequently situated in opposition to history. Maurice Halbwachs, a pioneer theorist of collective memory who was killed at Buchenwald, viewed the collective memory as a "living deposit" preserved outside academic or written history. For him the advent of history marked the end of a golden age when history and collective memory were the same, when what was remembered was absorbed into ritual forms of repetition like prayers and memorial ceremonies. In his posthumously published *La mémoire collective* (probably written in the 1930s), he argues that history begins only at the point where tradition ends, at a moment where social memory is extinguished. The need to write an historical account of anything, whether a period, a society, a major event or an individual, comes only when a living connection with the past is no longer possible. Halbwachs' work is an important source for defenders of memory against history, like Yerushalmi, who contrasts the "documents" of history with the practice of ritual observances that stress the "eternal contemporaneity" of the past rather than its historicity. History in this view can only give us a multitude of constructed and often contradictory versions of the past, always understood as something that happened in a "then." It cannot help constitute the social, collective, communal identity that provides the most authentic ground for human existence by means of redemptive and integrative ritual and recital. But as Novick points out, there is "a circular relationship between collective identity and collective memory" (7), in which the memories help to constitute the sense of collective identity itself, even while it is the collective identity that makes such a mode of memory possible. The opposition here between the values associated with memory and those identified with history is another longstanding one in Western discourses. It especially resembles the opposition between "oral" societies and "print culture" as articulated by Walter Ong. The valorizing of the oral, with its face-to-face negotiations, involving facial expressions, gestures, and general physical context, was based on the notion that communication in such a context involves meanings transparent to the participants. Print culture moves away from these presumed virtues of "presence" into a language separated from its "origins" and the signifieds of its signifiers.[16] This fierce ideological and psychological opposition between memory and history is ignored by those Klein speaks for when he says, "We sometimes use memory as a synonym for history to soften our prose, to humanize it, and to make it more accessible. Memory simply sounds less distant, and perhaps for that reason, it often serves to help draw general readers into a sense of the relevance of history for their own lives" (129).

Finally, no discussion of memory would be complete without a consideration of forgetting. In Orwell's *1984*, the allegorical architecture of Winston's world is full of "memory holes" for the instantaneous disposal of unwanted records. The mechanism is as apt a trope for the constructions of individual memory and collective memory as it is for a document-based history. In all cases what is *not* remembered is as crucial for the economy of memory and for its contents as what is remembered. Except for the special case of "repressed" memory in traumatic experience, there has been little attention paid to the importance of forgetting in memory discourse. Although of major importance, it seems to be a conveniently forgettable topic.[17]

II. Events Happen

Events, past and present—not social forces and historical trends, nor questionnaires and motivation research . . . —are the true, the only reliable teachers of political scientists, as they are the most trustworthy source of information for those engaged in politics.

Hannah Arendt, *The Origins of Totalitarianism*

We will use the term "event" in what follows, because it is the dominant term in trauma discourse, perhaps the most frequently deployed and most ambiguous term of all, universally chosen to refer to *what really happens*. Whether it is described as an "ontological event" (Wiesel, Langer, others), an "absolute *novum*" (Katz), a "*mysterium tremendum*" (Cohen), a "limit event" (Friedlander, others), a "modernist event" (White) a "literal event"

(Lang) or a "postmodern event" (Lyotard, others), the authors are striving to formulate an ontologically definitive degree of "eventness." "Events happen, whereas facts are constituted by linguistic description," writes Hayden White, and "we must not confuse facts with events" (1999: 18). But to get that snappy bumpersticker phrase, "events happen," White must have forgotten that a few pages before he had written: "A failure of historical consciousness occurs *when one forgets that history, in the sense of both events and accounts of events, does not just happen but is made*" (13, italics added). Elsewhere, knowing that "event" will not do the job on its own, White does what we all do, invoking "a real event" or "an event that really happened" or "the events themselves" or "past real events," what Deleuze calls "the event as such" or "the pure event," to let his reader know that his referent is the real thing, the *Event-an-sich*. Perhaps we need a new word to designate what really happens, or even better, what really *happened*, because "The event is . . . always already in the past and yet to come" (Deleuze 143).

As it so happens, the verb "happen" contains its own redundant ontology; it is formed by adding a verb ending to the noun "hap," which means what happens (e.g., fortune, fate). To say "events happen," is to be even more redundant; since an event is "anything that happens," we are saying "things that happen, happen," reaching in words for "that which occurs insofar as it does occur," in our desire for "a category of very special things: events, pure events" (Deleuze 143, 1). But a "pure event" would be like the *tohu wa-bohu* of Genesis, "without form, and void" (another redundancy) before the Divine Logos constructed a world out of it. Human ontology is made in the likeness of the divine, for we too epistemologize on an abyss, with our human logos on one side and *stuff* on the other. We poke through the stuff to find bits we call "facts," to use as evidence to confirm the reality of the "event" we are using to make sense out of the stuff, a circular process that convinces us that there must have been an event there to begin with; otherwise how could we have understood it as such; and this still leaves open endless debates about the cause of the event, its extent, its consequences, whether it resembles other events, and so on.[18]

At the same time that "event" is used for the real *before* it's framed into perception and meaning, it is used for events that are "constructed" in their origin, among them the Holocaust, which has been under conspicuous construction for several decades now. The situation is reminiscent of the creation of the Farnese Tower in Stendhal's *The Charterhouse of Parma*. The citizens watch it being built over the course of many years, only to find on completion that it had always been there:

> The Prince who . . . built this prison visible from all parts of the country, had the singular design of trying to persuade his subjects

that it had been there for many years: that is why he gave it the name of *Torre Farnese*. It was forbidden to speak of the construction, and from all parts of the town of Parma and the surrounding plains people could perfectly well see the masons laying each of the stones. (298)

The Holocaust that we speak of today emerged slowly as a separable, singular, paradigmatic event from the overall course of the war and the deaths of 50 million people in that war. Familiar as it is now, it was unknown at the time.

In 1956–57 Hannah Arendt could survey "the human condition" without mentioning the Nazi genocide, and the inaugural book on the subject, Raul Hilberg's *The Destruction of the European Jews*, went years without a publisher, until the assistance of a private subvention allowed him to print it in 1961. Now considered the first classic study of "the Holocaust," the book did not use that term to identify its subject. As Hilberg explains, "In the beginning there was no Holocaust. When it took place in the middle of the twentieth century, its nature was not fully grasped" (1988a: 21). Primo Levi's first book, *Se questo è un uomo*, was rejected by several major publishers, then published in 1947 in a very small edition (2,500) by a company that promptly went out of business. It took over ten years before Einaudi published it in 1958. In 1969, *The American Heritage Dictionary* provided a five-word definition of "Auschwitz": "The German name for Oświęcim" (*sic*). There are no entries for Majdanek or Treblinka. Dachau, Belsen, and Buchenwald are each "the site of a German concentration camp," but "concentration camp" is defined as "a camp where prisoners of war, enemy aliens, and political prisoners are confined." "Laager" (*sic*) is defined as "a defensive encampment." There are no entries for death camp, Zyklon B, Muselmann, Kapo, Kristallnacht, SS, Birkenau, Canada, and other terms now associated with the Holocaust.

In 2002, studying the Holocaust is recommended or mandatory in public schools in at least 17 states, prominent in all entertainment media, the theme of many museums. It is the subject of a flood of articles and books and media presentations, and endowed chairs in Holocaust Studies multiply at colleges and universities across the country. According to Alvin Rosenfeld, there are "more than 100 Holocaust institutions throughout the United States and Canada . . . which are dedicated to educating the public about the Holocaust" (1997b: 137–38). In 1989, Annette Insdorf identified 125 fictional and documentary films based on the Holocaust, and as of 1993 there were almost fifty different Holocaust testimony archives in the U.S., with the Museum of Jewish Heritage in New York boasting a collection of over 80,000 hours. For many the Holocaust has become more central to American cultural life than the Civil War. In 1980 George Kren and

Leon Rappaport suggested that in a few years "the accumulation of items concerning the Holocaust—books, films, poems, articles, stories—will equal or exceed the total number that have been produced about any other subject in human history" (1). Twenty years later their prophecy seems more than fulfilled, and to their list of genres we can add the categories of memorials, monuments, museums, video testimony archives, and "virtual reality" death camp tours on CD-ROM discs.

Just as it took several decades for the Holocaust discourse to reach its current state of construction, the witness discourse on Hiroshima/Nagasaki has grown through a series of stages or generations. As John Treat points out, it moved from a first phase of "rupture," focused on problems of description and imagination, through a focus on technology, power and ethics as social and political issues, to a third, contemporary state where it has become part of a worldwide comparative discourse of witness—except that where studies of Hiroshima/Nagasaki invariably mention the Nazi genocide, the reverse is seldom the case. The U.S. experienced a perfect example of the event as deferred retrofit in the November national election of 2000. When was it over? And when it was over, was it over? Had it happened? Is it over yet? What really happened in one sense could only be determined by assembling all of the facts, in the form of many thousands of votes, and determining precisely what was the status of each, a task that can never be accomplished. Meanwhile, when we use "event" to designate events like the Nazi genocide, or World War I, or decolonization, the French Revolution, the Renaissance, the fall of the Roman Empire, the advent of modernization, the splitting of the atom, it should be obvious that events of such complexity will always be under construction.

Only certain events have the power to interpellate witnesses; in ordinary life we look at things or watch the passing scene, but we *witness* an accident or a crime, incidents that seem to demand action and reaction, decision or judgment, where exactly what happened and how it happened are matters of extreme urgency. In a murder trial the victim is equally dead, whether as the result of negligent homicide or murder in the first degree. In trauma discourse the comparable issue is whether the traumatic event should be restricted to human infliction of trauma, which tends inevitably to raise issues of evil and moral judgment, or to include "natural" events as well. Paul Ricoeur traces the distinction to what he describes as the earliest discursive responses to evil—*lament* and *blame*, where lament is provoked by suffering from external causes, while blame is a response when there is discernible human responsibility for the suffering (1995: 250). This is comparable to Primo Levi's distinction between "the lamenting tones of the victim" and "the irate voice of someone who seeks revenge" (1996: 382). Kant considered the sublime under two categories, whether the feeling is generated by the mind's confrontation with an overwhelming natural force, like that of a hurricane, or by an internal disturbance of our thought by something that resists conceptualization—what Thomas Weiskel calls the hermeneutical sublime.

This crucial difference is important for a better understanding of witness, and has little or nothing to do with the degree or intensity of the pain experienced. Elaine Scarry argues that we react differently to pain inflicted by human agents and to "the pain that has no human agent, such as certain forms of cancer pain or burn pain." These "are every bit as horrible for the person who suffers them, and yet, we can at least work to heal that pain, and no one's confused about whether it's a good or not. The idea that actually willfully inflicting those kinds and levels of pain—if there is such a thing as evil, then that is what it is" (Geddes 81). In criminal law it is the *mens rea* (mental state, intentionality) of the defendant that makes all the difference, not the degree of suffering of the victim. The difference between the accidental transmission of smallpox to the Native American population, and the distribution of blankets deliberately infected with the bacteria, is the difference between ignorance or carelessness and genocide.[19] We tend to contemplate the horror of AIDS with a perspective different from that for genocide. In either case a large amount of human misery, suffering, and death may occur, but our sense of agency tends to make us put them in different categories. Another difference is in the status of the victim. When victims are considered innocent, like children, the violation is considered more heinous because of their state ("innocent" = incapable of inflicting harm, from *in-* = not + *nocens*, present participle of *nocere*, to harm, hurt); also the psychological component of trauma is considered different if a child is violated by a trusted relative instead of by a stranger. Finally, the trauma will be more affective the more the victims are like us.

Increasingly, and perhaps inevitably, there are gray areas where trauma is neither "natural" nor attributable to specific human agency, but is caused by the ways humans have organized political, economic, and institutional power. Kleinman, Das, and Lock call this "social suffering," and their collection of essays discusses various political, economic, and institutional applications of power ranging from the rape of Indian women by British soldiers during the struggle for independence, to the imposition of Maoism in China, to the Holocaust. Large-scale events like economic depressions and famines are particularly good examples of gray areas. Jasper Becker argues that the great famine in China in 1959–1961 was entirely man-made. No blight destroyed the harvest, there were no unusual floods or droughts, urban granaries were full, and other countries were ready to ship in grain. Mao realized in 1960 that there was a famine, but continued the pretense of bumper crops.[20] Robert Conquest, in *The Harvest of Sorrow*, has shown at length how the Kremlin under Stalin deliberately managed famine as a terrorist technique. On the 150th anniversary of the Irish famine, the governor of New York, George Pataki, signed a bill legally requiring high school students to study the Great Famine: "History teaches us," he said, "that the Great Hunger was not the result of a massive Irish crop failure, but rather a deliberate campaign by the British to deny the Irish people the food they needed to survive" (quoted by Tóibín 23). History had manifested itself to the governor in the form of Joseph Crowley, assemblyman from a largely Irish section of Queens, who sponsored a bill passed by the state legislature, mandating that the New York City school curriculum include a unit on the potato famine and the resultant mass starvation in nineteenth-century Ireland. Crowley's precedent was a 1994 law requiring schools to teach about human-rights violations, with particular attention to the inhumanity of genocide, slavery, and the Holocaust.[21] At any rate, the main axis of trauma discourse is concerned primarily with human-related trauma, not "natural," even though at times the distinction may not be altogether clear.

A) Is the Holocaust Unique?

Peter Novick, in *The Holocaust in American Life*, claims that the Holocaust uniqueness dogma has become "axiomatic," a "fetishism," and a "cult" in "official" Jewish discourse, dismissing it as a mystery religion that indicates a destruction of history. Jacob Neusner, in *The Aftermath of the Holocaust*, agrees with Novick that uniqueness is an especially American position and that it did not gain prevalence until after the 1967 Arab-Israeli war, when it emerged to become emblematic of American Judaism. It would take several volumes to review all the commentators who claim a unique status for the Holocaust, or for 8.6, or any of the other events for which such status has been claimed. We shall focus here briefly on the Holocaust discourse because it supplies an abundance of examples of the main issues. Of course, the Holocaust is unique, in the obvious sense that any event must be considered unique. Holocaust assertions are different, especially those that claim an ontological uniqueness, and insist on an altogether separate category for the event. These range from the obviously religious or mystical to the seemingly secular. The metaphysical or religious field is a crowded one, where Elie Wiesel is the best known, thanks to his famous response to the 1978 TV series *Holocaust*. In it he claimed that the Holocaust is "an ontological event," it is "unique, not just another event," and that "Auschwitz cannot be explained nor can it be visualized. . . . The Holocaust transcends history" because it is "the ultimate event, the ultimate mystery, never to be comprehended or transmitted" (1978). In a later formulation, he put it in the form of a rhetorical question: "How can one recount when—by the scale and weight of its horror—the event defies language?" followed by the familiar assertion: "An ontological phenomenon, 'The Final Solution' is located beyond understanding" (1989: xi). The form of the question is particularly interesting, since it points us to "the scale and weight" of the Holocaust "horror," not the event itself. This is the distinction Kant was making when he located the sublime not in events, but in the mind contemplating events, a hermeneutical sublime where he observed "imagination by its own act depriving itself of its freedom by receiving a final determination in accordance with a law other than that of its empirical employment" (91). Presumably the Nazis, who staged it as a scene of domination and horror, could contemplate the genocide with satisfaction rather than horror—and to imagine that satisfaction may also be a part of the horror for us. What confirms it as a phenomenon beyond understanding is the decision not to look

The view that the Holocaust is unique and without parallel in human history is closer to a doctrine or a dogma than to a reasoned discursive position. Its rhetorical form is usually an unargued assertion: "For Auschwitz and Treblinka there was no earlier historical analogy and there was no philosophical, or for that matter theological, frame of mind that could possibly integrate them into any system of thought. The Holocaust was an absolute *novum* lacking accountability in any rational terms" (Katz 33). It is usually accompanied by the claim that the Holocaust cannot be represented or rationally apprehended, and by the concomitant claim that any attempt to explain or compare it is to deflect its moral impact and confuse its meaning, or even to commit blasphemy and a betrayal of Jewish history. For Claude Lanzmann, the "refusal of understanding" is the only possible and acceptable ethical attitude to take in the face of the Holocaust conceived as "pure event," and anyone who attempts to understand it is engaged in a "perverse form of revisionism" (1991: 477, 484, 478). In *Denying the Holocaust* Deborah Lipstadt claims that the most insidious form of Holocaust denial is the attempt by historians to create "immoral equivalencies" (212). Thus the Truth of the uniqueness of the Holocaust is established not by detailed comparisons with other atrocities, or by argument, but by assertions that seem to call for an act of faith and to make intellectual labor directed towards "understanding" not only vain, but an insult or blasphemy. It is more like a religious position than an intellectual one, where the ontological gap between ordinary events and the Holocaust must be matched by a gap in intellectual processes, leading to an Augustinian *credo ut intellegam*.[22]

Numerous gestures towards argument or reason have been offered to support the doctrine of uniqueness. In his ontological proof Descartes argued that our idea of God is unique among all our ideas because it includes the *necessity* of God's existence. Alex Callinicos makes a similar move when, after showing an inability to understand Hayden White's position, he appeals to the Holocaust in order to defend history from the relativity of White's representational modes: "Once the referents of historical writing have been occluded, the boundary separating it from fiction is inevitably blurred. . . . But here a pressing problem emerges to confront the historical skeptic. For surely there are events which it would be simply outrageous to treat as constructs of the historical imaginary. The most obvious is that of the Holocaust" (66). Our idea of the Holocaust as an event, then, must include the necessity of its own existence. When Saul Friedlander claims that the Final Solution is "the most radical case of genocide in human history," he invokes the staggering numbers of victims, the intensity of site investment, and the industrialized sadism as reasons for considering it as the "limit event" capable of defining our notion of eventness (1993: 134). In his brief critique of Friedlander, Kerwin Klein misses the point of the "limit event" concept. He argues that "One could not claim that the Holocaust was the most radical genocide in history and simultaneously claim that it was incommensurable with other events. To describe the Nazi murder of European Jews as a limit-event implies some common measure since it must exceed ('transgress,' 'go farther than') the others" (149). The idea of a limit event is like the idea of the absolutely large, Kant's mathematical sublime that resists all comparison and is, as he points out, a dimension equal only to itself that can be encountered only in ideas. Klein sounds like a spokesman for the Toledo merchants stopped by Don Quixote, who demands that they "confess that there is not in the whole world a more beauteous maiden than the Empress of la Mancha, the peerless Dulcinea del Toboso." "Show her to us," the merchants reply, "and, if she is as beauteous as you say, we will most willingly and without any pressure acknowledge the truth demanded of us by you." "If I were to show her to you," replied Don Quixote, "what merit would there be in your confessing so obvious a truth?" (51). The merchants are making a category mistake, for such an assertion can only be made as an act of faith, not as the conclusion of an exhaustive series of comparisons. And in this sense advocates of Holocaust uniqueness are correct to reject any and all attempts at comparison in advance. To decide to make a comparison is already to have lost faith in the absoluteness of the metaphysical event. On the other hand, critics who resort to actual quantitative comparisons for asserting uniqueness are on very shaky ground. In terms of absolute numbers, horrible as it is, six million is not the largest genocidal tally in human history.[23] In terms of relative loss of population, estimates are that the Nazis murdered half a million Gypsies, or one third of their total population—the same percentage lost by the European Jewish population. But that, in turn, pales besides the total systematic destruction of the Tasmanians by the British, or the almost total annihilation of the Herero by the Germans, and other devastations perpetrated in the colonial expansion of Europe, including the calculated genocide of the Amerindians.

Another frequent claim for Holocaust uniqueness is typified by Geoffrey Hartman, when he claims that "it is crucial to stress that the claim of exceptionality refers to the implementation of an ideology that singled out the Jews for extermination solely because they were Jews. All were to be killed, whether by shooting, gassing, or working them to death—including the children. It is this fact, not numbers, which made the Nazis' war against the Jews an exceptional act of genocide, one we define by the special if inadequate term 'the Holocaust' " (1996: 138). On the one hand, this point is so obvious that it goes without saying. As the Tasmanians were slaughtered because they were Tasmanians, the Armenians because they were Armenians, the Bosnians because they were Bosnians, so the Jews. On the other hand, this position raises the awkward issue of pain. Is the suffering of Jews as Jews, because they were Jews, unique? And if so, how can we determine that to be so?[24] Roger Gottlieb calls this argument an "arrogance of pain" that "tends to ignore the fact that the Holocaust . . . did not happen only to Jews. Five million others—homosexuals, mental patients, leftists, gypsies, prisoners of war—were victims as well. There has been enough murder— both then and since—for us to renounce the social or emotional isolation of the special victim" (7). A somewhat different view of the racial or ethnic basis for considering the Holocaust to be unique was suggested by Aimé Césaire thirty years ago: what makes the Holocaust unique and unbearable is that "at bottom, it is not *the humiliation of man as such*, it is the crime against the white man, the humiliation of the white man, and the fact that he applied to Europe colonialist procedures which until then had been reserved exclusively for the Arabs of Algeria, the coolies of India, and the blacks of Africa" (13–14).

There is a secular argument for something in the instrumental modality of the Holocaust that makes it unique, and uniquely modern as an event. Hayden White claims that, "The notion of the historical event has undergone radical transformation as a result of the occurrence in our century of events of a scope, scale, and depth unimaginable by earlier historians and the dismantling of the concept of the event as an object of a specifically scientific kind of knowledge" (1999: 72). The twentieth century is itself unique because of "the kind of 'unnatural' events—including the Holocaust—that mark our era and distinguish it absolutely from all of the history that has come before it" (81), and of these events "the Holocaust of the European Jews" is "the paradigmatic modernist event in Western European history" (79). But White cannot demonstrate that there is an ontological change in the nature of events themselves, only a change in our "notion of the historical event." His repeated claim that prior historians could not imagine modernist events suggests the limits of their imaginations rather than a rupture in the nature of events, and sounds like the norm for historical progression in which one age can seldom anticipate the next.[25] Could the seventeenth century have imagined steam engines and Bessemer furnaces and power mills and steam-driven presses and what Blake calls the "Satanic Mills" of the industrial revolution? And how does an age—as opposed to an individual—imagine anything? Surely most historical subjects are incapable of imagining their own age, much less some future transformed by new technologies and social organizations; perhaps this is even more the case for the historians White invokes, who are more used to looking back to the past than imagining the future. We should not confuse human error about reality and human nature with an ontological shift or rupture in that reality. For example, the fact that the twentieth century has refuted Hegel's claim that the sum total of concrete evil had already been encountered in history, and that evil has not been able to maintain a position of equality in the ultimate design of the world, does not mean that the fundamental nature of reality has been ruptured because he failed to imagine the future correctly. Condorcet, at the peak of enlightenment optimism, was confident that the "Future Progress of the Human Mind" would cause reason to keep pace with that of the sciences, leading to the elimination of prejudice and superstition, and the perfection of human society. We do not imagine a fundamental rupture in human nature simply because he misjudged its potential. Or was he right? We are now equally in the position of those who do not know what the future will bring.

In general, it seems dubious and self-centered to make such universal assertions about what could or could not be imagined before our time, especially given the traditions of apocalyptic imagination in the West, and imaginations like those of Blake, Milton, Bunyan, Dante, and other notable visionaries. Our century may have outdone all previous ones in embodying what White, in the name of uniqueness, calls the utilization of "scientific technology and rationalized procedures of governance and warfare (of which the German genocide of six million European Jews is paradigmatic)" (1999: 69). But surely Dante's hell, with its vision of a calculating, engineering, bureaucratic God, using "scientific technology and rationalized procedures" in order to devise tortures to punish selected subjects in excruciating agony through eternity, shows an imaginative capacity equal to anything the twentieth century had to offer. We challenge White's position here not because of its weakness, but precisely because of its strength and his distinction as a theorist and historian. If White succumbs to the siren song of uniqueness, then it must have some strong appeal, and the other side of that appeal includes the very serious consequences of a commitment to the putative uniqueness of the Holocaust or any other traumatic event.

As already mentioned, there are increasing signs of dissatisfaction with the attempts by some commentators to segregate the Holocaust discourse from a larger historical and theoretical context of traumatic events. Gillian Rose is a good example of the aggressive mode this dissatisfaction can take. In "Beginnings of the Day," she mounts a vigorous critique of the practice of designating Auschwitz as an unrepresentable rupture in history, because it substitutes an indulgence in "Holocaust piety" for an inquiry into the social and historical conditions that made it possible. To do so is to "mystify something we dare not understand, because we fear it may be all too understandable, all too continuous with what we are—human, all too human" (1996: 242–43). Roger Gottlieb rejects arguments for uniqueness as "temptations to thoughtlessness," and argues that

> it will not do to encapsulate the Holocaust in a sterile shroud of mystery, regarding it as a permanently inexplicable and horrible enigma. This approach to the Holocaust is, paradoxically, another form of trivialization. Though there can never be a final truth about the Holocaust which will set our minds "at rest," there must be "truths for us" which will guide us in inner reflection and outer action. (3, 4)

To make such a total investment of cultural and intellectual resources in a single event, however significant it may be, is also effectively to distance us from other events that deserve our attention. Arthur Cohen makes this aspect of the "unique" position very clear in his invocation of the Holocaust as *mysterium tremendum*: "If we stand on the contention that thought is essentially incapable of compassing the *tremendum*, that it must fall silent and dumb before its monstrousness, there are additional consequences. . . . The first and most pressing is that the past that pressed against us before the *tremendum* is annihilated . . . and if, as is signaled by our language, *tremendum* means historical immensity for which there is neither a satisfactory analogue nor historical model, the history of the past becomes irrelevant" (37, 41). The ambiguity of the phrase "history of the past" is telling. What is history the history of, if not of the past? Or is it the kind of history that we had in the past, before the only "relevant" subject for history became the Holocaust, a new history with a single subject? At any rate, the *prima facie* moral unacceptability of this "moral" position seems to have escaped the many commentators who quote it as part of their *obiter dicta*. As Peter Novick emphasizes,

> talk of uniqueness and incomparability surrounding the Holo-
> caust . . . promotes evasion of moral and historical responsibility.
> The repeated assertion that whatever the United States has done to
> blacks, Native Americans, Vietnamese, or others pales in comparison
> to the Holocaust is true—and evasive. And whereas a serious and
> sustained encounter with the history of hundreds of years of enslave-
> ment and oppression of blacks might imply costly demands on
> Americans to redress the wrongs of the past, contemplating the
> Holocaust is virtually cost-free: a few cheap tears. (1999b: 15)

The claims for uniqueness of the Holocaust as event come towards the end
of a century that includes such a stunning array of horrible acts perpetu-
ated by humans against other humans that it may well have been the most
terrible period in human history to date. Featuring two nearly global wars,
a number of genocidal attempts, colonial wars, ethnically motivated violence, and innumerable acts of terrorism, this period and the beginning of
the new century would seem to demand a postenlightenment perspective—or a posthumanist one—in which the human condition is given serious reconsideration.

In the meantime, increasing numbers of critics and historians are approaching the Holocaust as an historical event, assuming that with study
and thought we can achieve some degree of understanding. To do so is to
shift from a theological or metaphysical question, essentially rhetorical, to a
sociological and historical one and to theories of social action, asking what
caused individual subjects to commit such acts and how those acts were determined or facilitated by cultural and social environments; to look for
analogues and for causes in social structures and social practices, rather
than invoking mystery, destiny, or some unnamable and unthinkable
causality. To do so is to view the atrocities of Nazism and the Holocaust not
as aberrations but as understandable, even logical outcomes of the origins
of European modernity, and to risk losing our complacent feelings of safety
in being different from them. Connections can be made between the final
solution attempted in the death camps and the U.S. final solution for the
war with Japan. Both the death camps and the atomic bomb were possible
only as secret bureaucratic efforts requiring the labor of thousands who did
not altogether understand the nature of their efforts. Both were awesomely
efficient achievements in the art of harnessing social organization with science and technology in order to produce massive human destruction and
misery in innocent civilian populations. The Final Solution was an attempt
at total genocide; the atomic bombing was a *symbolic* genocide, showing
that the U.S. was willing and able, if need be, to destroy the entire Japanese
population. Both were acts of industrialized mass killing which claimed

justification on moral grounds, and in both cases most ordinary citizens accepted the necessity of the actions taken as being essential for the good of the state.[26]

Comparative genocide studies have multiplied at a growing rate since Leo Kuper's *Genocide: Its Political Uses in the Twentieth Century* and other studies of the 1980s began to define the field.[27] Robert Melson, in *Revolution and Genocide*, provides one example of the move toward comparative genocide studies. He focuses on what he calls "total domestic genocide" in two contexts, the Armenian genocide and the Nazi genocide, taking a matter-of-fact approach to "the fact that genocide, mass murder, is part of human history, and thus in principle explainable in broadly historical terms" (xvi). While acknowledging that "for some any attempt at explanation or understanding is a form of transgression," he sets about producing "a careful comparative history that will demonstrate both the significant similarities and crucial differences between the cases compared" (xvii, 33). His first chapter provides a useful overview and extensive bibliography for some of the main issues in the comparative approach.

B) *Representing the Traumatic Event*

If we turn from issues of uniqueness and comparison of traumatic events, we find the Holocaust to be a useful paradigm for issues of representation and the difficulties of representing such events. To do so we must ignore the sacralizing tendencies of those who would prohibit or regulate representations. Here again Wiesel provides an extreme example: "One does not imagine the unimaginable. And in particular, one does not show it on screen." To make the attempt may "profane and trivialize a sacred subject" and be a form of "blasphemy" (1989: xi). Of course, language is always an inadequate medium for representing reality, which is one reason why so much writing is about writing. As Susan Stewart points out in *On Longing*, when language attempts to describe the concrete, "it is caught in an infinitely self-effacing gesture of inadequacy, a gesture which speaks to the gaps between our modes of cognition—those gaps between the sensual, the visual, and the linguistic" (52). These gestures, a staple in the rhetoric of the sublime, become more conspicuous in dealing with large-scale traumatic events. Primo Levi's statement that in Auschwitz the prisoners learned that "our language lacked words to express this offense, the demolition of a man" (1986: 22) is echoed by Takenishi Hiroko: "What words can we now use, and to what ends? Even: what *are* words?" (quoted in Treat 27). Both were anticipated a century before when a correspondent wrote from Ireland during the potato famine, "We have no language to convey to you any adequate idea of the amount of misery to be found on every side" (*Transactions* 188), and another contemporary made the same point more effusively: "No language is adequate to give the true, the real picture; one look of the eye into the daily scenes there witnessed would overpower what any pen, however graphic, any tongue, however eloquent, could portray" (Nicholson 9). An event that defies all representation will best be represented by a failure of representation, and this is in fact one of the oldest tropes of Western writing, what Kant called the negative or non-presentation of the idea of horror in the sublime. Representation seems to delight in "Speaking the Unspeakable" (Leak and Paizis), "Bearing the Unbearable" (Aaron), "Thinking the Unthinkable" (Gottlieb), and going "Beyond the Conceivable" (Diner), so it is not surprising that, as Tim Cole and others have noted, in the 1990s attention shifted from interest in the events of the Holocaust to interest "in the *representation* of those events" (xii). In the entire history of Japanese Literature, no subject has given rise to as much poetry as the bombings of Hiroshima and Nagasaki.

Artists have found many interesting and effective ways to combine representation of a traumatic event with awareness of impossibility. One thinks of Art Spiegelman's *Maus* comix, dealing so effectively and self-consciously with the mediated nature of his knowledge and the nature of his medium. Another American artist, David Lowenthal, represents the Holocaust by using miniature children's toys; he makes miniature SS officers, death camps, and camp inmates, then photographs them to reproduce well-known documentary scenes in a gruesome combination of the photograph as the medium for best representing reality, and dolls or puppets as conspicuous examples of the unreal or unnatural. Two English sculptors, Jake and Dinos Chapman, have created an ambitious and elaborate work along similar lines. Using more that 10,000 toy figures, hand-modeled and hand-painted over almost four years, they produced a swastika-shaped landscape with a volcano in the middle, surrounded by detailed scenes that include a death camp, battle scenes, and figures being crucified, disemboweled, and shoveled into smoking ovens. For exhibition purposes they comissioned a group of blown-up C-prints taken by the German fashion photographer, Norbert Schoner.[28] Canadian artist Vera Frenkel's *Body Missing* project (1994–1997) is a mixed-media installation that probes the relationship between aesthetics and genocide, focussing on loss and displacement in the context of the Kulturpolitik of the Third Reich, in particular on Hitler's plan to build a museum in his home town to house the works of art looted during the war.[29] Also there are inevitable examples of bad taste and poor judgment, as exemplified in the Jewish Museum exhibition "Mirroring Evil: Nazi Imagery/Recent Art" (opened March 17, 2002), featuring thirteen conceptual artists from seven countries. The low points of this show included English artist, Alan Schechner, who digitally inserts himself—conspicuously holding a can of Diet Coke—into a photograph of

Buchenwald inmates; Polish artist Maciej Toporowicz, whose video montage included body-beautiful Nazi propaganda films and Calvin Klein ads; Piotr Uklanski, also from Poland, created forty-seven color-saturated prints of famous actors like David Niven and Clint Eastwood in Nazi roles. The critical point here may be an equation between Nazism, the Holocaust, and consumer goods, but the works themselves seem to become consumer goods that make minimal demands on their consumers.

Whatever the medium of representation, realism is not always the most effective mode for representing trauma, nor is the power of successful cultural representation dependent on direct personal experience or eyewitness of the events represented. For example, when John Felstiner calls Celan's "Todesfuge" the Guernica of poems, he is invoking a cultural/aesthetic semiotic of atrocity that Picasso both deploys and contributes to in his painting. The power of artistic "witness" in that work is not due to Picasso's Spanish blood (i.e., authenticating a legitimate connection to the victims) or to a literal representation of the events. Rather, it is the disruption of conventional modes of representation—the visual rhetoric of rupture. In Paris at the time, Picasso based his painting on newspaper accounts, using precisely those techniques of rupture that are invoked as the authenticating signs of trauma. With its electrical flash from above illuminating a landscape of agony that includes a burning house, a soldier blown to pieces, a screaming woman, a neighing horse, a bull, and a dead baby, it can be read as an imaginary news photograph, with the wounded horse made of newsprint. One of the century's most familiar icons, it literally turned the stuff of newspapers into art, transforming it from a historical to a symbolic event.[30]

An interesting late twentieth-century mode of representing collective traumatic events is the archive of individual personal testimonies, a flourishing industry that seems to assume that the accumulation of witness accounts will somehow "add up" to a collective view, like the parade of witnesses in a trial, or like the collecting of artifacts in a museum designed to "represent" the "Holocaust experience." Hayden White has argued that synecdoche is an essential part of narrative, the "historicist trope of the real," in which it functions as the dominant trope for 'grasping together' (Greek, *synecdoche;* Latin, *subintellectio*) the parts of a totality apprehended as being dispersed across a temporal series into a whole in the mode of identification" (1999: 20–21). But whereas Thucydides had to rely on "eyewitnesses whose reports I have checked with as much thoroughness as possible"(24), modern technology can give us videotaped testimony of the witnesses themselves. Since the 1970s there has been a rapidly increasing worldwide trend in the collection of such documents, in an unending need for testimony from living witnesses of traumatic events. In Japan, novelist

Toyoshima Yoshio stated that what was needed in the wake of history was "human documents" *(ningen kiroku,* quoted in Treat 51). The genre of the *testimonio* is a related phenomenon, based as it is on the chronological narration of recalled experience from a single and unified first-person point of view wholly identifiable with the author, the testifying survivor. In this context the eye-witness subject can be seen as a rhetorical position, implicitly authenticating experience that is presented as coming from personal memory.

The factual status of the *testimonio* is subject to challenge, as the recent study of Rigoberta Menchú by David Stoll illustrates. Thucydides pointed out long ago that "different eye-witnesses give different accounts of the same events, speaking out of partiality for one side or the other or else from imperfect memories" (24). A major problem with recorded memoirs, especially when they are recorded many years after the events remembered, is that memory is so readily modified by later experience, including reading and desire.[31] "The greater part of the witnesses have ever more blurred and stylized memories, often unbeknownst to them, influenced by information gained from later readings or the stories of others" (Levi 1989: 24). This is even more the case with traumatic events, where the memory trace was compromised from the beginning, so that "their capacity for observation was paralyzed by suffering and incomprehension" (24). Geoffrey Hartman, one of the most avid supporters of recording survivor testimony, and instrumental in the founding of the Yale Video Archive (now the Fortunoff Video Archive for Holocaust Testimony), notes that "every Auschwitz survivor seems to have gone through a selection by Mengele, as if he manned his post 24 hours every day," and that "Survivor testimonies recorded long after the event do not excel in providing *vérités de fait* or positivistic history" (1996: 141–42). Shmuel Krakowski, the director of Yad Vashem, told a reporter in 1986 that most of the twenty thousand testimonies it had collected at that time were unreliable, because many of the witnesses "were never in the places where they claim to have witnessed atrocities, while others relied on secondhand information given to them by friends or passing strangers." (Barbara Amouyal in the *Jerusalem Post*, August 17, 1986, quoted by Novick 1999b: 275). What this means is not that all witness testimony is worthless, rather that it demands special modes of attention and interpretation. What survivors are witness to is their own suffering, in the past as victims and in the now of telling as survivors. They are also subject to the context in which they record their testimony and to the expectations of the interviewer. Dori Laub emphasizes that the listener "is a party to the creation of knowledge *de novo*. The testimony to the trauma thus includes its hearer, who is, so to speak, the blank screen on which the event comes to be inscribed" (57). No matter how objective an interviewer or videographer tries to be, the testimony will be to some degree influenced by the process and requirements of authentication themselves. A Spielberg interview, designed to produce a message of redemption, will be quite different from a Lanzmann one, and both will be different from Marcello Pezzetti, who is especially keen on capturing the "humor" of his Italian witnesses.[32]

There are almost fifty testimony archives now in the U.S., chief among them the Museum of Jewish Heritage in New York, with its collection of videotapes of survivors, taped by the Museum during the eight years before it opened in 1997, augmented by the Steven Spielberg Survivors of the Shoah Visual History Foundation, with over 80,000 hours of videotape accounts by survivors of the Holocaust, in their own words, without scripts.[33] In Los Angeles the Beit Hashoah—Museum of Tolerance—has a "Hall of Witness" with eight video monitors where we can hear recorded testimony. Surely from such a massive accumulation the Truth will emerge, in spite of inevitable mistakes, false memories, errors, and even downright lies. As a gigantic serial synecdoche, the massive accumulation of individual survivor testimony offers itself as the parts of a totality that can be grasped together in the apprehension of a totality perceived as a whole event. Primo Levi imagined combining all the survivors' stories into a single scripture of biblical proportion and significance, that would be

> A sorrowful, cruel and moving story; because so are all our stories, hundreds of thousands of stories, all different and all full of a tragic, disturbing necessity. We tell them to each other in the evening, and they take place in Norway, Italy, Algeria, the Ukraine, and are simple and incomprehensible like the stories in the Bible. But are they not themselves stories of a new Bible? (1986: 59)

But like Borges' fantasy library, the closer a collection comes to that imaginary totality the more it eludes our ability to experience it directly as a whole. In Los Angeles what we hear are scripts read by actors (so that the accents of the actual survivors will not distract the visitors) and in New York the accumulated testimony has been culled to three hours by Max Lewkowicz (of Rainmaker Productions) together with David Altshuler, the museum's director, and others at the museum. Even if we could somehow grasp all the available testimony, we would have all the flawed accounts together with all the true ones.

III. From Victim to Survivor to Witness

Without you there would be no events, and there must be events.
—Dostoevsky, *The Brothers Karamazov*

There is a special relationship between the traumatic event and its witness, and a special dependency, since whether or not an event is traumatic can only be established by the existence of witnesses whose trauma both authenticates them and the reality of the traumatic event. As traumatized trace, the witness is an indexical sign or symptom of the reality of the event, the experience of which prevents the witness from communicating in normal modes. This perspective challenges the common assumption that witness can be transparently based on an original event, and leads us to an understanding of the relationship between witness and event as an example of what Jacques Derrida calls the "logic of the supplement." This logic is a double logic, in which the witness as supplement is considered both as something foreign or extra to the essential nature of that to which it is added (the event itself), and as something necessary to complete an inherent lack or absence within that to which it is added—an essential condition of that which it supplements. The event cannot be separated from the experience of the event. An event can preclude the possibility of acts of witness, most obviously by killing the victim. For survivor witnesses, witness itself becomes a part of the trauma, since the pain of seeing others perish is added to the suffering of those who do not. With increasing media representation of traumatic events—most spectacularly in the 9/11 coverage—a category of voyeur witnesses must also be considered. In extreme cases the whole life of a victim can become living testimony to the traumatic experience, both physical and mental, the traumatized body and mind of the victim serving as evidence for the reality of a history that hurts, as the charred remains of a building witness its conflagration. "The most violent wrenchings in the world, that is to say, have no clinical standing unless they harm the workings of a mind or body, so it is the *damage done* that defines and gives shape to the initial event, the *damage done* that gives it its name" (Erikson 184).

Dubravka Ugresic has complained that "we are witnesses and participants in a general trend of turning away from stable, 'hard' *history* in favor of changeable and 'soft' *memory* (ethnic, social, group, class, race, gender, personal and alien)" (29–30). But under the new model of the traumatic event, we know that the "hard" history exists precisely because it inscribes itself in "soft" bodies and minds, thereby guaranteeing its and their certainty:

> [E]specially in therapy culture, talk shows, and memoir-mongering, trauma is treated as an event that guarantees the subject, and in this psychologistic register the subject, however disturbed, rushes back as survivor, witness, testifier. Here a traumatic subject does indeed exist, and it has absolute authority, for one cannot challenge the

trauma of another: one can only believe it, even identify with it or
not. In trauma discourse, then, the subject is evacuated and elevated
at once. (Foster 1996a: 123)

Ordinary epistemology is reversed, as Elaine Scarry suggests in her description of torture as the attempt to create physical pain "so incontestably real that it seems to confer its quality of 'incontestable reality' on that power that has brought it into being" (1985: 27). It has been a commonplace since Nietzsche to observe that in history writing there is no fact that is not preceded by a meaning, that there are no "facts as such." In the same mode, we can now say there is no event that is not preceded by a witness. Nietzsche's contemporary William James, in his *Principles of Psychology*, shifted attention from the question of what reality might really be in and of itself, to the question, "*Under what circumstances do we think things are real?*" (II, 291). If we follow his lead, we can see in *The Courage to Heal*, a popular book by Ellen Bass and Laura Davis, just how far trauma epistemology can go: "If you think you were sexually abused and your life shows the symptoms, *then you were*" (22, italics added).

Such overconfidence in the ability to read the semiotics of trauma led to a number of perversions of justice in the 1980s, and to the formation of the False Memory Syndrome Foundation of Philadelphia in 1992. There is considerable controversy over the issue of "repressed memory," as with memory in general.[34] Physical indexical signs—literal wounds, scars, tattooed numbers—tend to be more reliable than literary style for authentication of survivor status. In Japan, where survivors are entitled to medical and social welfare benefits, there are strict laws and procedures designed to enable bona fide survivors to obtain a "*hibakusha* certificate" that "verifies that the said individual is a survivor of the atomic bomb" (Yoneyama 93). There is also an attempt to maintain standards and a degree of precision by insisting on identifying victims by their distance from the ground zero of the blast.

It is hard to imagine so bureaucratic a procedure for verifying survivor status in the U.S., but there have been recent signs of an institutionalized awareness of the category of victim in the innovative form of the "victim impact statement," the result of a "victims' rights movement" that started in the late 1960s. VIS statements are intended to bear witness to the effects on survivor victims (e.g., children, spouses) in the form of continued suffering. Some form of victim impact evidence is now allowed in most states, designed to produce powerful effects on juries after guilt has been established, at the sentencing phase of a trial, by providing information about the consequences of the criminal act. Physical injury, economic loss, change in personal welfare or family relationships, need for psychological services, and any other evidence of the impact of the offense on survivors can be brought to bear on the punishment to be meted out. Paul Gewirtz claims that "no movement in criminal law has been more powerful in the last twenty years than the victims' rights movement, which has sought to enhance the place of the victim in the criminal process" (139).[35] The rationale was expressed by Justice Antonin Scalia, in the case of *Booth v. Maryland*: "Recent years have seen an outpouring of popular concern for what has come to be known as 'victims' rights'. . . . Many citizens have found one-sided and hence unjust the criminal trial in which a parade of witnesses comes forth to testify to the pressures beyond normal human experience that drove the defendant to commit his crime, with no one to lay before the sentencing authority the full reality of human suffering the defendant has produced—which (and not moral guilt alone) is one of the reasons society deems his act worthy of the prescribed penalty." Survivor witnesses of traumatic events do not provide knowledge or information in the usual sense; they are themselves the evidence, the knowledge, that we receive from their existence as survivors. Survivors of large-scale traumatic events become by extension witnesses for those absent and unable to bear witness themselves, and this is an essential part of the genre of *testimonio*, as exemplified in *I, Rigoberta Menchú*.[36]

To shift now from the relationship between witness and traumatic event to the relationship between the witnessing subject and those to whom the witness is addressed, consider this typical assertion by Lawrence Langer: "There is simply no connection between our ordinary suffering and their unprecedented agony" (1999: 115). Langer has just quoted a description by "an eyewitness to the slaughter" of a horrible incident in which a group of Jews was forced into a pit lined with quicklime then boiled alive by a liquid that had the effect of slaking the lime. "Nothing . . . can silence the cries of those hundreds of Jews being boiled to death in an acid bath," asserts Langer. But there are no cries to be heard; Langer takes his description from a book by Theo Richmond that quotes (in translation) from a protocol taken some months after the war by Soviets from the eyewitness, a Polish Catholic. There are two orders of empathy at work in this scenario. First, accepting the textual transmission as factual, there is the empathy of the witness for the pain of the Jewish victims. Without some kind of "connection" with them—in this case the imagination of what it would feel like to be boiled alive, even though the witness has never actually experienced that agony—the witness would not be able to describe the scene. It is his *affect* in the telling ("The cries were so terrible that we who were sitting by the piles of clothing began to tear pieces off the stuff to stop our ears") that makes the horror so vivid that nothing can silence their cries for Langer, who in turn seeks to transmit that affect to his readers through his retelling. Clearly the witness felt some kind of intense suffering in the episode, even though it was not the "unprecedented agony" of the victims. He seems to have felt that pain again in the telling, and the sensitive reader—who has not experienced the actual agony of witnessing the scene—feels some connection with his pain in the attempt to imagine both what it would be like to be burned alive and what it would be like to have to witness such pain, to hear their cries.

To understand what kind of "connections" are at work here, *pace* Langer, we must resort to the function of "imagination" in the experience of sympathy. The classic study of sympathy is found in Adam Smith's *Theory of Moral Sentiments*, where he argues that, given the impossibility of actually knowing or entering into someone else's "sentiments," our acts of sympathy are structured by a theatrical dynamic that depends on people's ability to represent themselves to others:

> Though our brother be upon the rack, as long as we ourselves are at our ease, our senses will never inform us of what he suffers. They never did, and never can, carry us beyond our own person, and it is by the imagination only that we can form any conception of what are his sensations. Neither can that faculty help us to this any other way, than by representing to us what would be our own, if we were in his case. . . . By the imagination we place ourselves in his situation, we conceive ourselves enduring all the same torments, we enter as it were into his body, and become in some measure the same person with him and thence form some idea of his sensations, and even feel something which, though weaker in degree, is not altogether unlike them. His agonies, when they are thus brought home to ourselves, when we have thus adopted and made them our own, begin at last to affect us, and we then tremble and shudder at the thought of what he feels. (10)

If the recreation of what another feels depends to this extent on the imagination, and on representation of another's feelings, resulting in a powerful reaction based on "the thought of what he feels," it is evident that the capacity of sympathy to bridge the boundaries between separate subjectivities is matched by its capacity for manipulation and its susceptibility to a theatrical staging.[37] Sympathy is a trope—the opposite of irony, which creates distance—that appears to abolish distance. Diderot's *Paradoxe sur le comédien* suggests that the most accomplished actor is the one who is most distanced from the emotion to be simulated because his detachment allows him to create that emotion from the point of view of the spectator, who alone matters. Sympathy may in this conception be the most artificial of emotions, the creation of a pure fiction. Thus sympathy is a slippery concept, especially if we ask what is the status of our feeling of sympathy when there is no actual corresponding fact, person, or event to be sympathetic with, as in the case of artistic fabrications. It is entirely possible for what we experience as sympathy to be a mode of auto-affectation.

The earliest reactions to survivors of the Holocaust saw them as passive victims of Nazi atrocity, and sympathy was not always an overwhelming response. Victims themselves often expressed feelings of shame at their condition, as when Etty Hillesum wrote: "They are playing a game with us, but we allow them to do so, and that will be our shame for generations to come. It is a complete madhouse here; we shall have to feel ashamed of it for three hundred years. The *Dienstleiters* [Jewish section leaders] themselves now have to draw up the transport lists" (1986: 87, 89). Emmanuel Ringelbaum, writing in the Warsaw Ghetto, echoes this note: "This will be an eternal mystery—this passivity of the Jewish populace even toward its own police. Now that the populace has calmed down somewhat . . . they are becoming ashamed of having put up no resistance at all" (333). Elias Canetti found no basis for sympathy in the image of Jewish victims he contemplated in 1945: "The suffering of the Jews had turned into an institution, but it outlived itself. People don't want to hear about it any more. They were amazed to learn that one could exterminate the Jews; now, perhaps without realizing it, they have a new reason for despising them. . . . They were degraded to slaves, then cattle, then vermin. The degradation worked" (71). In Israel, in the early years after the War, Holocaust survivors were referred to as "soap" because of the widespread rumor that the Nazis used the fat from Jewish bodies to make soap. Eventually the continuous display of victimization came to be seen as a form of triumph for the Nazis, in their systematic attempts to degrade and humiliate the Jews even as they worked towards their annihilation. Thus Michael Kimmelman could ask, apropos of the opening of the Museum of Jewish Heritage in New York, "Does depicting Jews in photographs of emaciated corpses and, inferentially, through piles of their abandoned belongings, remember them as they would have wanted to be remembered, or as the Nazis would have them remembered?" (B 1). A similar stage of humiliation and shame characterized the Hiroshima/Nagasaki survivors, who were marked by the bomb as if by a curse. Yoneyama describes at length how survivor identity was reduced to a "universal and anonymous identity of *hibakusha*" and the victims treated as objects of prejudice and discrimination (114). Given such degradation, a reluctance or refusal to speak about one's experience was long held in Japan to be an authenticating sign of the traumatic experience. Many were silent because of the harsh reality of discrimination against survivors when they sought employment or marriage partners, so that "Those who really suffered cannot talk about it" was a common attitude (88). "From the first, the average person treated the injured . . . almost as if they had always been dirty beggars. . . . I could not help being struck both by this psychology and also by the psychology whereby victims as victims became absolutely servile, as if they had always been pathetic creatures" (Ōta 217). The situation began to change dramatically in the early 1980s, with the emergence of a more active image and role for the witness as storyteller, due in no small part to the foundation of two survivor associations. The Kataru Kai association refused to use "*hibakusha*" in its name, with its passive connotations of subjection to the bomb and radiation. While the Tsudoi association included the term "victim" (*higaisha*) in its full name (Genbaku Higaisha Shogen no Tsudoi), its more common name is Assembly of Witnessing (Shogen no Tsudoi), with a pronounced emphasis on agency that matches the Kataru Kai (*kataru* = to narrate). Thus both with some urgency emphasize identification of their members as *survivors* who can have *active* roles as "witnesses" (*shogensha*) or "story-tellers" (*kataribe*). The emergence of "testimonial practices" (*shogen katsudo*) of these associations has led to a gradual change in status for survivors of 8.6. It has also led to a high degree of conformity, with narratives presented as factual and realistic congruent with assumptions about the possibilities of accurate historical reconstruction. The testimonies of *hibakusha* avow to tell the "actuality" of the event, "as it really was," and "with accuracy" and thus rest "upon realist and positivist assumptions about the possibilities of accurate historical reconstruction" (Yoneyama 211). In this they bear close resemblance to the first-person narratives of the *testimonio* genre.[38]

This change in the role of survivor in Japan is exemplary of one of the most striking changes in the last two decades of trauma discourse: the transformation of witness as victim to witness as survivor, and to witness as performer, telling the tale of survival as a form of self-therapy and inspiration for others. Although the traumata differ widely, these "survivor narratives" have a number of features in common, among them the idea that narrative testimony, in the form of an active remembering and telling, can enable a move from a state of helpless victimage to a mode of action and even potential self-renewal, demonstrating that new actions can still be possible in spite of the trauma of suffering. One of the earliest organized reactions to the AIDS epidemic was a concerted effort to replace the term "victim" with the term "survivor," then by PWA or LWA, an assertion of at least a minimal dignity for those who were perceived as losing almost everything else. At the same time some feminists were raising the flag of "power feminism" in opposition to what they saw as "victim feminism." Nowhere was the shift more dramatic than with images of Holocaust survivorship. As Henry Greenspan describes it, "our response to these survivors also underwent a transformation. Out of 'the Ashes' or 'the darkness' of 'defeat,' we began to look for heroes and victories and 'the joy of survival,' " in "a modern crusade" to collect and distribute in the greatest possible quantity new testimony on the Holocaust. Indeed, "so much do we celebrate the act of testimony—congratulating survivors for giving it and, perhaps, ourselves for getting it—that the specific content of that testimony is left as mostly background. That is, survivor's speech tends to be esteemed in the abstract—as the idea of testimony rather than the reality" (58, 59).

Like the story-telling in AA meetings, there are important social and therapeutic components to such testimonies, more significant by far than their evidentiary function. After World War I, Freud had speculated that trauma was caused by having lived through an experience so extreme that one had not in fact experienced it—that is, had not integrated it mentally and emotionally into one's sense of being. In *Unclaimed Experience*, Cathy Caruth describes trauma as a "double wound," because it "is not locatable in the simple violent or original event in an individual's past, but rather in the way that its very unassimilated nature—the way it was precisely *not known* in the first instance—returns to haunt the survivor later on" (4). To take an active role in story-telling or testifying can be a way to cope with the double wound of deferred trauma. As Judith Herman points out in *Trauma and Recovery*, "The physioneurosis induced by terror can apparently be reversed through the use of words" (183). There is a striking correspondence in the shift to this new configuration of testimony with the dynamics of Freud's famous distinction between the state of melancholy, with its passive feelings of worthlessness caused by overidentification with the lost object, and the active, agential state of the *Trauerarbeit*, the "working-through" of cathexes to the lost object, an active mourning that allows life to go on and new cathexes to be developed, as if in defiant and ironic response to the "*Arbeit Macht Frei*" motto hung over the gate at Auschwitz.

IV. Amnesia and Musealization

I can swim like the others only I have a better memory than the others. I have not forgotten my former inability to swim. But since I have not forgotten it my ability to swim is of no avail and I cannot swim after all.

—Franz Kafka

To forget the dead altogether is impious in ways that prepare their own retribution, but to remember the dead is neurotic and obsessive and merely feeds a sterile repetition. There is no "proper" way of relating to the dead and the past.

—Fredric Jameson

In the allegorical world of George Orwell's Oceania in *1984*, Winston Smith's job is to rewrite the *Times* on a daily basis in order to make the past "fit" the ongoing present: "This process of continuous alteration we applied not only to newspapers, but to books, periodicals, pamphlets, posters, leaflets, films, sound tracks, cartoons, photographs—to every kind of literature or documentation which might conceivably hold any political or ideological significance. Day by day and almost minute by minute the past was brought up to date" (163). We may be tempted to laugh at Orwell's crude allegory of the triumph of English socialism in the Ingsoc party in Oceania, but much of what he describes is as pertinent to the U.S. today as it was to Great Britain in 1949. After drinking their toast "To the past!" because "the past is more important," O'Brien asks Winston the crucial question: "Then where does the past exist, if at all?"

> "In records. It is written down."
> "In records. And—?"
> "In the mind. In human memories."
> "In memory. Very well, then. We, the Party, control all records and we control all memories. Then we control the past, do we not?" (205)

The main difference from this in our own reality is that we live in a system in which every party is presumably free to strive to produce the past it needs in order to establish the present it wants.

In the Book of Deuteronomy, Moses is instructed to write a poem before he dies, a poem that will live unforgotten in the mouths and minds of the people: "Now therefore, write you this poem, and teach it to the children of Israel; put it in their mouths, that this poem may be a witness for me against the children of Israel. . . . And it shall come to pass, when many evils and troubles have befallen them, that this poem shall answer them as a witness, for it shall not be forgotten out of the mouths of their seed" (31: 19–21). Harold Fisch discusses this text at length in *Poetry With a Purpose*, pointing out that the Hebrew word 'èd, "witness," is related to a root word 'ûd which includes the sense of persistent repetition. "It enters into the definition here as an aspect of the process of learning, of lodging the words in the memory. . . . But it also seems to refer to the process of the poem's evocation in the future time; it will then become *a nagging presence,*

returning upon those who have learned it with a disturbing constancy"
(51). One of the oldest and strongest aspects of an act of witness is that it
seeks to invade its readers or hearers, demanding their attention. When Job
cries out, "Oh that my words were now written!/Oh that they were printed
in a book!/That they were graven with an iron pen and lead in the rock for
ever!" (23–24), his desire is to find "redemption" in the possibility of an
endless series of repetitions of his story in mimetic sequence. The challenge
to the readers of Job, as Jonathan Lamb points out, is to enter into its want
of logic and to find there whatever evil or good they can. "The history of
the reading of Job is strewn with crises mimetic of those it describes, recurring at the same level of intensity as often as the book and its options are
taken up" (6). The Holocaust Memorial Museum attempts to exploit this
feature, with its "Identity Card Project," where each visitor is expected to
enter into an empathetic relationship with a Holocaust victim.[39] But Job rejects the kinds of consolation staged by the Museum, in order to insist on
the activity of suffering: "Therefore I will not refrain my mouth; I will
speak in the anguish of my spirit; I will complain in the bitterness of my
soul" (7:11). Job's telling here constitutes a passionate event, not an occasion for understanding, evaluation, interpretation or moral inspiration.
Witness must be repeatable, even tautological; it exists in fact *as* repetition
and echo, in a series of recurrences at the same level of intensity. Job wants
his story remembered and repeated, not just by one reader or group, but by
an endless chain of readers. Active repetition is crucial to witness, a practice
made urgent by the continuous danger of forgetting. Witnessing is like
treading water, it must keep on keeping on; if one stops one sinks out of
sight into oblivion.

If the logic and the dynamic of witness is that there can never be an end,
never a sufficiency, then there is always a terminal silence waiting for the
witness to run its course. Paradox: that the universally acknowledged inadequacy of words leads to the production of yet more words that can only
confirm their inadequacy because more is never enough. Another paradox:
nothing is ever added in this production; nothing *can* be added, in the
sense of contributing towards an advance, towards clarification, towards
some conceivable form or mode of closure. The best result that can be
achieved is something like a system of maintenance, the system of "haunting" and "spectrality" that Derrida has examined at length in *Spectres of
Marx*, or that Hannah Arendt describes in *Men in Dark Times*:

> Insofar as any "mastering" of the past is possible it consists in relat-
> ing what has happened; but such narration, too, which shapes his-
> tory, solves no problems and assuages no suffering; it does not
> master anything once and for all. Rather, as long as the meaning of

the events remain alive . . . "mastering the past" can take the form of ever-recurrent narration. (193)

To accept the role of reader or hearer is to accept a responsibility and obligation, to take one's place in a series of readers whose attention keeps the witness alive.

We are rapidly approaching a diachronic moment of crisis, when the earlier emphasis on authentic witness of the Nazi genocide and 8.6 involving actual experience reaches its limit of survivors, making the etymological sense of the word "holocaust" (total consumption) a grimly literal fact. What will be left then will be the discourse of witness, reaching back for ever fainter traces of experience, an idea in the mind produced by texts and images, not a memory of lived experience. What will happen then is that the discourse will continue in order to continue, the witness not of historical fact but of fact mediated by tradition and myth and text. Memory (of those living at the time) will give way to memorial (sign created for those not living at the time). We cannot be metonymically linked through witness to past events as events in the same way; we can only memorialize them in the form of what Derrida calls "*monumémoire*" or "monumemory," a portmanteau word, coined by him in *Glas* to designate a monument à la mémoire, a "monument in memory."

James Young suggests a reading of Art Spiegelman's *Maus* as just such a text: "Spiegelman does not attempt to represent events he never knew immediately, but instead portrays his necessarily hypermediated experience of the memory of events. This postwar generation, after all, cannot remember the Holocaust as it actually occurred. All they remember, all they know of the Holocaust, is what the victims have passed down to them in their diaries, what the survivors have remembered to them in their memoirs" (1998: 669). In this formulation Young conveniently ignores what he knows to be the case—that the primary witnesses also lack untainted direct access to what "actually occurred"—in order to prevent a structure of ever-diminishing mediation that would make witnesses line up in an entropic series, like the "magnetized" rhapsodes in Plato's *Ion*, dangling one after the other until the magnetic force finally fails. He does so by claiming that "testimony is an event in its own right," on the basis of which the secondary witness can produce "a new story unique to their [i.e., primary and secondary witnesses, father and son] experience together" (676). Thus instead of an ever-diminishing and aging story, we have a "creation" and a "generation" in the form of a new story "grounded" in a directly perceived reality, that of the "event of transmission" in the form of the artist's memory of the witness's memory in the form of "original interviews." Their "necessarily mediated" experience of the Holocaust gives way to an unmediated experience, "the truth of how they came to know the Holocaust" (699).

Shoshana Felman gives us a somewhat different version of the same dynamic of renewal. "To testify," she claims, is to "*produce* one's own speech as material evidence for truth—is to accomplish a *speech act*, rather than to simply formulate a statement" (1992: 5). As a performative act, the "original" testimony will somehow transmit experience directly to its recipient rather than describing or representing it. In this way Lanzmann's film *Shoah* can make "the testimony *happen* . . . as a second Holocaust" (267). Her co-author Dori Laub makes a similar point in terms of "The listener to the narrative of extreme human pain" (57). Testimony to the experience of trauma "includes its hearer," who thus "comes to be a participant and a co-owner of the traumatic event: through his very listening, he comes to partially experience trauma in himself" (57). Here Laub's modifier "partially" takes the edge off Felman's insistence on full reincarnation, and returns us to an entropic series. According to exhibition designer Ralph Applebaum, the original plan for using identity cards in the United States Holocaust Memorial Museum in Washington had a similar goal and rhetoric. The museum was designed to produce a complete identification between the visitors and the victims, "as they moved from their normal lives into ghettos, out of ghettos into trains, from trains to camps . . . until finally to the end." The goal is to have visitors "take that same journey," so that "they would understand the story because they will have experienced the story" (quoted in Linenthal 410). This is a double mediation, first because there was no "story" for the original victims to experience; the story is a narrativized fiction in place of the phenomenological chaos of actual "experience." And second, because museum visitors will have experienced *nothing more than* a "story," and one with quite a different end, where they return to their own "normal lives." As Berenbaum insists, "the Holocaust offers no happy ending, no transcendent meaning, no easy moralism" (1993: 2).

There is a difference, as Walter Benn Michaels emphasizes, between a history that is "learned" at second hand and one that is remembered from personal experience; such a history "can only be remembered by those who first experienced it, and it must belong to them" (189). The reason "replicants" in *Blade Runner* are replicants is that their identities are constituted by memories that don't belong to them. Spiegelman has made the same point in "Mein Kampf, My Struggle," a cartoon in a *New York Times Magazine* special issue on confessional writing. He points out that "remembering those who remembered the death camps is a tough act to follow." The phrase has an ominously double meaning. What can *he* do next, to follow his own act in *Maus*? And what can those do whose experience of the Holocaust comes from him—those who will remember him remembering those who remembered, those in the next generation of witnesses? Being a witness can itself be a form of victimization, and if the "secondary trauma" is sufficiently strong, one's whole life could become a mode of continuing witness. What Spiegelman remembers and what he represents in *Maus* is the scene of *his own* memory of his father's telling of *his* memory, and we can see that this is part of his emphasis on the mediated nature of his knowledge of the Holocaust. In "Mein Kampf, My Struggle," Spiegelman writes "My parents died before I had any kids" over a picture of his crying son, Dashiell, and he ends the cartoon with a statement of fact: "Dash's four years old, and his sister is almost nine. (Two of their grandparents survived Auschwitz.)" The subtitle of the first part of *Maus* is *My Father Bleeds History*, suggesting starkly the existential immediacy of his father's traumatic wounds, but also suggesting the gradual depletion and final exhaustion of a supply of life blood. As a father in his turn, Spiegelman must locate his mediated experience of the Holocaust in Mauschwitz rather than Auschwitz; he can only bleed the history of a history, and that in the form of a cartoon or comic book.

If we heeded the calls to witness that are being mounted on every side, the result would be to live in a permanent state of witness, something like that achieved during the cold war when millions of people learned to live as witnesses to the bomb. The peculiar apotropaic nature of witness in nuclear criticism, during the period when that theoretical/critical movement briefly flourished, was in the paradox of an anticipatory mourning of a present that the future might eradicate, and a grieving for all the human lives and events that would *not* happen if a nuclear holocaust occured.[40] In the early 1980s, E. P. Thompson coined the phrase "Extremism" to characterize his own generation as one that "had witnessed the first annunciation of exterminist technology at Hiroshima, its perfection in the hydrogen bomb, and the inconceivable-absolute ideological fracture of the first Cold War [and] had become, at a deep place in our consciousness, habituated to the expectation that the very continuation of civilization was problematic" (1982: 71). Thompson was immediately criticized for his negativity by many, including Raymond Williams, who protested that Extremism promoted "a sense of helplessness beneath a vast, impersonal and uncontrollable force. For there is nothing then left but subordinated responses of passivity or protest, cynical resignation or prophecy" (1983: 221). In nuclear criticism theory, witnessing was both retroactive and *a priori*, looking back to actual nuclear destruction in Hiroshima and Nagasaki and looking forward to the possibility of nuclear apocalypse. During the decades of the Cold War, the bomb was both a real object and an internal construct for those capable of integrating the idea and estimating its implications. We were all urged to meditate constantly on the bomb, so that we might all experience the

psychological conditions of permanent wartime, with casualties and muta-
tions suffered in imagination before the terminal nuclear blast, in rapt fascination and horror at imaginings of "things that melt eyeballs, blast bodies to
bloody fragments and burn the flesh to the bone of living people" (Soper
178). As a result, the bomb became a universal part of our individual and
collective mental structures, giving children nightmares. It would seem that,
in our post-9/11 state, we are being conditioned by threats of terror and a
pseudo "war" to exist in a similar state of perpetual fear.

In this light, Jameson's statement gains added force: "To forget the dead
altogether is impious" but "to remember the dead is neurotic and obsessive
and merely feeds a sterile repetition. There is no 'proper' way of relating to
the dead and the past" (1995: 103). Many commentators on the Holocaust
and trauma theory take these psychological terms seriously, and employ
psychoanalytic models for their understanding of the problems of memory
as a social/cultural phenomenon. The most frequently invoked concept at
this stage of the discourse is Freud's notion that one can "work through"
(*durcharbeiten*) the traumatizing effects in a "work of mourning," or suffer
an even more complete "loss of self" by lapsing into a fatalistic state that
Freud termed "melancholia." While it may seem that this set of alternatives
is the product of universal common sense, it has been put to work in sophisticated ways by critics like Saul Friedlander, Dominick LaCapra, Andreas Huyssen, and Avital Ronell, who appeal to Freud's concepts of
"melancholy" and "mourning," and their clinical applications in "denial,"
"acting out," and "working through," for an understanding of the problem
of memory and witness on the social level. In different ways they all agree
that the false termination of denial or the fixation on loss in melancholy
should be replaced by the therapeutic goal of working through. But they
also note "the interminable nature of working-through" (Ronell 290) and
the fact that "The therapeutic goal . . . may never be totally or definitively
accomplished" (LaCapra 1994: 48). Friedlander notes the impossibility of
redemptive closure at the individual level and at the public level an erasing
of unbearable events that creates "a tendency towards closure without resolution" (1992b: 54). As we approach the inevitable moment when all surviving witnesses of the Nazi genocide are dead, the stakes are raised and the
discourse becomes both more serious and more trivial. As a sign of seriousness, the French passed the *Loi Gayssot* in 1990, to make the denial of the
Holocaust a criminal offense, joining Germany in the prohibition. On the
other side, we have phenomena like the Oscar for best foreign film awarded
to *Life is Beautiful*, or the stunning popularity of the revival of *The Producers*
as a Broadway play. One can even have a Holocaust vacation organized by
Midas tours: "Day 3. This morning we drive out to the Death Camps of Treblinka, where up to 17,000 victims were murdered daily. Returning to War-

saw for the afternoon, we stroll through the pleasant and peaceful Lazienki Park, maybe to the strains of Chopin. Return to our hotel for dinner."[41]

In the 1990s three elaborate and expensive new Holocaust museums were opened in the U.S.: The United States Holocaust Memorial Museum in Washington, in New York the Museum of Jewish Heritage—A Living Memorial to the Holocaust, and in Los Angeles the "Beit Hashoah—Museum of Tolerance," bringing the total number of Holocaust museums and research centers in the U.S. to over one hundred. It is only in the latter, dedicated to setting the Holocaust in the context of modern racism and genocide, that we find attention paid to instances of mass slaughter other than the Holocaust, in the form of a film on genocide that shows brief scenes from Bosnia and Rwanda and examples of racially motivated violence in Germany, Israel, Russia, and the U.S., ending with an American girl being inducted into the KKK on her sixteenth birthday. The entire film lasts exactly eight and one half minutes, out of a two and one half hours guided tour. Meanwhile a $60 million expansion of the New York Museum of Jewish Heritage is under way, scheduled for completion in 2003. The existence of institutions like Holocaust museums serves the function of providing easy knowledge—easy because it confirms received ideas and fulfills anticipated emotional experience. Their presence leads Andreas Huyssen to identify the museum as a key paradigm of cultural activities and to coin the term "musealization" to identify the phenomenon. In a letter of invitation to become a "member" of the Washington Holocaust Museum, signed by Miles Lerman, chair, one reads:

> Then, finally, when breaking hearts can bear it no longer, visitors will emerge into the light—into a celebration of resistance, rebirth, and renewal for the survivors—whether they remained in Europe, or as so many did, went to Israel or America to rebuild their lives. And having witnessed the nightmare of evil, the great American monuments to democracy that surround each departing visitor will take on new meaning, as will the ideals for which they stand.

In spite of the noble goals of the Museum, this sounds like the description of an "attraction" at Disneyworld. Among the "great American monuments" within walking distance is the Vietnam Veterans Memorial, whose polished surface, covered with the names of American casualties, reflects the image of all Americans who go to see their loss there, but gives no hint of the three million Vietnamese killed during the U.S. involvement in Vietnam. Nor does it give any hint of the ARVN casualties, our dead allies, who cannot be honored in their own country where the Vietnam War is called the America War.[42] As Langer points out, there will always be the temptation to "pander to a hungry popular clamor for reassurance that mass murder had its redeeming features," and those who "would convert death in Auschwitz or Bergen-Belsen into a triumph of love over hate," for whom "nothing less than a renewal of the Golden Age" will suffice (1995b: 7). When the Holocaust is commodified as a spectacle for the entertainment industry, staged and graphically represented, marketed, and managed for vicarious experience and virtuous consumption, then the discourse of witness may become another aesthetic commodity, providing an alternative mode of entertainment. Then we may find ourselves back with Ezekiel, complaining that the people react to the words as if they were nothing more than a musical entertainment or performance:

> And they come unto thee as the people cometh, and they sit before thee as my people, and they hear thy words, but they will not do them. . . . And lo, thou art unto them as a pleasant voice, and can play well on an instrument: for they hear thy words, but they do them not. (33: 31–32)

While we anticipate the opening of the next Holocaust museum, we might also remember the scandal caused by the Enola Gay exhibition at the National Air and Space Museum on the fiftieth anniversary of Hiroshima, showing that even after fifty years, the full history of the devastation in Hiroshima and Nagasaki is not assimilable into official public discourse in this country.[43] Another instance of silencing the Hiroshima holocaust lurks in the most celebrated film of 1996, *The English Patient*. In Michael Ondaatje's novel there is a long background section on Lieutenant Kirpal Singh ("Kip") explaining how he came to be a superloyal sapper, devoted to the memory of his British mentor, Lord Suffolk. When Singh hears of the bombing of Hiroshima he instantly perceives the racist implications:

> American, French, I don't care. When you start bombing the brown races of the world, you're an Englishman. You had King Leopold of Belgium and now you have fucking Harry Truman of the USA. You all learned it from the English. (286)

Another character concurs. "He knows the young soldier is right. They would never have dropped such a bomb on a white nation." Singh's dramatic departure in the novel is a powerful gesture of solidarity with the brown races and a rejection of complicity with what he recognizes as a continuation of the colonial mentality. In the film, however, he simply hops on his motorbike and rides off without explanation.

It is perhaps too tempting to be critical of the "musealization" phenomenon, forgetting that *some* memory is better than *none*. While we agonize about the memory crisis of the Holocaust, we should not ignore the fact that advocates for forgetting are also having their way. One of the most striking instances came in 1985, when Ronald Reagan joined Helmut Kohl in an attempt simultaneously to commemorate the fortieth anniversary of the end of World War II and to free Germany from any painful memories that might be lingering on. Reagan's speech on that occasion calls for what Dominick LaCapra aptly describes as a "celebratory forgetting" that simply ignores all "problems of public acknowledgment, mourning, and working-through" (1994: 73):

> I feel very strongly that this time, in commemorating the end of that great war, that instead of reawakening the memories and so forth, and the passions of the time, that maybe we should observe this day when, 40 years ago, peace began and friendship, because we now find ourselves allies and friends of the countries that we once fought against, and that we, it'd be almost a celebration of the end of an era and the coming into what has now been some 40 years of peace for us. And I felt that, since the German people have been very few alive that remember even the war, and certainly none of them who were adults and participating in any way, and the, they do, they have a feeling and a guilt feeling that's been imposed upon them. And I just think it's unnecessary. I think they should be recognized for the democracy that they've created and the democratic principles they now espouse. (Reported in *The New York Times*, March 22, 1985)

In 1996 the Polish poet Wislawa Szymborska won the Nobel Prize for Literature. The last book she published before winning the prize was *Koniec i poczçatek* ("The end and the beginning" or "An end and a beginning," or simply "End and beginning"), in which she repeatedly suggests the desirability of a *forgetful* relationship to history. For example, from a poem called "No Title Required":

> After every war
> Someone has to tidy up . . .
> Someone has to trudge
> Through sludge and ashes,
> Through the sofa springs,
> The shards of glass,
> The bloody rugs

The Holocaust Memorial Museum can be seen as engaged in a different kind of tidying up, with the largest collection of "authentic" Holocaust artifacts or relics in the world, objects transformed by what Donald Horne calls "the special magic of museums" that "hallows the object in itself, so that often the museum provides . . . a collection of isolated objects, sacred in themselves"(16, 17). Phillip Gourevitch describes his experience after visiting the Holocaust Memorial Museum: "After I left the museum, I bought a soda and strolled along the Mall. When I finished my drink, I found a trash can and was about to toss in my bottle when I noticed a familiar-looking grey card sitting atop the garbage already there. . . . Holocaust museum identity card No. 1221, Maria Sava Moise, Gypsy, had survived the war, only to wind up as a part of the litter of a Washington tourist's afternoon" ("Behold" 60). In spite of having just visited the largest collection of Holocaust relics in the world, the tidy tourist had apparently anticipated Szymborska's message, that only when the junkyard rubbish of memory is cleared away can life go on:

> Those who knew
> What this was all about
> Must make way for those
> Who know little.
> And less than that.
> And at last less than nothing.
>
> Someone has to lie there
> In the grass that covers up
> The causes and effects,
> With a cornstalk in his teeth,
> Gawking at clouds.

The fact that Szymborska lived in Krakow, near Auschwitz (the German for Oswiecm) during the war, gives an added frisson to this image of blissful ignorance. If Thucydides was right when he claimed that "human nature being what it is" the "events which happened in the past . . . will, at some time or other and in much the same ways, be repeated in the future" (25), then we might as well know "less than nothing" for all the good it will do us. Or is it the case that we will eventually know less than nothing about events which happened in the past, no matter what Thucydides has to say?

A recent book by Timothy Ryback reads like an allegory of the contemporary witness discourse. *The Last Survivor* is focused on the modern city of Dachau and its past relationship to the death camp that bears its name, an identity many residents would like to forget, even though—or perhaps because—during the war the location of the camp was welcomed by them for financial reasons. Now the town is still benefiting from the camp, which attracts a large number of visitors each year, whom the local McDonalds tries to attract by putting English-language fliers on the windshields of cars parked in the death camp memorial site lot. Rybeck (an American living in Salzburg) writes about a citizen of Dachau named Martin Zaidenstadt, who has become a full-time survivor/witness, and denies the official version that the gas chambers in the camp were never used, maintaining daily to camp visitors (in multiple languages) that gas *was* used there, challenging all who question him: "Who was there? You or me?" Although Zaidenstadt claims to have been an inmate of the camp, his name does not appear on the records; but the records are admittedly incomplete. Ryback visits Zaidenstadt's *shtetl* in eastern Poland, a place called Jedwabne, but finds no adequate evidence of his identity there. Instead, he finds evidence in Jewish records that it may have been the Poles, still profoundly anti-Semitic even fifty years after the Jews "disappeared," who had packed all the local Jews into a barn and burned them alive. Confronted with this evidence, the town's historian replies, "The Jews have their memories, and we have ours," as blunt an acknowledgment of the politics of memory as can be imagined, and of the effects of time.[44] The most efficient way to avoid a memory crisis is not to have any knowledge to forget, a fact that motivated the Nazis in their suppression of information about the Final Solution. The possibility that the bombings of civilians in Hiroshima and Nagasaki may not have been necessary to achieve victory is only now beginning to find a place in history, as is the fact that U.S. and allied troops ruthlessly slaughtered unknown numbers of Iraqi troops in the Gulf War who were unable to fight or had surrendered or were retreating.

A few years before the Enola Gay controversy, another scandal had erupted when the National Museum of American Art in Washington, D.C., opened an exhibition on the theme of the American West in 1991: "The West as America: Reinterpreting Images of the Frontier 1820–1920." The same year saw the cancellation in cities across the country of a traveling exhibition on the Vietnam War called "As Seen By Both Sides," because of protests of those who objected to a reconciliation or even an acknowledgment of another side to the conflict.[45] It may be that the enthusiastic Americanization of the Holocaust is functioning as a Freudian "screen memory" (*Deckerinnerung*) that employs one traumatic memory in order to cover up memories of another traumatic event that cannot be contemplated directly, so that the fascination with the Holocaust could be read as a kind of screen allegory through which the nation is struggling to find a proper mode of memorializing traumata closer to home. The displaced referents of such memorializing may extend to events as distant as the genocide of Native Americans or as recent as the Vietnam War. Whether we agree with this particular analysis or not, the time when we will celebrate the opening of our Native American Holocaust Museum, or our African Diaspora or slavery Museum seems far in the future.[46]

CHAPTER **1**

The Menchú Effect:
Strategic Lies and Approximate Truths in Texts of Witness
ANA DOUGLASS

The consumption of testimonial literatures on American campuses, and the almost reverential treatment these texts have received, have recently come under intense scrutiny with the publication of an anthropological study of the single most celebrated text of witness of the last two decades, *Me llamo Rigoberta Menchú y asi me nació la conciencia.*[1] Menchú's account of her life as a political activist and spiritual leader altered the trajectory of history in Guatemala and beyond. On one level Menchú's autobiographical narrative exists as a textual record of the horrors enacted against the indigenous population of Guatemala by its right-wing leadership and stands defiantly, both on a political as well as a generic level, as an artifact based exclusively on personal experience. In her testimonial, Menchú presents a personal account of the political and economic repression she, her family, and her village suffered while living and working within a fundamentally feudal land system in Guatemala during the 1970s. Menchú describes how her parents, brothers, friends, and neighbors were subjected to horrific acts of torture and humiliation, in many instances culminating in death, as a direct result of their efforts to undermine the social and economic structures supporting the system of land distribution in rural Guatemala. Within American universities, Menchú's testimonial came to function as the definitive example of the value of testimonial literature, both as literary productions and as vehicles for informing an otherwise uninformed readership about human rights atrocities occurring around the world. A recent critique and, in places, direct refutation of Menchú's text, David Stoll's *Rigoberta Menchú and the Story of All Poor Guatemalans* raises fundamental questions, however, about the "truthfulness" of significant passages and events in Menchú's Nobel Peace Prize generating narrative.[2] Stoll's claims that Menchú's text contained numerous inaccuracies, if not conscious lies and acts of manipulation, unleashed a flurry of discussion in the popular press.[3] His research, whether we are in complete agreement with it or not, forces a rereading not only of Menchú's testimony—a product of the rhetorical stance of the witness—but also of the rhetorical constructs that underlie the primarily Western readers' assumptions *about* the witness—the notion that the witness is necessarily innocent, truthful, and above conscious manipulation in the telling of his or her story.

Considered as a genre, testimonials are more vulnerable than other personal narratives to the many social, political, and historical pressures from which they are generated. Typically, these texts purport to be the utterances—represented with a minimum of external intervention—of the indigenous voice, a voice otherwise rarely recorded, and otherwise never heard. These narratives represent for many readers an almost transparent account of the life and communities of indigenous people, generally from Third World contexts, whose lives and cultural fabrics are coming unraveled under the pressures of encroaching Western values and persistent political, economic, and social oppression from within. A common subtext of texts of witness is the theme of cultural loss as they chronicle the acculturating impact of various economic, political, and religious forces affecting the indigenous communities' previously "uncomplicated" lives. Read within this context, testimonial literatures stand as a kind of "pure" utterance and "authentic" transmission of experience in spite of theoretical trends of the last few decades that question the notion of "truth" within the unstable vehicle of language. These texts avoid the interpretive pressures of poststructuralism, not because they are somehow outside of contemporary models for understanding language and its relationship to concepts of "truth," but because of a perceived political necessity of their very existence. "*Testimonio*," John Beverley argues, "can never . . . create the illusion of that textual 'in-itselfness' that has been the basis of literary formalism, nor can it be adequately analyzed in these terms." Read in this light, texts of witness occur as "an extraliterary or even antiliterary form of discourse" (Beverley 1996a: 37). Any attempt to consider Menchú's persona as a rhetorical construct can be construed as a denial of the fact that human rights abuses occur in Guatemala. Such an act would be an abuse of practice in the name of theory, a cynical subordination of historical fact and political realities to the solipsistic pursuit of theory. To do so would be tantamount to dismissing Menchú's authority to serve as a witness to an undeniably "real" series of human rights abuses.

Thus, critics have tended to employ "a hermeneutics of solidarity" to generate "sympathetic" readings of texts of witness that account only for the political context out of which the text is produced.[4] In an effort to create this sense of solidarity with the politics of the witness, critics pay little, if any, attention to the rhetorical processes and aesthetic considerations influencing the production of texts of witness and often completely ignore the political climate affecting the readership's consumption of these texts. Such critics have evacuated the interpretive process in favor of a facile affirmation of the absolute "truth value" of the witness's account, ignoring many of the rules of textual analysis they would not hesitate to consider when reading a novel on the subject of human rights abuses from anywhere in the world.[5] Equally telling, the politics of consumption—the social, political, and economic conditions shaping the perceptions of the Western reader—have received very little consideration. The resulting criticism is more interested in building a sense of solidarity with the witness than in looking critically at the politics of production and consumption of the text itself.

In light of recent revelations that Menchú's text includes distortions and moments of false or inaccurate information, it seems that the time has come to revisit the forces that brought her testimonial to such prominence in the Western world and to reconsider notions of authorship and readership in her text and the relationship between the two. For my purposes, the politics that produce texts of witness and the politics that inform the way the readership consume texts of witness are inextricably intertwined. A second equally significant consideration, caught between the forces of production and consumption and implicated in both, is the issue of the primacy of the text itself, the need to hold in place the artifact with its rhetorical constructs and strategies, its capacity to stand in error and to stand in some proximity to truth. The issue of Menchú's "truthfulness" interests me less than the difficulties her "lies" present to the hermeneutics of solidarity informing the critical line on her text. I would prefer to ask the questions: what do Menchú's "lies" tell us about the nature of the readership of texts of witness, and how do "lies" function within the textual doubling "effect" that I see as a defining characteristic of the genre? Somewhere in between the politics of production and the politics of consumption of these texts, the witness establishes the witnessing "effect," a concept that should be understood both in terms of the noun—an "effect"—and in terms of its rarer usage as a verb—"to effect" change. Testimonials as artifacts include both meanings of the term. Whether or not readers can agree upon the "truth value" of their content, texts of witness create in their very existence a supposition of "truth value," an "effect" or, as Alberto Moreiras argues, an "aura" of truth that gestures at "absolute truth." Herein lies the power and value of texts of witness, the doubling effect that I am calling the "Menchú effect."

I. The Politics of Western Consumption: The "Rebirth of the Sacred," the Culture Wars, and the Defining of a New Genre[6]

In critical considerations of the politics informing the production and consumption of texts of witness, the other genres used for representing the events and transmitting the "truths" of a politically volatile situation are often forgotten—the less glamorous texts of governmental documents, the popular press, and human rights reports. Texts of witness take on a somewhat sacred role in discussions of international politics and human rights abuses. During the 1970s and 1980s, horrific human rights abuses occurred in countries throughout the world, but it was only with the widespread dissemination of texts of witness that Western readers began to consider the implications of the ongoing atrocities in a country like Guatemala. For a number of reasons, academics and their students preferred the single voice of the "eyewitness" over the governmental study, the human rights document, or the Western journalist's account. This preference for first person accounts fed directly into the essentialist belief system inherent in the emerging identity politics of the 1980s. In accordance with this brand of identity politics, the privileged status of the testimony ultimately stems from a belief within the readership, either implicit or explicit, that the eyewitness account gleans a kind of authenticity from the speaker's proximity to his or her culture and its traditions. The witness's credibility resides at least in part in a shared identity with those who are being victimized and, in some cases, even with those who are perpetuating the victimization of the witness and the community. From this privileged position of shared core identity, the witness speaks with a kind of authority that begins from the premise that the accuracy of the account resides first and foremost in the unimpeachable authority of shared identity—an authenticity of speech that can only come from a deeper shared identification with the victims. It is in the linguistic encounter with the "authentic other" that the reader can come to understand events and issues of another culture that would otherwise escape comprehensibility.

Western critics have recently tried to account for the 1980s' fascinated consumption of Third World literature, especially the vaguely defined genre of testimonial literature.[7] Precipitating what might loosely be referred to as the "culture debates" of the 1980s, texts such as Miguel Barnet's record of the life of Esteban Montejo, *The Autobiography of a Runaway Slave*, and *I, Rigoberta Menchú: An Indian Woman in Guatemala*, were embraced by the academic left as exemplary of a new "poetics of solidarity," focal points of "resistance literature" which not only served as a powerful resource for addressing issues of class, race, and cultural difference in the classroom but also as an equally provocative tool for applying pressure to the hegemony of the literary canon and the hierarchy of genre implied within it (Gugelberger 1996b: 1). With the widespread inclusion of Third World testimonials in core curricula across the United States, a debate ensued in which the academic left saw in the testimonial literature of Third World peoples a source of potentially liberating leftist discourse and a means of creating greater understanding of and solidarity with these emerging liberation movements. The sides of the "culture debates" loosely fell along "those who saw in *testimonio* a salvation, almost the proof that the subaltern *can* speak, and those who saw in the first wave of reception a flawed affirmation giving way to an implicit restitution of precisely that discipline that the originators of the discourse considered as being challenged by the *testimonio*" (Gugelberger 1996b: 6, emphasis added). In practice, this debate achieved a potentially undesirable and unexpected end for Western scholars, with the coopting at the level of ideas and language of the Third World by the First World, in a "Latinamericanism" similar to the "Orientalism" identified by Edward Said.[8]

In the 1980s, Western audiences were presented with a proliferation of first person accounts of the economic and social abuses perpetrated against various marginal communities throughout much of the Third World. At the same time, universities within the United States were engaged in an active attempt to "diversify" the curriculum.[9] The traditional Western culture course "appeared to many not only an anachronism but the exemplar of everything that needed to change in the new university" (Pratt 2001: 32). At many universities student- and faculty-led grassroots movements emerged, attempting to force curricular changes that would incorporate such texts into their Western traditions-based curricula. In his much discussed work, *Illiberal Education*, Dinesh D'Souza chronicles one of the most widely discussed and openly contested examples of this movement to incorporate testimonial texts into core curricula—the transformation by Stanford University faculty of their Western traditions core course to a "Culture, Ideas, and Values" course, a shift that marked a curricular move away from a traditional "great books" approach to one that reflected multicultural concerns. *I, Rigoberta Menchú* serves for D'Souza as "the text which best reveals the premises underlying the new Stanford curriculum" (71). Indeed, Pratt sees D'Souza's text as "the book that definitively established *I, Rigoberta Menchú* as a political target" (2001: 35). Describing Menchú as "a consum-

mate victim," a woman who "suffer[s] from multiple vectors of simultaneous oppression," D'Souza challenges the decision to use her testimony to
replace the "great works" of the Western traditional canon. "Rigoberta's victim status," he suggests, "may be unfortunate for her personal happiness,
but is indispensable for her academic reputation" (72). D'Souza's critique
of Stanford's move to replace Dante with Menchú lies with his discomfort
with what he calls the "paradoxical provincialism" of the "multicultural
project," the paradoxical impulse, he argues, for women and students of
color to want to study themselves rather than study such non-Western cultural phenomena as the influence of Japanese markets upon the world's
economies or the increasingly powerful presence of Islamic fundamental-
ism in Third World politics.

D'Souza's critique of Menchú herself and his understanding of her text
reveals his own conservative political agenda, which sees her and her text as
pawns of leftist campus politics. In a particularly misleading statement,
D'Souza argues that students see Menchú as "a modern Saint Sebastian,
pierced by the arrows of North American white male cruelty . . . her life
becom[ing] an explicit indictment of the historical role of the West and
Western institutions" (72). He asks the complicated question: "Whom does
she represent?" and offers the simple answer that she "embodies a projection of Marxist and feminist views onto South American Indian culture."[10]
D'Souza's criticism of Menchú as a political activist, however, ventures beyond simply disagreeing with what he perceives to be her Marxist and feminist beliefs. He even goes so far as to discount Menchú's suffering as that of
a person who "simply happened to be in the right place at the right time," as
if to find oneself in the midst of a genocidal moment in history could in
any way be read in terms of being "in the right place" (72).

While it is relatively easy to dismiss D'Souza's critique of Menchú herself
and of the value of texts of witness in general, his critique of the academic
left is a bit more difficult to discount given the widespread usurpation by
First World academics of the text to serve their Marxist and feminist agendas. Again, the distinction is one between the text itself and the politics of
consumption informing the reception of the text. D'Souza argues that
Menchú's testimony gets used by Marxist and feminist academics as "independent Third World corroboration of Western progressive ideologies,"
her words serving as a mere "mouthpiece for a sophisticated left-wing critique of Western society," a critique that is "all the more devastating because
it issues not from a French scholar-activist but from a seemingly authentic
Third World source" (72). It is here that D'Souza actually touches upon a
legitimate critique. He sees in the 1980s move to affirm texts of witness evidence that the academy was simply creating another professional pathway
for itself, another vehicle for replicating itself through the act of celebrating

texts that it decided are worthy of celebration. D'Souza's charge that the emergence of texts of witness during the 1980s is tied to a shift in the trends of scholarship in the humanities and social sciences and a need for those disciplines to reinvent themselves finds support when we consider the flurry of scholarship dedicated to defining the history and boundaries of the genre of *testimonio* within Latin American literature. Consideration of texts of witness "c[ame] to be an important academic activity in the context of Latin American literature . . . cultural studies departments," anthropology, and other literary traditions at precisely the same time when "high literature [was experiencing] a loss of cultural capital" (Moreiras 196, 198). This trend goes to the heart of the politics of consumption of texts of witness. At the same time that D'Souza and other conservative cultural critics were launching public attacks on what they considered to be the academic left's misplaced fascination and overvaluation of texts of witness, "the emergence of the 'Third World' genre of the *testimonio* on the (largely academic) markets of the First World" initiated a flurry of scholarship that quickly became a career path in the humanities (Gugelberger 1996b: 6). The first step in this movement to legitimize the scholarly pursuit of texts of witness was to define the boundaries of the genre and to chronicle its origins.

John Beverley gives the most often cited definition of the primary characteristics of the genre of *testimonio*.[11] Building upon Raymond Williams' argument, in "The Writer: Commitment and Alignment," that the emergence of new genres can be understood in terms of the emergence of new historical consciousness, and the assumption that "the forms of working-class consciousness are bound to be different from the literary forms of another class," Beverley suggests that the genre of *testimonio* performs a similar ideological task for representing the colonial and postcolonial consciousness of the modern era (Williams 1980: 25). Such an era, defined in part as it is by "the potential for transition from one mode of production to another" should expect "to experience the emergence of new forms of cultural and literary expression that embody, in more or less thematically explicit and formally articulated ways the social forces contending for power in the world today" (Beverley 1996a: 24). By "*testimonio*," Beverley means, "a novel or novella-length narrative in book or pamphlet (that is, printed as opposed to acoustic) form, told in the first person by a narrator who is also the real protagonist or witness of the events he or she recounts, and whose unit of narration is usually a 'life' or a significant life experience" (1996a: 24). While he acknowledges the role of earlier "*testimonio*-like texts [that] have existed at the margin of literature," he maintains that the full-blown emergence of the genre occurs in the aftermath of "two related developments: the 1970 decision of Cuba's *Casa de las Americas* to begin awarding a prize in this category in its annual literary contest, and the reception in the late 1960s of Truman Capote's *In Cold Blood* and Miguel Barnet's *Autobiography of a Runaway Slave (Biographia de un cimarron)*" (1996a: 25). It is, however, Beverley's inclusion of Che Guevara's *Reminiscences of the Cuban Revolutionary War* that reveals the broader cultural politics at work in the defining of the genre itself. For Beverley, Guevara's "direct-participant account" initiates a proliferation of *testimonio* by "combatants" in the 26 of July Movement and at the Bay of Pigs. While Beverley's assertion that *testimonio* is an "embryonic" form for reflecting the voices of various ethnic and national liberation movements might suggest that *testimonio* is without an extensive history, others have argued that we can trace the history of testimonial literature in the Latin American tradition back to the ethnographic texts of sixteenth-century explorers.[12]

In contrast to Beverley's literary definition of the parameters of the genre of *testimonio*, Amy Fass Emery suggests that various Latin American sixteenth-century texts reveal ethnographic documentation of the disappearing cultures, peoples, values, and rituals of Latin America, producing what might be considered the anthropological version of the genre of testimonial literature. In contrast to the literary scholars who emphasized the generic boundaries of testimonials, the anthropological model is more concerned with the ethnographic strain within these texts, their tendency to chronicle the rituals of cultures lost and diminishing in the world. Early ethnologists like Bernardino de Sahagun generated narratives from the "testimony" of native informants. Similarly, in the nineteenth century, proto-anthropolgists like E. B. Tylor and naturalists like Charles Darwin recorded, either as the focus of their studies or as significant observations in conjunction with other scientific studies, the life histories of various indigenous groups. These early anthropological texts, in part trafficking on the popularity of travel literature, marked an attempt to consolidate the rhetorical authority of an emerging discipline and at the same time they constituted an attempt by anthropologists "to popularize their craft, to make it accessible and alive for a broad audience."[13] In keeping with these earlier models for recording life histories, Oscar Lewis created the "first actual life histories to be produced in Latin America." Devoted to the idea of "mak[ing] social sciences readable for the layman . . . to merg[ing] art and science," Lewis actively invoked what he considered to be the "literariness of personal narrative" as a rhetorical strategy for combating the "dryness of the scientific document" (Emery 15). Lewis' work has been identified as a primary influence upon Miguel Barnet, who bears witness for what many consider to be the first modern *testimonio*.[14]

For George Yúdice, those qualities that distinguish the genre of *testimonio* are primarily ideological. *Testimonio* can be defined by the degree to which the narrator bearing witness "reject[s] . . . master narratives" in his or her search for "survival within specific and local circumstances" (44). In contrast to Beverley's definition, Yúdice places greater weight upon the circumstances in which the witness speaks, the social and political context rather than the historical generic precursors to testimonial. "Testimonial writing," Yúdice asserts, "may be defined as an authentic narrative, told by a witness who is moved to narrate by the urgency of a situation." The quality that distinguishes testimonials from autobiography is the way in which the witness "portrays his or her own experience as an agent (rather than as a representative) of a collective memory and identity." While begging the question of what constitutes an "authentic narrative," he goes on to embrace the quality of the testimonial that critics find most difficult to account for—the role of the auditor in the authorship of texts of witness. Yúdice privileges those testimonials written "as collaborative dialogues between activists engaged in a struggle and politically committed or empathetic transcribers/editors" (44). The emergence of the genre of *testimonio* is, for Yúdice, evidence that "there is a shift taking place in the very notion of the literary," a challenge to the "definitions of the literary as legitimized by the dominant educational, publishing, and professional institutions" (46).

Yúdice's celebration of texts of witness and their capacity to undermine the literary status quo is precisely the stance that troubles D'Souza the most. Regardless of the degree to which we might want to champion Yúdice's "hermeneutics of solidarity" over D'Souza's conservative cultural critique, Stoll's unearthing of the inaccuracies in Menchú's text necessarily forces a rereading of it. The identity politics of the 1980s determined to a great extent the way that Menchú's text was received and understood by the academic left. Viewed as an authentic and authoritative account of the troubles in Guatemala, Menchú's text was above criticism, resistant to any charge that other "witnesses" might tell a different story of similar events. The academic left had no difficulty seeing Menchú's account in the terms that Menchú herself wanted them to—hers was "the story of all poor Guatemalans" (Menchú 1984: 1). Commenting on the response that he received from his fellow academics for raising questions about Menchú's veracity, Stoll suggests that to raise the specter that Menchú's story "is not the eyewitness account it purports to be" and that "other survivors [could] give rather different versions" of events central to Menchú's text is "to verge on blasphemy," to be accused of "having an odious political agenda." Clearly having experienced this response first hand, Stoll notes that "to question her story and [to] experience some of the reactions is to experience the rebirth of the sacred in our supposedly post-everything academe" (Stoll 1998: 9). That Stoll should receive this reaction in the late 1990s suggests that the climate of the culture wars of the 1980s, defined as it was by identity politics and academic turf wars, still has a strong hold on the academy today.[15] Because the Western readership was and in many ways still is predisposed to see in Menchú a purer presence, an authentic voice of the victim, her text achieves "the effect" of representing "absolute truths," even as it performs its greater task, of "effecting" political change. The presence of inaccuracies, even "lies" may, in fact, be a critical, or at minimum, not an unexpected part of achieving this doubling effect.

II. Rethinking Menchú as Historical Witness
Guatemala: A Case Study in Repression

Rigoberta Menchú's testimony seemed wholly plausible to critics and lay readers alike because, when looking at Guatemalan social, economic, and political history, the content of her story seemed in keeping with perceived trends within her country.[16] "When the Spaniards conquered Guatemala in the early sixteenth century, they burned and looted Maya cities," creating, as Arias notes, "one of history's first holocausts" in which an "estimated . . . two and a half million Mayas died in the fifty years following the Conquest" (2001a: 3). In the twentieth century, genocidal moments continued to be a defining characteristic of the Guatemalan historical landscape. As Menchú and numerous human rights groups were reporting, indigenous bodies were disappearing into the night, only to be found tortured and disfigured at some later date. Entire Maya villages were destroyed, forcing many into exile. "Even prior to the more detailed report provided by the United Nations Commission for Historical Clarification (Comisión para el Esclarecimiento Histórico, CEH) in 1999," Arias notes that "both the human rights organizations and the army itself often spoke of the destruction of more than 450 Maya villages, more than a hundred thousand deaths, and more than a million refugees" (2001a: 4–5). The Truth Commission Report estimates that 93 percent of the violence was committed by the army and its supporters.

The history of Guatemalan human rights abuses and the social and political oppression of its people stands as a singularly tragic case in a region with a long history of indifference to human rights, especially those of its indigenous peoples. Excluding a decade of democratic governance between the mid-1940s and 1950s, the contemporary history of Guatemala is one marred by systematic repression of its indigenous populations. Next to Bolivia, Guatemala has one of the largest percentages of indigenous peoples in Latin America.[17] Central America's third largest country, Guatemala in many ways is its wealthiest nation in natural resources, a magnet throughout the twentieth century for foreign investment. While Guatemala has numerous natural resources, the distribution of that wealth within the country is shockingly unequal, especially when analyzed along ethnic lines. According to human rights reports, during the 1980s 79 percent of Guatemala's population was considered to be either "poor" or "extremely poor." The primary point of economic disparity between the Ladino land-owning minority and the indigenous Maya Indians is the distribution of land. According to the Agency for International Development (Richard Hough et al.) report, *Land and Labor in Guatemala: An Assessment*, in 1982, Guatemala had the worst record of land distribution in Central America, exceeding even the ratings of pre-reform Nicaragua and El Salvador. During the 1980s, some seventy percent of the land was owned by only two percent of the population, and from the mid-1960s through the 1970s, military leaders expropriated much of the rural highlands, the lands traditionally farmed by Maya communities, to form what has come to be known as the "Generals' Strip" or the *Franja Transversal del Norté*, a strip of land replete with natural resources that has become the site of a transnational roadway. It is this history of uneven land distribution that serves as the primary force behind peasant organizing in the early 1970s. Certainly for Menchú, her family's and neighbors' relationship to the lands they farmed in the highlands and the time they spent laboring in the coffee *fincas* was a central factor in their decision to join in grassroots agrarian cooperatives and political action groups.[18]

The history of Guatemala's uneven land distribution is a long one and a central issue of concern for Menchú. Beginning with the Spanish Conquest, the indigenous populations have "systematically been denied their land, then forced to work it, for pitiful wages, by Spanish landowners, the Catholic clergy, eighteenth-century coffee barons, and later, by the Guatemalan army, who transformed the military into a lucrative business in the 1960s" (Simon 20). In other words, with the growing economic success of the few primary landowners, corporate groups, and government and military leaders, the economic viability of the Maya majority and poor Ladinos showed a different trajectory of growth—one defined by increasing impoverishment, indentured servitude, and land displacement. Along with the history within Guatemala of consolidating land and resources in the hands of the few, Guatemala has an equally long history of abusive labor practices, especially when seen along ethnic lines. As far back as the sixteenth century, Guatemala had the "*encomienda*" laws, which were "a system of forced labor whereby the Spanish *encomenderos* were granted allotments of 'natives' to indoctrinate into the ways of the Church . . . and received the right to demand labor or payment in kind," and "*repartimiento*" laws, which amounted to "the allotment of 'Indians' for a specific task, usually to carry out public works" (Moore 55, 123). As late as the 1940s, Guatemala had what was known as the Vagrancy Law, a law "based on the familiar idea that work must be an obligation for all . . . [and that] required that all who had neither profession nor trade should be obliged to go to work (mainly on the plantations) for 100 to 150 days each year" (Pearse 26). Workers were expected to carry a book documenting the number of days spent working on a plantation. "Any person suspecting another person of 'vagrancy' could denounce him to the local authorities," and as a result of the basic illiteracy and inability to speak Spanish of the indigenous populations, this law essentially "delivered them bound to the local officials and the landowners, who could put them to work with the full support of the law." The indigenous populations were especially persecuted under the Vagrancy Law in that "it is implicit in the law that it is to be applied to the 'Indian' [groups], immediately recognizable by the appurtenances of ethnicity, and also already conditioned to accept such impositions, implying exclusion from the enjoyment of the rights of citizens" (Pearse 27). The most recent incarnation of this history of forced labor occurred during the 1970s. In an effort to control peasant participation in guerrilla groups, the army forced the male members of Indian communities to join civil patrols, pseudo-military groups designated to patrol for guerrilla groups. This process also created labor gangs to work on such projects as rural road development.

Ironically, it was an attempt by democratically elected President Jacobo Arbenz to create significant land reform that led to the beginning of some thirty-five years of systematic political and economic repression, a state of affairs that has defined Guatemalan society for the last four decades. In 1952, President Arbenz attempted to address agrarian reform with his Decree 900, a law designed to open up land ownership to the indigenous groups who were already working these lands without ownership. Arbenz's land reform efforts incited the opposition of various international businesses, the most powerful of which was the United States-based corporation, the United Fruit Company. The largest landowner in Guatemala, the United Fruit Company had enjoyed a tax-exempt monopoly of the banana industry since the turn of the twentieth century. Prompted by the economic interests of the United Fruit Company, the U.S. State Department initiated a "destabilization campaign and propaganda blitz" designed to undermine the credibility of President Arbenz (Simon 20).[19] With this campaign of disinformation in place, the CIA engineered a coup that resulted in the rise to power of Colonel Carlos Castillo Armas as President of Guatemala.[20]

Along with the distinction of having the single most inequitable distribution of resources in Latin America, Guatemala carries dubious honors when it comes to the issue of human rights abuses. Guatemala is the first country to have "death squads" within its borders, perhaps the most infamous of which would be the "White Hand" or *Mano Blanca*. As a result of groups like *Mano Blanca*, Guatemala became the site of another dubious distinction—the term, "*desaparecido*," first emerged in the Guatemalan press to describe the disturbing numbers of individuals who were killed or "disappeared" with the increasing political tensions within Guatemala. Indeed, the term "*desaparecido*," according to Simon, "acquired its grammatical versatility as both a verb and a participle ('to be disappeared,' 'he was disappeared') in Guatemala almost a decade before the term was exported to Chile and Argentina." The human rights statistics for Guatemala stand out in a region of terrible atrocities. Thirty-nine percent of "disappearances" in Latin America occurred in Guatemala. Moreover, the American Association for the Advancement of Science (AAAS) asserts that, during the 1970s and 1980s, "at least 100,000 political killings and 38,000 'disappearances' [had been] carried out by army, police, and paramilitary government forces" (Simon 14). In response to the politicizing of the indigenous communities, the Guatemalan government, the landowners of Spanish descent, and the army initiated a campaign of terror and repression that exceeded any seen in the region.[21]

In response to increasing governmental and military repression, grassroots peasant organizations began to form. Agrarian cooperatives have existed in Guatemala throughout the twentieth century, finding their moment of greatest acceptance during the Arbenz regime of the late 1940s and early 1950s. However, between the mid-1960s and mid-1970s, agrarian cooperative groups almost tripled in number and increased exponentially in terms of their political activities. Indeed, Vicente Menchú, Rigoberta's father, emerged as a political force within these grassroots agrarian reform movements. Encouraged in great part by the Christian Democratic party, a political party organized in 1955, and the Catholic Church—two groups who were interested in achieving change through less radical means than the military option reflected in guerrilla groups like the Guerrilla Army of the Poor (EGP)—these cooperatives were led by peasant "catechists." These cooperative "catechists," like Vicente Menchú and Rigoberta Menchú herself, were usually rural leaders who, in keeping with the teachings of Catholic Action and liberation theology, attended to the labor and spiritual needs of their communities, increasing through their actions the collective level of social awareness of their peers. In many respects, the term "catechist" serves as a kind of all-encompassing idea, the point of intersection between the imported and indigenous ideologies in Menchú's text.[22] As the text progresses, the term "catechist" matures along with Menchú's political consciousness as she becomes a kind of catechist to the rest of the world, spreading word of the Guatemalan conflict to places and people who otherwise would have remained ignorant of the atrocities being committed there.

III. The Politics of Textual Production: "The Result of Collective Labor" or "A Mere Instrument for a Foreign Storymaster"?

The context from which Menchú tells her story is the recent political and social history of Guatemala; it is equally important, however, to look at the history of the production of Menchú's text itself. The production of a text of witness can be considered in light of two primary issues: the discursive and theoretical forces that define the text as an artifact in hand, and the political and cultural politics in which the witness exists and out of which the witness attempts to record his or her experiences. The production of Menchú's texts, as with all texts of witness, necessarily reflects a collage of intervening presences—witness, editor, transcriber, translator, reader. Her text then reflects the different voices, styles of expression, perceptions of "truth," and political agendas of each and every participant in its chain of production. Texts of witness are necessarily heavily mediated by the author function of the initial auditor, in Menchú's case, Elisabeth Burgos-Debray. An anthropologist and political activist, Burgos-Debray recorded and transcribed Menchú's narrative. In contrast to Yúdice's romanticized notion of the nature of the working relationship between the activist and the "politically committed or empathetic transcribers/editors," Menchú's and Burgos-Debray's relationship has been one defined in recent years by conflict and disagreement, not by shared political commitment (Yúdice 44). Their relationship, both working and financial, has surfaced as a primary issue in reconsidering Menchú's text. A second issue—whether Arturo Taracena or Burgos-Debray served as the primary editor of the manuscript—has been a point of contention in the discussion of the complex authorship of the text as well. Menchú has a complicated, often conflicted response as to whether or not the text reflects her story as she told it, and whether or not she would have the world view the text as her unadulterated story. In December of 1997, in *El Periódico*, Menchú argues that the text "does not belong to [her] morally, politically, or economically," and that "anyone who has doubts about the work should go to [Burgos-Debray] because, even legally, [Menchú] does not have author's rights, royalties or any of that" (quoted in Stoll 1999: 178).[23] At other times, Menchú suggests that the text is "the result of collective labor," brought together "with the help of many friends from the Guatemalan Solidarity group," even as she argues that she was an active editor of her story (quoted in Stoll 1999: 182). In Menchú's second autobiographical narrative, *Crossing Borders,* she attributes a special editorial role to her friend, Arturo Taracena:[24]

> The taping of my testimony lasted around twelve days. Afterward, there was a Guatemalan solidarity collective in Paris that helped with the transcription. . . . Dr. Taracena participated greatly in ordering the book, together with Elisabeth Burgos. At the end, they

also selected the chapters together. With this, I would like to say that Arturo Taracena has a significant role in the book. . . . Afterward came the text already arranged. For two months or more, I took time to understand it. What one feels speaking is very different than when it is on paper. . . . I simply was not aware of the commercial rules when I wrote that reminiscence. (quoted in Stoll 1999: 301)[25]

In this case, Menchú does not argue that she was excluded from the editorial process; instead, she suggests that she spent "some two months" coming "to understand" the shape and content of the text. While Menchú has remained somewhat inconsistent as to whether or not she played an active role in structuring the text, she has been much more consistent in demanding her legal rights as "official" author of the text. In 1991, Menchú suggested that "what is effectively a gap in the book is the question of the right of the author, right? Because the authorship of the book really should be more precise, shared, right?. . . . An author was needed, and [Burgos-Debray is] an author" (Brittin and Dworkin, quoted in Stoll 1999: 187). Soon after making this statement, Menchú approached Burgos-Debray about signing over authorial rights so that she could initiate her own contracts. Burgos-Debray and the publishers, Gallimard, turned down Menchú's request, which in turn, according to Stoll, led Menchú to make very public charges that Burgos-Debray was defrauding Menchú of her share of the proceeds from the book.

Burgos-Debray tells a very different story. While she admits to "correct[ing] verb tenses and noun genders" and, as she openly states in her introduction to the text, to "giv[ing] the manuscript the form of a monologue," she denies changing the details of any of the fundamental events of the narrative (xx).[26] Stoll's research suggests that Menchú was not "a mere instrument for a foreign storymaster." Before speaking with Burgos-Debray, Menchú had been telling a very similar story, detailing the same events, even beginning her narrative in a similar fashion in other public documents. Stoll notes that, in a news bulletin from December 2, 1981, Menchú "anticipates the key claim of her Paris story" when she says: "My sorrow and my struggle are also the sorrow and struggle of an entire oppressed people who struggle for their liberation" (Stoll 1999: 183).

The issue of whether or not we are to "believe" or "disbelieve" Menchú's narrative to be a factual retelling of events she witnessed depends greatly upon our willingness to bracket off our awareness that other forces and authors are involved in the act of producing this text. For example, Stoll argues that those inaccuracies within the text reflect the story as told by Menchú and are not the brainchild of Burgos-Debray. Upon listening to some of the taped initial interview between Menchú and Burgos-Debray,

Stoll suggests that Menchú "sounds in control" and notes that he "heard little prompting from" Burgos-Debray. "From the start of the session," Stoll argues, "Rigoberta [was] creating a persona for herself as a Guatemalan everywoman." Stoll, therefore, sees in Rigoberta Menchú's assertion that she is metonymically a stand in for all poor Guatemalans evidence of her "manipulation" of the process of bearing witness; however, it is equally possible to see this rhetorical shift simply as a function of the genre—a statement that achieves the effect of making the presence of one body stand in for the absence of the many. In a final gesture of support for Burgos-Debray, perhaps somewhat misplaced in its own willingness to place all the blame on Menchú, Stoll discharges Burgos-Debray of any responsibility in promoting a text with documented inaccuracies, stating that "under the spell of [Menchú's] calm voice," he also "would have believed everything she said" (Stoll 1999: 188). Stoll clearly wants to maintain the image that the anthropological encounter between Burgos-Debray and Menchú— ethnographer and native informant—was conducted properly and within the ethical guidelines of the profession. In a sense, Stoll is displacing all "blame" for the textual inaccuracies onto Menchú. Ironically, by doing so, Stoll casts Burgos-Debray in the role of "victim" of the disinformation and manipulation of her own native informant; of course, this is a relationship that the anthropologist is supposed to be trained to negotiate. Stoll's position, however, is somewhat suspect. Menchú tells her story with a single purpose in mind—to bring worldwide attention to the larger truths of acts of violence in her country. That she would distort details and represent herself in a light that was not entirely accurate is simply part of the rhetorical strategies that go into creating the persona of the eyewitness, *the effect* of the act of bearing witness. That Burgos-Debray did not consider the possibility that Menchú could be representing her eyewitness account in less than perfectly truthful terms is not evidence that she was a "victim" of Menchú's manipulative ways so much as she is a "victim" of her own willingness to ascribe to Menchú an authenticity and authority to speak for a people and a politics that mirror her own identity politics. She was hearing what she wanted to hear, and like the Western readership as a whole, Burgos-Debray chose to emphasize her politics of solidarity with Menchú instead of following the recognized protocols of her professional training.

Even as Stoll's research complicates any discussion of authorship and the politics of production of the text itself, he in no way dismisses the fact that Menchú's text chronicles the essential events of Menchú's life and that the text played a critical role in bringing world attention to Guatemala. As a human rights document, Menchú's text achieves the "effect" of representing the hardships facing the indigenous populations during Guatemala's civil war. "Whatever is mythic" about Menchú's text "does not prevent it from also being historical," from documenting very real human rights abuses in Guatemala and from bringing the reader into some proximity of "truths" about those abuses, into an encounter with Otherness (Stoll 1998: 9). "There is no question," Stoll argues, "that a K'iché Maya peasant named Vicente Menchú organized a new settlement called Chimel or that he was persecuted by the Guatemalan army . . . that he, wife Juana and son Petrocinio were killed in the space of 5 months (December 1979–April 1980) or that tens of thousands of peasants were subsequently killed by the Guatemalan army" (Stoll 1998: 9).[27] Stoll also does not dispute that land ownership for Menchú's father and for Chimel residents was a central issue during the 1970s.[28] However, while these essentially historical facts are necessarily represented in the text, much of the text finds its voice trafficking on what may be considered more literary concerns—tropes in place of direct representation, a poetics of witnessing rather than a more literal accounting of daily events. This poetics of witnessing depends upon the readers' willingness to suspend their awareness that what the witness presents as "truth" may in fact be caught somewhere in between the perceived "absolute truths" of historical accounts and the "universal truths" reflected in the literary. The "effect" of texts of witness depends precisely on this willingness of the audience to collapse the difference between the historical and the literary.

In Menchú's text, this poetics of witness is most evident when examining the issue of Menchú's use of Spanish and the quality of her voice in the text. In 1982, Menchú sat down with Burgos-Debray to tell her story in Spanish, not her native K'iche' Maya. The significant difference in the quality of the first person voice in *I, Rigoberta Menchú: An Indian Woman in Guatemala*, a text generated out of obscurity, and Menchú's second text, *Crossing Borders*, a text that chronicles Menchú's life in exile as a player on the stage of international politics, suggests one of four options: Menchú's account is heavily mediated by her transcriber and translator; Menchú is actively creating a persona for herself that suits the political agenda of the moment; Menchú's language skills improve rather dramatically between the publication of her two texts; some combination of the three previous options. In the earlier text, Menchú's voice is that of a naïve innocent who is brought into political consciousness as a result of having witnessed acts of torture and murder. In her second text, however, her voice takes on an elevated consciousness (most obviously at the level of vocabulary) that reflects the political savvy and acumen necessary for the world stage of human rights activism.[29] In *I, Rigoberta Menchú*, the issue of Menchú's subjectivity is clearly intertwined with the issue of her use of the language of the colonizer, her claim that she has reluctantly turned to the language of her auditors to assure a hearing of her testimony. This is a claim the readership and Burgos-Debray were eager to hear and believe, as it fit with their preconceptions about who Menchú should be as an appropriate and authentic witness for oppressed indigenous groups everywhere. [30]

In her first text, Menchú appears as the authentic, innocent indigenous other, telling her story despite the limitations of her education and basic literacy. The strategic quality of this persona becomes even more apparent with Stoll's revelation that Menchú had received a much greater degree of education than her protestation of functional illiteracy in her first text would suggest. The shift in consciousness may be a reflection of the decade between these two accounts, or it may be a reflection of those inaccuracies in her first text—primarily the issue of the level of her education. Menchú was not illiterate when she met with Burgos-Debray in Paris, far from it. According to Chiantla school records, Menchú finished "*primero básico* (seventh grade in October 1979)," and further interviews with classmates suggest that she had begun the eighth grade only to be forced to leave when she went into exile in Mexico (Stoll 1999: 164). Menchú's educational history was also a point of interest to the other residents of Chimel. Stoll reports the reflections of a sibling who tells of Menchú's last visit to Chimel. According to the sibling,

> Her way of talking was no longer that of ours. She could speak Spanish well. . . . She admonished us to speak correctly. She always shared what she was studying there. . . . We were always taking it in, in case there was some court or lawsuit to attend. She always explained things to us. When she left we were always sad. (quoted in Stoll 1999: 163)

Burgos-Debray's introduction to Menchú's first text affirms an image of Menchú as a "political innocent," an uneducated indigenous person. Contrary to the report from the sibling maintaining that Menchú was quite literate in Spanish, according to Burgos-Debray, Menchú "ha[d] spoken [Spanish] for only three years" (xi). Regardless of whether or not Menchú deceived Burgos-Debray into believing she was a recent student of Spanish or whether Burgos-Debray chose to downplay the significance of Menchú's educational background because the text was initially recited in Spanish, it is still subject to the transforming effects of her transcriber, Burgos-Debray, and her translator, Ann Wright.

The Western readership was willing to suspend the question of what the effects of translation and multiple authorship would have on the accuracy of the text in favor of reading Menchú's text as an authentic utterance of the innocent indigenous witness. This willing suspension of critical inquiry goes to the heart of what I am calling the Menchú effect. In the absence of critique, the line between historical event and literary representation of these events gets blurred in the witness's account. Another powerful effect of the poetics of witness is the ability of texts of witness to transcend generic and disciplinary boundaries. Menchú's narrative stands out from others in its breadth of representation of not only the political tensions and subsequent atrocities of the 1970s and 1980s but also as an ethnographic text that chronicles the endangered traditions and rituals of K'iché Maya culture. In this sense, Menchú's text operates across different disciplinary registers; it is at one and the same time a human rights document, an ethnographic monologue and, as Stoll's research shows, in places a clear work of fiction.

The transcriber, the reader, and the witness engage in a cycle of bearing witness—the reader's act of bearing witness to Menchú who is bearing witness to Burgos-Debray. This cycle reflects its own kind of politics, the politics of the Western gaze and its tendency to ascribe to the Third World witness a presumed "innocence," a practice that has its roots as far back as antiquity and continues up through the practices of the twentieth-century ethnographer. Situated within this presumption of "innocence" is an equally artificial rhetorical construct, "authenticity." Admitting that Menchú's text, indeed texts of witness in general, tend to be subject to acts of willful manipulation in their construction and in their consumption is hardly grounds for dismissing them out of hand. "Many of the supposed idiosyncrasies concerning authorship that Stoll finds" in Menchú's text are simply "symptomatic of the vagaries of testimonial production in general" (Gelles 17). To be bothered by the inaccuracies within the text is in some ways to "confuse the category of 'testimony' (as in the court proceeding) with the literary genre of *testimonio*, which partakes of the former to some degree but is qualitatively different in terms of the construction and circumstances of the authoring" (Gelles 16). The value of Menchú's text, therefore, lies in its mere existence and in its enactment of the doubling effect of the witness—its capacity to transmit an "effect," the blurring of borders between historical event and poetic truth in its relating the details of human rights violations—and as a direct result of this "effect," the text's ability to "effect" real political change.

IV. It's Giuliani Time! Tortured "Truths" and Strategic "Lies" in Bearing Witness

What is most interesting about Stoll's defense of Burgos-Debray and his willingness to attribute inaccuracies in Menchú's text exclusively to Menchú herself is that Stoll is ignoring a fundamental tenet of the ethnographic encounter: native informants do not always tell the truth. The reasons for this could come from any number of legitimate explanations. The native informant might have a fundamental distrust of the anthropologist who sits as an implicit outsider to the informant's culture; the native informant might have a desire to control the terms by which the anthropologist represents the community in question. Menchú mentions repeatedly in her text that there are simply rituals she could not discuss as part of the code of behavior within her own culture. Sometimes the native informant simply cannot share the truth lest he or she betray the very community the witness is attempting to preserve by bearing witness at all. Any one of these reasons could have influenced the nature of the exchange between Menchú and Burgos-Debray, and any one of these possibilities should have prompted Burgos-Debray to investigate the "inaccuracies" that exist in Menchú's account.

That Menchú's text contains numerous inaccuracies, reflecting the "impossibility of mimesis" and the "loss of truth," is undeniable.[31] In a sense, these inaccuracies are a result of two unrelated phenomena, both of which are entirely predictable. First, the nature of the speech act itself and the witness's inability to control language and its meaning create within texts of witness a gap between intent and truth. Using Benveniste's concept of the *enounced* and the *enunciation*, Antony Easthope argues that "as signified is to signifier, so enounced is to enunciation" (43); with this comparison, Easthope articulates a linguistic model for addressing inaccuracies in Menchú's text. Analyzing a quotation in which Lacan argues that in the statement "I am lying . . . the I of the enunciation is not the same as the I of the statement (enounced)," Easthope shows how the "subject of the enounced and subject of enunciation are two different positions for a speaking subject" (44). This differentiation between subjects is a critical one because it displaces any notion that the relation between signifed and signifier is a transparent one determined by the intentions of the witness. Moreover, the notion that there are multiple subjects present in the social act of discourse also raises questions about the status of the unconscious— a psychic space that Lacan contends is the "real place of another discourse." Lacan argues that "language . . . escapes the subject in its operation and in its effects"(quoted in Dews 83). Therefore, even as Menchú identifies herself in and through language and perceives herself as the source of meaning, "language . . . escapes [her]," exposing the ontological precariousness of the subject and showing how Menchú's subjectivity is dependent upon the illusion of a stable signifier. The idea that language eludes the control of the speaking subject also highlights the degree to which Western critics have shown a willingness to suspend their awareness that the witness's account is subject to these same linguistic presuppositions about the relationship between truth, meaning, and the spoken word.[32]

The second reason for the inaccuracies in Menchú's text raises more questions about the audience's role in determining the truth value of a text than it tells us about the motivations of the witness. That witnesses choose "to manipulate," and embellish events to create a greater "effect," seems wholly plausible if we consider the strategic goals of telling the narrative in the first place. What motivates the witness to distort? Perhaps it is the witness's intuition that, without the embellishment, without the exaggeration and misinformation, the intended audience will not pay attention. Perhaps it is the witness's sense that telling a strategic "lie" in the name of "effecting" political change is a calculated risk worth taking because it will bring the readership into proximity of "truths," into an encounter with profound events outside of the purview of their daily lives.

The Abner Louima criminal and civil rights case of recent years is an excellent example of a case where, in an effort to get the public to pay attention, Louima, the lone witness to his own victimization, included a strategic "lie" in his testimony. On August 9, 1997, Louima, a Haitian immigrant, was arrested outside a Brooklyn nightclub. Within hours, Louima was taken to an emergency room where he was treated for damage to his colon and a ruptured bladder. Three days later, the Brooklyn District Attorney's office began an investigation into the report of two separate incidents of police brutality in the Louima case. First, four officers were accused of beating Louima in the police car on the way to the 70th Precinct station; the second and more horrific incident involved the claim that Louima was escorted into a police station bathroom where Officer Justin Volpe sodomized him with a three foot long stick while another officer, Charles Schwartz, reportedly held him down. The attack in the bathroom resulted in Louima's serious internal injuries, leading to three surgeries and a two-month stay in the hospital. In an interview conducted in the hospital just after the incident, Louima reportedly claimed that the officers chanted "It's Giuliani time" when beating and sodomizing him.[33] At a time when New York City was engaged in a very public discussion of mayoral acceptance and encouragement of what seemed like a pattern of excessive force within the greater metropolitan New York area police departments, Louima's claim attracted immediate media attention and initiated a relatively rapid response from the District Attorney's office to investigate the allegations. Mayor Giuliani, who had a reputation for being "outspoken in [his] defense of police officers," suggested immediately following Louima's hospitalization that any officer found guilty of such a brutal attack should be sentenced to prison for a substantial amount of time (McFadden and Fried, *New York Times*: May 25, 1999).

Louima later recanted his claim that the officers chanted "It's Giuliani time," explaining that he felt that he would never get the media attention necessary to force the District Attorney's office to pursue an investigation of the 70th precinct and its officers if he did not invoke the single most powerful and visible proponent of the police department—Mayor Giuliani. That Louima lied about this one aspect of the case is not in doubt; he acknowledged he told a lie. The larger and ultimately more interesting question is why did he have to lie? Moreover, situations like Louima's and his apparent need to tell strategic "lies" indicate that the nature of bearing witness, presumptions of "absolute truth" implied in the witness's account, and the role of audience and historical moment, are heavily implicated in the production of texts of witness. In Louima's case, he clearly believed that his account would fall by the wayside if he did not situate the attack in the larger context of a city-wide debate over the Mayor's consistent defense of the police department's use of force. Implicit in Louima's belief was his self-conscious awareness that the media would only pay attention to yet another report of police brutality if the Mayor's name was attached in some way.

Louima's assumptions proved to be not only politically expedient—the District Attorney's office initiated an investigation directly and the Federal authorities took over the case in February of 1998—but also reasonable if read in light of the 1994 Mollen Commission report on corruption in the New York Police Department. The Mollen Commission found that New York police officers frequently used excessive force "to administer what they believed was street justice" (Barstow, *New York Times*: June 9, 1999). They would then cover up their actions by insinuating that the victims initiated their beatings, falsely accusing them of resisting arrest. Moreover, the split verdict in the Louima case also suggests that Louima had reason to believe the public would be predisposed to dismiss his testimony. After four other officers testified that Justin Volpe had bragged about and brandished the three foot piece of wood he used in the assault, Volpe changed his plea from "not guilty" to "guilty." Believing Louima's credibility as a witness would be bolstered by Volpe's confession and, therefore, Louima's claims of having been assaulted in the police car by the other four officers would have greater credibility, the prosecutors devoted much of their closing arguments to retelling the events that occurred in the bathroom. The verdict was at best mixed: the jury exonerated the four officers accused of assaulting Louima in the police car, and only held Officer Schwartz accountable for assisting in Volpe's assault on Louima in the bathroom.

The verdict suggested the prosecutors had miscalculated regarding the public's willingness to take the word of the victim when he alone is the witness to his own victimization. "Even knowing that his most chilling tale of police brutality was no longer in dispute," Barstow argues, "jurors demonstrated their unwillingness to take Louima at his word" (*New York Times*: June 9, 1999). Indeed, Zachary W. Carter, the United States

Attorney who prosecuted the case, argued that the verdict demonstrated exactly what prosecutors have always known about police brutality cases. Carter noted that it is "historically difficult" to win convictions "where the only witnesses to the assault are the victims themselves." The jury only gave verdicts of guilty—Volpe and Schwartz—where, as Barstow suggests, "Louima's testimony was supported by the testimony of *other police officers* from the 70th precinct" (*New York Times*: June 9, 1999, emphasis added). No police officer corroborated Louima's claim that he was beaten in the police car. As a result, the verdict indicated a willingness on the part of the public—the victim's/witness's audience— to affirm Volpe's confession, not Louima's accusations. Louima's attorney claims that his client was a victim of what the Mollen Commission calls "street justice," a victim of the excesses of a police culture tainted by its abuses of power. The jury's verdict, however, reflected a more sanitized and localized condemnation of the renegade behavior of a single police officer. Mayor Giuliani's words upon hearing the verdict affirm this interpretation. Noting that what had occurred was "horrendous and perverse and sick," Giuliani goes on to argue he does not believe that "police officers in any way identified with the kind of conduct that was involved" in the Louima case ("Quotes on the Verdict in the Abner Louima Case," 06/08/1999, http://www.nytimes.com/library/national/regional/060999ny-louima-quotebox.html, 09/29/1999).[34]

Not unlike Louima, Menchú was faced with the problem of attracting international attention, of getting the Western world to pay attention to human rights abuses in Guatemala. From 1978 to 1980, an astonishing number of strikes, abductions, and massacres occurred, reflecting the degree to which Lucas García and the military had increased the pressure upon the population and the intensity of the response of these grassroots groups to the repression. Of these events, the occupation and subsequent death of some forty people (including Menchú's father) in the Spanish Embassy received the most attention from an international press otherwise oblivious to the ongoing events in Guatemala. In the words of the United Nations Guatemalan Truth Commission Accord, this "contemporary history of [the Guatemalan] homeland records grave acts of violence, disrespect for fundamental rights of humankind and suffering inflicted on the population," as a direct result of "the armed conflict" (*Guatemalan Truth Commission Accord*, 04/08/1999, http://www.stile.lut.ac.uk/~gyedb/STILE/Email000s048/, 04/22/2001).

Menchú needed to attract the attention of an otherwise indifferent audience. Her personal narrative, however, unlike Louima's, not only bears witness to events that directly affected her life but to a larger series of historical and political events that influenced literally hundreds of thousands of

Guatemalan lives. Menchú reveals in graphic detail events surrounding the deaths of family members and friends—even bearing witness to the horrific torture and death of her younger brother, Petrocinio. She begins by telling her readers that Petrocinio was "the first person in [her] family to be tortured" and that the details of his death made it "an unbelievable story" (1984: 172–73). Working as a labor organizer for the cause, Petrocinio was captured while walking along a road on his way to another village and was taken into custody with a group of suspected rebels and rebel sympathizers. Menchú tells how the army commander tortured and killed her brother and the other prisoners, an act intended to send a very public message to the rest of the community that a horrible death would be the fate of those who supported or joined the guerrillas. The army, according to Menchú, sent out a bulletin, demanding that the entire community bear witness to the event in the public square, stating that "any who didn't go to witness the punishment were themselves accomplices of the guerrillas" (175). In order "to see" their family member for a last time, Menchú relates how the family, including her father, "crossed long stretches of mountain country on foot" and "walked through some of the night, with pine torches, in the mountains," only to arrive early in the morning at Chajul, the site of the public execution.

The prisoners arrived "wearing army uniforms," and Menchú tells us her mother "recognized her son, [Menchú's] little brother, among them." Her brother had already been severely tortured. All of the prisoners "had no nails" and the army "had cut off part of the soles of their feet" (176). With the community gathered to witness the execution, the army commander then embarked on a lengthy speech, telling the people they "had to be satisfied with [their] lands" and they "had to be satisfied with eating bread and chile." The army commander "must have repeated the word 'communist' a hundred times," lecturing the people about the creeping communism that first began with the Soviet Union and then moved to the Carribean with Cuba and Nicaragua. Using the prisoners' bodies as evidence, the army commander "devoted himself to explaining each of the different tortures" (177). Menchú reports,

> This is perforation with needles, he'd say, this is a wire burn. There were three people who looked like bladders. . . . They were inflated, although they had no wounds on their bodies. But they were inflated, inflated. . . . All of them were missing part of the tongue or had had their tongues split apart. [She] found it impossible to concentrate, seeing that this could be. (177–78)

Menchú tells us her brother's body "was cut in various places," "his head was shaved and slashed," and he had "no nails . . . [or] soles to his feet."

Since he had been tortured over the course of "sixteen days," his wounds "were suppurating from infection" (178).

She describes her parents' reaction to her brother's state. Her mother "wept" and "almost risked her own life by going to embrace [her son]," held back by the male members of her family. It is her father, however, who comes to embody the silent rage of the community. Menchú says that she "watched him and he didn't shed a tear, but he was full of rage . . . and that was a rage we all felt" (178). In a final act of terror, the soldiers doused the prisoners with gasoline and set them on fire, "many of them begg[ing] for mercy," "some of them scream[ing], many of them leap[ing] but utter[ing] no sound" (179). Bearing witness to this final act, Menchú echoes her opening comments in describing the significance of her brother's death. "It wasn't just [her] brother's life," she argues, but "it was many lives, and you don't think that the grief is just for yourself but for all the relatives of the others." A defining moment in her life, witnessing her brother's torture and execution culminates in a profound shift in her consciousness. "That was precisely the moment," she notes "when [she] finally felt firmly convinced that if it's a sin to kill a human being, how can what the regime does to [the people of Guatemala] not be a sin?" (180). The details of Petrocinio's death are "a reality [she] can't forget, even though it's not easy to tell of it" (177).

While the villagers of Chajul debate the exact events of that day, no one doubts that Petrocinio Tum Menchú was tortured horribly and ultimately killed with a group of suspected guerrillas and guerrilla sympathizers. It was not unusual for "the army to humiliate and torture captives before they were killed, even in front of their families. . . . Nor was it unknown for the army to burn people alive" (Stoll 1999: 69). But other survivors' memories of the day of Petrocinio's death reflect a very different account from Menchú's. Leaving aside the specifics of the details—whether or not the prisoners were burned in the public square or outside of Chajul—the unavoidable problem with Menchú's eyewitness account is that evidence suggests she and her family were not in fact there to bear witness to the event. The most damning evidence of this fact comes from Vicente Menchú himself. In a statement titled *"Carta abierta"* signed by *"Communidades campesinas de Chajul, Nebaj, Cotzal y San Miguel Uspantán del Departamento de El Quiché"* and distributed by the Democratic Front Against Repression on February 1, 1980, a peasant delegation, including Vicente Menchú, reported the Chajul events in a significantly different way.

> . . . the army brought to Chajul seven campesinos whom it had kidnapped in Chicamán, dressed them all in olive green and forced them to go up the road that leads to town. A few meters away, soldiers were hidden and shot at the seven campesinos until they were

all dead. After that, the army threw down a pair of old shotguns without ammunition next to the cadavers and began to say that the dead were guerillas who had wanted to attack the garrison in Chajul. The cadavers lay there for many hours, until they were put in two holes in the Chajul cemetery, after [the army] burned one of the bodies with gasoline. (quoted in Stoll 1999: 69–70)

Whether or not Menchú knew about this document, the differences between her eyewitness account and her father's goes to the heart of the problem of the representation of "truth" in accounts of witness. Stoll provides further evidence that Menchú's and her father's accounts were not consistent with one another. In an interview given five days before Vicente's death at the Spanish Embassy, he clearly indicates that he is *uncertain* whether his son was killed at Chajul, saying that he "did[n't] know if they [were] alive or if [the soldiers] had already killed them" (quoted in Stoll 1999: 70). Indeed, Vicente's "uncertainty" about the status of Petrocinio can be directly tied to the fact "the bodies were never positively identified." With some discrepancies in account, the events at Chajul as reported in the "*Carta abierto*" is "the version of events that appeared in human rights reports" (Stoll 1999: 70).

Stoll is quick to note the discrepancy between the specific details in the human rights reports and Rigoberta's account of the events at Chajul is not in and of itself "very significant." Petrocinio was tortured and ultimately killed by the Guatemalan army. Her embellishment of the details and inclusion of a more graphic and sensationalized list of the details of torture diverge in part from other reports, but seen in a broader sense, her version "follows the others and can be considered factual." The real problem lies in the fact that Menchú's version "is not the eyewitness account that it purports to be." Moreover, there is little evidence to support Menchú's claim that both her parents and brothers also witnessed the executions. "The Chajules," according to Stoll, "only supposed that the seven victims were from Uspantán because the army said so." As to those who actually witnessed their murders, "no relatives were on hand to identify [the bodies], and Rigoberta was not there either" (Stoll 1999: 70).

For some readers, Menchú's strategic "lie" that she was an eyewitness to her brother's death undermines her credibility as a witness. It is, however, possible to see Menchú's strategic "lies" in quite a different light. Menchú's conscious manipulation of the facts of the event (not the essential acts themselves, but of who bore witness to them) reveals more about her level of awareness of the expectations of her readership and international politics than about her own character. In her recounting of the executions, Menchú authors for herself a persona, the only persona valued in the currency of international public awareness of human rights violations, the eyewitness. That her account of her own participation at the event is fictional, nothing more than an effect of the text, should not surprise us. Menchú is simply aware of a critical flaw in the way Western readers consume (or remain in denial about) information regarding human rights atrocities. Her strategic deployment of a constructed self reveals the fact that the Western readership's point of identification is with the living eyewitness, not the tortured and fragmented body of the victims of the execution. In other words, her use of the rhetorical construct of the eyewitness in this instance combined with her strategic "lie" that witnessing her brother's execution is "a reality [she] can't forget" plays fully on the Western readership's willingness to confuse the category of "testimony . . . with the literary genre of *testimonio*" (Gelles 16). Like Louima, Menchú knows she needs to tap into a larger context for situating the death of her brother in the Western readership's consciousness. In order to do this, the events of the execution shift to a symbolic register where the distinction between historical fact and literary truths breaks down. In this representation of the event, she becomes a victim (after all, she has lost her brother) who bears witness not only to the prisoners' victimization but to her own victimization; moreover, she makes her brother's death symbolic of the deaths of all the disappeared in Guatemala. By consciously using the rhetorical construct of the eyewitness, Menchú does what human rights documents were unable to do—she makes "an unbelievable story" believable to an otherwise detached Western readership (Menchú 1984: 173).

V. The Menchú Effect:
Witnessing and Approximate "Truths"

How can we talk about the witness and texts of witness in light of Stoll's revelations that one of the more "sacred" texts of witness contains false information and inconsistencies? The fact that Menchú's text, or any text of witness, contains inaccuracies, some willful and some accidental, is hardly grounds to dismiss the value of texts of witness. Nor should this fact motivate readers to retreat into the reactionary stance of a critic like Dinesh D'Souza, who would argue that inaccuracies in Menchú's text are simply an extension of what he would consider to be the exaggerated reaction of the academic left to human rights abuses in countries like Guatemala. It would be a horrible overcorrection of our critical approach to these important texts if we were simply to discount them out of hand. What we need to reconsider is the role of the Western reader in creating an unreasonable set of expectations for what constitutes "authenticity" of speech. What we need to rethink is the boundary between historical fact and literary truth, the belief systems that inform each version of truth—historical and universal—the politics that inform these belief systems, and how language represents (or fails to represent) truth.

Texts of witness are best talked about in terms of their proximity to "truths" and the various rhetorical strategies enacted to achieve the "effect" of representing in language events that border upon the unspeakable. The witness's speech is subject to the effects and limits of language, and it should be seen as a product of its historical context. When looking at the complicated linguistic structures of contemporary poetry, the reader distinguishes between *language* and *discourse*, between what Benveniste refers to as the "domain of language as a system of signs" and the other "universe [of the sentence] . . . whose expression is discourse" (quoted in Easthope 8). Poetic discourse for Easthope is a "product of history," but he is equally aware of the fact that it "consists of language . . . [and that] it is always the *product* of a *reader*" (24). Because of these inherent qualities of any discourse, Easthope argues that the "relatively autonomous practice . . . [of] a poetic tradition" should be analyzed in terms of its own historicity; perhaps even more crucial to any consideration of poetic discourse is the need for the reader to theorize beyond the level of the materiality of language and to attend to the social activity from which discourse is produced. In the case of texts of witness, this primarily involves an examination of the dynamic between witness, critic, and readership.

When reading a text of witness, the reader is necessarily caught between two reading strategies: the desire to believe the witness and the need to question her.[35] The impulse in witness discourse has been to privilege the former over the latter, to hold in place as securely as possible issues of "authority" and "authenticity" for fear the "real world" consequence of a more critical reading would in some way undermine the impact of these texts or compromise the reception of them in the Western world. As a result Marxist readings have predominated and have tended to move hand-in-glove with the grassroots revolutionary rhetoric and liberation theology espoused in many Third World texts of witness. However, as critics like Shoshana Felman and Alberto Moreiras have started to apply some pressure to the traditionally Marxist reading of these texts, other theoretical perspectives, centered on the nature of the exchange between speaker and auditor and based on a more critical consideration of the role of language, have provided a vehicle for reexamining these texts and the effect they have on the readership.

For Felman, psychoanalytic and performance theory provide at least two theoretical frameworks for considering text of witness and preserving a kind of (if not a definitive) "authority" for the witness. Felman's work on speech act theory and witness negotiates the ethical problems that arise when considering questions of "authority," "authenticity," and representations of "truth" in accounts based on personal experience. In agreement with Emmanuel Levinas, Felman suggests that for a subject "to testify—to vow to tell, to *promise* and *produce* one's own speech as material evidence for truth—is to accomplish a *speech act*, rather than to simply formulate a statement" (Felman and Laub 5).[36] Felman shows that the witness speaks from and about her own abjection, and as a result "does not have to *possess* or *own* the truth in order to effectively *bear witness* to it" (15). Narratives of witness, therefore, constitute a kind of performance during which it is not the absolute "truth" of the witness's experience but his or her experience of "speaking," the speech act itself, that confronts and exceeds questions of truth. Read in this way, Menchú's text disarms questions of whether or not her text reflects "absolute truth" even as it purports to represent nothing less. In other words, the representation of "truth" is the fundamental rhetorical strategy at play within her text, but the absolute value of the text need not be judged on the failure or success of this strategy to reflect "absolute truths." While Menchú does not "possess or own" the "truth," she effectively bears witness to "truths" by making herself "the vehicle of an occurrence, a reality, a stance or a dimension *beyond [her]self*" (Felman and Laub 3). Even as we need to stay vigilant to the fact that this is a role Menchú has authored for herself, a rhetorical strategy, we can also see the powerful "effect" of this rhetorical move.

In texts of witness, the figure of the witness—the "I"—articulates a fundamentally social space in which his or her testimony functions as the arbiter of a larger cultural experience, one that seemingly transcends individual experience; this movement from "I" to "we"—one that critics often describe in terms of a textual shift in which autobiography transforms itself into social biography—is frequently articulated in terms of tropes of the disintegration or fragmentation of the speaking subject's body and in its place the positing of a collective or social body.[37] Menchú's text enacts this transformation from autobiography to social biography. Beginning with the first paragraph of her text, Menchú wants her auditors to see her autobiographical narrative as a testimonial about the endangered state of a larger cultural body, as a social biography for the indigenous peoples of Guatemala.

> My name is Rigoberta Menchú. I am twenty three years old. This is my testimony. I didn't learn it from a book and I didn't learn it alone. I'd like to stress that it's not only my life, it's also the testimony of my people. . . . My story is the story of all poor Guatemalans. My personal experience is the reality of a whole people. (1984: 1)

In claiming that her testimony is "the story of all poor Guatemalans," Menchú politicizes the cause of her people while simultaneously minimizing the importance of her own involvement in the struggle. This movement towards "we" and away from the self-conscious "I" is a politically savvy move, but it is also, as Felman shows, a strategic move that gives the reader the impression that "the witness's speech is one which, by its very definition, transcends the witness who is but its medium, the medium of realization of the testimony" (Felman and Laub 3). In other words, we can see Menchú's "speech act" as an articulation of a larger social space in which the witness's testimony "do[es] not simply *report facts* but, in different ways, encounter—and make us encounter—*strangeness*" (Felman and Laub 7).

While Felman's psycho-linguistic understanding of the speech act of the witness provides a powerful explanation of what we might consider the psychological effect upon the reader of texts of witness, in its limited scope it misses in its explanation a more immediate effect of Menchú's insistence that her story is "the story of all poor Guatemalans." Menchú's gesture to see her story as emblematic of the story of all indigenous peoples of Guatemala opens up a critical space in which the reader can then come into some proximity to "strangeness," optimistically into some proximity of "truths" about an intolerably inhumane situation, and this critical move allows for feelings of empathy or solidarity in the absence of any tangible bridge or opportunity to understand another culture in a moment of profound crisis. However, what is missing in this critical reading premised upon a solidarity with the absent witness is any consideration of the possibility of reading the move from "I" to "we" as a conscious rhetorical strategy, an effect of texts of witness that speaks more to the politics from which the texts are produced and, even more directly, to the politics in which the texts will be consumed. These two explanations for the rhetorical shift from "I" to "we," a move that is at one and the same time motivated by the need to bridge the gap between experience and language's inability to represent experience, and by the critical necessity simply to be heard, are not necessarily mutually exclusive, but may in fact both be operative in the act of bearing witness and reading texts of witnesses.

As a natural complement to Felman's psycho-linguistic reading of texts of witness, Moreiras offers a compelling model for understanding issues of rhetoric and the limits of language in texts of witness. "The voice that speaks in *testimonio*," he argues, "is metonymically representative of the group it speaks for" (197). The critic's voice, as well as the translator and any other authorial intervention, exists in a paratextual relationship, creating a necessary rupture with the witness. The critic's voice, therefore, exists in "a metaphoric relation with the testimonial subject through an assumed and voluntaristically affirmed solidarity with it" (197). While the critical gesture of solidarity with the witness "is precisely the emotional apparatus that enables our metaphoric identification with the other," it also precipitates the paradoxical "double conversion of the other into us, and of us into the other," a move that may have "a strong emotional-political character, [even] ethical character," but one Moreiras maintains emphatically whose "epistemological status remains severely limited." According to Moreiras,

> Solidarity allows for political articulation, but cannot by or in itself provide for an epistemological leap into an-other knowledge, understood as a genuine knowledge of the other. . . . The basic consequence of this structural limitation is that the testimonial subject, in the hands of the Latinamericanist cultural critic, has a tendency to become epistemologically fetishized precisely through its (re)absorption into the literary system of representation. In other words, solidarity, which remains the essential summons of the testimonial text and that which radically distinguishes it from the literary text, is in perpetual risk of being turned into a rhetorical tropology. (198)

For Moreiras, this critical move within Latinamericanist circles to place testimonial literatures in the vacuum left when high literatures lost much of their cultural capital has created a fundamental problem; it has changed the epistemological terms out of which text of witness emerge by placing testimonial texts "paradoxically" and "dangerously" as "one of the main sources for a Latinamericanist 'aesthetic fix,' " "a sort of methadone in the absence of an effective literary critical practice." Such a move while producing a kind of high, a sense of unfettered solidarity with the witness, "does not produce solidarity," according to Moreiras, "but only a poetics of solidarity of a fallen and derivative kind" (198).

Like Felman, Moreiras is keenly aware that the problem for the witness lies fundamentally in the nature of the speech act itself—in the need to "speak" about that which is "unspeakable," to speak a "word [that] is founded on the continuous insistence on a secret that will not be revealed" (204). A product of the vexed act of speaking the unspeakable, texts of witness necessarily exist in this epistemological conundrum—texts attempting to articulate that which is seemingly beyond language to express. For Moreiras, the reconfiguration of the Latinamericanist literary tradition comes from "an auratic practice of the postauratic," a tropology in which the "problematic resurrection of the dead [read unspeakable]" becomes the defining characteristic of both a Latin American poetics and a Latinamericanist critical response (201). This auratic practice, or what I would reterm, the "auratic effect," opens up a space in which the reader can come into proximity with the "unspeakable," with what Felman would describe as "encounters [with] strangeness." The "auratic effect," however, should be understood as just that, an effect, a discursive product. For Moreiras, "auratic practice" is:

> ... the constitution of a self-legitimizing locus of enunciation through the simultaneous positing of two radically heterogeneous fields of experience—the experience of the dead and the experience of the living, my or our experience and theirs—and the possibility of a relational mediation between them through prosopopeia. It is a practice of the postauratic because the relational mediation between the heterogeneous realms is no longer based on mimesis, but it is based precisely upon *the impossibility of mimesis*: a simulation, then, a repetition, whose *moment of truth is the loss of truth* itself. (201, emphasis added)

The "auratic effect," therefore, emerges out of this collision of representations of experiences, an effect that Moreiras argues results in "the production of abjection" (201). Adopting Judith Butler's definition of the abject, Moreiras suggests that the production of abjection in texts of witness creates an "originary and founding outcasting whose most concrete task is to produce empowerment, but whose most precise discursive result is the constitution, or . . . the repetition of a realm of social unlivability" (201).[38]

Regardless of the existence of human rights groups and their efforts to document "the social unlivability" ongoing in Guatemala, the world paid little attention to the situation there. During the height of the violence, the daily events of Guatemala were relatively absent from the radar screen of Western public awareness. This absence of information in the popular press is a curious oversight if considered in conjunction with the overwhelming acceptance of Rigoberta Menchú's testimonial during the early part of the 1980s. The politics of consumption of the events of Guatemala appeared to find a more natural and "authentic" vehicle of expression in Menchú's personal account than in the eyewitness accounts of journalists or the composite reports of human rights groups. In this context, the testimonial as a genre became a more plausible and sympathetic vehicle for Western audiences to consume the details of the Guatemalan conflict, a better way to confront the extent to which acts of inhumanity could challenge the boundaries of what it meant to act humanely.

Read in light of both the politics informing the production and the consumption of Menchú's text, her "eyewitness" account achieves its "effect" and effects change because it bares the trace or "aura" of "truths" rather than serves as a transparent vehicle for, or explanation of the human rights violations it tends to chronicle. Menchú clearly "does not possess or own [truth]." She does, however, effect the "effect" of truth, and in doing so, manages "to effect" profound political change. Menchú's testimonial as a text-in-hand "effects" change in that it exists, for better or worse, in place of the human rights document, the reporter's exposé, the political report, as a privileged account of the state of daily life in war-torn Guatemala. In serving this purpose within global discussions of human rights abuses in Guatemala, Menchú's "eyewitness" account subsumes questions of "authenticity" and "truth" in its pursuit of the larger, intended goal of "effecting" political change.

In the act of telling her story, factually and in its moments of conscious manipulation, Menchú managed to bring international attention to the atrocities being committed against Guatemala's indigenous cultures, a feat that brought her from obscurity to the position of Nobel Peace Prize recipient. Contrary, however, to the views of many Western critics, the value of Menchú's text lies not so much in any assertion that Menchú herself offers the reader a direct line to "truth," or an uninterrupted glimpse of "innocence," or an opportunity to come into contact with the "authentic" voice of oppressed people everywhere. At best, she brings her readership into some proximity of "truths," into some dialogue with a distant "other." In this, Menchú's text has undeniable value. However, what is perhaps most revealing about Menchú's text is what its reception tells us about our Western selves and our naïve willingness to see Menchú as a kind of symbol for all indigenous peoples.

CHAPTER **2**

Excessive Witnessing: The Ethical as Temptation

JOSEBA ZULAIKA

> Now, if merely to be present at a murder fastens on a man the char-
> acter of an accomplice; if barely to be a spectator involves us in one
> common guilt with the perpetrator. . . .
>
> —Lactantius

However we may wish to characterize the contemporary "crisis of witnessing," the problem is not that we lack the very stuff on which to exercise our
testimonial powers. Living in this era of electronic media, watching/wit-
nessing seemingly everything in front of our eyes, loaded as we are with images of wars and starvation, asking ourselves where to draw the line
between reality and fiction, the problem is that we don't know what to do
with so much of it. It is this "excess" in the role of witnesses that we are confronted with in the contemporary world—excess in the dual sense of too
much horror leading to the impossibility, abolition, or futility of witnessing
(hence its "crisis"), but also in the sense of unreserved, transgressive, savage
obligation to tell the truth, a call born out of the pitiless awareness of the
absurdities and injustices that excuse such horrors. If Bataille thought that
economic production should be linked not to scarcity but to potlatch-like
excess, the political economy of witnessing is also better understood as the
problem of what to do with *la part maudit*, "the accursed share," the excessive "gift of death" central to our religious and military cultures.

Spectators, witnesses, accomplices, writers—the blurring of such roles was already denounced by the Christian apologist Lactantius, shocked as he was by the spectacle/scandal of the Roman circus. Excessive witnessing may be forced upon individuals by their political or social environment. This is the fate of people like the medical doctor Charles Clements witnessing the war in El Salvador.[1] There are also those who, perhaps repulsed by the spectacle of world affairs or just ashamed of being mere bystanders, are voluntarily drawn into active witnessing to the point of excess. Because of their journalistic or literary ambition, their religious convictions, their love of risk and transgression, or some other form of consciousness or passion for truth, all sorts of reporters, writers, conscientious objectors, and activists take upon themselves the burdens and rewards that derive from bearing ultimate witness. Perhaps their motives might be questionable, yet the role itself may carry them into unknown territory in the service of truth. I myself once fell under the spell of the call to excessive witnessing when I was willing to join Basque guerrillas for the sake of writing a book.

One can always translate such temptations for risk-taking into the rhetoric of knowledge. Writers in particular can easily justify their love of transgression and the complicities of witnessing as the obligatory search for truth. Embracing the truth game of witnessing in a radical manner soon confronts us with the "excess" in which the call for bearing testimony far outweighs our sense of professional duty and conventional morality.[2] The difficulties in admitting to our abysmal Western history are but the initial predicament for such testimonial consciousness. This is a history inextricably tied to our religious heritage, whose genealogy goes back to Abraham—father to Jews, Christians, and Muslims—and whose chilling legacy is a willingness to sacrifice his son as testimony of faith in God. This is the true ground for Isaac's, Christ's, and Socrates' sacrificial gift: "[T]he gift of death would be this marriage of responsibility and faith. History depends on such an excessive beginning" (Derrida 1999: 6). The initial and most serious problem for the witness is the very difficulty in admitting or even defining an ethics of responsibility for such religious and political histories. It is no accident that we find the enigmatic "dying for another" turned into the maximum expression of love and freedom, the ultimate triumph of life, at the center of Western thought from Plato to Heidegger.

Nowhere is the gift of death as massive, universal, and unconditional as in war. In the final analysis, whether we subscribe to Nietzsche's nothingness or Christianity's *mysterium tremendum*, the history of responsibility implies having to act and make decisions that, in their excessiveness, exceed theoretical knowledge. The moment of decision is beset by paradox, dissidence, heresy, and secrecy which become intrinsic aspects of such responsibility. It is when we decide to witness contemporary history as one of crime and sacrificial holocaust that we are confronted with the paradoxical excesses of the Kierkegaardian *fear and trembling*—the aporia of responsibility by which human sacrifice is the final duty, as well as a mockery, of ethics. Whether we decide to watch armies fighting for their national interests, or write an ethnography of indigent mothers letting their children die of hunger, whether we observe the consequences of racism and international politics, or simply take stock of our nuclear predicament, the sacrifice of Isaac becomes the most everyday common occurrence.

I. The Executioner as Witness:
Abraham, Genet, and the Temptation of Ethics

> And God tempted Abraham and said unto him, take Isaac, thine only son, whom thou lovest, and get thee into the land of Moriah, and offer him there for a burnt offering upon the mountain which I will show thee.
>
> —Genesis 22:1–2

In between Aaron Burr Hall, where I was writing my dissertation on Basque political violence, and the Firestone Library a few yards away, there was a chilling sculpture that marked my student years at Princeton. It was a realistic life-size portrait of a stiff Abraham, his left hand holding a bound Isaac, while his clinched right fist clutched a large, ordinary kitchen knife fatefully pointed at the heart of the son at the very moment of final sacrifice. For periods the knife would be missing. It didn't seem surprising that some onlooker found it too unbearable. With the knife restored to the sculpture, the sacrificial moment became once again agonizingly gripping.

The work had been made by sculptor George Siegel at the request of Kent State University in memory of the four students murdered by the National Guard during the Vietnam protests. Kent State decided it didn't want the sculpture and sold it to Princeton. The representation was too unmerciful, a tale of a father murdering his son, a tragedy too banal . . . too close to home in Ohio. The knife represented the brutality, familiarity, and intimacy of the murder. The tragic and everyday associations among modern warfare, youth resistance, home repression, university life, and Abraham's parable became indelibly engraved on my consciousness.

What was Abraham's "sin"? His exorbitant obedience to God, his unconditional passion for bearing witness to his absolute faith expressed in his willingness to sacrifice his son. He is at once the most moral and the most immoral of men. Abraham's paradox informs the ethical position of anyone radically committed to bearing unconditional witness to contemporary history.

Abraham's parable has captivated religious thinkers for centuries. Søren

Kierkegaard turned the story into a paradigm of transcendent faith. What happened on the mountain is unforgettable: "[F]rom that time on Abraham became old, he could not forget that God had required this of him"; he even "prayed God to forgive him his sin, that the father had forgotten his duty toward the son;" and, above all, "he could not comprehend that it was a sin to be willing to offer to God the best thing he possessed, that for which he would many times have given his life; and if it was a sin, if he had not loved Isaac as he did, then he could not understand that it might be forgiven. For what sin could be more dreadful?"(28–29).

Abraham's story condenses the "teleological suspension of the ethical"—the ethical is overridden altogether by a higher *telos*. For Abraham, despairing yet obedient to superior orders, and with knife in hand poised over his son, the ethical is that which might prevent him from fulfilling God's will—that is, ethics itself becomes a *temptation*: "What ordinarily tempts a man is that which would keep him from doing his duty, but in this case the temptation is itself the ethical . . . which would keep him from doing God's will"(70). Abraham's aberration testifies both to the existence of an ethical norm and to the need to transgress it for the sake of any transcendence. "Abraham is therefore at no instant a tragic hero but something quite different, either a murderer or a believer"(67). It is by resisting the "temptation" of being moral (that is, preserving his son's life) that he reaches the "suspension" of ethics in order to become the monstrosity of an absolute murderer/believer.

Can this theological tale help us understand the antinomies of contemporary witnessing? Consider for example Jean Genet, "The Black Prince of French Literature" as Cocteau called him, the infamous transgressor, the at one and the same time saint and *canaille* who during the last twenty-five years of his life wrote nothing but an hallucinatory report of his sojourn in Jordan and Lebanon among destitute and armed Palestinian fedayeen.[3] Whoever is the perfect candidate for the role of the witness, this *captif amoureux* acting "like a little black box projecting slides without captions," a literatus who "settled for witnessing" and produced a work that "is, disconcertingly, a surprising success" (Geertz 1992: 3–6) might be considered a candidate for our guide. The philosopher Gilles Deleuze could compare Genet's book to the Bible—with his stories about chosen homeless people, a book of memory that alternates serenity and hate, mixes history and poetry. Affection and empathy more than ideology bound Genet to the Palestinians' fate, yet his rejection of the existence of God at one point scandalized the "terrorist" fighters. The public debate between their leader Abu Gamal and Genet was settled with the bond of a final promise: "If a Jordanian soldier . . . threatened you, I'd kill him," to which Genet replies: "I'd try to do the same if he threatened you"(101).

As in the case of Abraham, it is the closeness between sanctity and murder that throws into relief the difficulties of theorizing and moralizing about bearing witness. There is no ethical posturing in Genet, no unctuous rhetoric of witnessing, no unquestioned memory or unreviewed truth. The last thing Genet wants to establish is his own innocence. The self-questioning is radical. He asked himself why they needed him there. For what purpose was "this grey, pink, round head forever in their midst? Use it as a witness? My body didn't count. It served only to carry my round grey head" (83).

Recently, anthropologists have also become absorbed with the role of witnessing and ethics in their discipline. Scheper-Hughes' paper "The Primacy of the Ethical" marks the militant position of a "barefoot anthropology" in which the anthropologist must above all be sensitive to ethical imperatives. She is inspired by the writings of the moral philosopher Emmanuel Levinas. I myself, accused of moral relativism for my work on political terrorism, have in the past placated my own sense of moral panic by reading Levinas and quoting him profusely.[4] His exorbitant ethical "asymmetry," one that goes far beyond a formal and private I-Thou reciprocity—in Alyosha Karamazov's words, "We are all responsible for everyone else—but I am more responsible than all the others"—presents for me as well the highest human ideal. Thus I admire Scheper-Hughes' call for Levinasian ethics. Yet I have asked myself repeatedly whether such borrowing of the moral high ground from an ethical authority succeeds in its attempt to make my work impervious to charges of banality. It is when I look through Genet's bare lenses that I become suspicious of such moral invocations.

Beware of Abraham. The road to violence, repression, and murder is usually preceded by calls to morality and martyrdom. It is by appealing to the ultimate truth of ethics that the military mandarin, the patriotic scoundrel, or the counter-terrorism zealot will engage in the most cruel forms of dehumanization. The disturbing question is how well-equipped is a moralist anthropology to record the many moral outrages committed in the name of morality.

For an example of the difficulty, if not impossibility, of formulating a *minima moralia*, consider the discipline of moral philosophy, where a leading figure like Alasdair MacIntyre could begin a chapter of his influential *After Virtue: A Study in Moral Theory* with the following statement: "The most striking feature of contemporary moral utterance is that so much of it is used to express disagreements; and the most striking feature of the debates in which these disagreements are expressed is their interminable character. . . . There seems to be no rational way of securing moral agreement in our culture" (6). Even Levinas' trenchant ethical discourse may not, in fact, be of much help in concrete situations of political conflict. It is one thing, for example, to maintain that, as a value of personal conduct, one should never question the injunction "Thou shall not kill." Yet the established morality tells us that there are political exceptions. The practical (and moral) rule for the military is the stark opposite: "Thou shall kill." Any citizen of a modern state is a potential soldier under the *ethical* commandment to kill. Asked whether Israel was innocent or responsible for the massacre at Sabra and Shatila, Levinas responded that, "Unfortunately for ethics, politics has its own justification" and "[t]he Zionist idea . . . has an ethical justification" (quoted in Hand 292). He spoke in terms "of the responsibility of those 'who have done nothing,' of an original responsibility of man for the other person. . . . This is the responsibility of those we call innocent" (quoted in Hand 290). Even Levinas' work, from which one can learn the most about the conflictive relationships between ethics and politics, is incapable of immunizing us against "the temptation of innocence" (250). If Abraham's story is for Kierkegaard a paradox without mediation, equally so for Levinas are the contemporary conflicts between ethics and politics. It is once again the predicament of being compelled to choose while the choice destroys its own moral grounds.

Lyotard refers to this predicament in general terms as "a *differend*," that is, "a case of conflict, between (at least) two parties, that cannot be equitably resolved for lack of a rule of judgment applicable to both arguments. One side's legitimacy does not imply the other's lack of legitimacy." Thus, in the same political situation, a soldier might feel morally compelled to obey the orders to kill, whereas another might feel as strongly compelled to disobey them. No ethical appeal can, in the end, alleviate the daunting prospect that, in such ultimate situations, "a universal rule of judgment between heterogeneous genres is lacking in general" (1988: xi). Not even Levinas posits a universal rule that might resolve, for example, the conflictive relationship between ethics and politics.

The worst scenario is censorship against witnessing, masked under the guise of ethical appeal. The case of Philippe Bourgois comes to mind. While searching for a fieldwork site, at the invitation of refugees in a Honduran camp he crossed the border into El Salvador with the intent of staying but 48 hours to assess the convenience of doing fieldwork there. Bourgois became caught up in the fourteen-day nightmare of a search and destroy operation conducted by the Salvadoran army with the aid of American Huey helicopters. While running for their lives at night and hiding during the day, he witnessed the massacre of 50 peasant civilians and their children, with another 50 wounded and 100 missing. Was such witnessing "ethical"? Bourgois soon found that he "had violated several of the anthropological/methodological ethics" and that the institutional consequence of having violated this disciplinary code was an attempt to terminate him as a graduate student, for "I had crossed a border illegally, thereby violating the laws of my host country government, I had not notified my dissertation committee of my decision to explore a new dangerous research site, I had notified the media and contacted human rights organizations, thereby violating the right to privacy of my research subjects" (50). The last charge— going public with his testimony of human rights violations—was particularly "unethical." The mockery of "anthropological ethics" could not be made more graphic than by obliging the ethnographer "to obtain informed consent from the Salvadoran government troops firing at us before photographing the children they wounded" (51). As Bourgois points out, "Most political economy studies can be defined as potentially unethical. A fieldworker cannot obtain important information on unequal power relations by strictly obeying the power structure's rules and laws." In the end, "in a real world context, the entire logic of anthropology's ethics is premised on a highly political assertion that unequal power relations are not particularly relevant to our research" (52). Here is a blatant, yet potentially common, instance of invoking the ethical to suppress research that implies radical witnessing.

Genet was a witness to the armed fedayeen, incautiously "responsible" for their fate beyond any personal reserve, yet quite conscious of the uselessness of his presence. He didn't need to dress up his writing as moral imperative. As he put it in a 1974 interview, "It was completely natural for me to be attracted to the people who are not only the most unfortunate but also crystallize to the highest degree the hatred of the West." He was "attracted but not blinded" by his subjects, "a prisoner of love" (viii). Yet he forced himself into watching the bulls, not from the safety of the stands, but from inside the fatal arena, while he kept recording the "kind of fascination that makes them jump off a cliff not to help but merely to follow those who have already leapt to their death" (88). By witnessing the immoralities of sacrifice, he was quietly defining the genesis of a people.

II. Confessions

A confession has to be a part of your new life.

—Wittgenstein, *Culture and Value*

Confessions and silences besiege the witness. Silence amounts to complicity when injustice is not denounced. Courageous writers have made their works "speak truth to power" by uncovering worlds of secrecy, violence, and domination. Yet confessional discourse also may become complicitous when it is apologetic of inexcusable wrongs.

Confession being, rhetorically, a verbal utterance, de Man writes about the "fiction" implicit in utterances that have no necessary link with a referent. In particular, he sees no harm in Rousseau's stealing of a ribbon while accusing a maidservant of having given it to him (an event Rousseau dwells on in his *Confessions*); there was no other wrong but the fact that its "essential non-signification" was not properly interpreted by his accusers. Yet Rousseau's confessional "absurdity" is far more convincing to the anthropologist as witness than de Man's innocence-granting fictional discourse and silence. An entirely textual approach like de Man's, that would completely deny the transparent relationship between language and its referent, would not do justice to those critical situations in which verbal utterances are ritualized to the point that the "fiction" becomes literal metaphor. Shamanism all over the world attests to the curative powers of confession. The whole point of a sacrament is that the fiction's absolute reference can never be questioned. A Quaker act of witnessing restores truth to a personal belief. Language considered rhetorically can isolate verbal utterance from its role in securing or initiating practical justice but, in the pragmatic everyday world, talking and repairing injustice are frequently one and the same act.

But "experience always exists simultaneously as fictional discourse and as empirical event and it is never possible to decide which one of the two possibilities is the right one" (de Man 293). That is why bearing witness is so relevant to truth. As much as anthropologists write about ritual (with its substances, formulas, gestures, acts, embodied symbols) being a partial correction of the "lies" of verbal discourse, so witnessing is a similarly indispensable "referential" activity. The witness's truth hinges on something as trivial as having been *there*.[5] It is an embodied activity in that one must "see" and "hear" and "smell" what is going on to then "speak" or "write" or "weep" at what one has perceived with one's senses. It is not mere talk in a theater of language, but recounting in the context of bodily presence—having been there to being here now—and intended as a ritualized truth-telling performance. The verbal dimension of the truth is only one aspect of the global testimony. Such witnessing goes far beyond the "fictions" of mere non-referential language. Contrary to the grammatologist, for whom all orality and unmediated community is suspect, for the ethnographer a message is most valuable when face to face with the person who utters it. Such embodied voice has the added dimension of performance and can speak from experience. In some cultures the speaker must qualify with a quotational "they say" all narratives in which the speaker's knowledge is not evidential; what the speaker has not witnessed carries a different truth claim. Contemporary political rhetoric takes place similarly in the newly oral culture of the mass media in which, as Robert Paine contends, "saying is doing." Thus, the link de Man acknowledges between cognition and performance in a *promise* (Rousseau's model for the social contract) is also present, although in a more problematic way, in the confessional mode.

It is the damaging connection between confessions and excuses that a close reading of Rousseau's text reveals—self-accusing turned into a mode of self-excusing which, in terms of truth, "ruins the seriousness of any confessional discourse by making it self-destructive" (de Man 280). Confession being a verbal act, how do we know it is *true*? We may not be able to know its ultimate truth in terms of textual reference (which is essential to law), but we can be certain of the truth achieved by certain confessions when we examine the circumstances in which they transpire, as well as their consequences. A man willingly confessing on his deathbed, because of religious terror, murders for which another has been imprisoned for thirty years is dealing with fundamental truth; nothing can redeem the murders or the injustice of the innocent's life in prison, yet the results of the confession are of utmost consequence for both men.

Contrary to the attitude of de Man, who delved into the deceptive truth of the confessional mode (*qui s'accuse s'excuse*) and concluded that in the end "the confession fails to close off a discourse" (282), it is noteworthy that both Wittgenstein (a thinker essentially concerned with the limits of "what can be said") and Foucault (adamantly opposed to the servitude of a confession that takes place in a power relationship) made highly unusual "confessions" that are among the most revelatory incidents of their lives. For Wittgenstein "*all* philosophy . . . begins with a confession" (Ray Monk 366). He often remarked that genuine understanding is frequently impeded by pride, not lack of intelligence: "If you are *unwilling* to know what you are, your writing is a form of deceit" (quoted in Rhees 174). And in 1936 Wittgenstein went so far as to prepare a confession of the moments in which he had been weak and dishonest. He read it to a number of his closest friends who were embarrassed by such an uncomfortable experience (Monk 367–72). His most serious sin was that he had lied when he was brought to court to answer charges of violence against his students as a schoolteacher in an Austrian village. Wittgenstein later went to the village to apologize personally to the adults whom he had physically hurt in their youth. The point was to dismantle his pride. We might say that Wittgenstein flirted with "absurdity" in his pathetic, almost religious, urge to eradicate his own cowardice, yet when we watch him testify publicly against himself we feel we are in the presence, not of deceptive theatrics, but of an act of truth.

Similarly Foucault, a thinker fascinated with transgression and concealment, who "had waged a kind of guerrilla war, in theory as well as in practice, against the imperative to tell the truth," most particularly against the duty to confess to a pastoral power, dedicated his last university seminar to the topic of *parrhesia*, or the art of truth-telling, and even confided secrets to a close friend he knew was likely to divulge them (quoted in James Miller 358). By teaching this course he "was conceding his own inability, when all is said and done, to escape from the duty to tell the truth" (358). Turned into an archetypal modern Cynic, Foucault devoted his last five lectures to the road to truth developed by the school of Diogenes and the Cynics. Cynicism was not organized around the study of texts but of exemplary figures whose radicalness consisted in the claim that a "person is nothing else but his relation to truth" (360). This was a truth that could only be embodied in the real life of a person, not handed down in the form of a text, law, or commandment. What Foucault admired in the Cynic was that he had made of himself "a *blazon* of essential truths." In particular, they exploited the lessons of "scandalous behavior" by turning their own breaking of laws and taboos into a source of public controversy. By exploiting the fight between different views, what the Cynics sought was not primarily the discovery of a new truth but rather to internalize the struggle for truth. The early Christian ascetics are, for Foucault, the agonizing example of such "immediate, explosive, and savage presence of truth" (361).

The "obligation of truth" forced Foucault not only to write of the atrocities of Western culture, but also dictated that, in the end, he tell the truth about his most hidden personal self. As he was facing death, he decided to confide his secrets to his friend Hervé Guibert who, in a short story entitled "The Secrets of a Man," written the day after Foucault was buried, speaks of the philosopher's three "terrible dioramas." The first shows the child witnessing the amputation of a leg by his surgeon father in Poitiers—an event that would rob the boy of his virility. The second scene has the young philosopher walking past a courtyard suffused with infamy—a sequestered woman had lived there on a straw mattress for decades, declared mad by her family after she had killed her illegitimate child. The third diorama had to do with the fantasy of the murder of Jewish children, war refugees from Paris, who overshadowed him at school, until they were taken to the concentration camps.

Nietzsche wrote that every great philosophy was nothing but "the personal confession of its author" (13). In his final interview Foucault, too, stressed that all his work amounted to a kind of autobiography. He went on to admit that in his latest book he was "trying to detach myself" from a certain philosophically evasive style in order to "use it as a field of experience to be studied" (quoted in James Miller 372). It is his own truth that he sought, and it is the brutal presence of the obligation for truth, tortuously embodied in their lives, that one finds so arresting in the works of these philosophers. This is far from a mere textual commentary followed by silence. Nor is it a prescription of ethics. Truth had to do with admitting that one's self is also full of deception, sin and potential murder. Even if no redemption came from speaking out, they each felt a duty to confess. The ethical was not the deceptive temptation of programmed virtue but reconciliation with one's own flawed life. By admitting guilt, redemption was possible; but by breaking the silence, another unfathomable silence was revealed.

III. Autobiography and Murder

Autobiography veils a defacement of the mind of which it is itself the cause.

—Paul de Man, *Rhetoric of Romanticism*

Anthropology, whose agenda has classically been, in the words of Clifford Geertz, "Looking into dragons, not domesticating or abominating them, nor drowning them in vats of theory," ultimately confronts its practitioners with issues of confessional truth games and the apologetic discourses they tend to generate (1984: 275). Even an anthropologist like myself, working in the supposedly most familiar of places, my own homeland, can discover plenty to confess and feel embarrassed about. This is my case while writing what follows.

My first contact with the Basque separatist armed group ETA (*Euskadi Ta Askatasuna*, "Euskadi and Freedom") dates back to December 1970. I was working as a porter in the old Charing Cross Hospital and it was during my routine lunch hour walk through London's streets that I was jolted by the presence of Basque emigrants staging a hunger strike in Trafalgar Square. Less than a hundred yards from the hospital, they were protesting the Burgos trial in which 16 ETA activists were being judged by a military court that would eventually condemn six of the defendants to death sentences for the murder of a Spanish police officer. My first reaction was to avoid any contact with the protestors. Only six months earlier I had escaped Spain by taking the ferry from Bilbao to Southampton and had immersed myself in the metropolitan anonymity of London. The last thing I wanted was that even in London I should be caught up in the heavily dramatized politics of Basque nationalism.

On that first day I succeeded in walking away. But the hunger strike endured for weeks. Eventually, I could not tolerate the guilt of observing the protesters obliquely day after day. Finally, I stopped at the tent where my compatriots were camping across the street from the National Gallery. From the moment I admitted to them I was Basque, a day without a visit was an act of betrayal. During the Christmas demonstrations, organized to protest the death penalty for the six ETA activists, multitudes joined the marches; the same was the case in other European capitals. The cause of the hunger strikers was morally right in the eyes of the public at large. Worldwide protests forced the dictatorial regime of the ailing General Franco to transmute the death sentences into 30-year prison terms.

The group of London refugees asked me to teach them the Basque language. So twice a week we met in the apartment of "Wilson" and his Serbian girlfriend. Wilson was one of the hunger strikers and, as I soon learned, a "liberated" ETA member (meaning, one of the few full-time salaried operatives dedicated entirely to the organization). The following summer I returned to the Basque country. So did Wilson, and he was soon requesting that we rent an apartment together in San Sebastian. I bluntly declined. I simply did not care about politics. William Blake, mythology, and writing were my only world. I was studying philosophy in San Sebastian and I remember one night walking with Wilson through the city's main streets, talking about life in London. The next morning there was a large picture of him on the front page of all Spanish newspapers as the most wanted ETA leader. That was the end of our encounters. He was at one and the same time a "terrorist" wanted by the Spanish police and a hero for a large part of the Basques. In the spring of 1975 he was captured in Barcelona by the Spanish authorities in a group arrest facilitated by a mole's tip-off. His comrade and lieutenant "Txiki," an immigrant from Andalusia, was arrested with him and executed in September of that year; it was believed that Wilson's impending execution was just months away.

Besides ETA, there was another military institution that had a far more definite claim upon my services—the Spanish army. While studying philosophy in Bilbao, I received my draft notice. I kept postponing my fourteen-months-long military service, since I was determined never to become a soldier in Franco's army. Still, while I was managing the postponement, twice they cut my long hair short, an initiation that I hated. When there was no possibility of further delay, I went to the army and faked insanity.

Anthropology was going to be my only truth game. Prior to my stay in London I had abandoned my religious vocation as a prospective Catholic priest. One year of reading Dostoevsky, Nietzsche, Unamuno, and Freud had undone everything my religious teachers had so patiently built up during years of nurturing discipline and idealism. I had lost it all as if by a stroke of bad fate. For me London was a period of unmitigated inner catastrophe that I survived by writing a long Blakean poem on Adam's fall from paradise. I knew then that I was a writer. The decision had been inescapable: I was going to become an anthropologist in order to study mythology and symbolism, the very realities that had betrayed me so spectacularly. Thus, in that very inflamed period in which all my friends were involved in the rebellious politics of antifascism, in 1975 I found myself in Canada, an escapee with the excuse of an anthropological vocation. And I was happy to have escaped, or so I thought.

In the summer of 1979, on a Sunday afternoon in the coastal town of Zarautz, almost a decade after our initial encounter in a tent at Trafalgar Square, I was again face to face with Wilson—the same man whose death by firing squad had seemed all but certain after he had been arrested, tortured, and kept in solitary confinement for months. But Franco's death in November of 1975 changed the course of events, and he had been released in the summer of 1977. In the meantime I had published my London book of poetry, I had written an ethnography of deep-sea fishermen in Newfoundland and now, as a graduate anthropology student at Princeton, I was eager to meet up with Wilson again.

Something unexpected had happened when choosing my fieldwork topic for the doctoral dissertation. This was the moment I had dreamed of as the opportunity to plunge into the study of some exotic symbolic system such as shamanism, prophecy, or witchcraft. My mentor was supportive but he insisted on something else—the advantages of returning to my own culture. I pondered the suggestion for weeks. One thing was obvious: the only way I could "return" to my culture was by confronting the agonizing political and moral dilemmas posed by the now endemic political violence. The opening revelatory incident of my ethnography would be that summer morning, in my natal village of Itziar in 1975, when I heard women neighbors crying in the street. I rushed down the stairs and found my mother pale and unable to walk after having just witnessed the murder of the alleged police informer of the village by two ETA militants. Soon I was in the street surrounded by horrified faces, being asked the unanswerable question: "But how can that be?"

Contrary to its classical "participatory" rhetoric, I envisioned "fieldwork" as a distancing device that would release me from real participation—a reminder that it all was simply writing and that, of course, I was by no means obliged to "solve" any of the actual political and moral quandaries. Thus all I had to do was to observe, not judge, at least not initially. In exchange for waiving my obligations to comment, I would become an unreserved witness. I had been uninterested in ETA's "cause" and unwilling to collaborate with it. Yet anthropology was taking me back to the very same people I had strenuously avoided years earlier. Now here I was, a graduate student, eager to seek contact with Wilson and to write about the same conflict I had fled before. Obviously, it was not primarily for the sake of the country that I was willing to do my work, but something much more conceited and banal—for the sake of writing a good ethnography. Still, I felt that the act of witnessing/writing was, in my case, in itself as radical as anything I could have done by participating in political revolt. Anthropology had allowed me this conceptual ploy, this game of truth, and I felt thankful to the discipline for it and for the protection it afforded.

Talking to ex-militants like Wilson did not present much of a problem, after all. In my own village, too, there were two former ETA members, youths who had joined the organization and made their first "actions" precisely in the company of Txiki, Wilson's lieutenant, and who had become radicalized beyond any point of return when he was executed by Franco in Barcelona. Fun-loving, raucous, absorbed by sex, fond of folk singers, I never suspected they were ETA militants. Now that I was back as an anthropologist in the summer of 1980, they, barely in their twenties, were willing to talk to me about their surreal odyssey—from village comradery to ETA membership, to killing, to arrest, to torture, to prison, to release and comradery again.

But one of the four had not been arrested. He later transferred to the more extreme "military branch" of ETA and died in a confrontation with the police in June of 1980. And the fourth one, Atxega, after leaving prison, had joined the "politico-military branch" of ETA—the one advocating political discourse as well as military operations. His village friends would regularly visit Atxega in southern France and so I, too, ended up seeing him in their company. My curiosity regarding his life was, of course, intense. As an old friend, he was willing to help out with my anthropological project. He was in fact one of the members of the ETA politico-military executive committee, and he would mention it to the rest. These were obviously "illegal" contacts with ETA. The real issue for me at the time was not, however, between legality and illegality, but between siding with the state's definition of the violence or the one upheld by the villagers themselves. As a student working in a foreign university, I could easily live by accepting one or the other definition, which did not commit me to any moral or political position. Yet as a writer committed to recording the true political pathos of a community, I knew that I would simply put myself outside their moral realm if I decided to espouse the definition of "terrorism" imposed by the State. A crucial consequence of such a legal and moral *cordon sanitaire* against political revolt, since Franco's times, was to taboo the role of the witness. Ethnography of "terrorism" was simply forbidden.

The dilemmas inherent in militarism are multiplied in the case of a "terrorist" group. My youthful respect for the members of ETA who had checked Franco's succession plans (Wilson was one of the famed commandos who assassinated Carrero Blanco) was a distant remembrance. I deplored the fact that ETA did not disband when Spain embraced democracy and matters could be decided in the ballot booth.

"But what do you want to prove?" they asked me time and again when, six months later, I was summoned by ETA for an interview arranged in a French hideout to which they drove me blindfolded. At issue were the limits of my contacts with them and potential participation in an underground "cell" of the organization. I told them I had no political goals of my own, no commitment to the cause of an independent Basqueland. I wanted to approach them with no preconceptions, I replied. I had nothing to prove. I simply wanted to be a witness to their lives before I wrote a book. Yet I was willing to assume all the risks of being a witness (which would immediately make me an accomplice to terrorism). Morally, the most troublesome prospect was one of being forced to commit murder, and I told my ETA interlocutors that I would not obey them if they ordered me to kill someone. They replied that once you are in, there is no separation between killers and non-killers. I realized that, if I joined them, the likelihood of direct or indirect complicity with murder was very real, yet I persisted. I had fallen into the abyss of excessive witnessing—one that entailed the possibility of putting at risk my own life and that of others, a decision which, had it led me into being dictated to by the actions of an armed group, exceeded all of my personal knowledge and morality.[6]

My ETA interlocutors were baffled by my presence. After discarding various hypotheses (such as the obvious one that I might be working for the CIA), they simply didn't know what to do with me. It was then that they decided to break off communications. I had failed the exam. I was discouraged and relieved. My truth game was over. For them such a witness was simply unnecessary and in the end unwanted. To me this meant that there was nothing exemplary to learn from their lives. I also came to realize that permitting or prohibiting the presence of a witness can determine the overall meaning and outcome of a course of action. The executioner does not want a witness, I concluded.

IV. From Silence to Writing on the Horns of the Bull

... to be a writer, a man of letters, is not enough. It is boring, pallid. It lacks danger. Leiris must feel, as he writes, the equivalent of the bullfighter's knowledge that he risks being gored. Only then is writing worthwhile. But how can the writer achieve this invigorating sense of mortal danger? Leiris' answer is: through self-exposure, through *not* defending himself; not through fabricating works of art, objectifications of himself, but through laying himself—his own person—on the line of fire.

—Susan Sontag, "Michel Leiris' *Manhood*"

Women who had just witnessed the murder of a neighbor faced me once with the question "But how can that be?" The horror in their faces demanded that I produce a "reason" for the murder. Yet it was a moment of inexcusable tragedy, of complete silence. Any word of response to the unanswerable question, any excuse for the act, would have sounded sacrilegious. Only complete silence was morally appropriate. When no excuse can undo unredeemable violence, all confession is a failure. Pleas of "innocence" are no less problematic when they lead to complacency regarding the truthfulness of one's testimony. It is such "temptation of innocence" that besets confessional discourses. Borrowing approvingly from a philosopher the moral high ground can also turn into a form of confession, as I know from my own experience with Levinas.

For Kierkegaard's Abraham ethics itself became a "temptation" in the lofty sense that transcendent commands may exceed even moral codes. But there is a less metaphysical and more commonplace way of understanding the temptation of ethics; that is, when "ethics" becomes a discursive formation susceptible of appropriation by the most opposed ethical stances. The soldier and the pacifist, the terrorist and the counter-terrorist, the scientist experimenting with the genome project and the one opposed to it, will all sincerely invoke ethics as their ultimate guide. Each will herald his or her own use of ethics as the unquestionable authority that should prevail and thereby resolve any dissonance among competing genres and legitimacies.

Counter-terrorism discourse, with its sustained strategy of dehumanizing the other fashioned as moral imperative, presents a good arena for observing the most dubious appropriations of ethics.[7] So does any military discourse. Not only did I fail to respond to "the Basque revolution" earlier as a young man, I had also thwarted the Spanish army's order to accept the inalienable duties of a Spanish patriot. I did eventually return to the Spanish army as a writer, and ended up publishing an essay on military conscription as the necessary condition for manhood in any modern state—an initiation ritual in the most literal sense.[8] Far from chastising the Spanish military as a murderous institution by borrowing from Kant an ethics of universal peace, what anthropology confronted me with was once again the universality of human killing as an ultimate duty of citizenship.

Such ultimate situations in the military or religious spheres confront us with the tension between bearing witness and silence, confession and failure. The author of *Fear and Trembling*, faced with the paradigm of such undecidability in his commentary on Abraham's sacrifice, disguised himself under the pen name "Joannes de Silentio." For Kierkegaard the excess of such a sacrificial gift remains inaccessible—a sort of scandalous *secret* submerged in silence. He calls our attention "to the difficulty Abraham had in saying anything at all. The distress and anguish in the paradox consisted . . .

in silence—Abraham cannot speak" (127). In Derrida's commentary, Abraham is not a witness, "in the sense that to witness means to show, teach, illustrate, manifest to others the truth that one can precisely attest to. Abraham is a witness of the absolute faith that cannot and must not witness before men. He must keep his secret. But his silence is not just any silence. Can one witness in silence? By silence?" (1999: 73). As argued by Bateson and Bateson, "*noncommunication* of certain sorts is needed if we are to maintain the 'sacred.' Communication is undesirable, not because of fear, but because communication would somehow alter the nature of the ideas" (80). Silence and secrecy are thus widely used as markers showing that we are approaching a sacred site. But can an anthropologist be silent when confronted with the injustices of the world we live in? Here one admires Scheper-Hughes' insolent call to ethics.

Terrorism presents a contemporary discourse that attests to the relevance of the role of the witness—both as a promise of redemption and as a failure—in the history of crime. The face-to-face confrontation with the killers and victims can radically affect the witness. Such a transformation was partially achieved in the town meeting that concluded my anthropological fieldwork, when my neighbors asked me to speak about what I had "found out" in the course of my investigation and I turned the meeting into a confrontation between the opposing views regarding the violence. Witnessing another's views and destitution was seemingly a unique lesson in history and ethics. In one sense there was a promise of resolution in the very act of an entire community bearing witness. "By provoking such dialogue between irreconcilable worldviews, I felt I was sharing with my Itziar neighbors and friends anthropology's subversive character," so that ethnography became "a distancing device by pointing out the 'otherness' of what people experience, the ethnographer included, within the boundaries of their cultural constructions" and, in so doing, the anthropologist was "inviting his culture to understand and ultimately question the role of the native" (Zulaika 1988: 350).

Yet were such confident intimations of a testimonial breakthrough signs of real transformation, or were they merely the mirage of a writer seeking redemption? The community of neighbors wanted to feel implicated in one another's lives, to assume mutual responsibility, and thereby find salvation in the very act of bearing witness to one another's actions. Accepting the risks in each other's presence was a revelatory event, in itself an act of transformation. That testimony to an unwanted history of violence and victimization seemed to provide a new awareness of the community's cultural meltdown; it could be regarded as a belated attempt at a collective confession and request for forgiveness.

However, another village meeting quickly dispelled such illusions about understanding and forgiving. The occasion was to consider the intention of a television producer to film a documentary on the violence in Itziar—based on the published ethnography. Confronted with the prospect of re-counting their recent history of division and murder to the unrelenting eye of the camera—that decisive witness in defining terrorism and its vic-tims—the anthropologist and the community failed miserably in their tes-timonial task. Old accusations of mutual victimization were brought to life. Former antagonistic scenarios became overpowering and, ultimately, the villagers refused to collaborate in a common narration of their political story. The community's earlier self-confessional spirit dissipated in failure. There were wounds that simply could not be healed. For the camera, that is, the external world, there was no community capable of witnessing. Such failure only underscores the problematic nature of the role of the witness.

In brief, the stance of the Itziar villagers was not forced initially by "ethics" *per se*, but something previous to it: the recognition of the exis-tence of their human community and the right and duty to witness and confront each other's lives. The testimonial meeting was, in a profound sense, an act of taking responsibility for the community's crimes. And just as important by removing the taboo from the role of the witness it was also possible to go beyond any illusion of communal redemption through ex-emplary testimony. It was by partially leaving aside claims of the greater value of one's own ethical positions that Itziar's communal encounter among antagonistic political stances was possible.

If anthropology is to continue bearing witness to the generalized sys-tems of death in the present age, it is the temptation of moralistic ortho-doxy and innocence that we should be concerned about. We are better off looking into Abraham's moral paradox and admitting that his sacrifice is not only the true basis of our religious and military predicaments, but also that his moral bankruptcy is the fate of even the most unconditional of witnesses.

Forced into so much witnessing, we may fall prey to a sense of moral panic. Weary of the ills of moral relativism, we resort to the radical ethical thinking of philosophers such as Levinas, whose privileging of the ethical is a way of thinking religiously without religion. Hegel, Kierkegaard, Heideg-ger are towering figures in that philosophical tradition. Yet, in the end, it is Abraham's religious paradox—his readiness to sacrifice Isaac for the un-compromising love of God—that subverts and reduces to silence their eth-ical thinking. Ethics, for Kierkegaard, is regulated by generality and demands the responsibility of involving oneself in it and speaking out to answer for one's decisions. Yet what does Abraham's sacrificial readiness teach us? Simply, that "the ethical is the temptation." In Derrida's commen-tary, "That far from ensuring responsibility, the generality of ethics incites

to irresponsibility. It impels me to speak, to reply, to account for something, and thus dissolve my singularity in the medium of the concept"
(1999: 61). All ethical generality fails before Abraham's insolent paradox.

The sacrifice of Isaac is what a writer is confronted with each time he or
she witnesses a "ritual killing." Each time a soldier is initiated into the myste-
rious realm of having to kill and die for an ethics higher than the individual,
the sacrifice of Isaac is being commanded. This is the scandal of our politics,
our militarism, our international law. We are faithful to our basic social and
national moralities by everywhere agreeing with the sacrifice of Isaac—the
very betrayal of ethics. Murder as an act of absolute love is what ethics cannot understand or tolerate. That is also Scheper-Hughes' story "on the political economy of modern love and infant death in the Brazilian shantytown"
where children are left to die of hunger and to turn into "angels" in a reenactment of Abraham's lesson of faithful killing (1995: 416). There is no redemption for the mothers, nor for the anthropologist, for sacrificing their
children to hunger. The force of Scheper-Hughes' ethnography springs from
the fact that she makes anthropology return "to its origins by reopening—
though in no way claiming to resolve—vexing questions of moral and ethical relativism" (1992: 21). One such question is that, in perpetual paradox,
the same invocation of ethics issued against the discipline's comfort level
risks itself providing that very moral comfort that might set anthropologists
apart from the moral predicaments of their informants. Veena Das asks:
"What is the form through which violence may be written about when its
foundation, as Bataille said, is that it exceeds limits?" (33). The special responsibility towards those who suffer should transform the anthropologist
into a witness, but a witness *à la* Abraham—horrified not primarily by some
evil out there in the world but rather by the abyss of one's own participation
in the murder.

CHAPTER **3**

Witness in the Wilderness: The Tropical Tryst of Claude Lévi-Strauss and Theodore Roosevelt

WILLIAM A. DOUGLASS

To witness without "bearing" (recounting) is a private act that poses a co-nundrum—can there be experience that is unshared, like the sound of the philosopher's solitary falling tree? For present purposes there is no dilemma, since I plan to compare two classic twentieth-century texts within that quintessential witnessing genre known as the traveler's tale—a literary form currently given considerable attention by the social sciences and humanities.[1] My subjects are Claude Lévi-Strauss and Theodore Roosevelt, authors of *Tristes Tropiques* (1973) and *Through the Brazilian Wilderness* (1919), respectively. Based upon expeditions into the same area of the Brazilian highlands, but a generation apart (Roosevelt in 1913–14 and Lévi-Strauss in 1935–37, 1938–39), the two witnesses produced accounts that differ profoundly even though they share certain common elements. I focus upon the writers as much as their texts in the spirit of Montaigne, who cited the Ancients to make the point that any traveler always takes himself on the journey and therefore perceives the world, no matter how exotic, through his own eyes.[2]

Lévi Strauss is a social anthropologist known for his structuralist approach to the study of culture. His work is discussed in a global intellectual circle whose circumference transcends the boundaries of his chosen discipline. However, his fame echoes largely within the halls of academia; his name is scarcely a household word. Conversely, Theodore Roosevelt led an ascendant United States into the twentieth century. A larger-than-life fig-ure, he was arguably the most flamboyant, and one of the most popular, of the American presidents.

It is their respective texts that tip the scales in favor of Lévi-Strauss for present purposes, since *Tristes Tropiques*, while attracting but limited read-ership upon publication, would become a classic that continues to be dis-sected and debated to this day (Lévi-Strauss and Eribon 58). Roosevelt's book, while widely read in its time, entertained and informed (but without challenging) the reader and now gathers dust on the shelves of a few per-sonal and public libraries.

If the fate of the texts recommends one over the other, there remains the question of which Lévi-Strauss wrote *Tristes Tropiques* and which TR wrote *Through the Brazilian Wilderness*? The former details the experi-ences of an aspiring anthropologist in his mid to late twenties, undergoing his discipline's mandatory *rite de passage* of fieldwork. The young scholar sojourned in Brazil in the shadows of obscurity while struggling to scale the foothills of what would eventually become the lofty peak of an illustri-ous career. Conversely, when he journeyed to South America, Roosevelt was in his twilight years, descending from the mountaintop of a public life that made him a battle-scarred veteran of many wars, both figurative and literal.

Claude Lévi-Strauss, a Brussels-born, Paris-raised Jew (though an unbe-liever), came from an obscure artistic family of modest economic circum-stances. Trained at the University of Paris in law and philosophy, he eventually gravitated towards sociology and the emerging field of social an-thropology. He embraced Marxism and became a socialist activist, though his commitment proved suspect and his involvement transitory.[3] This background not only failed to facilitate, but rather frustrated, his desire to enter the exclusive ranks of French academics. Relegated to a teaching post at a provincial *lycée*, in 1935 the young scholar welcomed the opportunity to teach sociology as part of the French contingent at the nascent Univer-sity of São Paulo. The posting provided him with the opportunity to con-duct the field research among Brazilian Indians that would become the basis of his doctoral dissertation.

Between 1935 and 1937 he made brief visits both back to France and to the interior of Brazil. The specifics are extremely sketchy, but by the end of his stint with the University of São Paulo, he appears to have spent a total of about five months in the field. These initial experiences were with the Caduveo and Bororo Indians, two tribes that were well on their way to as-similation within Brazilian society. He subsequently formed part of an ex-pedition into the Brazilian highlands that was financed by the French government and included at least two other scientists from different disciplines. Whether or not it was his exclusive responsibility under the terms of the grant is unclear, but at least one of Lévi-Strauss' duties was to collect artifacts for the *Musée de l'Homme*. The expedition lasted from June of 1938 into early 1939.

Lévi-Strauss returned to France on the eve of World War II, served briefly in the French army, was decommissioned and given a teaching post at a *collège* in Perpignan, from which he was promptly removed when the new (anti-Semitic) racial law took effect. He then moved to New York as part of the Rockefeller Foundation—New School efforts to extricate threatened intellectuals from Europe (Lévi-Strauss and Eribon 25–27). After the war he was named the French cultural attaché in New York City.[4]

In 1948 Lévi-Strauss returned to Paris to present his dissertation. He secured a "transitional job" as a *maître de recherche* at the Centre National de la Recherche Scientifique and was then appointed by Paul Rivet as assistant director of ethnology at the Musée de l'Homme (53). In 1949, and again in 1950, his candidacy for entry into the Collège de France was defeated.

> After this double disaster, I was convinced that I would never have a real career. I broke with my past, rebuilt my private life, and wrote *Tristes Tropiques*, which I would never have dared publish if I had been competing for a university position. (50)[5]

From the outset, the book received a warmer reception in literary and other intellectual circles than in anthropological ones. Indeed,

> The moment he opened *Tristes Tropiques*, Paul Rivet shut the door in my face. He was quick to anger, and after reading the first sentence, "Travel and travelers are two things I loathe," he must have stopped there and concluded that I was a traitor. (59)[6]

Clifford Geertz characterizes the work as a "combination autobiography, traveler's tale, philosophical treatise, ethnographic report, colonial history, and prophetic myth," which ". . . far from being a great anthropology book, or even an especially good one, is surely one of the finest books ever written by an anthropologist" (1973: 347). Marcus and Fischer note that the book is ". . . philosophical, elegant, and worthy of reflection and rereading, destined to be taught in literature classes as a model of *belles lettres*" (1986: 34).

Theodore Roosevelt was born into a well-to-do, socially prominent New York family.[7] He was the grandson of a real estate magnate and son of a civic leader (Brands 1997: 3–18). A sickly youth, he found relief from his chronic asthma in the outdoors and developed a passion for natural history that nearly determined his career choice and remained with him throughout his life.[8] In the summer between his sophomore and junior years at Harvard, he hunted and fished in the Maine wilderness. After graduation he and his younger brother Elliott went on an extended hunting trip to Illinois and Minnesota, just east of the Dakota Territory.

For the young naturalist, specimen collection, often with firearms, was a critical part of the scientist's trade—or what his biographer Brands calls his "armed science" (70). Roosevelt would later become a dedicated big game hunter and the founding force of the Boone and Crockett Club (189). In 1881, TR entered public life by winning a seat in the New York State legislature. In 1884 his first wife died shortly after giving birth to their first child and a devastated TR retired to South Dakota where he purchased a cattle ranch. It was there that he experienced frontier life for the first time and came to know and admire the frontiersmen. In 1886 he returned to New York, regained his Assembly seat, and remarried. He and his wife Edith would have five children (Roosevelt firmly believed it to be the duty of every white American to propagate for the sake of the "race"). In 1888 he left New York politics for an appointment in Washington, D.C. as the U.S. civil service commissioner, and for the next five years he reshaped what had been a perfunctory post through effective advocacy for equal treatment of every citizen under the law. In 1893 he ran for mayor of New York and was defeated. Between 1895 and 1897, TR served as the city's reformist police commissioner.

After Washington, D.C., New York municipal politics seemed provincial, so, in 1897, Roosevelt used his connections to gain an appointment as assistant secretary of the Navy. When he became acting secretary he all but provoked the Spanish-American War (1898), resigning his post to organize and lead the Rough Riders (a curious combination of Western frontiersmen and Ivy Leaguers) into combat. He returned from Cuba a war hero and that same year won the governorship of New York. In 1899 Roosevelt enhanced his national notoriety and popularity by publishing a book entitled *The Rough Riders*. It was but the latest in an impressive list of publications that had established his reputation as both a scholar and popular writer. They ranged from histories such as *The Naval War of 1812* (1882) and the four-volume *The Winning of the American West* (1889–1896) to biographies of *Governeur Morris* (1888) and *Oliver Cromwell* (1900), as well as adventure travelogues in the vein of *Hunting Trips of a Ranchman* (1885), *Ranch Life and the Hunting Trail* (1888), and *The Wilderness Hunter* (1893).

In 1900, after crossing the state's political bosses, TR was maneuvered into accepting the vice presidential nomination, an office that he regarded as political oblivion. However, in 1901 President McKinley was assassinated and Roosevelt became the youngest president in the nation's history. He then won reelection in 1904. As president, Roosevelt was a personalist, populist and paternalist. He was personalistic in the sense that Roosevelt-the-politician was a dubious party man, far more prone to value and heed his own counsel than that of others. He was a stern moralist who preached a combination of honesty, thrift, dedication to task, and patriotism which, taken together, equated to Americanism. TR also possessed a large ego that was but rarely assailed with self-doubt or shaken by adverse criticism.

Roosevelt's populism stemmed from his history as a political reformer and his firm belief that democracy was the essential element in the progress of any nation. It was also nurtured by his racial beliefs. While he shared many of the invidious racial and ethnic stereotypes of his contemporaries, he did not believe in the inherent inferiority or superiority of different races.[9] Rather, he was an equipotentialist, convinced that all human beings, given the right education and opportunities, were equally capable. TR believed that business and labor had a moral obligation to one another to ensure that there was a decent wage for an honest day's labor. The era's "robber barons" suspected him of being a pro-labor closet radical.

Domestically, Roosevelt was an imperial president in that he regularly tested the outer limits of his authority within the checks and balances of the American political system. In foreign affairs he championed what came to be known as the Roosevelt Corollary of the Monroe Doctrine. A foe of disorder and challenges to established authority, Roosevelt never hesitated to intervene in the domestic affairs of his nation's hemispheric neighbors. He was also committed to a colonialist manifest destiny, advocating his country's governance of Puerto Rico and the Philippines. The most spectacular example of his imperialist mindset was his role in engineering the excision of Panama from Colombia so that he could build the canal.

In 1908, and despite his immense popularity, TR honored his pledge not to run for reelection and anointed his friend and protégé, William Howard Taft, as his successor. In March of 1909, Roosevelt fulfilled a dream by departing for a year-long African safari along with his nineteen-year-old son Kermit. According to Brands,

> Sensitive to the charge of bloodthirstiness, Roosevelt took pains to cast his safari as a scientific expedition. He pledged his prizes to the Smithsonian museum; the animals, stuffed, would depict the large-mammal life of East Africa to future generations of students and other museum-goers. (643)

The "expedition" was underwritten by Andrew Carnegie[10] and Roosevelt negotiated a contract with *Scribner's* that guaranteed him the sum of

$50,000 for twelve articles to be written in the field, posted from Africa, and serialized in the magazine.

Free to devote time to other activities, TR luxuriated in his lifelong scholarly interests. While passing through England on his journey home from Africa, he was awarded honorary degrees by Oxford and Cambridge. He then gave the prestigious Romanes Lecture at Oxford University, speaking on the subject of "Biological Analogies in History." In 1910–11 he was elected vice president of the American Historical Association, and president the following year. He became a fund-raiser for the Smithsonian Institution and engaged in an acrimonious published debate "regarding the function and purpose of protective coloration in birds and other small vertebrates" (682).

Meanwhile, TR had become deeply disillusioned with Taft as the keeper of his legacy. His successor seemed too uncritical of the political bosses and vested interests for Roosevelt's taste. TR and his supporters formed the Progressive ("Bull-Moose") Party to contest the election of 1912. While on the campaign trail he was shot by a would-be assassin, but survived the attack. Roosevelt's challenge doomed Taft (who came in third) and elected Woodrow Wilson. Consequently, by early 1913, TR was *persona non grata* with the Republicans and leader of the fledgling Progressive Party. Sensitive that his party's greatest asset, should it wish to prepare for the election of 1916, was the Roosevelt personality cult, TR penned a series of autobiographical articles for *The Outlook* magazine that were published at year's end in book form. He also decided to launch another expedition—this time to South America—that would inspire *Through the Brazilian Wilderness*.

Lévi-Strauss' expressed hatred for explorers at the outset of *Tristes Tropiques* is clearly a rhetorical ploy to distinguish the anthropological text from that of the "mere" traveler's tale.[11] He abominates the adventurer who assembles

> lantern-slides or motion pictures, preferably in colour, so as to fill a hall with an audience . . . [for whom] platitudes and commonplaces seem to have been miraculously transmuted into revelation by the sole fact that their author, instead of doing his plagiarizing at home, has supposedly sanctified it by covering some twenty-thousand miles. (1973: 4)

As a quintessential binarist, if Lévi-Strauss eschews *adventure* as his organizing trope, he is left with *ennui*. *Tristes Tropiques* has, in fact, been analyzed as a text on boredom (Arshi, Kirstein, Naqvi, and Pankow 1994). Indeed, the very pace of the argument can be stupefying. The reader is taken on a seemingly interminable voyage that effects the transition from

Europe to a world of tropical languor. Rather than the adventurer's hyperbole designed to pique the reader's interest with vivid accounts of natural and cultural exotica, hard won through the narrator's assumption of considerable personal risk, *Tristes Tropiques* evokes images of a tropical world that is but a seedy and decrepit version of Western civilization converted into a corrupting global force.[12]

Before introducing us to the elusive (and illusive) primitives of the Brazilian wilderness, there is first an interlude in São Paulo, during which Lévi-Strauss assumes the (neither entirely self-conscious nor oblivious) role of "intellectual broker" as part of the civilizing French mission to the University of São Paulo (1973: 100).[13] His subsequent search for the primitive is rather like the peeling back of the successive layers of a rotten onion in the hope of finding an edible core. It begins in the suburbs of São Paulo, "but not among suburban Indians, about whom I had been given false promises, since the suburbs were inhabited by Syrians and Italians" (107). The working-class suburbs were inhabited by *mestiços* or "coloured people" (black crossed with white), *caboclos* (white crossed with Indian), and *cafusos* (Indian crossed with black). Fifteen kilometers away was a curious tribe of fair-haired, blue-eyed "natives" of German descent. Then there were the Japanese truck gardeners.

Further afield lay the "pioneer zone," a melange of European influences in which country life has a Mediterranean flair, while new cities "were totally nordic" (122). It is not until a third of the way through *Tristes Tropiques* that we visit the Paraná and encounter the anthropologist's first Indians, the Caduveo of the Rio Tibagy. They had been herded onto a reserve by the Brazilian government two decades earlier and provided with many of the accoutrements of Western civilization ("So to my great disappointment, the Tibagy Indians were neither completely 'true Indians', nor, what was more important, 'savages' ") (159).

To reach his first "real" tribe of passable Indians (that is, "a society which is still alive and faithful to its traditions") (234), Lévi-Strauss first ascends the Rio Paraguay in a steamboat, then travels cross-country by truck before spending more than a week canoeing into Bororo country. The description of his journey in part replicates Roosevelt's itinerary more than two decades earlier, and the two accounts are remarkably similar (217–33). Both possess a certain venture-into-the-Heart-of-Darkness quality.[14]

In formulating his standard ethnographic description of Bororo life, Lévi-Strauss employed Portuguese to interview informants. Missionaries and the Indian Protection Service had mediated and eliminated the previous conflict between the Bororo and the area's colonists. He notes that his village, Kejara, was one where the native culture had remained relatively untouched (234).

In 1938 Lévi-Strauss returned to Brazil to resume his search for the primitive. In a chapter of *Tristes Tropiques* entitled "Lost World," he tells us:

> My intention was to spend a whole year in the bush . . . and being more anxious to understand America than to study human nature by basing my research on one particular instance, I finally decided to take a sort of cross-section through Brazilian anthropology—and geography—by travelling across the western part of the plateau, from Cuiaba to the Rio Madeira.[15] Until recent times, this region had remained one of the least known in all Brazil. The Paulist explorers of the eighteenth century, discouraged by the desolate nature of the country and the savagery of the Indians, had hardly ventured beyond Cuiaba. At the beginning of the twentieth century, the 1500 kilometers stretching between Cuiaba and the Amazon were still forbidden territory. . . . It was only in 1907 that General (then Colonel) Candido Mariano da Silva Rondon began to explore and open up the territory; he was to be engaged on this task for eight years, during which time he established a strategically important telegraph line linking the federal capital, via Cuiaba, with the north-west frontier posts for the first time.
>
> The reports of the Rondon Commission . . . , one or two lectures given by the general, the account written by Theodore Roosevelt who accompanied him on one of his expeditions and finally a delightful book by the late Roquette Pinto . . . entitled *Rondonia* (1912), gave a modicum of information about the primitive communities discovered in the area. But since then, the old curse seemed to have fallen over the plateau again. No professional anthropologist had ever ventured across it. It was tempting to follow the telegraph line, or what was left of it, to try and find out exactly who the Nambikwara were, as well as the mysterious communities further to the north, whom no one had ever seen since Rondon briefly indicated their existence. (277–78)

In point of fact, the expedition lasted considerably less than a year and the parties "seem to have been on the move nearly the whole time" (Leach 1970: x).

His encounters with the Nambikwara, while clearly a less "contacted" people than either the Caduveo or Bororo, failed to satiate the anthropologist's appetite for what had become a relentless search for the truly primitive. He therefore set out to find the furtive Tupi-Kawahib of Rondon's earlier account. After journeying four additional days upriver from his remotest Nambikwara group, Lévi-Strauss encountered a community of about 25 people "who referred to themselves as Mundé," and "had never before been mentioned in any anthropological study" (379). However, the crowning moment actually left him "with a feeling of emptiness" and after a few days he abandoned the effort (375).

> I had wanted to reach the extreme limits of the savage; it might be thought that my wish had been granted, now that I found myself among these charming Indians whom no other white man had ever seen before and who might never be seen again. After an enchanting trip up-river, I had certainly found my savages. Alas! They were only too savage. Since their existence had only been revealed to me at the last moment, I was unable to devote to them the time that would have been essential to get to know them. . . . There they were, all ready to teach me their customs and beliefs, and I did not know their language. They were as close to me as a reflection in a mirror; I could touch them, but I could not understand them. I had been given, at one and the same time, my reward and my punishment. . . . I had only to succeed in guessing what they were like for them to be deprived of their strangeness: in which case, I might just as well have stayed in my village. (375–76)

There is, then, a sense in which Lévi-Strauss questions the feasibility and worth of the anthropological enterprise. *Tristes Tropiques* thereby becomes a precursor of the movement that would subsequently transform his discipline, clearly one of the reasons for its continued popularity.[16] It also stands alone within the body of the author's own work since, ironically, rather than abandoning both his field site and chosen field, he passed through that Mundé looking glass and became the main anthropological spokesman for, and practitioner of, structuralism. In summing up this intellectual progression, Geertz comments:

> For what Lévi-Strauss has made for himself is an infernal culture machine. It annuls history, reduces sentiment to a shadow of the intellect, and replaces the particular minds of particular savages in particular jungles with the Savage Mind immanent in all of us. It has made it possible for him to circumvent the impasse to which his Brazilian expedition led—physical closeness and intellectual distance—by what perhaps he always really wanted—intellectual closeness and physical distance. (1973: 355–56)

Whatever else it might be, then, *Tristes Tropiques* is retrospective musing in the service of self-reflection. The book was written nearly two decades after the events it describes and was dashed off in a four-month period of late 1954 and early 1955 (Lévi-Strauss and Eribon 1988: 58). It details the experiences of a youthful novice anthropologist, while giving voice to the angst of an embittered, middle-aged, and seemingly career-blocked scholar. Recall Lévi-Strauss's comment that he would never have written the book had he thought himself to be a serious competitor for a university position.[17] Asked if *Tristes Tropiques* was a summation of his work to that point, he replied, "Also, of everything I believed and dreamed about" (1988: 59).

At one point in the text Lévi-Strauss shares with the reader three pessimistic poems that he wrote while in the Brazilian wilderness, including one that "conjured up bleak memories of suburbia" (388). One can imagine him nearly twenty years later, at his wintry task of writing *Tristes Tropiques*, staring out a Parisian window while pondering the words of a Verlaine poem about ennui,

> *Il pleure dans mon coeur*
> *Comme il pleut sur la ville;*
> *Quelle est cette langeur*
> *Qui pénètre mon coeur?* (160)

Roosevelt's South American venture would embrace several activities and was, in many respects, a replay of his African one. As ex-president, he had received many invitations from around the world to lecture, including several Latin American countries. He decided to incorporate visits to Uruguay, Argentina, and Chile into his itinerary. His primary goal was to conduct a "zoogeographic reconnaissance through the Brazilian hinterland" (1919: preface). The expedition included two scientists from the American Museum of Natural History responsible for collecting birds and mammals. Roosevelt would again be accompanied by his son Kermit. The expeditionaries departed New York by steamship on October 4, 1913.

In his role as French cultural imperialist, Lévi-Strauss was both profoundly disappointed by, and paternalistic towards, Brazil.[18] It was, after all, the main source of his "tropical" (in both senses) malaise. Ironically, Roosevelt, the quintessential American imperialist who had invaded Cuba, coopted Puerto Rico, and all but stolen Panama (for its own good to be sure) was generous and ebullient regarding South America:

> Altogether the impression left on me by Bahia was not only one of beauty and picturesqueness, but of eager determination to succeed in manufacturing and commerce, and of the full realization by the leaders that there could be no success of the kind unless there was a

stable, orderly, and honest government, unless justice was meted out without favor, and unless energy, thrift, hard work, and intelligent enterprise were shown in the business world. If, as I not only hope but believe, Brazil can continue developing all these qualities, she has before her a future of limitless prosperity and development in the twentieth century. (*The Outlook*, December 13, 1913: 802)

Of Rio de Janeiro Roosevelt noted:

> . . . in Italy there is apt to be some revolting lack of cleanliness to mar even what is most beautiful, whereas around Rio the cleanliness and wholesomeness surpass that of even our northern cities. . . . I felt that Rio need fear no comparison with any modern capital, from New York to Berlin. (*The Outlook*, December 20, 1913: 840–41)

Indeed, the city changed his mind regarding the advisability of the European grand tour of his youth:

> Altogether it is difficult to write of this city of over a million people without expressing astonishment that both its beauty and its greatness are not more widely understood. . . . The people of the United States do not realize what a wonderful city this tropic capital is; wonderful not only in beauty, but in its extraordinary material activity and achievement. Fortunately, South America is becoming more and more accessible to the people of the United States. It is much to be wished that young Americans would visit their neighbors to the south of them before they make a European tour—just as it is much to be wished that dwellers on the Eastern coast would, wherever possible, take some trip at least as far west as the Pacific before they cross the Atlantic Ocean. (*The Outlook*, December 20, 1913: 837)

While in Rio, Roosevelt was invited by Brazil's minister of foreign affairs to team up with Colonel Rondon of the Telegraphic Commission for a trip down the unexplored Rio Dúvida (River of Doubt). TR would later reconstruct the invitation:

> Now, we will be delighted to have you do it; but, of course, you must understand, we cannot tell you anything of what might happen, and there may be surprises, not necessarily pleasant. (*The Outlook*, June 6, 1914: 283)

Roosevelt accepted on the spot, but first he had to attend to his speaking engagements. TR would continue to fashion his paean to South America as he visited Uruguay, Argentina, and then Chile. While acknowledging the abject poverty of Paraguay, as he closed out the "touristic" (and diplomatic) portion of his tour before exploring the Brazilian interior, he wrote from Asunción:

> ... we must beware of dogmatizing overmuch as to the inability of the tropics . . . to sustain a high civilization. . . . The twentieth century is the century of South America. (*The Outlook*, June 6, 1914: 308)[19]

The text of *Through the Brazilian Wilderness* begins on December 9, 1913, when the Roosevelt party departs Asunción to ascend the Paraguay River, in order to meet up with Colonel Rondon and the several Brazilian members of the formally designated Expedicâo Científica Roosevelt-Rondon. There follow a series of canoe trips and overland treks by oxen and mule train for which Roosevelt provides detailed description of the people and places visited. But, above all, his text is a pastiche of hunting adventures and naturalist observations. While recounting a jaguar hunt, TR conflates the two:

> A hunter of scientific tastes, a hunter-naturalist, or even an outdoors naturalist, or faunal naturalist interested in big mammals, with a pack of hounds such as those with which Paul Rainey hunted lion or leopard in Africa, or such a pack as the packs of Johnny Goff and Jake Borah with which I hunted cougar, lynx, and bear in the Rockies, or such packs as those of the Mississippi and Louisiana planters with whom I hunted bear, wild-cat, and deer in the cane-brakes of the lower Mississippi, would not only enjoy fine hunting in these vast marshes of the upper Paraguay, but would also do work of real scientific value as regards all the big cats. (1919: 119)

We have noted that *Tristes Tropiques* moves from civilization (São Paulo), through a buffer zone of European immigrant settlers, to the first contact with the (disappointing) Caduveo Indians. From there the benchmarks of the journey into the primitive are the progressively less assimilated tribes, first the Bororo, then the Nambikwara, followed by the quest for the Tupi-Kawahibs, culminating in the discovery of the Mundé.

Roosevelt's progression into the wilderness is similarly marked by encounters with increasingly primitive savages. First there were the Parecís, whom Colonel Rondon had civilized by convincing them to wear Western clothing and "to substitute for the flimsy Indian cabin houses of the type usual among the poorer field-laborers and backcountry dwellers in Brazil." His brief description of them is laced with ethnocentric commentary ("The women seemed to be well treated, although polygamy is practiced"), and as if this weren't enough to set the anthropologist's teeth on edge, most of his description of the Parecís waxes eloquent over an extraordinary game in which a ball is struck only with the head (196, 198–99).

The expeditionaries continued further into the bush, intent on reaching the headwaters of the Rio Dúvida where their exploration of the unknown would commence. According to TR, "From this point we were to enter a still wilder region, the land of the naked Nhambiquaras" (208). In his first encounter with them he observes,

> Nowhere in Africa did we come across wilder or more absolutely primitive savages, although these Indians were pleasanter and bet-ter-featured than any of the African tribes at the same stage of cul-ture. (222)[20]

For TR, these Indians were less an object of fascination than an obstacle to be warily traversed. He notes:

> At one camp three Nhambiquaras paid us a visit at breakfast time. They left their weapons behind them before they appeared, and shouted loudly while they were still hiding in the forest, and it was only after repeated answering calls of welcome that they ap-proached. Always in the wilderness friends proclaim their presence; a silent approach marks a foe. (229)

And again:

> After breakfast at Bonofacio a number of Nhambiquaras—men, women and children—strolled in. The men gave us an exhibition of not very good archery. . . . Several of the women had been taken from other tribes, after their husbands or fathers had been killed; for the Nhambiquaras are light-hearted robbers and murderers. (246)

On February 27, 1914, still in Nambikwara country, the expeditionaries put seven boats into the headwaters of the Rio Dúvida. More than six weeks later, on April 15, 1914, they reached their first human settlement in the lower reaches of the stream. They had lost two of their craft, endured food rationing, the drowning of one man and the near-drowning of Kermit, and a murder/desertion by a deranged expeditionary. TR suffered a severe injury and nearly failed to complete the ordeal himself. In mid-May, 45 pounds lighter and afflicted by a variety of tropical ailments, he reached New York. According to Roosevelt, in addition to mapping a previously unrecorded river course,

> Zoologically the trip had been a thorough success. Cherrie and Miller had collected over twenty-five hundred birds, about five hundred mammals, and a few reptiles, batrachians, and fishes. Many of them were new to science; for much of the region traversed had never previously been worked by any scientific collector. (1919: 347)

TR was immediately plunged into a round of frenetic activity regarding his expedition. On May 26, 1914, he traveled to Washington, D.C. to submit a report to the National Geographic Society. While there, he toured for the first time the Smithsonian's exhibit of the stuffed specimens of African fauna that he had collected in 1910. He then addressed a crowd of 4,000 people in Convention Hall regarding his South American expedition (*The Outlook* June 6, 1914: 282–83).[21] In July he traveled to London to present his findings to the Royal Geographical Society. There he also gave a public address to an overflow audience of more than a thousand people (*The Outlook*, July 11, 1914: 570–71).[22]

The dark side was that the trip down the River of Doubt had broken TR's health; he would never fully recover. He resigned from the Progressive Party and suffered the personal tragedy of losing one son and having another severely injured in World War I. In 1919 he died in his sleep of lingering illness. According to Brands, "The malady was diagnosed this time as inflammatory rheumatism but was almost certainly related to the persistent infections that had dogged him since his Amazon trip" (810).

Conclusion

If Lévi-Strauss was a French intellectual imperialist, Roosevelt was an American colonial one. The former was a professional anthropologist, amateur naturalist, and aspiring academic, the latter a respected naturalist, amateur racial theorist, and quintessential man of action. While both are highly educated and articulate products of Western civilization, Lévi-Strauss is one of its most acerbic critics while TR was among its most dedicated boosters.[23] The emblematic symbol for contrasting the spirit of the two texts is Rondon's telegraph line. For Roosevelt it was indexical, a Western technological triumph, a straight line through the wilderness pointing towards a glorious (Western) future for the Brazilian highlands:

It is an upland region of good-climate. . . . There is much fertile soil in the neighborhood of the streams, and the teeming lowlands of the Amazon and the Paraguay could readily . . . be made tributary to an industrial civilization seated on these highlands. A telegraph-line has been built to and across them. A railroad should follow. . . . Once this is done the land will offer extraordinary opportunities to settlers of the right kind: to home-makers and to enterprising business men of foresight, coolness, and sagacity who are willing to work with the settlers, the immigrants, the home-makers, for an advantage which shall be mutual. (1919: 195)

TR could not have been more favorably impressed by the people he met in the Brazilian interior:

In short, these men, and those like them everywhere on the frontier between civilization and savagery in Brazil, are now playing the part played by our backwoodsmen when over a century and a quarter ago they began the conquest of the great basin of the Mississippi; the part played by the Boer farmers for over a century in South Africa, and by the Canadians when less than half a century ago they began to take possession of their Northwest. Every now and then someone says that the last "frontier" is now to be found in Canada or Africa, and that it has almost vanished. On a far larger scale this frontier is to be found in Brazil—a country as big as Europe or the United States—and decades will pass before it vanishes. (1919: 333–34)

Conversely, when he visits the Nambikwara a quarter of a century later, Lévi-Strauss finds that

No one dared to close down the line but everyone had lost interest in it. The poles were allowed to collapse and the wires to rust; the last survivors manning the post lacked the courage to leave and indeed could not afford to do so, they were slowly dying out because of sickness, famine and loneliness. (1973: 291–92)

As if "telegraphing" a response to Roosevelt's ebullient Americanism, Lévi-Strauss concludes:

In the wake of Rondon's men as they established the telegraph line, a flood of immigrants was expected to invade the area and use its hitherto unsuspected resources to build some Brazilian Chicago.

The illusion was short-lived; like the north-east of Brazil, with its inhospitable wastes which have been described by Euclides da Cunha in *Os Sertões*, the Serra do Norte turned out to be desert-like savannah and one of the most barren areas of the South American continent. (291)[24]

Tristes Tropiques, then, exudes an Old World, post-civilizational pessimism that questions, fundamentally, the value of Western traditions:

Being human signifies, for each one of us, belonging to a class, a society, a country, a continent and a civilization; and for us European earth-dwellers, the adventure played out in the heart of the New World signifies in the first place that it was not our world and that we bear responsibility for the crime of its destruction; and secondly, that there will never be another New World. (Lévi-Strauss 1973: 448)

Indeed, I would argue that *Through the Brazilian Wilderness* is the foil for a significant part of *Tristes Tropiques*. In addition to the linkage of their antinomic conclusions, there are simply too many parallels between the texts to be coincidental. Whether in their similar descriptions of the rigors of riverine and overland travel, the purgatory inflicted upon the traveler by insects and tropical diseases, the immensity and sameness of a verdant ocean contrasted with the diversity and relief of their respective temperate homelands, escapism into Western literary classicism in order to maintain one's mental bearings, felt trepidation and precautionary measures when traversing Indian country, *Tristes Tropiques* is at times an elaboration and improvement on *Through the Brazilian Wilderness* while at others its contestation.[25]

Lévi-Strauss' work both postdates and benefits from Roosevelt's, a potentially sore point for the "serious" observer seeking to lay claim to being the first European to cross the Brazilian borderlands' intellectual and territorial frontier posts between civilization and wildness.[26] We might recall that there is but a single reference to Roosevelt in *Tristes Tropiques*, one that relegates him to a mere companion of Rondon on one of the latter's expeditions, fails to mention *Through the Brazilian Wilderness* by name, and then juxtaposes (while implicitly contrasting) it with Roquette Pinto's "delightful" account of the area.[27] In short, when Lévi-Strauss begins his text with the phrase "I hate travelling and explorers," we can glimpse the brash Roosevelt's ghost hovering in the background and sense the irony in *Tristes Tropiques*' acerbic opening denunciation of the explorer/adventurer who sanctifies his plagiarizing of platitudes and commonplaces, miraculously transmitting them into revelations by placing them in distant exotic settings.[28]

There are further contrasts and similarities in both the genesis and narrative styles of the two books. *Tristes Tropiques* is a retrospective account written two decades after the author began to experience Brazil and a decade and a half after he had last done so. Its pace, at least as a travel tale, is at times agonizingly slow. *Tristes Tropiques* permeates rather than penetrates Brazil. Its preoccupation with ennui seems to echo the boredom of a housewife's domestic existence. Indeed, Lévi-Strauss characterizes anthropological field research as a feminine undertaking.[29]

Roosevelt's text is a contemporary account written in crisp installments. *Through the Brazilian Wilderness* employs a curious combination of serious social and political commentary, interwoven with the adventures of the hunter/naturalist/explorer. The writing has a certain Frank Buck (Bring 'em back *dead*) tone that also anticipates the cinematic *Perils of Pauline*, keep-the-viewer-on-the-edge-of-seat (and, of course, coming back next week) quality in its serialization. Indeed, TR sets the stage in a discontinuous first chapter whose central theme is the danger of poisonous snakes to world explorers. We are taken to São Paulo's Instituto Serum-thérapico where venoms are extracted and converted into serums.[30] Roosevelt describes in great detail a manichean struggle in which a harmless mussurama snake kills and eats a venomous jararaca (Roosevelt 1919: 9–26).[31] Above all then, *Through the Brazilian Wilderness* is a "male" text, an adventurous thrust into the unknown in which Roosevelt's frequent understatement of obvious dangers and his generous comments regarding the mettle and accomplishments of his companions are clever props in staging the primary message: *I went there and survived.*[32]

While this meta-statement is palpable in both *Through the Brazilian Wilderness* and *Tristes Tropiques,* the two authors situate themselves differently within their texts. Roosevelt, the experienced politician, knows how to remain center stage without claiming all the credit. Like the main actor in a triumphant play, and like the consummate politician that he was, TR leads the sincere applause for the supporting cast. His text is sprinkled with detail and praise for the activities of identified fellow travelers—Colonel Rondon, Kermit, naturalists George K. Cherrie and Leo E. Miller, and others. At times we are even introduced to the "grunts" who transported the provisions and paddled the canoes as people. There is both a human face and sense of collective effort in the Roosevelt account.

Tristes Tropiques assumes an entirely different tone. It is an angst-ridden journey into the mind and soul of its author; one that is almost entirely lacking the presence of other named and developed characters. It is only through *Saudades do Brasil* that we belatedly learn that Lévi-Strauss' parents lived with him in 1935 in São Paulo (1995: 22). Like Roosevelt, Lévi-Strauss was accompanied, at least in part, by two other French scientists during his Nambikwara expedition, yet they are not mentioned in *Tristes Tropiques*.

Both texts address *doubt* in various guises. Both are in search of the primitive wilderness experience—the quest to transcend the boundaries of the unknown, to become the first "civilized" person to capture (and thereby domesticate) its essence. Despite his civilized cynicism and pessimism, until the very end of this retrospective account the anthropologist is driven by the belief that an unsullied primitive tribe must still exist somewhere "out there," yet to be discovered. For his part, Roosevelt sought (and found) "new" species (that is, those as yet unknown to Western science).[33]

But both men also faced doubt in another form. Lévi-Strauss ponders and then pontificates over the very wisdom and purpose of the anthropological enterprise:

> As he practices his profession, the anthropologist is consumed by doubts: has he really abandoned his native setting, his friends, and his way of life, spent such considerable amounts of money and energy, and endangered his health, for the sole purpose of making his presence acceptable to a score or two of miserable creatures doomed to early extinction, whose chief occupations meanwhile are delousing themselves and sleeping, and on whose whims the success or failure of his mission depends. . . . Above all, he asks himself questions: Why has he come here? . . . It is now nearly five years since I left France and interrupted my university career. Meanwhile, the more prudent of my former colleagues were beginning to climb the academic ladder: those with political leanings such as I once had, were already members of parliament and would soon be ministers. And here was I, trekking across desert wastes in pursuit of a few pathetic human remnants. (428)

While confronting doubt in the tangible form of the Rio Dúvida, the furthest thing from Roosevelt's mind was to question why he'd come. In matter-of-fact terms, and after stripping his stores down to the bare essentials before descending the river, he lays out his strategic thinking,

> If our canoe voyage was prosperous we would gradually lighten the loads by eating the provisions. If we met with accidents, such as losing canoes and men in the rapids, or losing men in encounters with Indians, or if we encountered overmuch fever and dysentery, the

loads would lighten themselves. We were all armed. We took no car-
tridges for sport. Cherrie had some to be used sparingly for collecting specimens. The others were to be used—unless in the unlikely
event of having to repel an attack—only to procure food. The food
and the arms we carried represented all reasonable precautions
against suffering and starvation; but, of course, if the course of the
river proved very long and difficult, if we lost our boats over falls or
in rapids, or had to make too many and too long portages, or were
brought to a halt by impassable swamps, then we would have to
reckon with starvation as a possibility. Anything might happen. We
were about to go into the unknown, and no one could say what it
held. (1919: 247–48)

TR was not only unconsumed by doubt; he conquered and then subsumed
its river, rechristened in his honor the Rio Roosevelt by a grateful Brazilian
government.[34]

Clifford Geertz has an abiding fascination with *Tristes Tropiques* (1973:
345–59). Not only did he analyze it in 1973, he later wrote "The World in a
Text: How to Read '*Tristes Tropiques*' " in his *Works and Lives: The Anthropologist as Author* (1988: 25–48). In the latter analysis Geertz reconstructs
Tristes Tropiques, arguing that rather than a commencement and aberration
within the body of Lévi-Strauss' work, it is actually its culmination. Geertz
believes that the book anticipates Lévi-Strauss' subsequent structuralism,
and indeed furnishes the clearest statement of it (37–38). He further argues
that *Tristes Tropiques* is actually five different "thin" books (travel tale,
ethnography, philosophical text, reformist tract, and symbolist literary
text) "wildly signaling to get outside this fat one" (33). Together they add
up to a myth that may be characterized as follows:

> The encompassing form of the book that all this syntactic,
> metonymic jostling of text-types produces is a Quest Story: the de-
> parture from familiar, boring, oddly threatening shores; the jour-
> ney, with adventures, into another, darker world, full of various
> phantasms and odd revelations; the culminating mystery, the ab-
> solute other, sequestered and opaque, confronted deep down in the
> *sertao*; the return home to tell tales, a bit wistfully, a bit wearily, to
> the uncomprehending who have stayed unadventurously behind.
>
> This too, of course, the Anthropologist-as-seeker myth, can be
> seen as just one more metonymically adjoined text, side-by-side
> with the others, the meaning of the whole lying in good structural-
> ist style (thus with good structuralist elusiveness) in the conjunc-
> tion rather than in the parts conjoined. (44–45)

While Geertz marshals his considerable rhetorical skills in defense of this thesis, in my view such analysis rather overwhelms and outweighs the text itself, which is more eclectic and free associational—a veritable farrago—than an integrated myth resulting from authorial intentionality.

Finally, in contrasting *Tristes Tropiques'* travel-tale little book with its ethnographic one, Geertz belittles the former as "one damn thing after another" while the latter is informed by a "thesis," the implication being that it is superior (37). Again I would dissent. Admittedly, there are many superficial travel tales. However, to judge and characterize the entire genre in such terms is akin to depicting cinema as weak plots, poorly acted. I have argued that the emblematic characteristic of the travel tale is first-person narrativity which translates into self reflexivity and self expression. In my view, this is present to some degree in the worst of travel tales and is paramount in the two superior ones that we have just considered.[35]

Finally, I would note that this kind of analysis, whether of a single text or in a comparative vein, constitutes its own form of witnessing. It places an additional filter between, in this case, the reader and the Nambikwara. It also brings the biographers of their chroniclers front stage and thereby makes the witnesses as much the object of analysis as that which they witnessed. In short, to analyze the traveler as well as the travel tale in this fashion introduces another form of witnessing, that of the witness of witnesses witnessing.

CHAPTER **4**

An All White Jury: Judging Citizenship in the Simpson Criminal Trial

CINDY PATTON

America is continually ridding itself of racism. While racism sometimes seems to "get better" or "worse," the rules for evaluation also change, moving up and down a conceptual hierarchy from the intensely personal to the abstractly political. From the 1960s through the early 1970s, the idea of "institutional" or "structural" racism dominated both liberal and radical political analyses. By the mid-seventies and well into the Reagan era, mainstream thinking more often located racism in the individual. Watching the U.S. media watch "our" reaction to the O.J. Simpson criminal trial verdict provided a way station for considering where post-Reagan America stood in relation to this ultra-American self-improvement project. The media touted the popular discussion surrounding the Simpson criminal trial verdict as a fresh opportunity for an improved relationship between Americans, their race and their racism.[1] But as the mainstream—largely white writers—implicitly revealed, there were, in fact, *two* trials, two juries, two verdicts. As the trial zigzagged through protracted technicalities to its final verdict, we saw judgment doubled. Opinions about the accused's innocence or guilt grew emotional, while opinions about the opinions—and about those who held them—turned nasty. Pollsters suggested that there were race and gender differentials in views about O.J. Simpson's innocence or guilt, roughly, Blacks were more likely to believe in his innocence, while white men—and to a great degree, white women—believed he was guilty.

But the secondary judgments—those made about the white and Black men and women who were demographically clustered in the primary opinions—began to reveal the fault line that made the trial so catalytic of discussions of the incommensurability of racism and sexism.

The cacophony of judgment was structured by assumptions regarding the level—ranged from individual to structural—at which the etiology of racism or sexism could be found, and by representational differences in the modes for *signifying* these polarities of hate. In the end, the several "verdicts" were rendered differently by the jury, and by the Black and white publics; differently by those who weighted structural racism (Black men in America cannot get a fair trial) more heavily than structural sexism (victimized women in America cannot get justice), or, saw the trial in terms of individual racism (of the cops) versus propulsive misogyny (men who beat their wives will escalate to murder). These underlying asymmetries in American discussions about race and gender pit "women's concerns" against "Black concerns," and many have commented on the destructiveness of this collision of the oppressed. Coverage of the criminal trial fell prey to and then offered the trial as a means to justify the impasse between thinking about—and representing—racism and sexism, intensifying a rift within civil rights efforts that benefits traditional power holders by providing the logic to exclude both women of "either" race and Blacks of "both" genders from fully occupying the category citizen. The first section of this essay will discuss the suturing of different orders of question that occurred in discussions of the O.J. Simpson criminal trial. In order to understand how Blacks were conceived as improper jurors, the second section will look more closely at the concepts of judgment that were used in popular descriptions of the trial verdict. Finally, I will discuss the signification of racism and sexism to show how women (regardless of race) are precluded from claiming status as a class parallel to that occupied by African Americans (regardless of gender) in certain kinds of civil rights litigation.

I. Speaking of Racism

For more than a century, activists have worked to obviate or end racial bias in the judicial system. Most white Americans turned a blind eye to the work of the law—and its administrators—in sustaining the racial caste system post-emancipation. Indeed, the idea that Blacks are particularly susceptible to criminal tendencies, and that Black communities are rife with crimes of their own making, permeates the stereotypes—held by white Americans and by non-Blacks around the world—about African Americans. This brutal, stultifying, and intransigent conception of Black criminality, and not the probability of racial bias in the law and its use, served—still serves—as the justification for higher rates of arrest, conviction, incarceration, and placement on death row for Blacks when compared to whites. Despite this long history of white use and perception of American justice, the Simpson trial suddenly made it unradical for white Americans publicly to discuss the racial dimensions of American law. But this apparent burst of white conscience was only possible because the phrasing of the questions under discussion was restricted to subsume the sticky issue of crimes against our rights, with their broad and diffuse effects, under more visually spectacular crimes of individual violence, which have a more defined character.[2] The dead victims and evil killers present a more elegant narrative—justice done or not—and are more easily adjudicated in a court of law than the complex attempts to redress inequalities by and within one of the institutions central to our country's definition of rights. The question of O.J.'s guilt or innocence dominated not only the coverage of the trial (it was, of course the purpose of the proceeding) but also enabled a particularly facile dialogue about the issue of racism in America. Through yoking these two levels of crime—individual and collective—the opulent talk of racism could appear earnest and yet fail in every way to challenge or change the reality that the race of an accused person is inextricably linked with the question of his innocence or guilt. Practically speaking, it was virtually impossible to raise the issue of racism without being assumed to be arguing for Mr. Simpson's innocence. Similarly, a belief in his guilt was taken as a refusal to believe that the American justice system is racist. Though I'm sure many white progressives believed that O.J. was guilty and also believe that the justice system is racist, this opinion was not to be found clearly articulated in news media. And so intertwined were the issues of race and guilt or innocence, that I cannot recall anyone suggesting the system is not racist, and that Simpson was innocent, although the white jurors seemed, in the end, to adopt this position. Sequestered and, perhaps, the least overwhelmed by brief unleashing of so many angles of view on the issue of racism in America and in the case at hand, they did not believe the prosecution had made its case; but not, as Mr. Cochran had argued, because their case was hopelessly tainted by the racism of the Los Angeles police department.

1) *"Did he do it?"*
    1a) *"Is the justice system in America racist?"*

The first question, put formally to the jury in *The People of California vs. Orenthal James Simpson,* was also the hook to the media audience and the home base for discussions. Consumers of legal thrillers and detective fiction know that the best person to answer this question is the victim. Unfortunately, the victim of a murder is never available to testify. So, as television programs like *Law and Order* tell us, the police and the government prosecutors must "speak" for the dead who can no longer speak for themselves. Or rather, the police and prosecutors read the dead body and the scene of the crime for signs that can signify the speech of the dead person. The next best witness would, of course, be the perpetrator. But unlike earlier legal systems, which used inquisition and torture, our laws protect us from being forced to testify against ourselves. Deprived by exigency and procedural rules from wresting the truth from those most intimate witnesses to the crime, the court oversees the series of substitutions that we call evidence and testimony. In the publicity surrounding the trial, reporters offered two different rules of judgment through which to read the questions of racism, sexism, and the relationship of both to O.J. and Nicole. These alternate rules tended to blur the differences between the readers or viewers and the actual jurors in the trial. Erasing the line between the official and unofficial judgments helped viewers and readers exaggerate their real role within the legal process and give a special legitimacy to the judgments they derived from the partial and sensational coverage they consumed. Of course, Americans are already high consumers of police and legal dramas. However, the rapid slide between an opinion about an ongoing current event and actually enacting judgment required an account of differences between the official and unofficial judgments, and encouraged viewers and readers to forget that in America we strive to make judgment ever fairer by employing highly technical checks and balances between the prosecution and defense.

The court applies a complex system of proof and considers the crime that engendered the case as a past event. The television audience deals in narratives of motive, and TV producers handle motive by altering time in order to give the viewer a glimpse of the perpetrator before the trial. In each case, "guilt" is the logical outcome of the gambit to suture a "defendant" to an act outside the courtroom, but television viewers can construct a narrative around the acts and personae with more liberty than can a jury.

Regardless of whether they were "playing to the camera" (after all, with respect to the legal outcome—the ultimate measure of their worth as lawyers—the most important audience was the jury), the lawyers in the Simpson case were not indifferent to the value of televisual conventions. The prosecution's premiere television moment occurred when a witness to forensic evidence vividly demonstrated how the fatal cutting was done. For the defense, the use of televisual conventions rested more importantly in rendering wife battering a fiction instead of a possible motive for the crime.

The tandem question (#1a, above), equally hard to turn away from, was primarily discussed outside the courtroom. However often the issue of race emerged in the trial, the criminal court had no formal mechanism to try itself for racial bias—that would be the task of another court, should it become an issue on appeal. However, racial bias could be—and was—introduced as a motive to explain why officers of the law would tamper with the evidence against Simpson. Proposing this motive assumed that the police are "fair" with white criminals: bias lies not in the kind of crime, but in the race of the criminal. As I'll detail in a moment, this theory of bias runs counter to feminists' charge: that a certain type of crime, and not the race of the perpetrator, allows a class of victims to go unavenged by the justice system.

The prosecution was in a tough spot: they had to put the body of Mark Fuhrman before the court, although they tried to limit the use of Mark Fuhrman to his place in the chain of evidence. But the defense argued that Fuhrman had violated his sacred trust to "speak for the victim." Because of his racism, they argued, he was a tainted link in the succession of witnesses whose job it is to authenticate the evidence before the court by testifying that it passed from their hands to those of another sworn officer. In effect, the defense used the allegation of Fuhrman's racism to break the link that allows physical evidence to stand in for the murder victim's unavailable testimony. Paradoxically, indicting Fuhrman, surrogate voice of the victim, left much of the evidence in the case, like Nicole, silenced on the other side of a gap.

The issues of motive and how and where to investigate bias were expressed quite differently through another pair of questions:

2) *Do men beat and kill their wives and girlfriends?*
   2a) *Is the justice system in America sexist?*

I leave these questions out of quotation marks to signal the difference in their status within the public debates surrounding the trial and, especially, its verdict. I recycled the first two questions: even though I didn't specifically attribute them, they were actually said. I ventriloquize the last two: they were thought, but never occupied the same kind of place within the public discourse; they did not survive the trial coverage with the crispness and authority of questions #1 and #1a. For at least some people, and in the prosecution's theory of the crime, #2 is actually a preface to #1: the prosecution tried to establish Simpson's past behavior as an indicator of the probability that Simpson had progressed from battery to murder. It differs from "Did he do it?" in considering whether attacking unrelated women is equivalent to attacking one's wife or girlfriend.

We know and accept that people murder, but we do not completely accept and are not able to discuss publicly the particular kind of assault and murder that happens to women at the hands of their husbands and boyfriends. When the court considered whether dull, simmering misogyny could escalate into murderous rage, the expert witness said not necessarily.

The prosecution's case began to wither, but they plugged away at this theory of the crime. This not only weakened the theorized motive for the murder, but it also removed this death from the category of hate crime, placing the prosecution at a double disadvantage. The murder of Nicole was made into an individual crime, while the allegations of evidence tampering continued to be articulated as a virtual hate crime. Second, deprived of the logic that built from battery to murder, harping on O.J.'s sexism was seen (and O.J. continues to take this position) as a banal distraction in the face of the spectacular image of slitting a throat. The media discussion centered more on the general question of wife battery (indeed, abused wives "came out" on talk shows in droves) than on the ways in which battery exemplified the gendering of justice. Even those who thought O.J. was guilty did not seem to view battery as a hate crime against women. In fact, O.J. later admitted to having abused Nicole, but considered it a normal part of the relationship, or at least "past" and trivial in relation to her death. The question of whether wife and girlfriend abuse is common ultimately had little bearing on perceptions of this crime, an erasure that was extremely complex: for whites uncritical of their stereotypes of Black masculinity (especially in relation to white women), there was little difference—except in degree—between a Black man beating and a Black man murdering a white woman. Black women were divided about whether to participate in the discussion of misogynist violence; they were most acutely aware of the ways historical links between race and sex overdetermined the Simpson-trial-related debates. Black men must have felt painfully implicated in their every move and opinion. White feminists quoted in the media often seemed oblivious to the legacy of racism that has framed every American women's movement.

Denise Brown's crusade about wife abuse, featured widely on television during the trial, was an attempt to raise the question of pervasive and fatal sexism in American society and law, to expose this asymmetry in the judicial system. Question #2a was answered again and again in feminist protests and on talk shows featuring women who had experienced—"been victimized by" or "survived"—domestic violence, but, beyond the appearance of the expert witnesses, the question, an issue of civil rights, was not officially addressed. That women are so often the direct victims of male violence collides in the white paranoid imaginary with the figure of the predatory Black man, and complicates both anti-racist and anti-sexist political strategies. Few truly understand the extent to which the weight of this phobia restricts the public and economic mobility of Black men, who are not unaware of the fear their presence may inspire in white people.[3]

Decades of work by feminist legal scholars notwithstanding, both the dominant and legal discourse privilege race as the object of investigation in the question of bias within the justice system. For several decades, social scientists have compared race differences in rates of arrest, indictment, and conviction for various classes of crime. Whether we unofficial jurors considered him innocent or guilty, the O.J. Simpson criminal trial reflects this emphasis in the judicial system. Attempts to stop lynching and other forms of systematic wrongful prosecution have sensitized some whites to the inequalities faced by Blacks processed through the criminal justice system. Women who are battered and murdered by men they know are in a structurally and ideologically different relationship to *another* bias in policing and criminal justice. To argue that the criminal justice system fails to serve women who have been victimized by men is to claim that one class of crime's direct *victims* is treated differently than another.

II. Hate Crimes: Narrating the Stories of Victims

From the turn of the century through 1947, when Harry Truman finally signed a federal anti-lynching law, African Americans engaged in major efforts to end lynching, an extra-legal activity conducted primarily by racist whites against African Americans and, to a lesser extent, Jews and other ethnic minorities. Especially in the South, these activities were not only not stopped by local authorities, but sometimes engaged in by them. Thus lynching, the most grotesque and visible example of individual hatred joined with state sponsored racist violence, became the central image of the myriad social, economic, cultural, and violent crimes against African Americans. As Clarence Thomas well knew when he described his hearings as a high-tech lynching, the image of lynching is the ultimate representation of racism in America. But images of violence against African Americans can either offer a vicarious space for white Americans, or they can be a sign of white racism. In films, for example, use of racial epithets as such was permitted until the late 1940s or early 1950s, when they were condemned, only to reappear as a sign of the racist, as I have argued at length elsewhere (Patton 1995). The doubleness of such representations certainly continues, but by convention whites are supposed to identify with the victim-hearer of the racist speech, not with the speaker.[4] When Johnny Cochran battled to have Mark Fuhrman's racist speech admitted to the courtroom, he sought to use it not only to show Fuhrman as a perjurer, but more important, to re-present and make newly present a signifier of racism. Fuhrman's speech, as an indicator of his mood while gathering evidence, along with Fuhrman's conformity to a screen image of the racist, suggested that the present trial was a very expensive lynching.

But no such signifer of the wife-batterer exists, dozens of series episodes and made-for-TV movies notwithstanding. There is not even general agreement on what would epitomize a sexist phrase. In fact, our emotional relationship to the vocalization of sexism is different. The prosecution's use of Simpson's workout tape, in which punching exercises are "jokingly" said to have the benefit of preparing men to handle their wives, did not have an effect like the Fuhrman tape. His "joke" is accepted as bad humor, but not as proof of Simpson's active role in a system of sexist violence. The dignified space of the court failed to demand an unequivocal interpretation of the tape as sexist, as it managed to do for racism, despite—or perhaps because of—the complex procedural discussion about how to admit Fuhrman's words. To some extent, white viewers may have vicariously enjoyed getting to say the N-word with Fuhrman, but we were supposed to distance ourselves (as the white commentators tried to do) from the kind of person who would say such a thing. I would surmise that the hurt Black people must always experience in the moment of hearing the word was *justified*, was transformed into a feeling of justification, since *this* hearing was in the service of proving not merely Fuhrman's guilt, but the racism of the entire judicial system. By contrast, O.J. "got away" with re-expressing his sexism in the context of the foiled prosecution strategy. The mere fact that the "sexism" and "intent" of the video ("It was only a joke, and anyway, not a very mean one") were in question, allowed the tape to slap women viewers, with little possibility of feeling that this insult was absorbed for the sake of making a greater point about sexism.

At the time of the criminal trial, wife beating was not perceived as a crime of hate. Only after the trial did it become legible that violence within "domestic relations" is in some way different in kind from beating anyone else. But despite some efforts to regulate the sale of guns to men convicted of domestic crimes, and a few proposals to enhance sentences for domestic versus "regular" cases of assault, the link between a broad system of sexism, and a general hatred of women (commonly called "misogyny"), is not recognized in the courts. Even if it rarely goes punished, the idea of white police producing trumped up charges or evidence against Blacks is recognized as a form of official racism. Unlinked from the public practices of the state, battery of women is not understood as a manifestation of a systemic bias against women.

A) The Victim's Body

The arguments in the trial pitted a proposed individual psychological trajectory (of escalating spousal abuse) against the history of racist actions by white authority figures.

The fact that American racism is so much more representable than American sexism—and that the defense's and prosecution's *arguments* became increasingly asymmetrical despite their common use of concepts of victimization and bias—depends on the emergence of different conventions for representing racism and the racist versus representing sexism and the sexist.

Americans already recognize the Black body as an entertainment spectacle. In U.S. popular culture, at least since the early fifties, racism is complexly figured through presentations of racists and their potential victims. The representation of a Black body invokes the discourse of civil rights, and the issue of racism broadly. But because of the open-endedness of the general charge of racism, the appearance of the Black body requires various white characters—as effectors of racism—in order to clarify and localize (often literally, in the South or a Southerner) who was and was not racist. On one hand, this indicated that America's index of suspicion has been raised: the possibility of racism floats freely. But this also makes individual disavowals more secure. Beating a person because he is Black is widely considered to be unacceptable, but to charge someone with racism for voting for policies which will cause Black children to starve is considered hyperbole.

The Cochran case rested on a syllogism: racist cops go after Black men; O.J. Simpson is a Black man; the cops went after O.J. Simpson. But since O.J. seemed to so many people to have evaded the ill effects of racism—indeed, he seemed to have melted into one corner of wealthy white America—the charge of racism had to be lodged first on the institutional level. But the general allegation of racism would only go so far. O.J.'s life with Nicole was the kind of racial boundary violation that had long anchored racist white imagination, but the prosecution raised the potentially related facts of O.J.'s history of abusing Nicole as if the question of the Simpsons' domestic relations were *unraced*. The prosecution was naïve to think that the fact of O.J.'s and Nicole's racial difference could ever be entirely stripped away from this historical imagination, and from the real history of lynchings that occurred when racist whites concocted accusations of Black men as rapists of white women and then enacted vigilante (and also state sanctioned) "justice." O.J. was always at risk from a shift in frame: if the logic of representing racism ruled, he was a victim, while if the logic of representing sexism prevailed, he was a victimizer—of women. Though not absolutely necessary—simply the setting of L.A. would probably have allowed the general charge of police racism to stick—Mark Fuhrman secured O.J.'s position as a Black body, and therefore a victim-body. And, because the icon of the racist was so well established, the defense didn't need to explain why Mark Fuhrman might go after O.J. in particular. Fuhrman stood for the possibility of the police state railroading a Black everyman—the character that O.J., especially in his silence, was desperate to take up. All O.J. had to do was appear Black, the indirect object of a racist system. Thus, it was best if O.J. did not speak: the case became his body—as a victim of racism—against Nicole's body—as a victim of sexist battery, and, according to the prosecution, sexist murder.

With the weight of history so stacked against a Black defendant, it was hard to see how the defense strategy could overcome the white racist fantasy of Black men's violence against white women. I suggest here that the defense was successful largely—and prompted the particular kinds of reactions by feminists and in unthinkingly racist commentary—because sexist violence has a different representational history. While racist violence has a long history as a spectator sport, domestic violence has only recently become a form of mass entertainment, no longer the invisible national pastime and instead masculinity's big embarrassment. This once most private of sports gained a spectatorship on the awkward heels of feminist efforts to get domestic violence addressed as an epidemic of national importance. But with no established visual code for the victimizer comparable to that of the racist, victimization of women is only representable through the body of the victim, often, in TV series and movies, through photographs of the crimes committed against her. In television series, we often see a woman sometime "after" her beating, accompanied by the photos of her bruised body. Together, the physically healed woman and the police photograph convey to the battered woman the status of speaking subject, which allows her to testify against her batterer. The need to make her presentable, dignified, and more clearly feminine, suggests that as a victim, she is not a legal entity. Unlike the Black body that continuously signifies its status as object of racism, the victim of sexist battery appears discontinuously, as before and after the crime committed on her body. She is only a victim when she is being beaten; even when she is persistently battered, her body is simply the object of repeated but discontinuous bouts of sexist violence. In the Simpson case, even whites seemed to accept that the Fuhrman tapes were an example of systematic hate, racism as defined under the law. But few interpreted the battery photos or 911 tapes as evidence for an equally pervasive culture of hatred towards women. The dead Nicole and the beaten Nicole were treated as discontinuous, possibly both victims, but from different *forms* of violence—wife abuse, on the one hand, but non-gendered murder on the other. Despite the claim by many that "O.J. had never been Black until the trial," he managed to produce and sustain the mask of his Blackness in such a way that Nicole—or the prosecutors on her behalf—were unable to sustain her position as a victim of sexism.[5]

The titling that opened the 1995–96 weekly television drama *Murder One*—explicitly modeled on the languid progression of the Simpson trial—featured the brutalized and dead body of the murdered woman, the solving of whose murder was the focus of the series. Mainstreaming the titling scheme from *Twin Peaks*, which seemed quite sensational and counter-cultural the decade before, the credits underscored Laura Mulvey's famous quip that "sadism demands a story." *Murder One*'s triumph was to prove that once the generative sadism was visualized, an audience could get by on the slimmest plot. Images of her death appeared, were repeated, and were reproduced in different media as the drama unfolded. The color photos from which the sepia credits were produced (the diegetic "real" from which the proscenium "frame" is made) appear later as evidence in the fictional trial. A lost video, recovered in the final episode of the season, reveals the "truth" of who killed her. She is represented as most alive in service of suturing the viewer to the diegetic time of the murder. The dead woman's body is read and reread through the trial—not for signs of the cause of her death, but for the motive that would point to her killer.

In "real life," Nicole Brown Simpson was similarly unavailable to testify about her killing, but her body was not admissible as evidence of her victimization. The jury disregarded the photos of her earlier bruised and battered body as part of the basis for motive: in order to testify to wife battery, Nicole had to be alive. But the photos of her murdered body were also unassimilable: so brutal and "realistic" were the photos that the defense tried to have them barred from admission as "prejudicial," and several jurors, when they finally saw them, became ill. But these final pictures of Nicole's body, which so upset the jurors, did not give her the last word. In arguing the case as domestic abuse escalated to wife murder, the prosecution proposed Nicole's brutalized body as *his* signature.

This reading of the differential construction and representation of victims' bodies both extends and raises questions about Foucault's work on penal systems and on the power of discourse to produce and discipline the juridical subject. *Discipline and Punish* eloquently describes the shift from a regime in which the King exercised power over the populace by displaying his capacity to torture, mutilate, and take the life of the body. By the nineteenth century, this aspect of what Foucault would later detail through the concept of "governmentality" had given way to a form of power exercised through scrutiny of the body and promiscuous admonitions to normality. Foucault calls this "biopower," a system which allows for the production and control of life, of individuals and of populations. This regulatory regime is finally internalized through techniques like psychoanalysis and Marxist concepts of repression and false consciousness, whose critique he undertook in the Introduction to *The History of Sexuality*. While evidence of carceral society abounds, how are we to understand the ways in which the King's Law (as capital punishment) and penality each still operate? Foucault did not provide many clues for understanding the workings of multiple, coexisting forms of power relay. But American justice—both the courts and the broad perceptual grid of rightness which legitimates it—demonstrates that there are at least two policing systems which produce different requirements for the visibility of juridical bodies. Foucault deals mostly with perpetrators of crimes, rather than the differential mechanisms for producing crime's victims. In the American system and its popular representation, with asymmetrical pairs of juridical bodies—perpetrators and victims—each enters the court through different rules, accused of and liable to fall prey to different orders of crime.

In this sense, because the sign for the racist is more visually specific than the sign for the wife abuser, either the victim or the victimizer could establish the presence of racist motive, but not sexist motive. We did not need Mark Fuhrman to establish that Mr. Simpson represented the kind of person who could be racism's object: his visual presentation as a Black person was sufficient to invoke the possibility of his accuser's racism. By contrast, the sign of the wife abuser is much hazier—at present—than the sign of the battered wife: there is no codified image of the batterer. Even though the pictures of a battered Nicole and the 911 tapes of her terror each identified a specific perpetrator, her ex-husband, whose body was before the court, the prosecution could not rely on visual codes to link a husband-type to Nicole's murder. Unlike the popular knowledge which "racist" invokes (Fuhrman seemed straight out of central casting), no popular representation seemed able to link a smug batterer with O.J. as "the kind of guy who'd do something like that."

III. Americans / Jurors

> "You know," said a young [white] man, "After Tuesday I walk
> down the street and I wonder what Blacks are thinking. Do you feel
> like an American?" he asked the Black woman.
> "Some days," she said. (Rosenblatt 44)

As many commentators noted during the Simpson criminal trial, the law and the media collapsed into each other. The voluminous media coverage suggested that everything and everyone was try-able: O.J. Simpson, white women who marry Black men, Mark Fuhrman, the judicial system, Judge Ito, even the media itself was on trial in the media.[6] However, the sequestration of the jury meant that the extent to which the media became a theater of adjudication far exceeded the trial of the media in the courts. Consideration of whether and how video cameras might be in the courtroom and of the problem of leaks prompted by the erroneous reporting of the sock incident were the principal official moments when the court "tried" the media.

A lot of business was accomplished in the easy conflation of court and press. I want to open that reduction by suggesting that two forms of judgment, different in kind, not in degree, happened in and around *The People of California versus Orenthal James Simpson*. One form was a specific verdict, rendered by a specially selected group of Los Angeles citizens called the jurors. This judgment concluded a procedure called "criminal trial." The second complex of judgments is still being made by a non-selected and unspecified mass of "Americans." Here, questions about race relations, the state of criminal justice, the prevalence, distribution, and acceptability of "domestic violence" are linked to each other to produce complex statements about national identity and social processes.[7] A closer consideration of the popular representation of the jury, the "audience," and their respective judgments reveals how the official jury, with its mere plurality (over the course of the various sitting and removed members) of Black members, became a "Black jury," while the unofficial jury—the "audience"—became white in its locutory and material effects.

As I edge towards a discussion of the differing mechanisms that exclude African Americans and women from American citizenship, I might seem to be headed toward the recent revisions of Habermas now implied in uses of the term "public sphere." Recent work in popular culture studies has used this idea to address questions concerning the location and participation of Blacks in production and consumption of national and sub-national media worlds. For an obvious example, the essays in the 1995 Black Public Sphere Collective volume consider the utility and limits of concepts like "public sphere" and "counter-publics" for understanding the all too efficacious racial division of America's economic and imaginary lives. But as some of these authors note, the analysis of race relations in America becomes problematic when it relies too heavily on the idealized speech situation drawn from Habermas' early work. Developed from an at best debatable understanding of the historical emergence of European bourgeois civic culture, the ideal speech model is hard to jibe with our historical conditions where speech and the literal capacity *to be* in public space are continually circumscribed by structural and individual racism. My own reservation about the Habermasian frame has to do with its failure fully to materialize something like the "structure of feeling" embedded in the different ways people exchange ideas and constitute their subjectivities—their "good life" in Diawara's terms. These affective differences are crucial to any discussion of "communication" between racially identified and designated groups in America. It seems unlikely that there can be any kind of meta-space or bridging discourse that can do justice to these differences. The early Habermasian focus on the scene of communication freed from distortion imagines a kind of space—coffee shops, public squares—whose literal histories in America cannot ever be said to have been one of free exchange. For Habermas, the hazily conceived spaces are finally less significant than the mentalities of the new locutors who emerge within them. In this sense, the *space* of the public sphere, at least in the early Habermas, is ideal. But in America, especially in the American South, "public spaces" and the forms of locution attaching to them—sale of slaves, militating against slavery, provision of state-sponsored housing—are in no way extricable from a material history of asymmetrical race relations of the bloodiest and most inexpressibly corrupt sort.

Instead of publics, at least in Habermas' sense, I will speak of "audience" and of "viewers," which should also read differently from each other. "Audience" implies a real but phenomenologically self-reflexive group of addressees, a conglomerate of people who, while they may never meet, experience themselves as those to whom the media speak. The "viewers" is the specific, if indeterminate sum of persons who manage to receive the media, an objective sociological grouping who are considered without regard to their sense of belonging to an interpretive community. The dense "we" of the audience excludes but then fails to recognize its dissonance with those who are merely *numbered* among the totality of viewers. Extending Lyotard's concept of *le differend*, I want to argue that those who naturalize themselves as addressees exist on one side of an affective gap—they cannot recognize why the other viewers do not feel a part of the "audience."

My interest in audience may seem like a return to an older, more content-analytic framework, perhaps suggesting that my project should have produced a comparison of Black community versus mainstream (shall we simply say white?) media coverage. Such an analysis would go to an argument different from—though not incompatible with—the one I make. While I have elected not to undertake a detailed comparison here, I am quite sure that differences in coverage were common. I also believe the opinion polls that so often show racial differences in those political attitudes that are most closely articulated to the differences in economic and legal conditions of Black versus white Americans. But I am less sure how to understand any relationship between these two "facts" of racial difference. The relative poverty of Black community news gathering resources, differences in investigative style, and the reliance, in syndicated reporting, on individuals rather than organizations (like UPI, Reuters, and so on) means that the national fabric of Black news production is structured differently from the major, white dominated organs (and differently again from other subnational news enterprises—gay, Arab-American, feminist, anti-vivisectionist). The Black media may effectively sustain an "imagined community" with a characteristic interpretive frame that no doubt also influences a Black audience's reception of Black reporters and of race-related stories in the mainstream media.[8]

Exploring the generation and durability of mediated forms of being-in-public requires qualitative research of the kind undertaken by Lewis and Jhally, for example, in their study of Cosby Show reception. My small, textually-based undertaking here is intended to suggest how the mainstream media coverage reproduced its racialized address—its presumption of a white audience—in the same breath that it represented Black opinion. Despite the vivid recording of the reactions of Black individuals—folks in bars and schools giving their opinions on the case—the unspoken reference point for what the "audience" knows and believes was, I want to suggest, white.[9] This elided difference between a *represented* audience and a *referent* audience is what allows white viewers to perceive their world as multi-culturalized, despite overwhelming evidence that the racial-caste system in America is growing more extreme.

Many commentators noted that the *exhaustiveness* of the television coverage—from live coverage to shortened repetitions, reviews and commentaries—helped American viewers imagine that they were the jury in the trial. The discussion of race within the TV diegesis intermingled with other textual elements from American history and mythology to create a major crisis in audience identification. Are "we" one with the jury who is delegated to enact our justice? Given the historic means for excluding Blacks from juries and the photophobia of cross-race identifications, the actual jury and the emerging audience-jury were on a collision course. As the jury turned blacker, the audience turned whiter. This creeping and incomplete racing meant that upon issuance of the verdict, the media could easily and credibly (to the white-raced audience) "explain" why "most Americans" rejected the findings of the official jury, ejecting the "Black jurors" from the realm of "good men and true."[10] At best, the jurors were seen as testifying to racism in the judicial system, but even here, they were not fully credible witnesses. Denied status as unbiased jurors because they are presumed too close to the experience of racism, Blacks are thereby said to be possessed by a race-based paranoia; they "see race" where it is not, and therefore they cannot "tell" whether racism is actually present. The unbiased juror can only pass judgment if race is un-thought: in this set of assumptions about the influence of the experience of racism, Black individuals can only serve as jurors if they renounce judgments that their experience as Black might inform, that is, if they exorcise the raced dimension of experience they alone are presumed to have in order to exercise *common sense*.

There were several versions of this rejection of Black judgment as categorically biased. Some lawyer-commentators and many persons on the street suggested that the jurors were underclass mouthpieces smuggled into the sacred halls of justice by a corrupt Black lawyer who would do anything for his rich Black client. The white underclass jurors, on this account, were intimidated by the Black jurors. In assenting to a "not guilty" verdict, they did not exact a race-traitor's judgment, but were victims of Black thugs. This logic allowed cathartic identification between outraged white viewers and the "jury" and gave a specific reason to reject the judgment and even the citizenship of the Black jurors. Disgruntled white interviewees—devices to suture the audience to the speaking space within the news commentary—called the Black jurors reverse racists, intimating that the jury's actions were tantamount to a hate crime, a new legal concept of the 1990s.[11] Designed to punish individuals for carrying out free-lance nastiness that was once (still is) a form of micro-policing sanctioned by the state, the concept of hate crime required establishment of particular kinds of bias as the motive for particular crimes. But how would you *know* if hate underlay a crime? How can an external observer make a judgment about a feeling known best to those who have it and those who are subject to it?

It ought to be the case that the presence of hate could be established by either witness to it: the words of the perpetrator (Fuhrman had to say it) or the wounded psyche of the victim (Blacks in L.A. had been ripped apart by it). But since the idea of reverse racism came into vogue before hate crime procedures were fully established, a victim's testimony was never above suspicion. The false charge of racism or rape, now a stock plot in television dramas, was almost immediately viewed as itself a lesser form of hate crime, or rather an illicit use of grudge, of individual animosity, as *hate*, a now legally categorized emotion. Morally disabled by the idea of reverse prejudice, Black experiences of racism can no longer be witnessed by its victims. Always now liable to charges of mistaking and abusing a grudge, the only people who can pass judgment on hate are those who have not experienced it. However, given the logic of hate in America—the understanding of hate as a couple, hater and hated—the person who cannot be victim must be victimizer. Thus, as *jurors*, Blacks cannot even express an opinion about racism, lest they betray a feeling whose valence under the law they can no longer control. The demand to be unbiased and fair cannot, at present, be reconciled with *speaking* about race. Having avoided connection with *being racist* by refraining from speaking about race, the white audience alone can rise above the petty reversal of hate that illicit charges might turn against it.

But this state of *being un-racist* is unstable, largely comparative rather than absolute, and thus rests upon the iteration of racism outside itself. It should not have taken much to convince most Americans that the already nationally shamed LAPD was racist: all we needed was to hear Mark Fuhrman *say* it. When he refused to perform racism in the courtroom, the defense (after a lengthy series of hearings on admissibility) used taped interviews Fuhrman had made while consulting on a screenplay. Furhman's attitude, the tapes, and whether either would appear in court were much discussed in the media. The prosecution hoped to mitigate the damage of a charge of bungled evidence handling—especially for racist reasons—and the audience waited with intense anticipation not merely to see Furhman testify, but to watch him react to "hearing himself" on the tapes.

Fuhrman's position was that he was "performing" the role of racist cop in his role as script consultant, that he was not actually a racist cop, but had experienced second hand the emotional expressions of racist cops, a displacement of racist feeling and "hearing" that identically recurred in the event of his testimony. The delay—that is, Fuhrman's silence—dragged on too long, and Cochran was able to widen the accusation of racism to the media and white viewers. Indeed, as the vortex of accusations of racism accelerated, Cochran was able to turn the charge of racism toward the judicial system as a whole. The white media, unwilling to side with Fuhrman (the audience needed to construct him as the particular racist in order to distinguish ourselves as "un-racist"), turned on the defense. This momentary shift in the media's sympathy was not an endorsement of Mr. Simpson's innocence, but rather, a well trained (through TV shows like *Law and Order*) resentment toward that hazy thing called the "criminal justice system" and toward the liberals who had hamstrung the system through procedural constraints designed to protect the "rights of criminals" (as opposed to "rights of the accused"). At this point, the media paralleled Cochran's claims, but with different meaning: Simpson's trial became evidence of everything wrong with the judicial system—not its racism and classism, but its failure to produce "common sense" outcomes.

The tension over Fuhrman and his tapes resolved into a complaint about the appropriateness of introducing the question of racism in the first place. Whites quoted in the news coverage often suggested that someone had to introduce racism in order for it to become an issue in the trial. To raise the issue of race is impolite, from the standpoint of a white America that has only just become able to tolerate—and barely at that—the *j'accuse* uttered by Black Americans. Charges of racism are to be handled in their appropriate forum: civil rights commissions and legal procedures. Use of the derogatory phrase, "Play the race card," suggested that Cochran had thrown a civil rights wrench in the gears of a criminal trial, forcing the wheels to turn in the wrong direction. But Cochran did not bring something foreign into the trial, he merely gave voice to the reality of racism in policing. As I suggested earlier, because Black experience of racism is only marked as "bias," the moment the issue of racism in the justice system explicitly emerged in the coverage of the trial, the audience and the imaginary unbiased juror became white.

The audience was not produced as white only through juxtaposition with suspect Black jurors. Once the audience became a site of legal judgment, Black viewers were also ruled out of "the audience" as meta-jurors. This move did not resort to simplistic stereotyping formulae; instead of relying on the figure of the Black minister to represent Black political opinion, reporters reserved Black clergy as moderate commentators on the appropriateness of the represented Black responses to the verdict. With these "primary opinions" and the clerical commentary on it displayed and displaced, the media could (as white uncle) provide the "unbiased" meta-commentary but also a terroristic threat in the guise of objective social forecasting: there would be a white backlash, they predicted, if whites' role as perpetrators in America's racist history was not allowed to slip from view.

Much of the representation of Black opinion of the trial and its outcome featured poignant stories of individual victimization that were proposed as the real, ordinary experience of the average Black American. I found this burst of expression of Black experience perplexing in the context of the larger coverage: at first glance, this seems like a dramatic admission that Blacks have been subjected to systematic white racist oppression. But these ritual tales of racist trauma were not introduced as the history that white America wants to have forgotten. Suturing the represented Black viewer with the jurors, these individual stories were fragments of the screen through which the jurors were said to have read evidence in the trial. Black *history* was not, finally, validated, but produced as a bias so disabling to Blacks that they are unfit to judge in cases involving race. Thus, the trebling of Black opinion—from its "expression" to its interpretation by Black clergy through the final commentary and editorial decision making about its representation in the white media—was seamlessly linked to the rejection of the Black viewers, whom one would have thought should be part of the audience for—indeed, the most authoritative witnesses to—the unveiling of the truth of racism in America. Black viewers were not in any way "represented" in the visage of their Black brothers and sisters; indeed, the means through which Black opinion was represented constituted Black viewers as unfit for the adjudicatory audience precisely because they inescapably live the connection between the historical or experiential fragments to the story at hand.

The devastating paradox of media invocation of Black experience in order to discount Black citizenship was the tragedy of the jury itself: the fact that there were so many Black members is a complex testament to the success of civil rights efforts to remove specific barriers to Black participation in U.S. administrative apparatuses. However, the trial coverage, and especially coverage of the verdict, dealt a severe blow to the image of Black dignity on which white acceptance of Black personhood seems precariously to rest. As a trial of Black citizenship, the mainstream coverage of Black opinion slowly and insidiously built into a minstrel show, staged through this refractory system of judgments and juries, which finally allowed whites, if they wished, to consume and disdain Black presence. "Ignorant" was the audience's judgment of the jury's verdict. "Bad taste" was their judgment of the represented Black reaction to the "not guilty" verdict. But while this sentiment was widespread among whites—I felt it myself— the liberal media were savvy enough not to pass this judgment directly: the charge was usually rendered as quotes wrested from Black clergy, who seemed concerned that Black rage or Black joy would overtake Black dignity. The hyper-representation of Black emotion, starkly juxtaposed against the seething and stereotypically muted feelings of whites, made it clear that while it was critical to have Blacks visibly represented, they, and their response to the case, were outside "the audience." The represented taking-up-of-space by Black bodies was not frightening to whites: Black rage has become consumable for whites, who experience it not as criticism, but as a lingering sentiment from a past for which few whites feel individually or nationally responsible. Black rage is just another form of Black hyper-emotion, like rap music or the blues or the L.A. riots, or else it is frankly pathetic, too late to do any good, immaturely misdirected at Blacks' white contemporaries.[12]

Unhappy lawyers said the jury had engaged in "nullification," a rare but accepted practice in which jurors set aside the instructions of the court and decide a case on another, presumably "higher" principle. Since there are civil rights laws, argued several commentators, the jury had no capacity to include racism in their consideration of the truthfulness of the police. Especially as a Black jury, the issue of race was untouchable; since jurors who "saw race" should have been excluded from the jury as biased, juries who now "saw race" must have been lying during *voir dire*. It should be noted, however, that once the jury had recovered from its ordeal and spoke to the press about its reasoning, it became clear that the twelve people exiled from the massive, mediated world did not believe they had nullified, but had executed their instructions to the letter: they doubted the prosecution's case. They were not ignorant illiterates; they were committed, if exhausted, citizens. The Black jurors were not "reverse racists," but proud Americans who, while enduring the virtual prison of the "trial of the century," nevertheless had the courage to challenge the day to day racism encountered during their sequestration.

In the gap between who the jury understood themselves to be, what they understood themselves to have done (apparently the white members felt fine about their verdict until they got out of their box), and what the media described them as doing (injustice) and being (a "Black" jury) lay the adjudicatory audience, the "we" who, however critical of the trial and/or its coverage, nevertheless were affectively compelled to reject the official labor of the "actual" jury. As a critical white viewer, I could find no happy place within the ultimately constituted audience, and yet, so great was the media's identificatory pull—the pleasure of "being audience" but also validation in mass culture of my status as "citizen"—that I could not turn away. For the duration of the Simpson criminal trial and for some time after, it seemed necessary to *judge*, a noisy compulsion that ultimately eclipsed that fact that Black people, indeed, the actual Black women who were jurors, had been robbed of their citizenship in the very act—of judging—in which our progressive denouncement of the hydra-headed racism and misogyny of the trial coverage indulged.

My emphasis on the procedures for racing the audience and jury has suggested that the mechanisms usually envisioned in liberal representation politics—in both senses—actually worked to turn the "authentic voice" of Blacks into evidence of Blacks' unfitness for citizenship, an extremely unhappy outcome for a politics of experience, authenticity, and visibility. This occurred in a way that both legitimated "what (white) women believe" (that the crime was one of sexist passion) but also used a semiotic regime that excluded women from the legal usefulness of the logic of the enduring victim whose negative side was used here to argue that Blacks are intrinsically biased jurors. If Blacks could not make judgments because they were mute, continuous witnesses to racist victimization, women, though they might be intermittent victims, could *pass judgment*, but could not witness to their fate at sexist hands.

IV. We Need Some Communication

Everyone agrees that the answer lies in talk and more talk, but the conversation has to be candid. . . . It might even be said, or discovered, that deep in their newly pained hearts, Blacks and whites know that they do not really live in different countries after all, that they have together made the same country, which has always been a complex of heaven and hell, as alert to its failings as it has been intent on repeating them. The Black American Dream shares much with the white American Dream; one could never be realized without the other.

But perhaps something else will happen this time—a change of direction, a pilgrimage together toward another country—undertaken by the great majority of Blacks and whites, who, beneath the skin, know perfectly well that hatred destroys the one who hates, and this is an immutable law. (Rosenblatt 45)

The invocation to honest talk employed two symbiotic dyads: the "two countries" that cannot live without each other, and the intransigence of the hater-hated relation. Recognizing our place in the former would produce a whole, productive America. Continuing to grovel in the latter would result in the economic downfall of the putatively greatest nation on earth. The idea that the economic interdependence of most Blacks and most whites is a two-way street is the worst kind of political lie. An entire history of social and economic relations had to be evaporated in order really to imagine that Blacks would gain if they abandoned the memory, codified in civil rights law, of their legacy as objects of hate. Imagining that whites' race hatred, if given up, would affect the class and culture structures that enlist it might assuage the guilt of some whites, but only by pretending that racism needs its most emotionally expressive forms to survive. Reporters—even in this case—are not oblivious to these pathetic little lies.[13] So why, after enduring such a complex trial, did they resort to such utterly vapid tropes when commenting on the final result? A succinct answer: the media are *racist*.

It is worth lingering here in order to avoid forgetting a simple truth. In my discussion of precisely *how* the media participated in an ongoing gambit to reproduce American racism and its deadening effects—particularly and materially on Black people—I hope not to absolve us of our ongoing responsibility to the "two countries" asymmetrically bound together in a spiral of racial hatred, especially the "us" who, as white readers of the mass media, were so seamlessly positioned as arbiters of Black citizenship. Even more particularly, the "us" whose income is partially derived from publicly indicting the racism that our labor sometimes only pushes to a level of greater convolution—or cynicism.[14]

The media *are* racist.

I want us also to consider the simple truth that the media are sexist. But I must argue cautiously if this succinct insight is to survive in a form that is not misleadingly parallel to our indictment of the media's racism. This "us" who are white women have an especially tricky legacy to contest; from rhetorical justifications of lynching through attempts to suppress rock 'n' roll music to the Simpson trial and beyond—the white patriarchy enlists "us" as the victims of Black men or Black culture more diffusely. That *this* victim position has grown less racially stark, that Black women can sometimes also be enlisted as victims of Black men or Black culture, is no comfort in the fight against sexual oppression, or in the struggle to rid the analyses and practices of feminism of *their* collusion in white racism. Working out how to analyze and disassemble the link between American racism and American sexism has been central to the Black feminism and Black womanism that evolved over four hundred years. Any small light I can shed on the question of how *this* trial played off two knotty and knotted problems relies on that legacy of experience and thought. As I explore intransigent racism in relation to the newly public embarrassment of sexist violence, I hope to unlink elements in a logic that connects Black men and white women as "two problems" that, while not extricable, wreak their havoc on the parties to the conflation in importantly different ways. The O.J. Simpson criminal trial coverage offers a window on the current political means through which both African Americans of either gender and women of both races are excluded from the category of citizen. In the case of African Americans, this will occur in the impossibility of serving as a juror, a mark of inadmissiblity to the category of universal subject of reason and compassion. In the case of women, the exclusion will be enacted through a refusal to convey a transcendent status to episodic enactment of sexist oppression, thereby robbing women of the chance to achieve civil consideration or compensation as *victims in principle* of specific acts of male violence.

The Bias of *Bias*

We often proceed as if all biases are structured the same way, manifest and represented through a common semiology of oppression. While racism and sexism in the justice system are historically related, they are companions not analogues, and they have different genealogies. It is not necessary to dishonor the tremendous efforts to change racial bias in order to begin addressing gender bias. But it is also not possible to duplicate this activism and employ it on behalf of women. Victim-witness support programs and proposed sentence enhancements for those convicted of violent crimes against their "domestic" associates are significant steps. But we must also reconsider how we represent—in narrative and in court—the bodies and voices of a class of victims whose experience is not yet accepted as real, not even, as in the case of African Americans' experience, disablingly real.

The relocation of the etiology of racism in the 1980s enabled the concept of "reverse racism" to blur the difference between the making of racial distinctions by those with traditional sources of power and by those without it. With the sociological idea of structural racism floating as a dim figure from the past, talk of "reverse racism" relegated individuals'—especially whites'—racist sentiments to something like a personal "preference." A structural analysis reemerged on the right in the form of an assertion that the government had instituted racial quotas that required employers to "prefer" Black candidates without regard to "capability." The resulting amalgamation of individual and systemic "racism" allowed the charge of "reverse racism" to disguise the social patterns that had produced different ways of being and defining "capable." The idea that "Blacks could be racist, too" deeply warped a hard-built sensitivity towards historical power differences. Racism was no longer the ultimate humanist frontier, but the very ground of equal opportunity: one man's hate was as good as another's.

The coverage of the O.J. Simpson criminal case verdict was a highly mediated version of a longstanding nativism in which whites view Blacks as perpetual outsiders, despite the fact that many African Americans trace their families' arrival in the New World to a much earlier date than many white families. From the standpoint of the trauma of the middle passage, the survival of a rich "Black" culture, much more so than the contributing European cultures, has defined what it means to be American in the late twentieth century. It is a cliché to speak of a Black cultural identity perpetually under siege in relation to the prominence of the Black contributions to dance and music in American culture. On another level, Black philosophers like Harriet Tubman, Ralph Ellison, and W.E.B. Du Bois inaugurated and detailed the "dual consciousness" that allows a fragmented, tense set of identifications to nevertheless produce deep allegiance to a general and plural idea of human-ness. This idea, reworked by both civil rights activists and Black Power advocates, produced the idea of cultural pluralism that enabled the later multiculturalism to prevail where a stultifying melting pot had once regulated American identities.

While now only a memory for many people, the coverage and ordinary discussions surrounding the Simpson criminal trial put into play many different means for expressing and exposing individual versus systemic racism—and sexism's complex relationship to them. But the talk did not finally move white Americans to honestly confront our responsibility for past and present racism, but only dug America deeper into its photophobic hole. Most major news organs insisted that Blacks and whites became even more wary of each other. Middle class whites were bewildered, angry, betrayed by their conviction that "race doesn't matter to me"; they felt humiliated that the "Black rage" associated with ghetto youth was also close to the surface of their apparently prosperous and happy Buppy colleagues. The massive coverage of Black law students, beauty parlor attendees, and bar patrons leaping around in revival-like frenzies of "joy" doubly exposed middle America's racial exclusivity: Black bodies were featured as spectacle—even to the point of inciting more white rage—while newspapers and news magazines reported that Blacks were unwilling to discuss the Simpson case with whites they know. And despite some feminists' attempts to have Nicole recognized as a casualty of misogyny, she lived on in popular memory mainly as a misguided gold digger who crossed racial lines because she could not find a suitable mate within her race and class.

Looking back these years later, I can only echo Lyotard's insights that the law is largely a space in which a few reluctantly achieve compensation for damages, while the real wrongs can never be compensated, often cannot even be spoken. Whatever we individually now believe about the "verdict," we can, I hope, see once again that few Americans continuously possess that thing we call "citizenship," and even fewer can use to their advantage the fragile status they have. If nothing else, the travesty of stolen citizenship that I have documented here should make us think long and hard when we watch the many trials that lie ahead. What is being protected, in the wake of September 11th when we are asked, *as citizens*, to willingly give up the procedures and political norms that were only marginally achieved for so many?

CHAPTER **5**

Poetry, Witness, Feminism
HARRIET DAVIDSON

The world we live in today is characterized by a new role for the imagination in social life. . . . The image, the imagined, the imaginary—these are all terms which direct us to something critical and new in global cultural practices: *the imagination as a social practice.*
—Arjun Appadurai,
"Disjuncture and Difference in the Global Cultural Economy"

What I cannot imagine stands guard over everything that I must/can do, think, live.
—Gayatri Spivak, "In a Word: Interview" with Ellen Rooney

I. Musings

Poetry never stood a chance
of standing outside history
—Adrienne Rich, "North American Time"

One of the curious idioms of the English language is the expression "to stand a chance." We tend to use it synonymously with "to have a chance," itself a nuanced use of the meaning of "to have"; for having a chance is not the same as, say, having luck (*la chance* in French), a property we assign to our more fortunate neighbors. Having a chance is the most provisional of properties, something we in no way own at all, but a situation we inhabit, something that opens out in front of us. In fact, chance is not anything at all, only the abyss of the random and indeterminate. But *a* chance is a determinate moment, a confluence of events, a context which gives us a chance and seems to undermine chance, too. *Having* a chance ties chance even more to the situation of a particular possessor. A skilled team has a chance to win; an unskilled one has little chance of winning.

Standing a chance is even more determinate, almost defiant. To stand is a simple verb of position and location; but it is also a richly figurative word: stand by me, stand up for, take a stand, stand your ground, how do we stand, stand on my rights, I can't stand you ("stand" has one of the longest entries in the *OED*). That familiar, material act of standing is closely retained in these metaphors as a sign of dignity, assertion, strength, or affirmation. Stand is also the root word in understand—*verstehen* in German—suggesting a foundational connection between standing and knowledge (comprehension). Standing asserts a physical presence, a stubborn thereness which seems to stand in opposition to indeterminate chance. When you stand, you have a context, a place in history, a wealth of determining factors arrayed before the abyss of the next moment. Standing a chance suggests realizing a chance, arresting chance, making a chance not too chancy. Still, we call it a chance, giving chance its due, the unknowable accident by which the poor team sometimes wins, the colloquial affirmation of a liberating or frightening unknown. Standing may be an anchor, but it also gives chance a place to operate. Standing a chance is a combination of chance and necessity residing in the literal stand; there, where you stand, your location, situation, context, there gather the forces of necessity, of what brought you there, there where you stand with chance opening out before you.

Adrienne Rich writes in "North American Time" that "poetry never stood a chance/of standing outside history" (1984: 324–28). There are two figurative stands here, both denied in a curious mix of metaphors turning on the chancy repetition of forms of "stand." As in all mixed metaphors, the literal reasserts itself in often nonsensical ways, and the words are vertiginously unable to resolve themselves into proper and improper meanings in spite of the rather straightforward sense of the lines (as in the sportscaster's description of the rookie younger brother of the National League batting champion: "He'll have his hands full trying to fill those shoes"). Rich's lines suggest both rational forces and chance meetings, two finely balanced octosyllabic lines, pulling colloquial rhythms into an irregular iambic pattern, equating, finally, the rhythms of the words "poetry" and "history." Both history and poetry may be seen as stories, as highly determinate forms. Yet the line break equates chance and history too, around the more and more literalized standing. Here history is thrown open to non-idealized process, to the vagaries of chance. What are we to make of poetry and history, chance and standing in these lines? The entwining of chance and determinism binds history, poetry and standing. There is no *exstasis*—standing happens in a determinate moment of history; but because of history as process and change, standing is always standing a chance.

Rich's poem continues:

> One line typed twenty years ago
> can be blazed on a wall in spraypaint
> to glorify art as detachment
> or torture of those we
> did not love but also
> did not want to kill
> We move but our words stand
> become responsible
> for more than we intended
>
> and this is verbal privilege

What happens to poetry after we write it? What life does it have in the world, if any? For a political poet, these questions are not only about an immediate result, if poetry can ever be said to have that. The line of poetry, read in a book or blazed on a wall, is a material mark that stands in the world, arresting chance and giving it a place to operate. But while the standing of words places them firmly in history, it also makes them exceed both intention and ideology. The standing paradoxically allows change, as it opens itself up to chance, to the deviations that throw together new contexts that will mutate the meaning of the words as the words mutate the context. How can this perilous standing, the material mark so open both to manipulation and chance, become what is most important for this feminist poet—responsible? How can standing a chance become taking a stand?

My interest in this question leads in several directions. I have been interested in incorporating chance into a theory of subjectivity and agency, something I made a stab at in an earlier article.[1] Now I want to look at how poetry itself stands a chance and takes a stand. The following sections meditate on the relation of contemporary poetry to its audience, a discussion aimed at literary issues about how poetry is defined and taught; on the role of poetry in the women's movement, particularly in relation to "consciousness raising" as a feminist methodology, a more speculative than historical discussion; and on the category of a poetry of witness as providing one way to think about the relation between experience, subjectivity, and social change. In summary, I think that witness is a useful category of subjectivity for feminism because, as I hope to explain, it powerfully melds the unimaginable with imaginative vision; the nonfoundational with commitment to truth; the split subject with agency.

II. The Situation of Poetry

For many readers, Rich's power as a poet and essayist comes from her willingness to take a stand; this willingness is also at the basis of most critiques of her as a poet. Rich is immensely talented, well trained in the "masters," brilliant in handling image and prosody, and at the well-formed line and the just-right word. I could say I was attracted to her for the same reason I love poetry in general—because I am (as she once said about herself) easily entranced by rhythm and sound in language. But that is not the only reason why I read her, nor why I often read many other recent poets, a few of whom would not, by traditional standards, be called great or even very good poets. These other poets, often women poets or poets from other "marginalized" groups—black poets, working-class poets, lesbian poets— range dramatically in technique and power, but they often share a deliberate lack of subtlety in taking clear political positions with a clarity seen by many professional readers as unforgivable. Typical is a review of Rich's poetry in the *New York Times* where the reviewer denounces her as too "ideological," saying she is "lost to poetry." This reviewer along with many others wishes to see poetry precisely as standing outside of history, as not taking a stand, as not being openly ideological. As a long-time reader of Rich I would argue that in many ways she is the most subtle of thinkers—she is historical, cultural, and deconstructive in both her essays and her poetry. But even her feminist supporters tend to categorize her in simple ways; for many she represents the essentialist feminist camp, a position which argues for the stability and universality and superior value of a female self. This is manifestly not her position, but I am interested in the misreading. Why does taking a stand put her beyond the range of poetry and theory alike? What does she do that elicits this response from both friend and foe?

I face what I see as a related question in teaching poetry. Poetry with clear positions and a certain truth value (of the "this is what happened to me" variety) tends to be what my students love more than any other, even after being taught and sometimes seduced by the intricacies of prosody and complex language, of ambiguity and personae. The majority of students wish to read poetry that speaks clearly and directly from the author about her or his experience. They respond strongly and personally (which they are often taught is the "wrong" way) to Sylvia Plath's anger at both men and her own body, to Langston Hughes' anger about inequality, to Lucille

Clifton's humor about her body, to Philip Levine's poignant narratives about his working-class family. The formal properties of the language and images of these poets can be analyzed structurally, and sometimes their poems even achieve that New Critical goal of unity and resolution. But more often they seem a bit more ragged than the stately ending of a poem like Keats' "Ode on a Grecian Urn" where beauty conveniently is truth. After doing this kind of analysis, I feel we have not yet touched on what students love about such poetry. Do they like a simple political message? Does their desire for accessibility indicate lazy minds, as many teachers think? Why do they so want to use the poetry as a way to talk about the author's personal life and then, more urgently, their own lives, their own feelings? Informal surveys of my classes always indicate two things: first, unsurprisingly, a majority of students report an aversion to reading poetry and feel it is boring and obscure. Second, a majority of them also report writing poetry at times in their lives and of liking rhyme and rhythm, which they mainly associate with children's verse and song lyrics. This sense that they dislike "poetry," but still write "poetry" and respond quite strongly to certain poems, suggests several different social meanings of poetry.

The New Critics largely responsible for the establishment of English as a discipline saw poetry as the privileged literary form. The poem was the art object pär excellence, the poet was the arbiter of value, and poets were the chief critics and theorists of Anglo-American modernism. The fact that this disciplining of English poetry occurred at the same time as the experimental ferment in modernist poetry has been much commented on in postmodern debates along Frankfurt school lines. Whatever transgressive value this poetry had was swallowed up in the formalist critical language that dominated criticism by the fifties. Many of the experimental techniques of modernist poetry were associated with radical political movements and avant-garde rethinkings of human subjectivity (from anarchist, progressive, communist, and fascist perspectives) exploring links between language, representation, and society. The importance of breaking with the past, of establishing the new man or woman, in probing the unconscious, all suggested the possibility of a revolutionary role for cultural production in modernism. But modernism, especially in the U.S., became associated with an elitist and reactionary separation from society and the common person. Recent work by Cary Nelson on the place of poetry in the progressive labor movements of the thirties in the U.S. suggests that modernist techniques were used toward progressive ends in this poetry, along with the more expected traditional, populist forms and the realism favored by many Marxist critics. What is important in such work is the discovery of how ubiquitous poetry is in the printed and verbal forums of the leftist movement, so thoroughly erased is this poetry from the literary history which came to dominate discussions of poetry after World War II. The formalism, impersonality, and difficulty privileged by this literary history still define "poetry" as students expect it in the classroom.

The dilemma for the poet of postmodernism was not how to write a shocking or experimental poem after modernism, but rather how not to write this kind of "poetry" at all. Both the new "confessional" poets of the fifties and sixties and the Beat poets were seen in their time as insufficiently distanced and formal to be writing poetry at all. Many of these poets saw their forum as the coffee house, the music club, and the political rally, further questioning definitions of poetry—is this a poet, a singer/musician, a performer, a politician? Also starting in the fifties, poetry engaged the battles over the body and its location—women's bodies in the poetry of Plath and Sexton, black bodies in the Black Arts movement, and homosexual bodies in Beat poetry. These poets' struggle to represent lives that because of oppression, or because they are a hybrid (as with the Beats black/white, straight/gay mixing), have yet to be represented. The attempt to censor Allen Ginsberg's homosexually explicit "Howl" came in the same year as the peak of hysteria over rock 'n' roll and the attempts to censor records and Elvis' sexy pelvis. Ginsberg was the first to notice and exploit this connection, bringing performance centrally into his work and identifying himself with the rock scene. The confessional and Beat poets had enormous influence on an emerging popular sense of poetry as a non-literary form. Poetry was coming to be seen by many not as a discipline to be learned, studied or appreciated, but as a practice widely available to the masses.

By the eighties, poetry had written its way so far out of the academy that the gulf between intellectuals and poets seemed unbridgeable—theorists found the poetry too simple and untheorized to warrant their attention, poets found the theory to be simply more of a kind of discourse that, whatever its content, worked to stabilize unruly practices. Many essays have been written recently bemoaning the loss of a literate audience for poetry, noting the sad decline of circulation in poetry journals and lamenting the lack of national, dominant poet-critics, like Frost and Eliot. But never, I would like to argue, have so many people written poetry. One critic cites the "grim" fact that a small poetry journal has only 1,000 subscribers, even though it gets over 40,000 submissions a year. Forty thousand submissions?

To reckon with this social fact, we need to redefine poetry as a practice which is not only aesthetic but also includes something that detractors might call the therapeutic and/or the ideological, but I will put under the category of witness. Indeed, poetry writing is now a staple of therapeutic work with children, the elderly, prisoners, the homeless, in addition to the neurotic (Anne Sexton began writing poetry at the suggestion of her analyst) and the disaffected or lovelorn students in my classes. Poetry workshops proliferate in the schools, political poetry is being studied again, and even the media have opened up to the spoken word movement. In addition, the poetry reading is a contemporary phenomenon which has yet to be analyzed in terms of performance, community, and the use-value of poems which create a social space and never gain immortality in the anthology. Poetry critics mostly dismiss this poetry as something they don't want to read—or indeed, even as dangerous to the "purity" of poetry (powerful Harvard critic Helen Vendler criticized the very popular Dodge festival here in New Jersey for lowering the standards of poetry), but its audience is growing, revealing a paradigm shift in our social understanding of poetry. There is probably an interesting subversive operation going on here; money for many of these non-academic poetry programs is raised under the aegis of the "higher" aesthetic and moral values associated with an elitist notion of poetry, even while its use tends to subvert those values. In the past few years, with the high visibility of slam poetry, rap poetry, and street poetry, the institutional support for poetry programs tends to justify them by appealing to liberal values of self esteem, which is not, I hasten to add, wrong-headed, only reductive about what this poetry can do. Poetry is one of the places where a rewriting of subjectivity can happen. In other words, I would like to argue that the cultural meaning and use, the cultural place, of poetry in the U.S. has changed in contemporary times from the modernist paradigm.

III. Feminism and Poetry: Imagination as a Social Practice

By way of illustration I want to argue that poetry has a distinctive role in the second-wave feminist movement, where reading and writing poetry have become part of the community building and consciousness raising so important to feminist politics and the creation of a counter-public sphere of discourse. Miriam Schneir's 1994 collection *Feminism in Our Time: The Essential Writings, World War II to the Present*, a companion to her widely used 1972 collection *Feminism: the Essential Historical Writings*, includes four poems: Sylvia Plath's "Purdah," Audre Lorde's "Who Said It Was Simple," Muriel Rukeyser's "The Poem As Mask," and Anne Sexton's "In Celebration of My Uterus." Though I could quarrel about her choice of these particular poems as most important for the development of the women's movement in the U.S., the inclusion of poetry seems unremarkable. In such a collection, especially after twenty years of feminist work and recovery, the choices facing an editor trying to select representative texts must seem daunting; but few would question her decision when she writes that, "A handful of poems were chosen as exemplars of the remarkable renaissance in women's poetry that has occurred during these years" (xvi).

More tellingly, one of the first popular anthologies from the second wave movement, Robin Morgan's *Sisterhood is Powerful: An Anthology of Writings from the Women's Liberation Movement* (1970), includes a section of poetry, called "The Hand That Cradles the Rock: Protest and Revolt: Poetry as Protest" (*The Hand That Cradles the Rock* was initially the title of the entire book, which was changed after protests from S. J. Perelman, who had used that title previously), and Morgan ends her introduction with a lengthy poem. I don't read this poetry as merely illustrative or entertaining, but as a cultural practice important to and furthering the radical goals of women's liberation to reshape society.

The intense contradictions of the personal and the political, identity and difference, and experience and discourse in feminism are heightened in a genre making claims to both authenticity (sincerity) and extreme artificiality, being defined in different historical moments as either meditative or performative, and in contemporary times being valued for expressing the most personal and idiosyncratic subjectivity and at the same time the most universal of sentiments. Poetry, partly because of generic and formal histories, engages the problem of experience and representation so important for understanding the consciousness raising of feminism. Of course, other forms of cultural production play with the same contradictions; the only argument for the popularity of poetry in the U.S. is its availability in material terms: you need no elaborate apparatus and very little time to write a poem, and poetry is relatively easy to distribute for a collective impact—either in a reading to a group, a use in chants or songs, or copies to circulate.[2] The inclusion of poetry in the anthologies, in the rap sessions, in the heart of the women's liberation movement is a sign of the multiple and varied issues, stances, and strategies of a movement that is now often viewed as rather monolithic and naïve. Poetry writing provides a myriad of women a practice which intersects privately and publicly with the consciousness raising of feminist groups; and in poetry's formal constraints, its insistence on attention to mediation regardless of who is writing, allows issues to develop in sophisticated theoretical ways which extend other political work.

Indeed the number of anthologies devoted to women poets, and the sheer number of women poets publishing and winning awards, is testimony to a social shift not only in the number of women writing poetry, but in the social use and value of poetry. Women poets have moved onto a public stage as women writing about women, part of the political and social change of second-wave feminism. Of course many poets who are women do not write about women's issues, and should not be expected to, though they may owe their institutional acceptance more to the women's movement than many of them wish to acknowledge. But the increase in the number of women in a field dominated not only by men but by aesthetic theories hostile to politics *and* the personal is more than just affirmative action. Today it is not outrageous or even uncommon to argue that the top-five list of major poets writing in the U.S. since the fifties would be dominated by women—something that would be unthinkable even today in any other literary period. In spite of grumbling by reviewers, the stature of poets like Adrienne Rich, Sylvia Plath, Gwendolyn Brooks, Elizabeth Bishop matches any comparable group of male poets, especially as innovators, as well as in popularity.

The rise of confessional poetry in American with its much denounced shift in focus to the personal, embodied, "authentic" voice coincides with the rise of feminism and women writing in the U.S. in a way that complicates vectors of causation. While the women's liberation movement and its focus on "consciousness-raising" clearly led many women to write poetry, the widely read confessional poetry (perhaps the first poetry movement to be dominated by women, and driven in the popular imagination by the sensational and tragic lives of Sylvia Plath and Anne Sexton) provided poetic models taken up in second-wave feminism. But both the poetry and the women's movement rise from similar critiques of subjectivity in post World War II America. The growing awareness of the Holocaust, the threat of nuclear annihilation, the pressures to conformity spurred most visibly by the McCarthy hearings, and the visibility of mass culture (and maybe even the media-spread tenets of existentialism) are only a few of the elements of U.S. culture in the fifties and sixties that led to a widespread rethinking of the efficacy of the liberal subject—rarely expressed in just that way, of course. Surely man was no longer master of his fate. Those abject others of history—some women, homosexuals, and those stigmatized because of race or ethnicity—who were never much inclined toward believing in autonomous selves in the first place (classic cases of interpellation gone astray) found some alliances here, but more importantly began to find an emergent collective voice among the fissures in subjective wholeness. Confessional poetry was named that by hostile critics; the poetry itself bears little resemblance to a confession of wrongdoing. Instead, it most often details the disintegration of rational authority and the corresponding rise in awareness of the body, as well as a heightened emotional rawness.[3] Confessional poetry involves both abjection, on the one hand, and self-assertion on the other, often in varying degrees. For instance, Ginsberg opens out a state of abjection—as gay, crazy, drug addled—into a visionary power, while Robert Lowell, from a hegemonic position of power as an upper class, old money, white male, charts the disintegration of his own rational authority over himself, as well as the loss of cultural authority of his class, and repeatedly tries and fails to identify with marginal others, especially African Americans. Plath performs a slow bodily dissection of herself in her poetry, even while creating scathing voices of self-assertion: "Out of the ash/I rise with my red hair/And I eat men like air."[4]

I wish to get away from the term "confessional," and from the more recent and more pejorative "victim art" for this poetry. This poetry is not primarily confessional or self-pitying, nor does it fit any of the other generic categories like historical, meditative, elegiac poetry. Instead, I would like to subsume this social use of poetry under the larger theoretical category of a poetry of witness. Even early discussions of feminist consciousness raising sessions cite the moment of testimony and witness as crucial to the functioning of consciousness raising. Most assume, I think, that this is a moment of transparency, of immediate knowledge or unmediated experience which is the "raw" material of analysis—what must be "raised" in higher or wider awareness by the mediation of political thought.[5] But many thoughtful discussions of consciousness raising suggest more: for instance, Sheila Rowbotham prefers to use the term "consciousness moving," saying "your own perception is continually being shifted by how other women perceive what has happened to them" (59). And how do we gain another's "perception"? "Analysis is not enough alone, for we enter the beings and worlds of other people through imagination, and it is through imagination that we glimpse how these might change" (218). Drucilla Cornell, too, introduces imagination into consciousness raising, contrasting herself with Catharine MacKinnon, who claims that consciousness raising is *the* feminist methodology:

> In contrast to MacKinnon, I believe consciousness raising does not involve the revelation of our ultimate situation as women. Rather, I understand consciousness raising as the endless attempt to re-imagine and re-symbolize the feminine within sexual difference so as to break the bonds of the meanings of Woman that have been taken for granted and justifiable as fate. . . . Consciousness raising engages the meaning of representation on at least two levels. First, the truth that arises out of consciousness raising is representative, in that it represents a view of the world that has come to be shared by a group. Second, such a truth involves a representation of reality, particularly of the strictures of gender identity, so that what has faded can be drawn into vivid outlines, what has been invisible can be seen, what seemed natural can be challenged and imagined differently. (1995: 82)

Like Rowbotham, Cornell wants to stress imagination rather than analysis. But Cornell also recognizes the "limits of our imaginations" and proposes a performative theory of politically engaged change which she describes as the "enactment of mimetic identifications" which "is a rhetorical and artistic device for both the engagement with and the displacement of the boundaries that have limited our imaginations" (97).

These writers are struggling with the feminist dilemma of the need both to use and to critique a notion of "experience." Like many others, they use the concept of the imagination in both ordinary and specialized ways to suggest something different from analysis or explanation, using imagination to connect for Rowbotham to the other's "being," suggesting an access to embodied experience, and for Cornell to both a complicated interaction with the unconscious (through enactment) and, more traditionally, to visionary change. The imagination is a pivotal point in either case, suggesting both limits and possibilities not entirely covered by conscious and analytical thought. The concept of the imagination is explored in a large discourse from literature, as well as a discourse on the image, and in the hands of someone like Cornell, the imagination is connected with the Lacanian Imaginary, often implying a hermeneutic plenitude. I would like to include in the concept of the imagination the moment of testimony or witness which moves away from the image to a dynamic with the audience (and also critiques the power of the imagination).[6]

IV. What I Cannot Imagine: Witness and Poetry

Gayatri Spivak's statement that "What I cannot imagine stands guard over everything that I must / can do, think, live" contains within it the imaginative figure named personification, as she makes what she cannot imagine into a ghostly figure standing guard—a mute witness, in my own imagination. Here again, the word "stand" indicates a kind of stubborn insistence of presence, not only against a chancy future, as in the Rich example, but more broadly against what I cannot imagine—the future, yes, and the Other, others, the unconscious, death, another's pain.[7] I'm asking the poetry of witness to do a lot of work with this: to safeguard that unimaginable from appropriation, to make us aware of the limits of our imaginations, and to make it stand guard, imaginatively, over our beings.

Much work has been done recently on clarifying the features of testimony and witness in the literature of the Holocaust, as well as in the Latin American *testimonio* tradition and the testifying in the Black church. The key features of Latin American *testimonio* as discussed by John Beverley in *Against Literature* are its appeal to truth, thus breaking with literary traditions of distance and narration, and its address both to and from a communal situation; that is, while dependent on the individual witness, it speaks from the position of the group experience, and wishes to impel future action by the group.[8] Shoshana Felman, in *Testimony: Crises of Wit-*

nessing in Literature, Psychoanalysis and History (co-authored with Dori Laub in separate chapters), starting from an interest in Holocaust stories but ranging into many different literatures, probes the paradoxes of witness more thoroughly, particularly the paradox that the witness is often invoked as someone speaking of what is too hard to be spoken and/or not ever meant to be spoken; here the literally unimaginable horrors of the Holocaust, with its attempt to eliminate all witnesses, remains definitive for her. She defines witnessing "as nonhabitual, estranged *conceptual prisms* through which we attempt to apprehend—and to make tangible to the imagination—the ways in which our cultural frames of reference and our preexisting categories which delimit and determine our perception of reality have failed, essentially, both to contain and to account for the scale of what has happened in contemporary history"(xv).[9] The archetypal witness for her is to a situation of unspeakable pain or suffering, to situations beyond ordinary language, and often to a situation where no one is supposed to be left to witness at all. Dramatically reducing the richness of Felman's discussion, I would highlight the main points as I interpret them: First and foremost, the witness speaks from urgency—something demands a voice, something essentially non-identical with the speaking subject.[10] As a corollary to this, the witness is an encounter with strangeness—witness may "speak ahead of knowledge and awareness and break through the limits of its own conscious understanding" (21). The witness may be to one's own experience, but that experience is created in the witness as non-identical to the self. Second, the witness is crucially about a speaker *and* a hearer and must create an addressee when it does not have one; this is not solitary, meditative, or soliloquizing speech. Both speaker and hearer are witnesses to what is said; indeed each needs the other to hear or speak. This implies that as an encounter, the witness is a speech act, not a discursive statement, which attempts to communicate, in the sense of transfer, urgency—to make something happen, to turn the hearer into a witness too. In this way the witness, while perhaps speaking of the past, is most concerned with the future. Not surprisingly, since she is a literary critic, Felman finds that her ideas of witness are most thoroughly carried out in art. She cites Adorno's well-known assertion about the impossibility of writing poetry after Auschwitz, but goes on to endorse his affirmation in "Commitment" where he worries that, "It is now virtually in art alone that suffering can still find its own voice, consolation without being immediately betrayed by it" (34; Adorno 1985: 312). While the force of Felman and Laub's work, especially the sections of the book written about psychoanalytic narratives, suggests that witness can also happen in the psychoanalytic situation (and I would argue also in religious contexts which she does not explore), nevertheless she focuses our attention on how art can create the two things most crucial for the witness—the address to and creation of the other, and the emotional urgency resulting from the encounter with strangeness, with knowledge we do not know we know.

The act of witnessing, as a performative act, unsettles established boundaries between writer and reader (or speaker and audience), between fiction and history, between experience and ideology, even between the past and future of memory and desire. The positions of speaker and audience are crucial here, and in fact testimony establishes a contract with its audience different from a literary one. The testimony demands belief (though it may not always get it), though not in the historical accuracy of its story. The testimony is not a recital of history, but is the creation of a history through an intersubjective process in which both the speaker and hearer gain their witnessing subjectivity through the new knowledge of a shared situation. Both subjectivity and knowledge are created in the testimony. Witnessing and testifying are always, in literature as much as in the legal system, performative acts, relying on complex notions of being *here* and being *there*.

A theory of the witness seems to break open the stalemate in postmodern theories of subjectivity caused by the merging of poststructural thought with the politically and ethically inflected work of feminist writers, Black writers, and Marxist writers. The need for a subjectivity that somehow escapes the binaries of essentialism and pluralism, a subjectivity with a clear identity and agency which is not an essential identity, is a common theme in postmodern work such as that by Judith Butler, Paul Gilroy, or Homi Bhabha. A recurring problem has been how to deal with experience and history, both shown by poststructural analysis to be suspect categories, mediated by countless forces and thus difficult to use as the basis for identity or politics. In Felman's psychoanalytic model, the act of witnessing reconfigures subjectivity as intersubjectivity and resuscitates experience by paradoxically placing the past into the future—experience is validated as truth in the act of witnessing and in the chain reaction of this act which compels testimony into the future. This is a performative way to think about both subjectivity and history, though Felman and Laub tend to focus, given their psychoanalytic approach, on the model of subjectivity more than history, thus opening themselves to the critique that their work insufficiently grapples with the moving target of historical, cultural, and political specificity.

The essence of the act of witness may be its difficult relation to historical truth in that it tries to speak of the unspeakable, of acts of horror or oppression that the power of dominant ideologies tries to hide, sometimes by eliminating all witnesses. In such testimony the unspeakable is spoken in such a way that the affective clings to the speaking, so that what is given is an ethical and ultimately political imperative toward understanding not

166 • Witness and Memory

just the past, but also the future. In this way, the witness is distinguished from the bystander who may see or even have the experience without the compulsion or ability to witness it. The act of witnessing begins in a personal raid on the inarticulate and creates a chain of witnesses each of whom receives this newly wrought history, charged with the affect which compels its retelling.

Testimony often witnesses the destructiveness of discursive contexts for specific lives or sites, particularly lives marked by extreme physical and psychic oppression. Through the witness, the unspeakable comes to speech as a contextualized and communal event; thus the literature of witness is often deeply and pointedly political. This, for Elie Wiesel speaking of the Holocaust, is the voice of our time: "If the Greeks invented tragedy, the Romans the epistle, and the Renaissance the sonnet, our generation invented a new literature, that of testimony" (1997: 9). The literature of testimony which Felman calls "omnipresent in our recent cultural accounts of ourselves," is central to much contemporary poetry, which presents a self wishing to express a seemingly unspeakable situation, and through an intersubjective contract, make it speakable, real, and political (Felman and Laub 6). The witness faces toward the future, gathering together a new knowledge of the past in the intersubjective performance of the present.

I am clearly arguing for a transformative power to the testimony or the poetry of witness: the power to open up a new space for social change. While this claim, indeed my whole discussion of witness, remains speculative, I hope that by going back to poetry I can at least clarify what I mean by the witness of poetry. My definition of a poetry of witness is that it combines a sense of historical and personal urgency (about more than yourself but about yourself) with a performative mode. It is poetry that is primarily contextual, dependent on its audience, and crucially future oriented, that is, while this poetry may often be about the past, its direction is toward the future as a warning, a call to action, an impetus to more poems or speech. In this it is primarily rhetorical—it wants to move, persuade, touch the audience—rather than formal or figurative or even realist. It wants an audience that believes and feels. Its primary trope would have to be metonymy—which figures so strongly in postmodern theory—that chain of speaking which can't ever speak the final word.[11]

Some things I might also look for in a poetry of witness would be a refusal of the traditional literary in some way—its desire for "historical" truth (and a historical speaking subject), its sense of its use-value in a social context, replacement of image with rhetoric. I would look for that pact with the reader, or creation of the reader in a present time of reading. Also, I would look for a shattering of subjectivity before the unimaginable situation; and for its reemergence as a witnessing subject.[12]

Let me go back to one of the representative poems from Schneir's anthology. The 1970 Audre Lorde poem "Who Said It Was Simple" might be read, contra the title, as a simple experience poem about the problem of racial solidarity in feminism, though it is also a poem critiquing this simplicity of experience:

> There are so many roots to the tree of anger
> that sometimes the branches shatter
> before they bear
>
> Sitting in Nedicks
> the women rally before they march
> discussing the problematic girls
> they hire to make them free.
> An almost white counterman passes
> a waiting brother to serve them first
> and the ladies neither notice nor reject
> the slighter pleasures of their slavery.
>
> But I who am bound by my mirror
> as well as my bed
> see cause in color
> as well as sex.
>
> and sit here wondering
> which me will survive
> all these liberations.

This poem begins with an image—the tree of anger—which quickly dissolves into rhetoric. The image is incoherent: what are the branches of the tree of anger meant to bear? more anger? but isn't it the anger that shatters the branches *before* they can bear? is the shattering good? or is the tree a symbol of feminism fed by anger to blossom in change, which taps into Black anger destroying feminism? The purpose seems to me rhetorical finally—to get her anger on the table as unbounded by the image, not imaginable. The narrative which follows, historically grounding itself in a real place—Nedicks—challenges literary distance. We read the speaker as the writer; and the historical Audre Lorde grounds the truth of her self-identifications later as Black and more obliquely as lesbian; in fact some readers feel they need to know she really is Black and lesbian to read the poem. But the truth of experience narrated here points to the mediation of experience by race. The poem catalogues what she notices and the other women do not, bringing what is invisible to them to light. She affirms a solidarity with the word "brother" and starts to distance herself from the women by calling them "ladies" even while closing a circle of identification with them by calling ironic attention to their "slavery" as women. The poem shifts tone with the third stanza, where she first uses the word "I": "But I who am bound by my mirror / as well as my bed / see cause in color / as well as sex." These lines not only point out the difference in experience between herself and them, but also, when it first introduces an I, introduces fissures in her self. The powerful mirror image is a Lacanian moment of the imaginary when the I of the enunciation is "bound" by the image of the I, the enounced. Her own experience, too, becomes an issue. She is bound by her race, differently bounded by her sexuality and yet split by both—the discursive formations of race and sex tell only part of the story of who she is. The strangeness of herself and the situation leaves her "wondering": "which me will survive / all these liberations." It is an urgent question of survival, asked of the unknown, chancy future, a future which splits her from herself as much as the discursive formations.

Who is this "I" who wonders and sits "here," and where is "here"? There seems to be a deliberate separation from the viewing subject of the second stanza who is never named "I"; so that "here" does not refer to the narrative situation in Nedicks, nor to the past at all, given the present tense of the grammar. Instead, it seems to refer to the writing situation: "here" in the writing of this poem, thinking about survival. Now this is an old trick of avant-garde poetry which we see often enough in feminist poetry. The historical and discursive space time of narrative and the absented space time of abstract thinking are joined by a third space time of the performative now: "These poems know poetry is a contact sport! The poem is not written until you read it!" Bob Holman writes (1). This is the moment of the only "I" in this poem; the I speaking now to us here, really, in this historical moment as we read the poem. Here I think a witnessing subjectivity emerges.[13]

In this poem the self is fragmented and undermined, only to be pulled back together as an agential "I" by the context of the reading. The poem's "I" is validated by ours; as ours is by its. We lend it our own reality; it lends us an identity and knowledge we cannot and do not possess. The boundary between reader and writer, history and literature, gets crossed as a matter of her, and our, survival. This highly political poem, articulating the race problem of feminism in 1970 long before it gets generally raised in theory, though lived and discussed in feminist work for years, creates a witnessing subjectivity, witnessing her own anger, confusion, and incoherence, even as we witness it too. We are created together as witness to what was for white feminists an invisibility—race—standing guard over what we must do.

I turn back to Rich for one more example. We left her in the midst of her poem "North American Time" (1984: 324–28), a poem written at the same time as her widely influential essay "Notes Towards A Politics of Location" which moves her feminist thinking to a complex grappling with difference.[14] The poem is a meditation on the impossibility of knowledge and the necessity of action; it seems to plead with her readers to read her as witness, not ideologue, and to enter with her into a witness of what we cannot know. She begins with a rare flash of humor:

> When my dreams showed signs
> of becoming
> politically correct
> no unruly images
> escaping beyond borders
> when walking in the street I found my
> themes cut out for me
> knew what I could not report
> for fear of enemies' usage
> then I began to wonder

Rich's protest against the rigidity of an ideology does not, however, lead her to reject her political stance; rather she focuses on how a political stance necessarily involves the "unruly" by leading us through a number of subject positions demonstrating the inadequacy of our knowledge. But the impossible breadth of knowledge demanded here pales next to the demands of the future. Rich not only catalogues the ways that our language can be misused in the future (quoted in my opening section), escaping our intention, but also how the future disrupts language, taking the difficult position that our words are held accountable to a future we cannot know. For her North American time is "stuck fast in the deep freeze of history" never acknowledging anything beyond its founding myths; feminism too, she worries, is in danger of a similar immobility, if not accountable to the future.

> It doesn't matter what you think
> Words are found responsible
> all you can do is choose them
> or choose
> To remain silent.   Or, you never had a choice,
> which is why the words that do stand
> are responsible
>
> And this is verbal privilege

Like most writing about writing there is a vertiginous quality to the self-reflection here: to what words does "words" refer? The flatness and repetition
of the language point up the seeming contradiction: thinking doesn't matter / words are responsible; you can choose / you never had a choice. But
the silence enacted in the overly large space after the word "silent," a breakage reflecting the impossibility of knowledge, the paralysis of action, the
failure of the imagination, is refused in this poem, as in all of her poems.
The force of her lines suggests both that most women have no choice other
than enforced silence, and also the sense of being compelled to speak. Rich
uses a language of urgency, again to suggest the forces which bind us and
push us—what "is meant to break my heart and reduce me to silence" she
writes in the penultimate stanza—and also the pushing back necessary for
survival, for any "I" to exist at all. The poem ends, after an imagistic passage
and another break in spacing, with a characteristic self-assertion:

> The almost-full moon rises
> timelessly speaking of change
> out of the Bronx, the Harlem River
> the drowned towns of the Quabbin
> the pilfered burial mounds
> the toxic swamps, the testing-grounds
>
> and I start to speak again

The traditional poetic image of the moon—so often a female imaginary—
is located in New York, then in the historical past of Native American set-
tlements, then in a political and discursive place of "pilfered" burial
mounds, toxic swamps (New Jersey, of course) and more metaphorically
the testing-grounds, an enigmatic image of destruction and challenge (also
a self-reflexive reference to a previous poem of her own "Trying to Talk
with a Man" where she refers to testing bombs). But this is primarily imagistic, not rhetorical work—no pronouns appear, only a tightly controlled
aesthetic mastery over sound and rhythm—the rough regularity of seven
syllable lines, the iambic rhythmic base with meaningful substitutions.
(The first line quoted has a rising iambic rhythm, while the second line
substitutes two dactyls to emphasize the irregular regularity of "Timelessly
speaking of change.") After the break, in the performance time of the
poem, the force of "start" and "again" gets highlighted. Hasn't she just been
speaking? Why would she need to start speaking again? Is the aesthetic
work of the preceding passage somehow not "speaking" in the way she
wants? And why is there no period, nothing but blank space after that line,
a spacing figured earlier in the poem as silence?[15]

The speaking subject who will now speak seems to leave the poem for historical reality, away from the aesthetic project to a social one. Once again, in the now time of the poem we, the readers, are lending that "I" of the last line our historical time, while it gives us a vertiginous identity which must and will speak, haunted by the need to communicate what it cannot know, by a ghostly figure standing guard.

CHAPTER **6**

Poetic Witness: Writing the Real
THOMAS A. VOGLER

And it shall come to pass, when many evils and troubles are befallen them, that this song shall testify against them as a witness;
for it shall not be forgotten out of the mouths of their seed.

> —Deuteronomy 31:21

Those of us who did manage to keep control over our personal affairs before it was all over are obviously not going to testify anyway.
What would we have said? That we confronted the monster eyeball
to eyeball and blinked first but only after a decent interval had
elapsed and were then excused from completing the examination
before defenestration became an issue?

> —John Ashbery, *Flow Chart*

Commenting on what makes literature different from the "true story" or
the "poetry of testimony," Vladimir Nabokov claimed that "Literature was
born not the day when a boy crying 'wolf, wolf' came running out of the
Neanderthal valley with a big grey wolf at his heels; literature was born on
the day when a boy came crying 'wolf, wolf' and there was no wolf behind
him" (quoted in Charlton 9). Nabokov was wrong; what we think of as literature was born when someone *told this story* and there was no wolf and
there was no boy, either. Even so, there are boys, and there are wolves who
would eat the boys if they had the chance; and there may be important implications in a story that is not literally true. Consider the case of a recent
avatar of the poet of witness, Araki Yasusada, a Japanese postal clerk whose

family was wiped out by the Hiroshima bomb, but who lived on to die of cancer in 1972. His strange and fascinating notebooks were discovered years after his death, and in the 1990s selections from them began to appear in English translation in *Aeriel, Conjunctions, First Intensity, Grand Street, American Poetry Review*, and other magazines, provoking the interest of anthologists and the possibility of a publishing contract with Wesleyan University Press. According to Eliot Weinberger, Yasusada was well on his way to a posthumous career as " 'our' primary poetry witness of nuclear disaster" (8), until a spate of rumors of his non-existence spoiled the game.[1] Part of the scandal of Yasusada's non-existence is that he and his works entered so easily into the subgenre of "witness literature," one that of all literary kinds is most bound up with notions of authenticity and referentiality, a poetry that puts us in touch with raw *facts* of existence rather than *effects* produced by rhetorical technique. With their umbilical connection to reality severed, the same words suffer a radical transformation of value. As Bradford Morrow, editor of *Conjunctions*, puts it: "If it was written by a Hiroshima survivor, as a literary response to that experience, then it's an amazing historical document and certainly a remarkable technical achievement," but if it's "just someone being empathic in another culture fifty years later" it's "not as interesting" (quoted in Nussbaum 84).[2] Clearly, then, a special relationship between the poet and poem and reader is called for if we are to have a poetics of witness. A special attitude (faith, belief) in the reader is necessary in order to produce an authentic reading; and there must be special signs in the production of the text signaling the reader that the poem deserves such a reading. This is the literary equivalent of what economists call a "fiduciary system," in which consumers exchange pieces of paper worthless in themselves for goods of real value.

In one of his most ambitious film-poems of witness, *The Gaze of the Gorgon*, Tony Harrison locates his voice of witness in a statue of Heine—poet, syphilitic Jew, outcast, somehow surviving to bear witness to a century of atrocity. Late in the poem the poet finds his way to the "crying wolf" trope, and the inevitability that at the end of the century many feel that the danger is over:

> The Gorgon who's been running riot
> through the century now seems quiet,
> but supposing one who's watched her ways
> were to warn you that the Gorgon's gaze
> remains unburied in your day
> and I've glimpsed her even in the USA,
> you'll all reply he's crying wolf,
> but in the deserts of the Gulf

steel pediments have Gorgon's eyes
now grown as big as tank-wheel size
that gaze down from her temple frieze
on all her rigid devotees.

Taking advantage of the rhyme between "wolf" and "Gulf," Harrison identifies the 1991 Gulf War as one of the latest in a century of atrocities, suggesting that the complacency with which the "civilized world" contemplated the wholesale slaughter of a retreating enemy may be the latest effect of the Gorgon's gaze.[3]

The "Gorgon" in this poem is Harrison's name for the paralyzing power of force used by humans against humans: "The Gorgon under the golden tide / brings ghettos, gulags, genocide." Harrison heads the work with a quotation from Simone Weil ("To the same degree, though in different fashion, those who use force and those who endure it are turned to stone." *The Iliad, or the Poem of Force*) and one from Nietzsche ("Art forces us to gaze into the horror of existence, yet without being turned to stone by the vision." *The Birth of Tragedy*) in order to set up an ongoing confrontation between the power of the Gorgon and the potential of art: "If art can't cope / it's just another form of dope, / and leaves the Gorgon in control / of all the freedoms of the soul." Primo Levi found his way to the same image in *The Drowned and the Saved*:

> I must repeat: we, the survivors, are not the true witnesses. This is an uncomfortable notion of which I have become conscious little by little, reading the memoirs of others and reading mine at a distance of years. We survivors are not only an exiguous but also an anomalous minority: we are those who by their prevarications or abilities or good luck did not touch bottom. Those who did so, those who saw the Gorgon, have not returned to tell about it or have returned mute, but they are the "Muslims," the submerged, the complete witnesses, the ones whose deposition would have a general significance. They are the rule, we are the exception. (115–16)

Writers like Harrison and Levi share Bertholt Brecht's sense of urgency that compels the poet to confront the danger and use the power of art to cry wolf!

They won't say: when the walnut tree shook in the wind
But: when the house-painter crushed the workers.
They won't say: when the child skimmed a flat stone across the
   rapids

But: when the great wars are being paid for.
They won't say: when the woman came into the room
But: when the great powers joined forces against the workers.
However, they won't say: the times were dark
Rather: why were their poets silent.

This 1939 poem, like its title ("In Dark Times"), suggests two contrasting views of art, and a later poem ("Bad Time for Poetry") makes the conflict explicit: "In my poetry a rhyme / Would seem to me almost insolent. / Inside me contend / Delight at the apple tree in blossom / And horror at the house-painter's speeches. / But only the second / Drives me to my desk."

To identify a moral and political role for poetry in this manner, to insist that it is the poet's duty to cry wolf when there *really is* a wolf, is to go against a longstanding tradition of art as a form of creativity free from the compulsions and contingencies of the temporal. In his *Poetics* Aristotle distinguished poetry from history, as capable of a universality lacking in the specificity of mere history; and the late eighteenth century saw a rejuvenation of this notion of a universal truth of poetry that gave support to the modern belief in the autonomous realm of the aesthetic.[4] A genre will inevitably be defined by the canonization of particular authors in anthologies, textbooks, histories of literature, and university curricula, a process that since the Romantic period has caused "poetry" to come to be synonymous with "lyric poetry" for mainstream readers and critics.

> From 1744 or so to the present day the best poetry internalized its subject matter, particularly in the mode of Wordsworth after 1798. Wordsworth had no true subject except his own subject nature, and very nearly all significant poetry since Wordsworth, even by American poets, has repeated Wordsworth's inward turning. (Bloom 1982: 287)

For critics like Harold Bloom and Helen Vendler, the epiphanic "personal crisis lyric," with its ahistorical, subjective, self-contemplative focus, constitutes an official verse dogma.[5] It is a poetics of subjectivity that is valued precisely for its "universality," its distance from any contingent historical context, so that the more lyrical a writer seeks to be, the more strictly all historical matter will be excluded. Romanticism is a crucial moment in the development of this concept of poetry, coming when the late eighteenth century fostered the ideal of an aesthetic realm of timeless formal beauty and emotional authenticity. Bloom's absolutes ("best," "significant") are inherited from a Romantic aesthetic of expressivity, where the only subject matter is the poet's inner state, where a disinterested commitment to formal beauty and emotional authenticity can be located in a site separated from history and from the commodifying pressures of the market place. Thus Blake and Byron, two great Romantic poets who did not turn away from issues of the moment, and who aspired to address a large public audience, are often not considered as major practitioners of the *lyric* mode. When Bloom was given the opportunity to select and edit *The Best of the Best American Poetry: 1988–1997*, based on ten annual volumes of "the best American poetry," he not only did not select any work from Adrienne Rich's 1996 selection of "the best," he devoted his whole Introduction to an insulting harangue against her selections that pointedly did not even mention her name.[6]

The last two decades have seen signs of change in this status quo, suggesting the widespread emergence of a desire for a different kind of poetry, one that can bear authentic witness to historical events in the real world. Early in the 1980s, Marjorie Perloff was criticizing the paradigmatic modernist lyric—both its practice and its criticism—for reflecting a narrow, reactionary and doomed view of poetry. In *The Dance of the Intellect*, she identified in poetic postmodernism "the urge to return the material so rigidly excluded—political, ethical, historical, philosophical—to the domain of poetry, which is to say that the Romantic lyric, the poem as expression of a moment of absolute insight, of emotion crystallized into a timeless pattern, gives way to a poetry that can, once again, accommodate narrative and didacticism, the serious and the comic, verse and prose" (180–81). In her widely praised and cited *Poetics of Postmodernism* (1988), Linda Hutcheon drew parallels between current works in literature and in painting, sculpture and architecture, claiming that literary postmodernism is "resolutely historical and inescapably political" (4). Already in the 1970s the subgenre of the *testimonio* was beginning to emerge in Latin America, presented as the authentic testimony of the colonized and oppressed. Twenty years later it had become a staple in the academic marketplace, advertised by Duke University Press as "The 'Real' Thing."[7] In "Beyond the Cave" Fredric Jameson anticipated the current mood:

> The idea of the autonomy of the work of art—which at first seemed a proud boast and a value to be defended—now begins to look a little shameful, like a symptom into whose pathology one would want to inquire more closely. At this point, then, we are tempted to ask, not whether literary works are autonomous, nor even how art manages to lift itself above its immediate social situation and to free itself from its social context, but rather what kind of society it can be in which works of art have become autonomous to this degree, in

which the older social and cultic functions of literature have become so unfamiliar as to have made us forgetful . . . of the power
and influence that a socially living art can exercise. (116–17)

We are now in a period where even a formalist critic like Helen Vendler,
who complains of all the "cant about . . . 'the poetry of witness,' " is not
averse to embellishing her *New Yorker* portrait of Seamus Heaney with a
hint of its cachet, claiming him as a poet who illustrates "the quarrel between the urgency of witness and the urgency of delight" (1995a: 84).
Shoshana Felman, who in 1980 was arguing that consciousness is a fantasy
effect and that literature teaches us that all authority is "a *language effect*,
the product or the creation of its own *rhetorical* power" (1980: 8), now
writes urgently about what she calls an "encounter with the real" and her
desire "to move on, as it were, from poetry into reality and to study in a literary class something which is *a priori* not defined as literary, but is rather
of the order of raw documents—historical and autobiographical" (1992:
42). Carolyn Forché writes in her anthology, *Against Forgetting*, that in 1980
"something happened along the way to the introspective poet I had been,"
causing her to turn her attention to poems that "bear the trace of extremity
within them, and [that] are, as such, evidence of what occurred." In spite of
her American contemporaries, who argued "against any mixing of what
they saw as the mutually exclusive realms of the personal and the political,"
she persisted in becoming "a repository of what began to be called 'the poetry of witness' " (30).[8] Hal Foster has noted that in contemporary discourse "a special truth seems to reside in traumatic or abject states, in
diseased or damaged bodies," and identified what he calls *lingua trauma* or
trauma discourse, where "especially in therapy culture, talk shows, and
memoir-mongering, trauma is treated as an event that guarantees the subject, and in this psychologistic register the subject, however disturbed,
rushes back as survivor, witness, testifier. Here a traumatic subject does indeed exist, and it has absolute authority, for one cannot challenge the
trauma of another: one can only believe it, even identify with it, or
not"(1996a: 123–24). In his aptly named *The Return of the Real*, Foster discusses at greater length these issues and the rebirth of the author, after
thirty years, to a position of authority.

As critical movements based in feminist and ethnic perspectives were
discovering an enormous range of writing that deserved attention because
of its subtlety and complexity, as well as its vitality and power of human interest, it began to seem that the criteria of literary and social history had
functioned to suppress such writing, and that the most useful criteria for
suppression were historical specificity and moral interestedness. The conviction that "any poetry which is merely political—and nothing else—is

shallow poetry" (Ostriker 213) begs the critical question: what constitutes the "something else" that marks the difference? An inability or unwillingness to recognize and appreciate the context of a cultural creation, dependent on an authentic collective life and on the vitality of an organic social group, leads Bloom inevitably to visions of doom:

> We are destroying all intellectual and esthetic standards in the humanities and social sciences, in the name of social justice. . . . Expanding the Canon, as I have said more than once in this book, tends to drive out the better writers, sometimes even the best. . . . Nearly everything that has been revived or discovered by feminist and African-American literary scholars falls all too precisely into the category of 'period pieces,' as imaginatively dated now as they were already enfeebled when they first came into existence. (1995: 519–26)

In the 1990s pressure to connect literature with a positivist sense of history had increased, even to the point where Cary Nelson felt the necessity for a timely warning, that "the last thing a politically committed criticism needs to do—perhaps the major temptation it should avoid as we near the end of this relativistic century—is to reassert a stable, positivistic sense of the availability of historical facticity and adjudicable literary meaning" (13). Fredric Jameson too, even while diagnosing the autonomy of art as a pathological symptom, warns his readers "that there is something quite naïve, in a sense quite profoundly *un*realistic, and in the full sense of the word ideological, about the notion that reality is out there simply, quite objective and independent of us, and that knowing it involves the relatively unproblematical process of getting an adequate picture of it into our own heads" (1998b: 121).

Significant changes in theoretical postures were also making their presence strongly felt. When Robert von Hallberg edited a special edition of *Critical Inquiry* devoted to "politics and poetic value," he sought to illustrate "the current trend toward political interpretation" by assembling "a collection of practical essays without any purely theoretical pieces" (1,5). But the results showed the impossibility of a complete separation of the "practical" from the theoretical, and it is understandably difficult to dissociate an emerging poetic and critical desire for "the real" from its theoretical context. The 1960s and 1970s had seen theoretical attacks mounted from several quarters on "naïve" theories of reference, on the "transparency" of language and on historicism in its unreflective modes. Foucault was one of the most vigorous and notorious of those who argued that all access to reality is mediated by language, and that history can better be understood as composed of texts than events. For Foucault, structuralism formed a "systematic effort to evacuate the concept of the event, not only from ethnology but from a whole series of other sciences and in the extreme case from history." The opposition between event and structure defines the event as "what always escapes our rational grasp, the domain of 'absolute contingency'; we are thinkers who analyze structures, history is no concern of ours, what could we be expected to say about it?" (1980: 114). Although nowhere near as dominant as its opponents maintained, poststructuralism in its various forms gathered a considerable following among literary critics who came to regard the distinction between an "objective" knowledge of history and the subjective mode of literature as untenable, because historical accounts of events, structured in language by the same devices as literary texts, share the same unreliability of linguistic mediation. With some understandable exaggeration, Perloff called this an "official academic dogma," for which "what counts as a fact is determined not by its existence in the world but by the discursive practices that make it possible for something in the world to serve as a fact within a certain discourse" (1993: 122). The result was a widespread misperception that an emphasis on the linguistic devices used to produce meaning, and on the difficulty of establishing a stable meaning for any text, can only lead to the unreal and unacceptable notion that language and literature cannot "refer" to anything at all, leaving all texts cut off from historical reality. Ignoring the meaning and point of the positions they condemned, hordes of "realists" rushed in like Samuel Johnson to kick the rock, and thereby offer themselves as witness to a reality that can be witnessed by textual means.

A number of questions should give us pause to reflect on the emergence of such an aggressive desire for the real, with often more weight given to assertion than to argument and demonstration.[9] Can the desire of critics or poets *make* the practice of lyric poetry change from its ahistorical paradigm and aesthetic? Should we emulate the Russian practice of socialist realism under Stalin? Must we throw out the whole lot of canonical lyrics that do not serve the function of historical witness, or contrive ever more clever critical ways of "historicizing" them to produce new readings replete with historical significance? If we replace our ahistorical canonical poems with historical ones, will we be gaining greater access to historical knowledge? Will we not in fact always be verifying the historical dimension of the poem by referring to more reliable historical sources? Is there anything in the potential nature of poetry—however defined—that makes it especially qualified to serve a historical function? If we want to know what really happened, would we ever select a poem as our "witness" unless there is no prose narrative account? If we want to know what really happened in the bombing of Hiroshima, will we turn to Jiro Nakano's tanka anthology, *Out-*

cry from the Inferno? ("One reads it with amazement," exclaims Weinberger. "Did not one of these poets feel that the tanka's five lines and counted syllables were somehow inadequate to their experience?"), or to the *Atomic Ghost* collection edited by John Bradley, or to Tony Harrison's *The Shadow of Hiroshima*, or to the notebooks of Araki Yasusada? Or will we not rather turn to books like William Schull's *Effects of Atomic Radiation*, or Kensaburo Oe's *Hiroshima Notes*, or Michael Hogan's *Hiroshima in History and Memory*?[10]

Do the special skills involved in writing "good" poetry, combined with the necessary reading skills, have anything to add by way of witness to narrative accounts, photography, film, and video? Forché and Lawrence Langer (and every other anthologist I've read) claim that a primary concern in their selections was literary quality. Thus Langer insists: "My main principles of selection are the artistic quality, intellectual rigor, and physical integrity of the texts" (1993: 8). We might well wonder how such "quality" can exist apart from some system of qualities and values, but this does not bother a critic like Bloom, for whom "The only pragmatic aesthetic" is that "some poems intrinsically are better than others" (1998: 24). Since Langer, Felman, and Forché do not define what they mean by quality, we must assume that they too resort to some sense of intrinsic poetic value, and we are back to an Arnoldian aesthetic circle where those in positions of intellectual power determine what is "the best that is known and thought in the world" and reject anything that is different (Arnold 256). Does this "quality" make the poems function better as witness? If not, is witness a surplus added on to literature; or is the literary/poetic added on to witness? Is poetry serving witness, or is witness serving poetry? If what is added is the aesthetic dimension, do we not begin to feel uneasy as witness moves inevitably towards its subject-matter of human inequity and horror? Are readers to become consumers and arbiters of "witness," voyeurs of aestheticized events? If it is embarrassing to take one's aesthetic pleasure in the contemplation of an innocent person's suffering, how much more so in a poem dealing with genocide? For art critic John Berger, to confront the misery conveyed by the drawings and paintings of *hibakusha* (atomic bomb survivors) published in *Unforgettable Fire*, is to suspend his aesthetic professionalism: "Clearly, my interest in these pictures cannot be an art-critical one. One does not musically analyse screams. . . . These were images of hell."

Adorno denounced the act of writing poetry after Auschwitz as barbaric, and some early readers of Paul Celan were disturbed at finding in his work "Auschwitz as soil for art, the victim's death-cry in perfectly harmonized verse," objecting that the poet took "far too much pleasure in art, in despair turned 'beautiful' through art."[11] Understandable as such reactions are, they miss the point that one of Celan's obsessive concerns is precisely the human ability to juxtapose atrocity and aesthetics. The "pleasure" such readers object to is their own, for to take pleasure in a poem like "Todesfuge" is to risk becoming like the camp commandant who orders the inmates to play for his pleasure, and then to blame Celan, whose response to Adorno and similar critics was, "[W]e finally know where the barbarians are to be found" (Felstiner 225).

An equally disturbing possibility we must contemplate in dealing with this topic is that we may be experiencing the intellectual equivalent of a consumer desire for change at the level of style or fashion, along with the desire to have poetry seem more important, more real, than has been the case.[12] I find the kind of rhetoric that graced the editorial pages of a journal like *apex of the M* in the mid-1990s more disturbingly authoritarian, with its abundance of "musts" and "shoulds," dismissing "theories of language purchased at the expense of an originary, immediate, and therefore revolutionary use of words," because "We are interested in a radical transparency of language that maintains particular ties with mimesis and narrative."[13] "Poetics should be less concerned with the free-play of the signifier and the reading subject than with the possibilities of justice for and vindication of the subjected," we are told. "The language of poetry must put into focus a role for the human in the deliverance of victims" and "language must ultimately yield to the dangerous life-force in memory and hope." Most disturbing of all (or should we simply be amused?) is when the death trope is invoked: "The dominant poetries of our time are in no way as threatening, or as excessive, as language should be. At no moment in recent history has poetry so clearly suffered for the refusal of those who partake of it to sacrifice their lives." There was a grim period during the "confessional poetry" era, where it seemed that a serious suicide attempt was necessary to authenticate a poetics of personal angst. Now, it would seem, the only good poet is a dead poet, provided the death was a sacrifice made for the sake of poetry. Perhaps the "M" in the journal title stood for "martyr," a word that originally meant "witness," in the sense that the death of the martyr gave witness of a willingness to die for the faith.

I. The Horror, The Horror!

> Who, after all, speaks today of the annihilation of the Armenians?
> —Adolf Hitler, 1939

When Robert Pinsky claims that witness "involves the challenge of not flinching from the evidence" and that "society depends on the poet to witness something," it turns out that what he means is the banal paradox that "real works revise the received idea of what poetry is" and succeed in being poetry by not being *poetic* (11, 12). In order to avoid this trivializing use of "witness" as just another way to repeat familiar platitudes about poetry, I propose now to take a closer look at the works by Felman, Forché, and Langer already mentioned, in order to give serious consideration to the possibility that the subgenre of witness poetry may be most meaningfully identified as poetry concerned with a specific kind of subject matter and a definable range of strategies and tropes.[14] If we want to find some function for a poetry of witness, where poetry is not handicapped by its limited ability to represent historical events and provide information, it makes sense to follow Forché's focus on what she calls "situations of extremity," in particular to those situations whose horror exceeds the ability of any form of language or any genre to describe or communicate adequately. In such cases the subject matter is not identical with a specific historical event; it is rather an idea of the event, and an idea that evokes the magnitude of the event precisely through an inability to encompass it fully. In this case, the limitations of lyric poetry as history or description lead to a failure that can succeed, by showing that the enormity of its referent exceeds its grasp.

It can also succeed by being *pathetic*, in the original sense of inducing an emotion and state of discomfort or suffering. A common notion of witness poetry is that it is pathological, or "disordered in behavior," thereby inducing a state of pathos in the reader. Even so, shifting from communicating information to producing affect does not allow for adequacy of expression in the usual sense. Any affect produced in the reader, however great, will always be inadequate compared to that of the original witness, whose affect will in turn be inadequate to the full horror of the event. Thus Weinberger's complaint that in Nakano's *Outcry from the Inferno* the tanka's five lines and counted syllables were "inadequate to their experience" misses the point. That small volume exploits a strategy that suggests by its starkly minimalist form the fragmentary inadequacy of *any* act of witness. No human writing can compete with the inscription of a bomb that wrote its own poetry of horror on human flesh and in the genetic text of its "survivors."[15]

I still hear their voices
crying in agony—
scorched bodies
clinging to the iron wires
of the burnt prison. (Chie Setoguchi)

The large skull
is the teacher's.
Gathered
around it,
smaller skulls. (Fumiko Shòji)

The nearly anonymous individual *hibakusha* who wrote these tanka have joined the dead victims, evaporated into language, but not without conjuring up the countless others who are also absent. Their simultaneous presence and absence, in inconceivable numbers, produces the effect of the Hiroshima holocaust as an enormous and unrepresentable event.

Although the term "holocaust" is capable of extended application, there is a universal tendency to identify "holocaust literature" with the specific events of the Nazi genocide, which then comes to be called "the Holocaust."[16] In my discussion of the three works at hand, I use the term "holocaust literature" in a general sense, suggesting mass destruction of human life by human agency, even though Felman and Langer invoke "*the* Holocaust" in its limited specific sense, to refer to the Nazi genocide directed against the Jews.[17] Forché tries to avoid the narrowing tendency by using a more general term "poetry of extremity" and opening her collection to a whole century, but this cosmopolitan gesture of inclusion produces the opposite effect when we perceive the provincial narrowness of her range of references. All three authors are involved not so much with a particular group of artifacts and texts, or with the establishing of historical facts, as with an ongoing discourse, a loose, evolving system of arguments and selective examples and readings that is rapidly becoming institutionalized under the name of "poetry of witness." As the legal concept of witness is inextricably linked to the formally established legal processes designed to determine rules of evidence and determinations of fact, so the literary discourse of witness has evolved its own procedures and rules of evidence, with critics functioning as judges who instruct the reader-jurors in the proper performance of their duties as witnesses of witnesses. Felman, Forché, and Langer have assembled what can be identified as the rudiments of a poetics of witness, while hinting at an aesthetics of witness, and conspicuously deploying a rhetoric of witness that is appropriately unacknowledged, since rhetoric is an art that hides its artfulness. All three make bold claims for newness, but most of what they contribute to a discourse on witness is quite old, already an explicit part of Classic, Romantic, and Judeo-Christian practice.

All three authors base their poetics of witness on a notion of subject matter and on a moral identification with the victims of mass destruction. As Forché shows, the subject matter does not have to be specific; but it does have to be *extreme*. If we identified a category of "nature poetry" dependent on its subject matter, we would know that the nature in question was more than the sum of an assortment of natural objects, that it depended on a shared concept of nature and the natural. In the case of trauma witness poetry, crucial parts of the concept are that the suffering be on a very large scale, that it be human-inflicted, and that the victims be considered innocent. This means for example that AIDS poetry does not find a place in Forché's collection, and that the Irish Potato Famine, if considered as a "natural" event, does not qualify. All three authors agree that in selecting examples of witness, distinctions of quality can be made, and that it is important to do so.

The criteria of documentary veracity and personal experience mean that a great many witness texts will be accessible to the Anglo-American reader only in translation, which greatly attenuates precisely those refinements of language, style, and structure typical of lyric poetry at its highest development. Ordinarily we feel that more is lost reading poetry in translation than reading a novel or work of informational prose. It is difficult when interpreting a translation to make meaningful comments about stylistic detail, but that transitory aesthetic part is the least important for the function of witness, so that the fact of translation makes it all the more plausible to speak of poetry as if it were entirely a matter of theme and content, information securely contained in the poem and not affected by the language in which it is conveyed. Also the reduction of aesthetic pleasure reduces the level of guilt we might experience, or blame we might address to the poet, and some of the stylistic features that are most easily captured in translation are ones that work well with features privileged in the witness mode: direct address, direct statement, narrative, parataxis, names, lists.

Dana Gioia claims that the translation boom in the last twenty-five years has made little or no effort to reproduce the prosodic features of their originals, thus tending to produce work that is formally vague and colorless, so that

> One can now read most of Dante or Villon, Rilke or Mandelstam, Lorca or even Petrarch in English without any sense of the poem's original form. Sometimes these versions brilliantly convey the theme or tone of the originals, but more often they sound stylistically impoverished and anonymous. All of the past blurs together into a familiar tune. Unrhymed, unmetered, and unshaped, Petrarch and Rilke sound misleadingly alike. (38)

In the case of witness poetry, translation into an already available and homogenizing style helps to create the effect of an identifiable body of work, and gives no sense of how formal effects may have been integral to the originals. The Yasusada hoax was possible in part because the fictive witness had supposedly been influenced by Jack Spicer and Roland Barthes in the 1960s. This nicely anticipates the question of how he comes to sound like them, and how his project to be called *After Spicer* sounds so much like Spicer's letters and "translations" in his *After Lorca*. But the work is also "pre-translated," replete with bits of translationese that give it the familiar quality of the witness subgenre. As with the translations of many other poets of witness, Yasusada's work was accompanied by a brief survivor biography, recounting the catastrophic destruction of his family and his own deferred death from radioactivity-induced cancer.

Another effect of the free verse homogenization is that with some notable exceptions witness poetry tends to be very easy to read. Its subject matter may be unfathomable, but its style and formal features and diction are not. Lawrence Venuti has coined the phrase "fluent strategies" to describe the pervasive tendency of translations in the English-speaking world. These strategies include the preference for linear syntax, univocal meaning, current usage, and a tendency to shun unidiomatic constructions, polysemy, archaism, or any effect that draws attention to the materiality of language. Fluent strategies ultimately obliterate the linguistic and cultural otherness of the source text, making it intelligible and already familiar to the target-language reader. Another consequence of "fluent strategies" of translation is that the translation becomes transparent and the translator invisible, with no indications of the extent of transformation required to render what can be radically dissimilar lexical, syntactic, and phonological structures. It is as if there were no significant difficulties in translating from one language into another, in spite of the fact that there are almost insurmountable difficulties when the text to be translated is a densely crafted lyric poem.

A quick look at a passage from Miklós Radnóti's "Hetedik Ecloga" ("Seventh Eclogue") can help make these generalizations more concrete. Gyula Kodolányi notes that Radnóti, who is "perhaps the most widely translated Hungarian poet in English-speaking countries," brought a contemporary edge to the deployment of classical Greek meters in his work, exploiting the flexible syntactic structures and variety of short and long sounds in Hungarian to give lines in those meters an unconstrained quality (718). The "Seventh Eclogue" is a poem written in "Lager Heidenau, above Zagubica in the mountains, July 1944." Addressed to his wife, it was one of the poems in a notebook found in a coat pocket by her when his body was exhumed from a mass grave in 1946. Forché includes a translation of the poem by Emery George, which begins:

> Look how evening descends and around us the barbed-
>   wire-hemmed wild
> oaken fence and the barracks are weightless, as evening
>   absorbs them

As the darkness settles in, difficulty and uncertainty mount for the poet:

> Oh, does that home still exist, now?
> Still untouched by bombs? as it stood, back when we re-
>   ported?

And will the men who now groan on my right, lie left,
  make it home yet?
Is there a home, where people can savor haxameter [*sic*]
  language?

No diacritics. Just one line under another line: groping,
barely, as I am alive, I write my poem in half-dark,
blindly, in earthworm-rhythm, I'm inching along on the
  paper.
Flashlights, books: the guards of the *Lager* took every
  thing from us,
nor does the mail ever come. Only fog settles over the
  barracks.

Another version, by Clayton Eshleman with the help of Gyula Kodolányi,
begins like this:

Do you see? Evening falls, fringed with barbed-wire
the hacked-out oak fence and barracks waver, sucked up
  by dusk.

and continues through the same lines:

                    O *is* our home still there?
Maybe no bomb touched it? Might it *be*, as when we were
  drafted?
The one groaning on my right, the one sprawling on my
  left, will they return home?
Tell me, *is* there still a homeland where this hexameter
  will be understood?

Without accent marks, feeling out line after line,
here, in the dusk, I write this poem just as I live,
blindly, a caterpillar inching my way on the paper.
Flashlight, book, everything taken away by the Lager
  guards,
and there's no mail—only fog settles on our barracks.

The poem in Hungarian is written in hexameters, which are relatively easy
to write in that language but still represent a deliberate emphasis on aesthetic and historical formalism, as does the name "eclogue" (from *eklegein*,

"to choose," hence a poem in a collection, "a choice poem") which was first applied to Vergil's bucolics. The name suggests a pastoral dialogue or soliloquy, with the setting described in some detail, written in highly finished verse, smooth and melodious. Thus the title and form play a crucial ironic function in the poem and make the hexameter reference in line 13 particularly difficult to communicate in modern free verse, where the translation itself may provide a negative answer, even if it manages to spell "hexameter" correctly. This is clearly the line that puts most pressure on the translator, and the one that challenges the reader who is reading the poem in a place that may or may not be a home (*haza*) where the hexameter may or may not be understood:

> Mondd, van-e ott haza még, ahol értik e hexametert is?
>
> — ‿ ‿ — ‿ ‿ — ‿ ‿ — ‿ ‿ — ‿ ‿ — ‿
>
> Mondd, van-e | ott haza | még ahol | értik e | hexamet | ert is?
> [Tell me! is there home still where ⌠they would⌡ hexameter also
> ⌊understand⌋

George does work hard to approximate the effect of hexameter verse in English, without falling into caricature:

> — ‿ ‿ — — — ‿ ‿ — ‿ ‿ — ‿ ‿ — —
>
> Is there a | home, where | people can | savor hax | ameter | language?

But there is hardly any effect of formal verse in the English, and he must stoop low ("nor does the mail ever come"; "lie left") to do his duty. It might work better here to translate into the iambic pentameter of blank verse, in order to produce a verse effect in English comparable to that of the hexameter in Hungarian. The Eshleman/Kodolànyi translation makes no effort to produce formal verse, so that their version with its deictic emphasis ("Tell me, *is* there still a homeland where this hexameter will be understood?") verges on absurdity.

A translation by Steven Polgar, Stephen Berg, and S. J. Marks does achieve absurdity with the deployment of "this": "Tell me, is there still a home where they understand all this?", followed by the even more absurd translation of line 14 ("Without commas, one line touching the other,"), where the commas that the poem says it is "without" are inserted to contradict the explicit statement of the poem. I have not seen the original manuscript, but it would seem obvious that the point here is that the poet, writing in the dark, cannot see well enough to place the usual diacritics in his text. Their absence thus becomes a meaningful sign, as is the presence of the hexameter form. It may be plausible to substitute "without commas" for "diacritics," since English has them; but then to put in the commas is as strange as to say the poem is in hexameters when it isn't.[18] On December 21, 1957, Nelly Sachs wrote to Paul Celan, saying that his reading and understanding of her poetry gave her the sense that "I have a homeland" (Celan and Sachs 10). Without a comparable sense of the urgent investment in form, the labor of writing, Radnóti's poem will not find a comparable homeland, whatever the language it finds itself in.

Like most critics of witness poetry, Felman and Forché and Langer assume as given, without any need for argument, a firm connection between literary text and historical reality. Thus for Langer the artist's task is "the problem of converting the murder of European Jewry into poetic vision" (553). For Forché, "the poem might be our only evidence that an event has occurred" (31). When Nazim Hikmet writes in a poem that "the water jug no longer freezes," she claims: "Of course, the fact that the jug freezes indicates just how cold the cell is" (34). Felman claims repeatedly to find in literary texts "an encounter with the real," and can find it even in Camus' allegorical novel *The Plague*, thanks to a "new, transformational relationship between narrative and history" (95), through which "the literary testimony of *The Plague* offers its historical eyewitnessing in the flesh" (109). All three share the problem of defining the essential criteria for an authentic witness, and share some equivocation about these criteria in actual practice. Forché's poets "must have personally endured such conditions" of extremity (30), and she includes biographical notes to establish each poet's credentials and right to witness. Felman maintains that the task of witness is to impart "a firsthand, carnal knowledge of victimization," (111) but finds ways to bring Mallarmé into play as an example of "precocious testimony" (21). For Langer, the ties joining poets to the Nazi genocide experience vary, and he includes biographical notes to establish the links for each one. Obviously, "closeness" is a strong factor, but it can be difficult to spell out with precision. In spite of her explicit criteria, Forché acknowledges that "I was hard pressed to find a significant poet who could not be included, who in some important way or another did not bear witness to the ravages of our time." After reviewing the wide variety of cases that seem to fit her specifications, Clayton Eshleman exclaims, "How much terror must I experience to justify my speaking for someone who is in agony or who has died from torture?" (225).

II. I Wrote the Hole Thing

[A] bullet hole is a sign that a gun was fired. As an index, the sign is not determined by the interpretation; it is determined historically, by the event that produced it.

—Charles Sanders Peirce

The theoretical foundation implicit in most of these considerations is a semiotic one, the assumption that a poem can be read as an instance of what C.S. Peirce identified as the indexical sign, defined as "a real thing or fact which is a sign of its object by virtue of being connected with it as a matter of fact" (2: 359). Such signs have the strongest "motivation" possible, since they establish a direct physical link between the sign and its signified. This makes indexical signs crucial in medical diagnoses (symptoms of disease), and in criminal trials, where the referent of narrative accounts is crucial, and competing narrative discourses try to establish what "really happened" by means of evidence in the form of indexical signs (fingerprint, footprint, DNA, retina and iris scans, voice prints, etc.) of the actual presence of the person in question. In law there are elaborate procedures for establishing the admissibility of evidence, and rules governing the construction of stories that can be presented to juries.[19] One of the reasons photography can communicate the effect of witness so powerfully is its aura of ontological authenticity, and our willingness to take the photograph as more than a representation, as an actual trace of the experienced world. Peirce was one of the first to make this point, claiming that "they belong to the second class of signs, those by physical connection" (2: 281). For Susan Sontag, "A photograph is not only an image (as a painting is an image), an interpretation of the real; it is also . . . something directly stenciled off the real, like a footprint or a death mask" (154), and for Roland Barthes photography is a medium in which "the referent adheres" to the image, producing the effect of a place in which "I can never deny that the thing has been there" (1981: 76). When critics speak of the poem of witness, we often find the same claim, as when Forché reads "poem as trace, poem as evidence" written by poets who "have themselves been marked" by "the impress of extremity upon the poetic imagination." Thus "These poems bear the trace of extremity within them, and they are, as such, evidence of what occurred." But the statement that a poem "is itself evidence of the experience it describes" would be absurd if applied to all poetry, so we have here another indication of something special about the subject matter of the poetry of witness (31, 32, 33). "Holocaust poetry, because it emerges from an experience so contaminated itself, exerts a special pressure on the poet's imagination" (Langer 558). In what amounts to a reversal of the ordinary dynamic of witnessing, the incontrovertible reality of the Nazi genocide as referent confers credibility on the poem if we choose to read it as a poem of witness. But in order to be sure that we have a poem of witness in this sense, we must have an authentic poet of witness, and we are back to the biographical and contextual materials needed to establish that fact, and the poet's identity or biography are of equal or greater importance than the poem.[20]

The only way there can be an indexical effect in writing is if it is on the material writing itself, or the materials of writing—shaky letters indexing the movement of a carriage, bloody pages a nosebleed—but even these effects can be faked. Once a text is set in print, as I showed with Radnóti's "Eclogue," they tend to disappear altogether, becoming indistinguishable from the verbal artistry of the poet, or an effect of that artistry. In Book IV of his *Aeneid*, when Vergil wanted to show how really upset and deranged Dido was, he wrote:

> Litora litoribus contraria, fluctibus undas
> imprecor, arma armis: pugnent ipsique nepotesque.
> [May shore with shore clash, I pray, waters with waters, arms with arms; may they have war, they and their children's children.] (628–29)

Here the last syllable is extra-metrical, showing that Dido's curse "runs over," reflecting her mental agitation. Almost two millennia later, Helen Vendler's fascination with such effects in her *The Breaking of Style,* and Spielberg's insistence while shooting *Schindler's List* on using a very crude technical manner in order to create the effect of mistakes and imperfections, show the same technique still at work. It would seem that only a willful blindness to how poetry and language work could lead so many critics to make so many claims for traumatic traces in the poems they discuss. Lea Fridman offers a particularly extreme example when she invokes Peirce's famous example of the bullet hole as an indexical sign that a gun was fired (a sign therefore determined historically by the event that produced it), then goes on to claim for literary texts an "unrepresentability" that is "not rhetorical but substantive," that is an "absence" that is "outside the play of symbolic form."

> To be touched by such an absence or silence is to experience a hole in the fabric of language, a hole and not a symbol of a hole, a hole that is the effect of extreme traumatic experience, even if not the experience itself. . . . The "hole in the fabric of language" . . . is a sign of historical trauma in a manner that is different from the way that an image or word is a sign or substitution for its referent. Traumatic narratives are structurally dissimilar from narrative as we conventionally understand it because such narratives have an existential and indexical, instead of merely a "representational," relationship to their subject. The hole to which I refer, the breakdown of the very

possibility of symbol-making, is the consequence of the experience of historical trauma and horror irrespective of, and prior to any and all interpretation. . . . For the purposes of criticism, we might indeed say that a work . . . is aesthetically successful to the extent that it is able to give visibility and "referential force" to the "hole" of unrepresentability. (131–33)

I quote Fridman at length here because she makes so egregiously explicit the kind of thought process and rhetorical practice that can't tell a hole from a "hole." When a bullet hole is *there*, it is also something that is *not there*, a vacancy created by the passage of a bullet that *was there*. We might say of Fridman's "hole in the fabric of language," that there is no *there* there. "—As for me, I had at first imagined that cinders were there, not here but there, as a story to be told. . . . One might dream that the word 'cinder' was itself a cinder in that sense, 'there,' 'over there' [*là, là-bas*], in the distant past, a lost memory of what is no longer here . . . the cinder is no longer here. Was [*fut*] it ever?" (Derrida 1991: 31).

Poets who strive to bear witness are often more aware of these problems than the critics who scan them primarily for their content as testimony. Poets can use a wide array of techniques to create the effect of first hand experience as the ground of their textual production; or they can more openly acknowledge the impossibility of authenticating authorial subjectivity within the poetic text itself. When poets do make such acknowledgment, their efforts are often ignored in the kinds of readings we find in even the best critics of witness poetry. As an example, Langer's commentary on Abraham Sutzkever's poem "Burnt Pearls," written in 1943 in the Vilna Ghetto, shows that much of what he seems to be finding in the poem is what he has brought to it. Here is the text of the poem as translated by Seymour Mayne:

> It is not just because my words quiver
> like broken hands grasping for aid,
> or that they sharpen themselves
> like teeth on the prowl in darkness,
> that you, written word, substitute for my world,
> flare up the coals of my anger.
>
> It is because your sounds
> glint like burnt pearls
> discovered in an extinguished pyre
> And no one—not even I—shredded by time
> can recognize the woman drenched in flame

for all that remains of her now
are these grey pearls
smouldering in the ash—

                Vilna Ghetto, July 28, 1943

According to Langer, the poet "has left us a powerfully concentrated illustration of the tentative relationship between culture and genocide during
the period—but it has nothing to do with resistance" (1995a: 62). He finds
in it "confrontation driven by an inviolable spirit of authenticity. The broken hands, the sharp teeth, the darkness and anger, the pyre, the flame, the
ash, the time-shredded poet himself, and the indistinguishable corpse of
the victim, violated by fire—these are the timeless emblems of Holocaust,
and language cannot undo the vehemence of their cruelty." The poem is
"art of the highest order" and it "reflects the power of word and image to
immortalize anguish: not to celebrate the victim's transfiguration into a
glorious example of spiritual defiance, but to mourn verbally her disfigura-
tion, her disintegration, her change from flesh into ash. Culture here is not
a collection of shining white pearls dazzling the future with mementos of
heroic endurance, but mere burnt grey ones, of precious if diminished
value, testimony to an irretrievable loss, imperishable substitutes—but
only that—for a world that is no more. If meaning is to be found in such
loss, it must be searched for in the tentative bond linking the burnt-pearl
remnants of the victim's death with the vital, glinting memories inspired by
Sutzkever's words" (62–63).

Langer's response is a remarkable flight of rhetoric that takes off in two
distinct directions. On the one hand, he finds in "broken hands . . . sharp
teeth . . . darkness . . . anger . . . pyre . . . flame . . . ash . . . corpse of the victim" what he calls "timeless emblems of Holocaust." He does not take note
of the poem's conspicuous figuration, in which the "broken hands" are a
trope for the poet's words ("my words like broken hands . . . like teeth"),
and the "written word" is a "substitute for my world." It is the *sounds* of
these words the poet says that glint "like burnt pearls/discovered in an extinguished pyre," and it seems clear that one of the insistent emphases of the
poem is on its existence in written language, made even more emphatic by
Sutzkever's taking the title of this poem as the title for his whole volume, for
which it functions as a *poetics*. Although he writes of the poet's words,
Langer does not take note of the fact that the whole poem is so emphatically
concerned with his *words*, as all that the poet has to work with. The "timeless emblems" that Langer finds are ones that the critic has brought with
him, not ones that Sutzkever could have known in 1943 as he struggled for
survival in Vilna. The point can be made by comparing Langer's list of
"timeless emblems" with a passage from Ron Sukenick's novel *Up* (1968):

> Screen fade skeletal barbed wire corpses hand impaled
> on electric fence stiffen naked in snow robbed of canvas
> inmate pajamas lie denuded in charnel stockpiles (147)

Sukenick's carefully composed collage of impressions here is not the stream of consciousness of an individual psyche but rather a global barrage of images which resist the ordering of syntax and grammar that could bring them into articulate form.[21] Meditating on the possible origins of Celan's "Todesfuge," Felstiner writes, "Its true origin, the only one we really need to know, we know already: 'l'univers concentrationnaire,' Nazism's 'concentrationary universe' " (27). Sukenick's images penetrate and surround the reader until s/he feels linguistically imprisoned in the same way, in a paratactic universe of horrible images that will never reach a period.

Langer's reading also moves towards a specificity of reference, by reacting to "broken hands" as actual hands rather than as a simile for words that "quiver/like broken hands." Certainly it is a calculated effect of the poem, to evoke images of a fragmented and destroyed body; but Sutzkever is emphasizing that he must do this in spite of the absence of any material evidence of any kind. The violated body that could provide the evidentiary basis for a witness of truth and testimonial against agents of atrocity is absent. The burnt pearls that Langer says are "imperishable substitutes" for "shining white pearls" are an implicit trope for the teeth of a cremated corpse, but explicitly a trope for the sounds of the poet's words—words that "sharpen themselves/like teeth." The point is not that the burnt pearls are substitutes for shining ones, but that the "written word" is a substitute/trace for the "burnt pearls" that are a trace of the "woman drenched in flame." Whatever the "glinting memories inspired by Sutzkever's words," they cannot be memories of this individual woman, because she has no identity. Thus the "bond linking the burnt-pearl remnants with . . . glinting memories" is the linguistic link between the poet's words as signifiers and a signified that has been utterly lost, for "no one—not even I—shredded by time/can recognize" her now. Derrida's meditation in *Cinders* is again relevant: "I have the impression now that the best paradigm for the trace [is] the cinder (what remains without remaining from the holocaust, from the all-burning, from the incineration the incense). . . . In writing this way, he burns one more time, he burns what he still adores although he has already burned it, he is intent on it" (43).

On a more personal level we can see that Langer's reaction to the poem is guided by his own passionately austere and powerfully articulated opinion on what we can learn from poems like these. For him, "the challenge of this literature is to discover and *accept* the twisted features of the unfamiliar without searching for words, like 'suffering,' to shape what we see into more congenial façades" (6). He is severe with those who "feed deep and obscure needs in themselves having little to do with the truth" by converting atrocity into some form of hope or triumph, and chooses instead a form of existential estrangement that resists the "comforting notion that suffering has meaning" (5). He is also convinced that "Incidents of resistance and uprising, courageous as they undeniably were, existed within a larger framework of loss" (6), and that acts of resistance were counterproductive. Thus the possibility that this poem, with its words sharpening themselves like teeth, its words that flare up the smouldering coals of the poet's anger, could lead to action or resistance, must be resisted. For Langer the poem "has nothing to do with resistance . . . it does not 'resist' genocide; it is born of it." Instead of inspiring resistance or anger or revenge in the reader, its function is "to immortalize anguish" and "to mourn verbally" what must be accepted as "an irretrievable loss." It should be possible to respect and share Langer's convictions in these matters and still see that they predetermine what he considers acceptable as authentic witness and lead him to a narrow and superficial reading of the poem.

Given their desire for the intensity of the witness poem as indexical sign, it is not surprising that all three critics under consideration here are constantly engaged with formalist concerns—so much so that the form of the poem is the most frequently invoked authenticating trope. For Langer, "the problem of converting the murder of European Jewry into poetic vision . . . means nothing less than finding a form for chaos by including chaos as part of the form" (553). For Forché, "Extremity, as we have seen, demands new forms or alters older modes of poetic thought. It also breaks forms and creates forms from those breaks. . . . [This] might well be the feature that binds this anthology together" (42). The implicit connection is that the *form* of the poem is an indexical sign of the poet's mental state, and the "broken" state of the poet's mind is a sign of real "conditions of extremity," responding to a force outside itself. "The narrative of trauma is itself traumatized, and bears witness to extremity by its inability to articulate directly or completely" (Forché 42). This is the mimetic convention that led the novelist Richardson to print Clarissa's "mad letters" in crooked fragments on the page, imitating the torn fragments of the letters she wrote, expressing her inner state.[22] Again, we are returned to the need for external evidence to establish the fact that disruptions of form are related to specific experiences—unless, like Felman, we can construe Mallarmé's "crisis of verse" as an *a priori* concrete and specific expression of "Celan's particular historical reality and his literally shattering experience as a Holocaust survivor. *The breakage of the verse enacts the breakage of the world*" (Felman 25). Vendler has written a whole book, *The Breaking of Style,* which shows that one can argue allegorically from formal observations to show almost anything. For example, in discussing a Hopkins poem, she suggests that "putting the mimesis psychologically instead of cosmically, one could say that the spondees represent the impressions of a poet who receives the stimuli of daily life as a series of unforeseeable and unsettling assaults. The regular measures of ordinary verse simply did not seem to Hopkins to represent the felt texture of his experience. . . . After the sullen dullness of the English winter, for example, Hopkins reacted with what was almost a pathology of ecstasy to the first bright day" (15). But if feeling good made Hopkins break his style for Vendler, feeling bad made him break it even more: "When the mind becomes one gigantic cacophony of groans, in eight-beat sprung-rhythm lines prolonging themselves into one undifferentiated monosyllabic vocal disharmony, we have come to the last agony of the stylistic body of poetry. Without Hopkins' remaking of the body of style, we would not come to know any of these things with that mimetic accuracy—one not only of visual representation but of structural and rhythmic enactment" (40). Perhaps Hopkins experienced psychic traumas as intense as those of Celan, but they were not caused by Holocaust experience. The fact is that poetic structure as elegantly and precisely constructed as that of Hopkins and Celan is not something that *happens to* the poet, like getting run over by an experience. The "breaking of form" is not evidence of a loss of control, but of an *exercise* of control designed to produce particular effects.

If witness poetry requires an authenticating "breaking of form" to indicate its true status, then we will be reduced to an extremely small body of work. Andrea Reiter notes that only about two per cent of all survivors of the Nazi genocide managed to express themselves in writing, and of those very few did so in verse. She confirms Michael Moll's finding that those few who did write had "a highly traditional form and a content usually concerned with everyday life in the camps" (85). In general, she finds in all forms of written expression a "weak impetus to originality, even among survivors who were accomplished writers. The overwhelming majority of the testimony takes over a structural model without adapting it in any way" (85). James Young, too, has pointed out that "the Holocaust, unlike World War I, has resulted in no new literary forms, no startling artistic breakthroughs; for all intents and purposes, it has been assimilated to many of the modernist innovations already generated by the perceived rupture in culture occasioned by the Great War" (2000: 5). John Treat, Lisa Yoneyama, and Kyo Maclear all emphasize how thoroughly conventional the vast majority of atomic bomb witness literature is in its formal dimension. "Indeed, for many Japanese artists in the immediate post-Occupation period, the choice of realist forms such as memoirs, figural representations, and documentary fiction was strongly influenced by the demand for evidence. . . . Realizing how generally accessible and appealing realist forms can be, many artists and writers continue to mobilize them in hopes of dramatizing the ongoing significance of the atomic bombings within a matrix of present-day political and social concerns" (Maclear 23).

III. The Silence of the Iambs

Mimetic expressivity of form was also a staple of the tradition of the sublime, as formulated by Hegel in his *Lectures on Aesthetics*, in the chapter "The Symbolism of the Sublime." Derrida gives a vivid paraphrase and description of Hegel's main point, that "The content . . . destroys the signifier or the representer. It expresses itself only by marking in its expression the annihilation of expression. It smashes to smithereens . . . the signifier which would presume to measure itself against its infinity. More precisely, form, the act of forming (*Gestalten*), is destroyed through what it expresses, explains, or interprets. That's the sublime. . . . The content operates in it and commands the sublation of form" (1987: 133). In the *Lectures* Hegel is condensing a century's discourse on the operation of the sublime as the representation of the unrepresentable, or the representation that there is *something* that is unrepresentable.[23] Poetry of witness can be understood as a recent reincarnation of the notion of the sublime, a name for the effect produced when the failure of representation is taken as evidence that there is something that exceeds the power of representation.[24] This something is not a physical thing or natural object or phenomenon; it is an idea or mental state that has been produced in the poet by some overwhelming cause. What the witness communicates in the sublime mode is the failure to encompass; as a single individual, the reader can identify with the poetic point of view of the witness, and can also become a witness. Thus witness will always be a witness of its own inevitable failure, and it is that failure to represent—rather than the actual representation of specific events—that produces the witness-effect.

One of the strongest indications of the operation of the sublime in the discourse of witness poetry is the prevalence of exaggerated rhetoric, suggesting an understandable desire of the critics to wrap their own writing in the aura of witness, and to participate actively in the discourse. For Longinus, the citation of a work gives evidence of its impact on the hearer, and that impact confirms the view that the work itself is evidence of a similar sublime impact on the poet. Even critical commentary, as part of the discourse of the sublime, will try to work by expressing the quality it aims to convey and to mimic the action it conveys, being sublime on the sublime, making the criticism itself a passionate event, rather than a calm instance of understanding, evaluation, or interpretation. Here is an example from Felman:

> Celan's verse, 'No one bears witness for the witness,' is in effect so
> charged with absolute responsibility and utter solitude, so burdened
> with the uniqueness of the witnessing, that it becomes itself not a
> simple statement but a speech act which repeats, performs its own
> meaning in resisting our grasp, in resisting our replicating or recu-
> perative witnessing. It thus performs its own solitude: it puts into
> effect what cannot be understood, transmitted, in the mission of
> transmission of the witness. It is the resonances of this bearing, of
> this burden of the performance of the witness, that will become, in
> all the senses of the word, the burden of this book—its leitmotif. . . .
> Celan's verse will indeed itself return through the various chapters
> of the present volume, like a compelling, haunting melody, like a di-
> rected beacon, an insistent driving force in the quest toward some-
> thing which is not entirely within reach. (3)[25]

Felman is so involved here in trying to say that what she's trying to say can't
be said, that she forgets that she is in fact bearing witness for Celan's witness, and that her co-author Dori Laub has declared that "being a witness
to the testimonies of others . . . [and] being a witness to the process of witnessing itself" are "distinct levels of witnessing in relation to the Holocaust
experience" (75). Langer describes a progressive development of affect as
the diligent reader of poems of atrocity gradually "develops a sense of the
idiom required to encompass atrocity and of the struggle to find a verbal
shape and form to mirror the unspeakable. If the results numb more than
they inspire, leave us frozen rather than inflamed with admiration, this
should be no cause for surprise or dismay" (558).

At times the critical rhetoric employed to discuss witness literature is
reminiscent of a slightly earlier period that showed a pervasive tendency to
elevate some form of "madness" to the status of a modernist sublime, seeing in it both a transcendental transgressionism and a "source" that answered a need for cultural and aesthetic renewal. "The self-reflexivity of
language in modern writing is a discovery of a 'madness' in language; by
purifying language of all obedience to 'discourse,' writing articulates the
'mad' source of experience, and so transcends or transgresses its limits"
(Rajchman 44). Michel Pierssens praised those mad writers who exhibit
"logophilia" as "examples of a linguistic, social and historical *practice* capable of undoing codes, redistributing discourse, uprooting structures, subverting the illusions that blind our culture. These writers form the priceless
heritage of an experimentation with language which a writing of the future
could well address as a resource for answering its most pressing questions"
(lx). This period saw the eruption of Deleuze and Guattari's concept of
"schizoanalysis" and their invocation of the schizophrenic as the embodi-

ment of a desire or polymorphous libidinal energy whose fragmentations are perpetually subversive to the codes of capitalism. The schizophrenic desiring machine was said to manifest itself as a force of fragmentation, confronting both a "totalizing" capitalism and the "master discourse" of psychoanalysis. At the same time Roland Barthes was praising the "text of *jouissance*" (also id-driven) as "one that imposes a state of loss, the text that discomforts . . . , unsettles the reader's historical, cultural, psychological assumptions, the consistency of his tastes, values, memories, and brings to a crisis his relation with language" (1975: 14). Foucault had defined madness as if in anticipation of the trauma discourse as a "formless, mute, unsignifying region where language can find its freedom . . . where thought is extinguished, where the promise of origin interminably recedes" (1970: 383). Felman wrote a book in the mid-1980s addressing "the significance of madness as a crucial question in the current cultural scene," critiquing the "inflation" of the currency of madness in "an era pervaded by discourses on madness" (1985: 12). Looking back from even so short a distance, we can see enthusiasm for the topic of madness as the symptom of a cultural predicament or a fashion, the sign of its time. The valorizing of madness as a state of being in which an especially high degree of authenticity inheres anticipated certain features and much of the rhetoric of trauma discourse. Both enthusiasms must face the fact that the essence of an internal state of madness or trauma, unless it is or remains literally silent, must be mediated by language. Any subjective state which is posited as the "origin" or the "cause" of value and meaning is itself known only as an effect of discourse, and therefore, like all other authenticisms (honesty, sincerity, imagination, the unconscious) is subject to appropriation as rhetoric or style in the service of the very forces of cultural repression or manipulation it seems to defy and resist.

Another thing that unites these three approaches to the same topic with many others is that they ignore the fact that authenticity in witness is not a spontaneously produced effect of reading, but is established by elaborate codes or systems that include books like theirs. Even if we agree with Wordsworth, that authentically motivated tropes are the ones "excited by real events" and expressive of "real passion," we must acknowledge with him that it is possible for poets "desirous of producing the same effect, without having the same animating passion," to learn the code and adopt the figures of speech to produce the same effects (1966: 63–64). It is even possible to argue for Diderot's *Paradoxe sur le comédien*, which claims that it is an advantage to be distanced from the emotion to be expressed, because detachment allows the artist to create the emotion from the point of view of the spectator, the one who really matters. Felman's claim that we are living in an "age of testimony" (5) resonates with Foucault's in *History of*

Sexuality, Vol. 1, that ours is an age of "confession," since both witness and confession are culturally agreed on systems for the production of truth. Like the poem of witness, "The confession is a ritual of discourse in which the speaking subject is also the subject of the statement" (61).

For a reader to negotiate an authenticating causal relationship between what Forché calls "the experience of extremity" and a poem of witness, requires recognition of a significant difference between that poem and other poems one may encounter, and a different protocol of reading appropriate to that poem. When Shelley writes, in "Epipsychidion," "I pant, I sink, I tremble, I expire!" we do not read the line as we do the first two lines of Pagis' "Autobiography" in Langer ("I died with the first blow and was buried / among the rocks of the field"), because Langer has provided "a precise Holocaust context" that informs our reading (584). When Shelley writes, in "Ode to the West Wind," "I fall upon the thorns of life! I bleed," we are advised by Donald Reiman that "Behind Shelley's image—besides other literary references—lie Jesus' crown of thorns and Dante's metaphor of life as 'a dark wood . . . rough and stubborn' " (Shelley 223). When we read in Langer the lines: "I undress. / Start dancing, / Dancing, / Dancing, / Till the thorns flower with my blood" from Abraham Sutzkever's poem "Black Thorns," we are inclined to read those metaphoric thorns as growing on a real grave of his dead mother ("On my mother's house / Thorns grow—") because of the context established by Langer and our expectations. When we read in Forché's collection the first two lines of Edith Brück's "Childhood" ("Your milk was already poisoned / by dark foreboding") we can take it as a psychological metaphor, and augment that sense with the information that "Brück spent part of her childhood in a concentration camp, an experience addressed in these poems" (388). Similarly, when we read Celan's famous lines from the "Todesfuge," ("Black milk of daybreak we drink it at sundown. . . ."), we benefit from Felman's guidance on how to connect the "figure" with "the literal concreteness of the death camp blood and ashes . . . the specificity of history—of the concrete historical reality of massacre and race annihilation" (30), as she explains that "The performance of the act of drinking, traditionally a poetic metaphor for yearning, for romantic thirst and for desire, is here transformed into the surprisingly abusive figure of an endless torture and a limitless exposure, a figure for the impotent predicament and the unbearable ordeal of having to endure, absorb, continue to take in with no end and no limit" (30). But when we read in Langer's collection Sutzkever's lines about an infant drinking poisoned milk ("That drop of poison extinguished your faith— / you thought / it was warm sweet milk") we are instructed by Langer to read the lines literally, because his wife "gave birth to a son, but the Germans poisoned the infant; the poem 'For My Child,' . . . alludes to this painful episode" (562). In this way, editors and critics of "Holocaust literature" are trying to make them appear to give the reader an unmediated, personally observed or experienced factual account of events and the effects produced by those events. This is why Weinberger is so upset with the fact that "witness poetry is entirely dependent on biographical background, and is ultra-empirical in a way perhaps unprecedented in literary history" (8). But all poetry is equally dependent on a context of intertextual allusions and a sense of framing discourse that we bring to our reading.

These, then, are some of the staple aspects of the discourse on poetry as witness to tramatic experience. There are other things they share that I find more thought-provoking and disturbing. For critics who are dedicated to preserving the real, to history and memory (both collective and individual), they show a surprising lack of historical perspective and a tendency to make exaggerated claims for the uniqueness of the Nazi genocide. This can lead to limited readings of poems, as when Forché collects four poems by Don Pagis and writes that "These poems bear witness to his camp experience," or when Langer cites Pagis' poem "Written in Pencil in the Sealed Railway-Car" as an example of how "The poet has concentrated into a title and six lines . . . the dilemma of finding a poetic language to speak truly about the destruction of European Jewry" (557):

> here in this carload
> i am eve
> with abel my son
> if you see my other son
> cain son of man
> tell him that i

Langer is taking the deictics of the text ("here"/ "this") in an extremely narrow and literal sense, even though he acknowledges that in other cases Pagis' poetry "resists the temptation of concrete historical or autobiographical allusion" (584). In my reading, the poem is indeed concentrated on the here and now of Jews being transported by rail to the death camps, but it is both specific and universalizing. The imagined speaker is a universal mother, calling out to all men that the "brothers" of humanity are still killing each other, and each reader can find the universal address both personal and intimate.

In words that Felman quotes with approval, Elie Wiesel claimed that "If the Greeks invented tragedy, the Romans the epistle and the Renaissance the sonnet, our generation invented a new literature, that of testimony" (1992: 5–6). But is it in fact the case that the Nazi genocide is "uniquely devastating" as Felman claims (xvii), or that it is only "in the last one hundred years," as Forché believes, "that atrocities have taken place on an unprecedented scale" (32)? Langer sees "the Holocaust" as "the murder of European Jewry" (553), ignoring the fact that the Nazi genocide included multitudes of the "handicapped," and of the so-called "Gypsies" (Roma and Sinti) and homosexuals, as well as the Jews. Forché suggests that "the Holocaust" was directed against the Jewish religion, suggesting a rather limited grasp of Aryan eugenics. Langer claims that without the moral impact of Holocaust literature "history itself . . . would plunge us back into the moral innocence that legend ascribes to the Garden of Eden. Its unsettling contours help us to face the estrangement of the world we live in from the one we long to inhabit—or the one we nostalgically yearn to regain" (7). A different view suggests that, without mitigating in the least the horror and reality of the Nazi atrocity, we should resist elevating it to unique status precisely because that helps us to remain in a false state of "moral innocence" with respect to other atrocities in which we may be implicated. An exclusive focus on "the Holocaust" makes it unique more by the amount of cultural capital invested in it than by its infliction of suffering on innocent victims, and contributes to an implicit system of control of trauma discourse in which "we" are always identified with the innocent victims, empathizing with the horror of their suffering. We thereby create a secure place of innocence to view atrocities from, atrocities that are always acts of an Other, different in essence from ourselves. There is more than a little danger of complacency here, of settling for a surrogate culture of witness in which the representations of atrocities and political struggles in places like Ireland, Spain, South Africa, Eastern Europe, India, Pakistan, Cambodia, Guatemala, Rwanda, or Bosnia provide the primary basis for much of the politically conscious cultural argument widely disseminated in the public sphere. Forché writes that "As North Americans, we have been fortunate: wars for us (provided we are not combatants) are fought elsewhere, in other countries. The cities bombed are other people's cities. The houses destroyed are other people's houses" (32). Forché has to forget one of the bloodiest wars ever (The Civil War) as well as the U.S. destruction of Amerindians, in order to make a statement that is all the more questionable after 9/11. But she also has to ignore the fact that often those bombs dropping on "other people's cities" are our bombs.

Felman claims to be writing a study that "defines at once the common ground between literature and ethics" (xii), and her emphasis on the unspeakable and inarticulate allows her to find even in the "silence" of Paul de Man evidence of the effect of the real, making him like "the survivors of the holocaust themselves, who have continued, willingly or not, to be 'the bearers of the silence,' the very bearers, that is, of the secrecy and the secret of contemporary history," so that the "failed confession" of Albert Camus' *The Fall* "can be read as de Man's unspoken autobiographical story" (xviii–xix). More than half of the Felman/Laub volume is devoted to Felman's discussion of Camus and de Man in the context of literature and ethics. In her de Man chapter, she finds "History as Holocaust is mutely omnipresent in the theoretical endeavor of de Man's mature work" and that "de Man's testimony in his later writings invokes the Holocaust as the very figure of a silence . . . which a certain silent mode of testimony can translate, and thus make us remember" (140, 164). By similar maneuvers, Camus is read as being silent in order "to make, precisely, of the *silence* both of the historian and of history a *sign*" (202). Silence, of course, is the favorite instance of the sublime, when "a naked thought without words challenges admiration, and strikes by its grandeur" (*Longinus* 28–29). Longinus gives the silence of Ajax in the eleventh book of the *Odyssey* as an example; as Samuel Monk observes, it is "an example that is repeated *ad nauseam* in the eighteenth century" (15).[26]

The reader of Homer has a good sense of what Ajax is being silent *about*, without any elaborate explanations; but until Felman identified it as a sign, had the silence of de Man and Camus signified the ethical freight of "the Holocaust" to any readers? When one is not speaking, how do we identify the particular thing that the person is *not speaking about*? Does the fact that Felman does not mention the fact that Camus is also silent about the French colonial tyranny in his native Algeria mean that she is bearing (silent) witness to his (silent) witness of French atrocities? To say that de Man and Camus are "silent" is of course a trope; they wrote abundantly and eloquently about a wide range of topics, and in his posthumous autobiographical novel, *Le premier homme*, Camus explicitly addressed the Algerian situation. To claim that their silence about any particular topic "invokes" that topic, is to trope on the trope, to *create* a "silence" that allows the critic to assume the sublime of language. Surely it is possible to choose not to speak about a topic, or to forget its existence, or not even to know it exists, in which case that silence is not a "sign" of invocation but of avoidance. When Brecht writes, in the poem I quoted earlier, that the question to be asked is "why were their poets silent," he implies a responsibility that cannot be satisfied by silent communication. Edmond Jabès makes the point even more emphatically:

> I believe a writer is responsible even for what he does not write.
> To write means to answer to all the insistent voices of the past and to one's own: profound voice, intimate, calling to the future. . . .
> But what do we not altogether say in what we say? Is it what we

> try to keep silent, what we cannot or will not say or precisely what
> we do want to say and what all we say hides, saying it differently?
>   For these un-said things we are gravely responsible.
>
> (quoted in Waldrop 46)

When Langer suggests that a "vital role" for "Holocaust literature" is to
keep us from plunging back into moral innocence, we have another version
of silence, in which to speak of one atrocity is *not* to speak of others, so that
the Americanization of "the Holocaust" may give us a righteousness that
helps maintain a false sense of moral innocence. I don't mean to identify
the silence as Langer's personal burden or responsibility. He is participating
in a discourse in which, as he writes, "a vast body of Holocaust literature already exists" (3). I am simply pointing to the *absence* of a vast body of literature, or discourse, on other instances of atrocities that should have an
equally compelling moral and human interest. Where Felman asks, "*Why
has testimony in effect become at once so central and so omnipresent in our recent cultural accounts of ourselves*," I am suggesting that we consider what
objects that testimony has chosen to address, with such exclusivity that the
word "testimony" (and its fellow "witness") can be assumed to belong to
"the Holocaust," so that it *goes without saying*.

Forché draws a much wider circle in her collection, aiming to survey all
the twentieth-century atrocities she can under the rubric of "extremity."
But her World War II poems (the largest category in the collection) have no
representatives of poetry from or about Hiroshima and Nagasaki. She begins her gathering with the assertion that "Any twentieth-century history of
human rights and genocide must begin with the massacre of Armenians,
then the largest Christian minority population of Turkey. Between 1909
and 1918, approximately 1.5 million Armenians were massacred by order
of the Ottoman Turkish government" (56).[27] But to begin with the persecution of the Christian Armenians by the "savage" uncivilized Muslims is to
be silent about one of the most appalling of this century's forgotten genocides. In 1904 Generalleutnant Lothar von Trotha ordered the complete extermination of the Herero in Southwest Africa, for contesting the
appropriation of their lands to be turned over to German immigrants and
colonial trading companies. The act was inspired by the examples of European colonialism, and is thus a connecting link between the colonial genocides and the Nazi genocide, forged in part by the preeminent German
ethnographer Friedrich Ratzel, who traveled to North America in the late
nineteenth century and was struck by the ease with which colonizers had
eliminated the indigenous population. This encouraged him in his theory
that certain peoples were genetically "passive" and "inferior." In his 1897
Politische Geographie, he classed together Jews, Gypsies, and "the stunted

hunting people in the African interior" (i.e., the Herero) in the category of "scattered people with no land" (35, 121). Ratzel's book impressed Hitler when he read it in 1924, the year he wrote *Mein Kampf*.[28] Almost a million Herero died when they were driven out into the desert, and the few thousand who were left were worked to death by hard labor in "concentration camps" (this marks the first use of the term *Konzentrationslager* in German). The omission of the Herero genocide by Forché is not a small matter, even if we consider the fact that there is no available Herero poetry of witness, only the report of the General Staff that "The month-long sealing of desert areas, carried out with iron severity, completed the work of annihilation. . . . The death rattles of the dying and their insane screams of fury . . . resounded in the sublime silence of infinity."[29] It is of the same order of omission that Winston Churchill committed when, in his August 24, 1941, broadcast to the nation he denounced the German treatment of the Jews: "Since the Mongol invasions of Europe . . . there has never been methodical, merciless butchery on such a scale, or approaching such a scale. We are in the presence of a crime without a name" (quoted in Gilbert 4). Admirable and humane (and rhetorical) as Churchill's support of the Jews was, it is still stunning to hear a sweeping summary that omits the invasion by Europe—and particularly by England—of the greater part of the globe, and the massacres of countless millions under the rationale shared by Hitler that superior races had the right to displace inferior ones. Langer suggests that "We are still wrestling with the loss of stature that a disaster like the Holocaust imposes on our ideal of civilization" (5). Perhaps we should be wrestling with the history of *all* holocausts, including the many inflicted by Europeans and Americans against people who had the misfortune to be unlike us.[30] Our continued complicity with the ignorance imposed on us through miseducation and political design is worse than a loss of stature. It reveals much of our academic posturings about topics like witness poetry for the self-centered and self-serving practice it truly is.

CHAPTER 7

The Burning Babe: Children, Film Narrative, and the Figures of Historical Witness

TYRUS MILLER

In a climactic scene of his 1985 film *Come and See*, a harrowing account of a thirteen-year-old's passage from boy to seasoned partisan during the Nazi occupation of Belarus, Elem Klimov breaks with the basic realism of the rest of the film and inserts a shockingly unrealistic device. While the battered and traumatized youngster Flor shoots at a picture of Hitler left behind by the marauding SS troops, viewers watch interpolated newsreel footage of Stuka dive bombers, marching troops, Nazi rallies, street parades, and World War I battles—accelerated and run in reverse. The scene ends only when the documentary footage has been "blasted back" to a still photograph of the toddler Hitler with his mother, his uncanny, piercing dark eyes staring out from the faces of both mother and son, eyes familiar from countless pictures of the psychopathic dictator and mass murderer. Seized with horror, Flor stops shooting, perhaps recognizing the resonance of his own cathartic symbolic violence against the photograph with the literal murder of women and children he has witnessed in a genocidal SS raid against a village.

At the same time, in hesitating before this first trace of Hitler's historical existence, Flor marks a limit to his ability to eradicate the facts of history, through subjective fantasy and personal acts of will. Hitler has already long been born and grown to adulthood, the Nazis are occupying Flor's country, and it is not through individual revolt against an image that this fact can be revoked but only by realizing this figural revolt through the collective violence of the partisan army. Flor is brought out of his absorption in the fantasy of rolling back history by the call of his comrades who are pulling out and retreating to their camp in the forest. The film ends with the boy joining them and disappearing into their ranks.

Finally, however, Flor's halt before the document of Hitler as child also marks another limit, self-reflexively related to the filmmaker's own retrospective position in narrating this crucial historical struggle against fascism, *the* foundational myth of the post-World War II Soviet Union, in a linear, realist narrative. In making Flor regress through the documentary material from the narrated present of occupation, genocide, and partisan resistance to the past of Hitler's infancy, and in allying his hero's subjective consciousness with his own highly artificial intervention into the narrative presentation, reversing its linear flow, Klimov confronts the comprehensibility of history as a causal sequence. In what sense, he asks, could the baby Hitler with his mother in the photograph also be the architect of the bloody attempts to enslave and eradicate the Slavic peoples? It is only the intervening mediation of a vast impersonal structure of history, a complex and contingent web of factors, that can bridge this incomprehensible gap. Klimov does not attempt to provide a narrative explication of the intermediary links, for he suggests that such an explication is essentially impossible. It is only possible to mark the gap figurally, as a place to return to, to witness for oneself, and to ponder. Klimov's answer is not a causal or a logical one, but rather, in a physiognomic and rhetorical sense, an analogical and *figural* one. It speaks through the eyes, the horrified eyes of Flor in gazing at the fixed stares of baby Adolf and his mother in the old photograph. The figure Klimov offers his viewers is the very organ of witnessing and of repeating that act of witnessing by viewing, retrospectively, the events narratively presented in the film. *Come and See,* he entitles the film, and this imperative is indeed the figural meaning of the film as a whole.[1]

In this essay, I take this kind of "figural" answer to a problem of historical representation and explanation as characteristic of a body of films that I consider "modernist" both in their aesthetic approach and—in a sense I will soon explain—in their approach to history. In my reading of these films, I follow Hayden White's recent work in which he discusses the notion of a historical figuration "in which and by which reality is at once represented as an object for contemplation and presented as a prize, a *pretium*, an object of desire worthy of the human effort to comprehend and control it" (1999: 88). In other words, the figures of history that White is considering and that I believe these films articulate are at once attempts to grasp historical reality and to project that grasp into a time in which the historical fact or event may be recalled and redeemed, the past's power drawn upon in a present moment of resistance or its violence dispelled in a new moment of retrospective revaluation. White suggests that it is particularly modernist texts that embody this figural doubleness to comprehend historically and to transcend projectively, in distinction to nineteenth-century claims for realist narrative and factual historicism. "In modernism," he writes,

> literature takes shape as a manner of writing which effectively transcends the older oppositions between the literal and the figurative dimensions of language, on the one hand, and between the factual and fictional modes of discourse on the other. Consequently, modernism is to be seen as setting aside as well the longstanding distinction between history and fiction, not in order to collapse one into the other but in order to image a historical reality purged of the myths of such "grand narratives" as fate, providence, *Geist*, progress, the dialectic, and even the myth of final realization of realism itself. (1999: 99–100)

In particular, I will discuss a group of films that explore the reciprocal relations between the heightened figural imaginations of child protagonists or narrators and the problems of narrative representation of traumatic historical events such as fascism, political repression, revolution, and war. I hope to suggest the extent to which child consciousness has been a crucial means for filmmakers in gaining imaginative purchase on the "modernist event" of twentieth-century history. At the same time, this very attempt to depict children's experience of history has also proven to be a particularly intense fulcrum of formal innovation in filmmakers' narrative treatment of historical events, a powerful impetus to a modernist reimagination of the forms of historical narration and testimony and the status of historical truth. I also wish to delineate the figural patterns into which these filmic representations of childrens' experience of history as falling into an identifiable and consistent set of narrative types. These narrative types, I suggest, correlate figuratively with the phenomenological character of children's experience, especially their particular mode of embodiment and the crucial role of mimetic behavior in their processes of interpreting the world and acting in it.[2]

I. The Pure Witness

In the opening chapter of *Cinema II: The Time-Image*, Gilles Deleuze argues that the neo-realist cinema of Roberto Rossellini, Luchino Visconti, and Vittorio DeSica represented a decisive break with the presuppositions of classical realism, despite the misleading name. Classical realism, as Deleuze had discussed it in the first volume of his cinema studies, *The Movement-Image,* is characterized by the centrality of action in a milieu, in which the action of characters and the situation that an action produces in its context are proportionally and organically related. Realism highlights the efficacious actions of characters as considered responses to the situations confronting them; in turn, these situations appear as directly affected by the struggles and efforts of characters. In contrast, Deleuze argues, neo-realism "is a cinema of the seer and no longer one of the agent" (2).

The neo-realist protagonist is no longer primarily a protagonist of an action that will effect some sort of change in the historical situation, but rather a protagonist of witness—a point of entry into the central imperative of these films to "come and see." The objects, events, and settings take on a heightened sensory intensity—and therefore an intensified affective potential—yet at the cost of immobilizing the character and dispossessing him or her of the capacity to act as an individual in the situation witnessed. "The situation," Deleuze writes,

> is not extended directly into action: it is no longer sensory-motor, as in realism, but primarily optical and of sound, invested by the senses, before action takes shape in it. . . . Everything remains real in this neo-realism . . . but, between the reality of the setting and that of the action, it is no longer a motor extension which is established but rather a dreamlike connection through the intermediary of the liberated sense organs. It is as if the action floats in the situation, rather than bringing it to a conclusion or strengthening it. (4)

This dispossession of the individual agent's sensory-motor action on the milieu and the compensatory heightening of the subjective element—the imaginative and affective intensities—is crucial not just as a phenomenological characterization of neo-realism. It also suggests that the "realism," the truth or testimonial claim, of this mode of cinema must reside in something other than the realistic reflection of objective material reality. It introduces a figural or fictional element not necessarily opposed to the truthfulness of the images, but indiscernibly blending subjective and objective components of that truth's advent to the viewer:

> As for the distinction between subjective and objective, it also tends to lose its importance, to the extent that the optical situation or visual description replaces the motor action. We run in fact into a principle of indeterminability, of indiscernibility: we no longer

know what is imaginary or real, physical or mental, in the situation, not because they are confused, but because we do not have to know and there is no longer even a place from which to ask. (7)

In introducing this mode of indiscernibility, neo-realism thus serves as a point of departure for a much broader range of subjective cinema. In opening up the image to subjective and objective components presented in a single indeterminate complex, neo-realism becomes for Deleuze the gateway to a number of different innovations in the handling of time in cinema.

Taking up the specific focus of my considerations, the figural role of child protagonists and narrators, it is easy to see how readily child characters fulfill the conditions for the role of "seer" dispossessed of the possibility of action and for the imaginative confusion of objective and subjective aspects of the witnessed scene. In Roberto Rossellini's *Germany Year Zero*, which dramatizes the plight of a young boy in bombed-out Berlin after World War II, the protagonist Edmund is portrayed as being blocked in many practical situations by his physical immaturity and age and at the same time subject to deluded, perverse ideas about the circumstances in which he lives. For example, in one of the first scenes of the film Edmund is being chased away from a work site—digging graves—because he is underaged. This scene is repeated several times in the film in new variations: when he is tricked by an adult buying goods for the black market; when he is taken advantage of by the ex-Nazi, pederastic schoolteacher to peddle Nazi memorabilia to British soldiers; when he is swindled by another young thief whom he has been helping; when he is chased away by older boys from the sexual play they are engaged in. In one of the cruelest scenes, towards the end of the film, he is even rejected by younger, smaller children who are playing with a ball; here his *larger* size is an ironic reversal of his fate through most of the film of having too small a body to assert himself effectively. In each of these instances, we see Edmund pushed to the margins of the world of work and action, even those of the criminal and sexual underworld, because of his not yet adolescent stature. This physically marked marginality forces him to be the witness of his family's fate at the hands of an unscrupulous landlord and eventually to abandon his older brother and sister and wander through the surreal shell of the destroyed city, with its ruins, its prostitutes, and its construction sites.

The two major exceptions to the film's barring of Edmund from action—Edmund's poisoning of his chronically ill father and his suicidal leap from a building under reconstruction—confirm Deleuze's argument concerning the indiscernibility of subjective and objective elements of the depicted events. The poisoning occurs when Edmund literally applies his schoolteacher's rote Nazi-Darwinian phraseology about the strong surviving and the weak having to die. The horror of Edmund's act of parricide is thus compounded by the viewer's sense that the father was killed by the ghost of ideology past possessing his son. Rossellini, furthermore, allows the actual death to take place off-screen, in the distraction created by a police raid looking for unregistered returned soldiers.[3] The event's lack of visible presence underscores the implication that this is as much a crime of Edmund's misguided thought as of his violent hand.[4] Similarly in the case of the suicide with which the film ends, the crucial change in Edmund, his recognition of his crime and resolution to kill himself, occurs with very little external registration. After his long nocturnal wandering through the city, he climbs the stairs to a building under reconstruction across the street from where his father's body is being taken away for burial. We see him playing on the construction site, hanging his jacket up on a beam before he slides down, so as not to get it dirty. He looks out over the houses around him and the street, throwing rocks; suddenly, with a look that indiscernibly mixes weariness, impassivity, and recognition, he jumps from the building and falls to his death. There is no outward transition from play to this most serious final act. His jacket still hangs on the beam, unsoiled by either his play or his fatal plunge to the street.

Elem Klimov, in *Come and See*, takes this principle of indiscernibility to a more radical extreme than Rossellini's moral complexes of historical damage and spiritual perversion in *Germany Year Zero*. For Klimov, ultimately, wants to depict for his audience the spiritual transformation of the naïve boy Flor into an experience-hardened, anti-Nazi partisan and to invite them to participate through film viewing in this inner conversion. As I have already suggested, the crucial force of transformation lies with what Flor witnesses, his "passion," rather than his actions directly.

Two scenes in particular underscore his placement in the role of the pure witness, in both cases because of his immaturity and boyishness. Having left his mother's house to join the partisans, Flor is left behind when they go out on campaign, and his boots are appropriated by a more experienced man whose shoes are worn out. Together with the commandant's young consort Glasha, Flor is temporarily deafened by an artillery bombardment of the woods where the partisans had camped. The scenes that follow take on a lyrical or even hallucinatory quality as they unfold against a subjectively focalized soundtrack of muted and damped sounds. For example, Flor stares in wonder at a German paratrooper dropping "silently" into the trees above him and struggling to free himself from the tangled parachute. The surreal image of the sky filled with slowly drifting parachutes, followed by the strange image of a man suspended in the branches, is set into relief by the eerie soundlessness. Psychologically, the scene effectively renders the stunned wonder of the boy at the spectacle and his momentary oblivion to the danger it implies for him and his people. The next day, having fled deep into the woods, in a scene of childish self-abandonment to gleeful play, Flor and Glasha wash themselves by shaking down rainwater from the trees. The visual lyricism of the scene—sunlit droplets falling down over the laughing youngsters—is heightened by the non-naturalistic sound, again motivated by the ringing of Flor's ears following the artillery concussions.

This oddly idyllic set of scenes has its harrowing counterpart later in the film, in the orgy of violence that the captive Flor is forced to witness as the SS massacre and burn a village. Having seen women and children brutally killed, Flor himself is randomly spared death by the whim of his captors, who pose for a picture around him with a gun to his head, but shoot off only the camera and not the pistol. After a moment of shocked recognition that he has survived, he loses consciousness and collapses. The entire scene is a fury of sight and sound: the barking of dogs, the laughter and shouts of the SS men, the rattle of guns and grenades, the roar of motorcycles and trucks, the smoke and flames of burning buildings, and the bursts and scattered trails of the flamethrowers' gasoline. The camera pulls back to reveal the helpless and traumatized boy in the midst of fire, smoke, and withdrawing columns of Nazi soliders. Yet in the scene that follows, in which the partisans have captured some of the SS officers and their men in an ambush, Flor is able to redeem this passive view of historical events. It is he who is able to bear witness against the Nazi killers, telling that they burned the people of the village alive, leading to their execution by the partisans.

II. Mimetic Games

The category of the "pure witness" pertains to film narratives centered on characters barred from any effective, proportionate response in action to their situation. Children, because of their limited horizon of experience and the physical limits of their bodies, are easily cast as this type of character. Yet the intensification of sensory experience that compensates for the loss of active agency and the dream-like indiscernibility of subjective and objective dimensions of the experience point beyond passive witnessing towards a new domain of agency residing in imaginative processes. These range from the lowest level of play or ritual-like processes through bodily metamorphosis and travel through time. Taking as examples René Clément's *Forbidden Games*, Neil Jordan's *The Butcher Boy*, and Goran Markovic's *Tito and Me*, I will describe the entry point of these imaginative processes by which agency can be recaptured beyond the pure witness state: the detouring of action into mimetic spaces of play, ritual, and theater.

I am suggesting that in the group of films represented by these examples, mimetic behaviors may function in a number of distinct ways to bridge an initial divide between the child as potential agent and the situation in which he or she might act. Such activities may focus the narrative on the *genesis* of a conscious, active subject and reveal the mimetic behavior of this subject-in-formation to carry the figural marks, the stigmata, of the historical situation in which it was enacted. The mimetic activity may be presented as predominantly *hermeneutic* in nature, a form of pre-understanding appropriate to an immature view of the world, a fictive or figural grasp of the historical circumstances in the absence of articulate concepts and language to formulate a more adult understanding. Or it may primarily depict a nascent *mode of action* in which the figural dimension—the adoption of roles and the constitution of virtual, theatricalized, imaginatively bracketed spaces of enactment—is inextricable from the action's potential efficacy in the world.

These functions are, of course, not mutually exclusive, since the emergence into conscious and active subjectivity is a dialectical process in which mimetic activity, in its dual dimensions as figural representation and figural enactment, plays a central role. In his book *Role-Playing and Identity*, the phenomenologist Bruce Wilshire, for example, argues that the formation and sustenance of personal identity should be understood as the result of a dynamic and ongoing negotiation of mimetic relations with others. Our capacity to project ourselves bodily into the embodied activities, gestures, modes of speech, and forms of life of others keeps us from rigidifying into closed and impoverished monads. Yet we must also develop ways of disengaging from mimetic involvements to avoid "engulfment" and to allow individual thought and decision. Wilshire looks to fictionalized representation and "staged," theatrical redoublings of primary, unreflective mimetic involvements as crucial possibilities for dialectically binding engulfment and disengagement into individualized identities in formation. He writes:

> When we see what the actor does onstage we see that at which the child is aiming, however unwittingly. If another can be enacted by a body—in the other's absence—then that body must realize both that it is a *person*, for it is the other person that it mimetically resembles and all recognize that only persons enact persons; and that it is *a* person because no one need be present to enact the other but he himself the actor! Moreover, he must realize that he is a free person, an agent, for the other is present merely as an enactment; no causal coercion plays from him to the actor. This behavior, then, must tend toward maximalization of individual identity. (200)

Put otherwise, fictional or theatrical reenactment allows the subject and his/her formation to be affected by the relation to others, but shifts the relation from a directly physical causality—a compulsion to act in such and such a way—to the "figural causation" of potential fulfillment, as defined by Hayden White. As important for Wilshire as the indirect connection that figural causation allows is the partial distance from necessity allowed by the "virtuality" of the figure, the weakening of more direct forms of influence: "It is the force of the fiction that breaks the power of the other without simply losing it" (200).

René Clément's *Forbidden Games* presents the ritualized play of the two children, the Parisian war orphan Paulette and the farm boy Michel, as a symbolic way of grasping and psychically binding the incomprehensible fact of death in war. At the beginning of the film, as the Parisians flee along the roads from the Nazi invaders, Paulette's parents are shot down and the little dog she has been carrying is killed as well. Another result of the attack on the columns of refugees is that a horse escapes and runs off to the fields; Michel's brother gets kicked by this war horse and after several days of suffering, dies from the blow. Paulette is temporarily adopted by Michel's family, and the bond between the two children grows as they build a pet cemetery, with the first grave devoted to Paulette's dead puppy. The children adorn the graves with crosses, and in one case, with a necklace taken from the nest of an owl living in the rafters of the old mill where they construct their cemetery. Later, as their cemetery becomes increasingly full of dead chicks, kittens, and other animals, and the arrangement becomes more elaborate and ornate, the children become dissatisfied with homemade crosses. Eager to please Paulette, Michel steals crosses from the church and churchyard cemetery to adorn their own childish counterpart of the adult sacred ground. The trouble that results leads to Paulette's being sent to an orphanage and Michel's destruction, rather than return, of the stolen crosses.

Clément's narrative focuses precisely and movingly on the binding force of the symbolic enactment, the children's game, their *play* with death as a source of vitality, joy, and love in the face of inexplicable fate and violence. The gentle irony of the film is that the children's seemingly morbid game represented a living relation between them, their loving cooperation in a kind of shared artwork against death. In turn, the forbidding of the game and the separation of the children is a belated victory for death: figuratively, the death of both children in the undoing of the figure articulated by their rituals and tokens of mourning. Michel's ultimate destruction of the cemetery and his return of the necklace to the owl's nest memorializes his loss, the "death" of Paulette to him, her passing from his life. Paulette's final scene is even more haunting: about to be taken into an orphanage, she hears the name Michel and runs off looking for him, calling his name. But realizing that it was not *her* Michel that was being addressed, she begins to call in desperation for her mother. Paulette's calling for—and suddenly *re-calling*—her mother, after the parenthesis of her time with Michel, drama-tizes the unraveling of the symbolic binding of death that the game with the crosses represented to her. At the end of the film a frightened little girl with no one in the world, Paulette has been brought back to the sheer un-bound fact of the loss of all those who have mattered to her—her mother, father, and now Michel as well.

Neil Jordan's *The Butcher Boy* (adapted from Patrick McCabe's novel) and Goran Markovic's *Tito and Me* both represent ways in which historical situations shape the formation of personal identities through their precipi-tation in the imaginative play of children. At the same time, however, they illustrate the deviation and potential freedom from the model that may fol-low from historical material being transformed through childrens' mimetic roles, rituals, and enactments. In *The Butcher Boy*, Francie Brady creates a world of play and imagination, at first defensively, to escape from the squalid realities of his life and to hold onto a sense of identity against his drunkard father, his mentally ill mother, and the social institutions of town and reformatory. We see him, for instance, living out various roles bor-rowed from comic books and television, along with his best friend Joe. Yet even as they remain modulations of this defensive play, Francie's imagina-tive projections and enactments of roles—the amazing Francie Brady, the Apache, the Fugitive, the Pig, and the Butcher Boy—begin to become shockingly active and effective as instruments of self-assertion and revenge against those he perceives as his enemies. As the film presents it, the erratic violence of his inner life appears to mirror the atmosphere of fear, para-noia, mass media hysteria, and real violence of the Cold War. In the time leading up to Francie's brutal murder of his putative archenemy Mrs. Nu-gent, he sees and hears news reports of the escalating Cuban Missile Crisis taking the world to the brink of nuclear destruction. In fantasized scenes, Francie imagines his town destroyed by a nuclear bomb and the residents replaced by ghastly mutants living within the wreckage and rubble. It is in-structive to note that this scene echoes—but in a fantastically transfigured way—the wanderings of Rossellini's Edmund among the rubble and the human underworld of postwar Berlin. Yet whereas the hallucinatory quali-ties of Edmund's night roaming followed from the heightened sensory in-tensities of the pure witness as he looks out over the objectively shattered landscape of the city, Francie's destroyed town really *is* a hallucination, mimicking the plots of the science fiction films that Francie loves to watch. Francie's sedative-induced vision gives the viewer figurative access to the inner, subjective mutation caused equally by the death of Francie's father and the traumatic fears of the historical moment.

Markovic's comedy offers a wry historical commentary on how the cult of personality around Tito, with its demand for hyper-identification with the heroic leader, could have given rise to the distinctly unheroic cast of adults that were presiding over the breakup of Tito's Yugoslavia forty years later. The story transpires in 1954, when the lumpish ten-year-old protagonist Zoran wins, to everyone's surprise, a writing contest about why he loves Marshal Tito. His poem, full of fervent praise and patriotic spirit, wins Zoran the honor of being included in a hike of young Pioneers around the countryside where the great partisan leader grew up. His teacher is disconcerted that the most desultory and slovenly student has been chosen to represent the school. His anti-communist relatives are concerned about Zoran's zeal for the communist chief, and his parents are worried by the line in his poem that says he loves Tito more than Mom and Dad. Markovic humorously presents Zoran's obsession with his hero. Zoran religiously imitates Tito's gestures from newsreels at the movies, while Tito is a tutelary presence in Zoran's erotic daydreams about the war orphan and schoolgirl Jasna, with whom he is deeply infatuated. On the Pioneer march, however, the communist attempt to create good little Titoists through mimetic identification—revisiting the mythic sites of Tito's childhood—goes awry, mostly because of the failure of the epicurean Zoran to appreciate the ennobling effects of physical discomfort and discipline and his "base" instincts for food, rest, and sleep. Continually in trouble with the ridiculously authoritarian troop leader Comrade Raja, Zoran's passive resistance leads the children to an ultimate revolt and to the troop leader's being taken away by the secret police. The film ends with the children having been invited to Tito's birthday celebration. Zoran, however, slips away when the photo session begins and samples the luscious spread of food set up in one of the adjoining rooms.

The dates of the fiction, as well as that of Markovic's film, are significant to the film's overall historical meaning. Set the year after Stalin's death, a crucial turning point in the history of world communism, it depicts Tito's alternative personality cult in full bloom. Ten years old at the moment of the film's events and its interpolated newsreel footage, Zoran had been born with the new Yugoslavian federation that arose out of the partisan struggle against Nazism and is associatively identified with that new state. He is the human clay, rather soft and lumpy, of the communist and nationalist ideal projected by Titoism. In 1992, the year of the film's release, Zoran would be forty-eight and an adult witnessing the dismantling of Tito's Yugoslavia. Implicitly, then, the film asks the question, who are we, who grew up under the deified Tito and now are to oversee the final dismantling of his creation?

Despite his Tito-mania, however, at heart—and in his roly-poly stomach—little Zoran remains an unheroic proto-bourgeois more interested in food, a bit of comfort, and a happy family than inspiring patriotic rhetoric.

Markovic does not simply satirize the communist ideal, however; he shows how the very mechanisms by which communist man was putatively to have been shaped lead to failure. No one could be more obsessively imitative of his exemplary hero Tito than little Zoran. Yet this mimetic identification, which first individuates him and estranges him from his family and school-boy friends, also provides him with a sufficient sense of personal individuality and freedom to resist Comrade Raja (and by extension, Titoism itself) at a critical point during the disastrous "March Around Tito's Homeland." Fallible human material and flawed methods in handling it collaborate to produce the disengaged young consumer who prefers tasty cakes to a photo op with the great man. In presenting Zoran as the ultimate, very un-utopian realization of Yugoslavia's Titoist "new man," Markovic also suggests a kinder, gentler road, alas, not taken, in the breakup of the Federation that would occur shortly after the film's release. Zoran offers an exemplary image of an essentially private, ironic, tolerant, and non-committed bourgeois, incapable of sustaining much nationalistic or ideological fervor for long. Instead, the conflicts he portends, like the constant but inconsequential bickering in his family's overcrowded Belgrade apartment, are not deadly, political, and ethnic ones, but petty domestic quarrels that need not preclude continuing to live together and need not draw blood.

III. Monsters of Innocence

I have suggested that the child protagonists of the films discussed above come to understand their historical situation and to act within it through the *figural* mediation of mimetic activity. Within this basic framework, there is a wide variety of mimetic modes, ranging from the ritual play of the children in Clément's film to the identificatory role-playing of Zoran in *Tito and Me*. But the extremes of Francie Brady's fanciful self-projection, his hallucination of the nuclear destruction of the town and its occupation by insect-like mutants, touch on my next category: the imaginative objectification of monsters as figures of the child's understanding of violent or traumatic events. The monster figure, in *The Butcher Boy* as well as in the two examples I will discuss below, is drawn from the iconography of popular culture and transferred onto adult figures in the child's environment. In this way, the monster comes to personify the child's fear, its lack of understanding, its sense of persecution, or even its ambivalent desire for an alliance with a power that exceeds its own weakness.

Victor Erice's *Spirit of the Beehive*, released near the end of Franco's rule in Spain, relates the story of two little girls, Maria and Ana, the daughters of two Republican intellectuals in internal exile in the countryside shortly after the Spanish Civil War. When the two girls see James Whale's *Franken-*

stein at the village cinema, the younger sister Ana is deeply troubled by the scene in which the monster first befriends a little girl, then kills her, eventually leading to his own violent death at the hands of the village mob. When Ana asks her sister why the people killed the monster, Maria tells her that it was just a movie and the monster didn't really die. But she goes on to make up stories about the monster to scare Ana. She tells her that the monster is a "spirit" and cannot be seen during the day, but that if you are its friend and call to it, it will come. She further embroiders her tale by showing Ana an abandoned hut with a well that she claims is the spirit's home. Ana begins visiting the hut to see if the monster is there, and one night she sneaks out to look. To her shock, she finds her "monster" laid out in the straw: a hungry, tired, wounded fugitive, a Republican soldier on the run. She brings him food and her father's jacket, which has his pocket watch in it. That night, the police catch up with the soldier and he is shot. The father is called in to the police, who have found his watch and jacket, and though he is not implicated, this is clearly an uncomfortable and potentially dangerous situation for him as a Republican intellectual hibernating in the countryside. Without saying a word about it, at breakfast the next day he opens his pocketwatch, which has a musical device. Maria, knowing nothing about it, makes no reaction, but Ana is fearful and appalled. She goes to the hut and finds nothing but traces of blood on the straw where the monster lay. Stepping out of the hut, she is confronted by her father, who sternly calls her. She runs away, staying out all night. She finds a mushroom, which her father has earlier told her is deadly, and takes a bite. In a puddle of water, she sees first her own face, then the face of the Frankenstein monster, with the features of her father. She loses consciousness and is found, shocked and exposed, though alive, the following morning. The film ends with Ana's rising from her bed at night and stepping outside, hearing the sound of a train whistle and calling to her spirit-monster and invisible friend, "I'm Ana, I'm Ana."

At nine or ten years old, Ana has very little experience with which to understand the terrible dislocation that has broken her parents' lives, forced them away from friends and the life of the city, and left them cold and estranged towards one another. Nor can she understand the larger forces at work in the coming and disappearance of her "monster," the fugitive Republican soldier. She cannot even grasp why her father might be upset by the disappearance of his jacket and its discovery by the police, except that he must in some way be responsible for the vanishing of her ally and spirit-friend. The monster serves as a complex narrative figure—a "spirit"—for a content that cannot be made discursively present in the film. This suppression of statement in favor of figural presentation is at once motivated by the use of a child as the center of the film's narrative consciousness and necessitated by the censorship operating in Fascist Spain at the time of the film's release. But at least three interpretative aspects of the figure can be discerned.

First, the monster figure seems to suggest that Ana has internalized into her personal identity—"I'm Ana," she calls—that which was externally represented by the runaway soldier: the residue of resistance, the traces of the revolutionary spirit for which the Republican army fought. In this sense, like Markovic's Zoran, Erice's Ana becomes a prefiguration of a political subject to be fulfilled in the near future of the present in which the film is being viewed. In other words, Ana, a child in 1940 and the beginning of Franco's reign, would be an adult in 1970 near its end; she points to the possibility of an historical connection of what came before fascism with a life-to-come beyond fascism. Moreover, allegorically, she represents the possibility of reforging the broken link between the educated middle-class intellectuals (such as her father) and the revolutionary masses who were literally the army of the Republic—a bond symbolized in her gift of her father's jacket and watch. Second, echoing the scene from Whale's *Frankenstein*, she hallucinates the face of the monster in the pool after having confronted the death of the fugitive and attempted suicide by eating the mushroom. The monster functions in this way to figure Ana's confrontation with death and specifically her fear of her own death. The final scene suggests that in overcoming her fear of the monster's power to kill (the little girl's death in the Whale film), she comes to view the monster as a protector and ally. Although in itself this is existentially and psychologically resonant, it also carries over into the level of submerged political allegory. The final scene suggests that Ana may now have the courage, the mastery of her own fear of death, to see beyond the face of monstrosity imposed by fascism upon its political enemies and to ally herself with them. Finally, the disquieting isolation and longing of Ana at the end of the film may also harbor a utopian content. Her father and mother are shown throughout the film as increasingly resigned, and in fact, they are likely never to be able to enjoy the love and the freedoms they tasted before the Republican defeat. Ana's very discontent, the psychic loneliness into which her experience has cast her, stands as a painful desire for something else, unfulfilled in the present, for which her parents no longer allow themselves to hope.

More recently, Phillip Ridley's film *The Reflecting Skin* offers an American Gothic counterpart to Erice's Frankenstein figure. Ridley's film has at its center the ten-year-old Seth Dove and the experience of familial, sexual, and historical violence immediately following World War II. Set on the Western prairies and dominated by a landscape of wide, flat, undulating wheatfields, *The Reflecting Skin* focuses the child's anxieties on a figure combining national foreignness and desirous female sexuality: Dolphin

Blue, the English widow who lives near the Doves' home and gas station. Out on the roads running through this rural landscape, a group of leather-jacketed sexual predators are driving around in a shark-finned black Cadillac, and Seth's friends are disappearing and being found dead. Made fearful by Dolphin Blue's hysterical outburst about her dead husband and confirmed in his alarm by a chance resemblance between her and a picture in his father's pulp magazine, Seth comes to believe that Dolphin is a vampire. She, he believes, is the "monster" responsible for the death of his friends.

Two further events enrich the meaning of the vampire figure with political and historical connotations. After the death of one of Seth's friends, the police come to the Dove house to interrogate Seth's father. Suspicion has fallen upon him because of an incident deep in his past in which he was caught in a sexual encounter with a teen-aged boy. The policeman taunts and threatens him, and rather than face the shame of a reopening of his past, Seth's father drenches himself in gasoline and sets himself on fire. The loss of his father and the violence of the police give Seth nowhere to turn, even after he witnesses a friend, later found dead, being pulled into the roving Cadillac. So in his helplessness, Seth disavows his knowledge of the truth and displaces his fears all the more intensely onto the "vampire," Dolphin Blue.

Still more significant than the death of his father, however, is the return of his brother Cameron from the Pacific, where he has been a sailor involved in the tests of the hydrogen bomb. When asked what he did in the "pretty islands," he answers, "Blew 'em up. That's about it." Yet he has come back discontented with the life to which he has returned and, unknown to him, sick from radiation exposure. The onset of his illness—which leaves him fatigued, thinning, and losing his hair—coincides with his developing love and sexual relationship with Seth's nemesis, Dolphin Blue. In a highly stylized, subjectively focalized scene, Seth witnesses Dolphin and Cameron in a sexual embrace, but interprets it as her biting Cameron and sucking his blood. After this act of "eye-witnessing," Seth will use any means necessary, including the real culprits for the murders that are happening, to destroy the vampire. When he meets Dolphin on the road and sees her accepting a ride from the Cadillac-driving killers, he makes no attempt to warn her and looks on with a sense of victory as the car speeds away. The next day, her body turns up in a ditch. Cameron collapses in an agony of grief, and Seth runs deep into the fields, recognizing what he has done in the final cry of guilt that closes the film.

In *The Spirit of the Beehive*, the Frankenstein figure serves as a figure of relation to the Republican past and to the revolutionary masses that precedes Ana's more active understanding that may come with her adulthood. In contrast, *The Reflecting Skin* uses the imposition of the vampire figure on

Dolphin Blue to highlight the tragic effects of misrecognizing and disavowing the real social, political, and historical sources of violence. The child's adoption of the monster figure is initially an innocent, if unfortunate, failure of understanding. At this stage, as in *Spirit of the Beehive*, it serves a primarily hermeneutic function, allowing Seth to grasp a perplexing and frightening situation and to focus his actions on the tangible goal of protecting himself from the vampire. If, however, Erice shows Ana passing from this hermeneutic use of the monster to an ethical and (prefiguratively) political alliance with him, Ridley shows Seth failing ethically by self-interestedly holding on to the figure of the vampire as explanation long after it has lost any credibility. As events unfold, the vampire figure, as Seth imagines it, becomes an actively maintained self-deception about the murders. The results are tragic—the death of Dolphin Blue and the spiritual destruction of Cameron with the death of his love and the destruction of his plans. Yet the film also suggests that Seth, because of his disavowal of the truth and his clinging to his pulp mythology about his foreign neighbor, is morally implicated in the terrible things that happen and must live with the awareness that he was a more-than-passive accomplice in Dolphin Blue's murder.

IV. Embodying Witness

In the previous three sections, I have discussed the figural expression of the child's relation to its historical situation as *external* form, however much that externality is qualified by subjective tones emanating from the child-witness and agent. In the type of the pure witness, the objective scene is lent a perceptual intensity that reflects the passive, "affected" condition of the immobilized seer, up to a limit of evoking a dream-like indiscernibility between the subjective and objective facets of a unitary perceived event. In the case of mimetic games, the figure takes on externalized form in the embodied activity of playing, making theater, or performing ritual. While the body is necessary and involved in the production of the objective form— the role or performance—it also remains distinct from it, as an actor's body does from the character it supports and signifies. Similarly, although the figure of the monster represents a powerful imaginative and affective investment, it is projected outward onto another body, which may become the guardian or antagonist of the child. In this section, I will explore a self-reflexive turn that renders more problematic the externality of the figure, a new figural type in which the bodily involvement of mimetic games and the monstrous metamorphic powers of the imagination converge on the child's own body. Under the rubric of "embodying witness," I will consider instances of the literal metamorphosis of the child's body itself, its own embodied "figure," in response to a traumatic historical circumstance.[5]

Joseph Losey's first feature film, *The Boy With Green Hair*, provides a transparently allegorical, though by no means simplistic instance of this figural use of the child's body. His framed narrative begins with the protagonist, Peter, in a police station and notably without any hair at all. After resisting speaking to the policeman, Peter begins to open up to a kindly psychiatrist and tells the story of what happened to his hair and why he ran away from home. Peter's parents, humanitarian workers with children in London during the war, were killed in a bombing, and he was sent from relative to relative to live until he arrived at the home of the goodhearted "Gramps," a former circus-artist and showman. Everything was going well in Peter's new life until two events struck at the heart of his well-being. Working with his classmates to collect clothes for war orphans, Peter only belatedly discovers that he himself is a war orphan; hoping to allow him to adjust to his new circumstances, Gramps had held off breaking the news to him that his parents were dead. Soon after this insight into his special and stigmatized social identity, the utterly unforeseen happens: Peter wakes up one morning with a full head of green hair. His new hair causes murmuring, discontent, and eventually fear in the people of the small town, and despite the best efforts of Gramps and the enlightened schoolteacher, a mob-like sentiment grows against Peter. Narrowly fleeing attack, Peter runs away and stumbles upon a place in the woods where he falls asleep and has a dream or vision. The children he has seen on the posters—war orphans from Germany, Yugoslavia, Greece, and elsewhere—speak to him and tell him that his green hair is a good thing and has a meaning. It is a sign to tell people that they must work to stop war and to keep from making more war orphans like himself. Peter returns to the town fired with missionary zeal. But the town is no more assuaged, and after one particularly narrow escape from a gang of boys, he gives in to the pressure to have his hair shaved. Deeply disappointed in himself and in Gramps, who in the end acquiesced in the town's intolerant demand, he ran away and was picked up by the police. The psychiatrist who has been listening rhetorically says that he doesn't believe a word of it, because he thinks Peter doesn't believe it himself; if he did, he wouldn't have given up so easily. Peter agrees to take up the cause again, grow his hair back, and live the role of the sign and messenger for peace. The psychiatrist opens the policeroom door to reveal the town's three enlightened members, the doctor, the schoolteacher, and Gramps, ready to bring Peter home again. The psychiatrist's parting exchange with the doctor underscores the *figural* truth of the story the boy has just told. He says it doesn't matter if Peter had green hair or not; he believes in what Peter was trying to say.

Losey's film is clearly a parable about racism and nationalism as the fundamental causes of war. Comprehending the pacifist meaning of Peter's embodied difference will require the members of this typical small town to confront their almost instinctual fear of difference, expressed immediately as racist prejudice and more mediately in the kind of nationalism that leads to war.[6] Losey's framing of the story and filtering of it through the child-narrator effectively motivates the simple, parable-like, and often fantastical nature of the story. More sophisticated, however, is his dramatizing of the social and personal struggle around Peter's body as a *sign*, the way in which Peter's difference, his having and being a marked body, becomes a site of meaning and of a conflict of interpretation. Peter ultimately claims his body by taking it as a meaningful sign, and this sign in turn allows him consciously to accept and enact what he objectively is, a war orphan. Yet as the framing narrator, he also is able to organize his experience around this embodied sign in the form of a coherent, teleological, autobiographical narrative that only requires the final encouragement of the psychiatrist to bring it to its symbolic fulfillment in his reconciliation with the enlightened community of elders. Any questions about Peter's factual reliability as a historical narrator ("Do you believe his story?") are secondary to the figural truth of his achievement of individuality and identity through narrative ("I believe in what he was trying to say"). Losey presents Peter's ultimate transformation through narrating his story as reabsorbing the bodily figure of change, the green hair, into his less visible but more decisive *consciousness* of having been "the boy with green hair." As character, Peter suffers a dialectical movement from receiving a bodily mark of indeterminate meaning, through a struggle for the meaning of the mark, to the erasure of his difference and alienation from his body under the domination of others; his colorless, bald head at the beginning of the film is the visible sign of his loss of identity. Yet as narrator, he completes the dialectical movement of the film in a final reclaiming of his identity in his reconstitution of the erased sign through language and narrative. The viewer knows in the end that it doesn't really matter if Peter's hair grows back green or even whether it was ever green at all. What matters is the conscious claim he makes on the *meaning* of his green hair as sign, his grasping of his own embodied difference and social individuation not as a deficiency but rather as a potential for positive change.

Völker Schloendorff's adaption of Günther Grass's celebrated novel of Nazi-era Danzig, *The Tin Drum*, offers a more ambiguous figuration of history in the body of its protagonist and diminutive tin drummer, Oskar Mazarath. The story revolves around the parallel between the childhood of Oskar and the rise and eventual fall of Nazism in the Polish-German Danzig area. Allegorically significant is Oskar's deliberate fall down the cellar steps at the age of three and his subsequent failure to grow any larger, despite his increasing psychic and even sexual maturation. Oskar has also been gifted with an extraordinary vocal capacity: his high-pitched scream, usually accompanied by a tattoo on his tin drum, can break the glass of tableware, cabinets, and windows even at a great distance. This imagery of Oskar as the infantile, destructive drum-beater and shouter brings him in contiguity with the figure of Hitler. One scene in particular suggests this juxtaposition. Up in a tower overlooking the city, Oskar drums and screams his glass-breaking cry, shattering windows around him. The scene ends with the voiceover of a Nazi orator addressing a crowd about the German-ness of Danzig and the arrogance of the Poles in trying to take over the city.

Elsewhere, however, the identification of Oskar with the Nazis gets re-versed, becoming satiric or pathetic in its connotation rather than allegori-cally representative. In one scene, for example, Oskar disrupts a Nazi rally by hiding under the bleachers and drumming off-time from the marching bands at the festivity. He manages to shift the rhythm from a goose-step-ping march to a waltz, thus thoroughly destroying the political effect of the mass event. Even more significant is Oskar's wandering through the streets during the events of Kristallnacht. Here Oskar's previous glassbreaking ap-pears both magnified to gigantic scale and radically outdone by the racist violence unleashed by the Nazis. Viewed against this organized, collective terror, Oskar's acts of destruction appear not as its allegorical counterpart but as the expressions of a childish and individualistic anarchism, moved by a spirit different from that underlying the Nazi violence. Moreover, Oskar undergoes a decisive inner change on that day with his discovery of the dead body of the Jewish toymaker Sigismund Markus, who had sup-plied Oskar with his tin drums. Although he does not grow any larger, the death of Markus is symbolically also the end of Oskar's childhood. With this passage out of his arrested childhood, in spirit if not yet in body, Oskar's mirroring of the Nazis in dwarf-like form no longer appears un-conscious and allegorically representative, but rather deliberately and strategically adopted on his part. In the ensuing events of the film, Oskar will thus become part of the entertainment troop of the older dwarf Bebra and will tour occupied Europe wearing diminutive uniforms, amusing and parodying the occupying Nazi army.

The ambiguity of Oskar's figure is intentional, bearing a number of different historical and political senses at once. Oskar's deliberate stunting of his growth and refusal to become an adult clearly hints that Nazism may be seen as an expression of Germany's political immaturity, the desire of a people to refuse historical change and to believe in a childish fantasy of omnipotence. As already mentioned, Oskar's shattering voice seems to echo Hitler's oratorical histrionics. Yet as his conversations with the circus dwarf Bebra make clear, Oskar also offers an image of the "little people," the weak, marginal, foreign, or freakish who would suffer the Nazi genocide.

And crucially, he also represents little *peoples*, such as the Kashubians and other ethnic groups that fit nowhere neatly into the geopolitical divisions of a nationalized Europe. As Oskar's grandmother remarks near the end of the film, the Kashubians have been kicked around by both the Poles, for whom they were not Polish enough, and by the Germans, for whom they were too Polish. In his mixed heritage—carrying his German father's name but probably the blood paternity of his Polish uncle, the lover of his Kashubian mother—Oskar serves as a warning against taking outward signs (his German name) as reliable gauge of national and personal identity. In the final scene of the film, Oskar, who has suffered another fall and has begun to grow again after passing eighteen years in a three-year-old's body, is being loaded aboard a train to Germany, deported from the Russian occupied territory because he is of "German" paternity. As the train pulls away to take him to a new life in Germany, he calls out for his grandmother the name "Babka"—not the German but the Polish or Kashubian word for "grandmother."[7]

V. Time Travelers

With my final type, the figural representation of an historical situation through the embodiment and consciousness of child characters reaches a maximum of imaginative latitude. In the films of this type, not only are spatialized relations between the child as perceiving subject and its surroundings rendered fluid, as the child engages in intense acts of witness and mimetic games, it personifies affects as monstrous figures, and self-reflexively transforms its own bodily figure according to its subjective response to historical circumstances. Also temporal relations are drawn into the reconfiguration of personal identity, in its various dimensions of embodiment, memory, imagination, and affect. In this last group of films, personal identity and the body are put in play across temporal as well as spatial divides. If we think, for instance, of mimetic activity as implying a virtual play-space in which some of the ontological characteristics of everyday reality are put in suspension, then so too time-traveler narratives play with time and its normally divided compartments of past, present, and future. Time becomes a volumetric "theater" in which virtual roles can be adopted, played out, perhaps also understood and criticized. For just as the fluidizing of identity in mimetic games may leave the actor changed and more aware, so too the time traveler may achieve an insight or gain a power not available to him or her before risking the encounter with the other in time.

The narrative figures that result from such encounters across time are versions of what Deleuze identifies as "time-images" in the second volume of his *Cinema* studies. Unlike classical realist narration, which presents a narrative time indirectly through the variations that emplotment lends to the linear succession of causal linked events, in these films narrative structure derives from the orders of time that are juxtaposed, blended, interlaced, or rendered indiscernible. Similarly, whereas in classic narration, the narrative foundation allows a hierarchical assignment of ontological value to memory (past), action (present), and imagined anticipation (future), in the latter case, the ontological values derive from the relations of time as concretely presented in the time-image. Thus, for example, in such films, memories, dreams, or imagination may be a means of effective present action, precisely when the body is immobilized or otherwise constrained from its normal active role.[8]

My specific focus on time in this final section brings to the fore an aspect implicit in all the types I have discussed. Once the basic premise of the pure witness is recognized—that the disengagement or blockage of effective action renders subjective and objective features of a perceptual experience increasingly indiscernible—then this indiscernibility can be seen to unsettle not just the objectivity of space, but also its temporal correlates in objective, linear, homogeneous, irreversible time. In Klimov's *Come and See*, for example, despite the relatively straightforward "realist" narrative sucession, there is a strongly accented dissonance between the objective time-span and the character's subjective experience of it. Only a few days pass in the film, yet Flor passes from boyhood to a kind of premature old age in that brief span. This paradoxical structure, of course, is most poignantly registered in the one sequence that dramatically breaks with realist narrative time, the climactic sequence with the shooting of the Hitler picture and the reversed newsreels: Flor's young face, worn, rigid, and etched with shock, gray with frost and grime, is juxtaposed to the motionless face of the infant Hitler in the arms of his mother. Similarly, in the manic subjective narration of Jordan's *The Butcher Boy*, the fusion of past and present, narrator and narrated character, make it difficult to neatly account for the temporal dimensions of Francie Brady's narrative. Most strikingly, Oskar's bodily figure appears as a complex temporal image of eighteen years of history and provokes problems of narrative coherence as a result. At the moment of his birth, for example, he is represented as having had the full consciousness of the voiceover narrator of the film. Later, he uncannily spans the range from toddler to adolescent to adult in the same small boy's body. As a result, we see the grotesque image of the puny Oskar in adolescent sexual play with his housekeeper Maria or being seduced by an older woman; and the strangely moving spectacle of his "mature" love affair with Roswitha, with whom he forms a kind of miniature parody of a married couple.

In the time traveler films, however, this interfusing of subjectivity and time structure is made explicit in the premise of a kind of mental communication and traffic across time. In Vincent Ward's *The Navigator: A Time-Travel Adventure*, for example, the narrative links the miners of medieval, plague-ridden England with the industrial workers of twentieth-century Wellington, New Zealand, through the visionary time travel of an epileptic boy in the English village. When the plague threatens to come to their Northumbrian village, the visionary boy and his adult friends set out to burrow through the center of the earth to the other side, where they believe the city of God must be. They find an unknown shaft and an engine for blasting through and begin a descent. Only later do we discover that the boy has fallen into a trance and continued on in a vision; the film indicates the break with objective, medieval reality to the dreamed modern reality only with the change from the original black-and-white to color. The miners in the boy's vision take copper to the "city of God," modern-day Wellington, New Zealand, and find a foundry that is being shut down because of layoffs. They recognize their fellows in the foundry workers and convince the skeptical modern workers to forge a cross to erect on the cathedral as an offering to God. In the process of setting the cross atop the spire, however, the boy slips and falls, plunging back into his dreaming body in the pit and awaking unharmed. He and his comrades return to the surface to find that the plague has passed over their village. Yet just as in his vision the boy has sacrificed his life to make the tribute to God, so too in real life he will become a sacrifice for his village. He alone will become infected with the plague and die of it, while the village is spared the epidemic.

Ward's film seems primarily concerned with developing a narrative analogy between the destructive and ineluctable spread of the plague and the unconstrained speed of military and media technology. In both cases, these "epidemic" infections are seen to undermine the bonds of community and the values that underlie it. The scene in the foundry, with the workers forging a link of shared feeling across time, suggests a convergence of Christian and working-class values that have been eroded by the forces of post-industrial modernity. It is an image of a good industrialism of the virtuous craft worker, rooted in a deep-seated Anglo-Saxon tradition going back to the Middle Ages. This traditional industrial working class, soon to disappear altogether, appears as the last bastion of the sort of putatively organic community from which the time travelers have come. Accordingly, three contrasting images of technology suggest the dangerous forces proliferating out of control and threatening to consign the foundry workers to the same oblivion as the latter-day heirs of the medieval British miners. First, one of the time travelers must run terrified through a nightmarish scrapyard in which huge mechanical claws grasp and clutch at the refuse of the industrial process. Second, having commandeered a rowboat, the questers are caught in an epic sea battle with a veritable "leviathan," when a nuclear submarine surfaces unexpectedly in the harbor. And finally, the visionary boy is hypnotized by a wall of television sets in a lobby and is "saved" from the evils that appear on the screen (among them, the submarine) when one of his friends smashes the TVs with an ax. This scene evokes a postmodern information and media society, in which all points of the globe are interlinked both by communicative flows and by the nuclear threat. Making this message still more explicit, Ward incorporates a news commentator talking about the idealistic but ultimately deluded attempt to make New Zealand a nuclear-free zone. Ward makes this media spectacle one of the obstacles and potential traps for the boy in his quest to raise the cross and save his village; television transmission is, in a sense, the Satanic double of his pious vision. The filmmaker thus implicitly suggests that only a return to traditional values of work, community, and faith can offer any hope of salvation against a postmodern condition undermining tradition with ever-increasing intensity.

Two films by Eastern European filmmakers suggest further alternative possibilities for time-image figures of history in relation to children. Andrei Tarkovsky's *Mirror* presents an intricate, complex, semi-autobiographical narrative figure of Soviet history from the early 1930s to the present of the film (early 1970s). Present-tense scenes of an unseen male voiceover with his estranged wife and their son shift unexpectedly and without clear points of orientation back to the 1930s and the war years, with images of the unseen man's mother and of himself as a child. In addition, there are interpolations of additional material, including television and newsreel footage from various periods. Two aspects of the film profoundly undermine the viewer's attempt to establish a temporal and ontological baseline from which the other materials can be considered second-order departures in fantasy or memory. First, similar or clearly related scenes sometimes appear in the mode of straightforward film narration (usually in color), sometimes as narration marked as subjective by a voiceover (for instance, as a memory being recounted), and sometimes in dreams (at certain points simply presented in surreal black-and-white images, at other times recounted by the voiceover). In the end, *all* the narrative material of the film appears to emanate from the unseen speaker of the voiceover, and there is no reason to favor the straight narrative passages over memory or dream on the grounds that it is "more objective." Each of the bits of this mosaic-like narrative seems equidistant from its subjective source. Tarkovsky furthermore undercuts the apparent objectivity of the narrative passages with a peculiar and challenging device: he uses the same actors to play characters in different parts of the voiceover figure's life. The mother in the 1930s and the wife in the 1970s are played by the same actress; similarly, the boy in military training during World War II and the son of that boy, now thirty years older, are played by the same young actor. Tarkovsky heightens the uncanny resemblance and repetition structuring the relationship between the generations—at least in his voiceover figure's subjective consciousness—by setting in resonance events from the past and in the present. For example, the voiceover figure's mother (during the war) and his wife (in the present) both drop a handbag and sit on the floor picking up the contents; the son (in the 1970s), in helping his mother pick up her things, has a sudden feeling of *déjà vu*, as if he were being haunted by the father's experience thirty years earlier.

If Tarkovsky's narration unfolds a complex image of history out of a highly personal nucleus of time, a pre-differentiated subjective time from which the differences between memory, imagination, dream, and perception flow, András Jeles' film *The Annunciation* presents a visionary panorama of history literally from the biblical fall of man to the modern age—all played by children between the ages of eight and twelve. It begins with a scene of the temptation of Adam and Eve by Lucifer in the Garden of Eden. Once they have been tempted and expelled from the garden, Adam wants to know if his knowledge has been worth losing paradise, and he asks the impish Lucifer to reveal the future of mankind to him. Lucifer lays him asleep with Eve in a pile of leaves and takes his spirit through a series of dream-visions into history—Ancient Greece, Byzantium, Kepler's Prague, the French Revolution, and nineteenth-century London. In each of the visions, the action is staged by the same cast of children, in a grotesque combination of children's games, theater, and dream. Adam sees in history an uninterrupted spectacle of scapegoating, intolerance, religious and political fanaticism, superstition, mob action, poverty, cruelty, infidelity, and violence.

Like Tarkovsky's *Mirror*, the film shifts time-references while using the same actors and providing limited exposition of narrative material. We see a set of almost dreamlike tableaux of history enacted by this group of child actors, recostumed for each shift in scene. There is even some contamination between historical periods in the visions, as when the Greek general from the Athenian scene inexplicably appears in eighteenth-century Paris to announce to Danton "there will be no beheading this time," thus shifting the scene to London. Just prior to this strange transition, Jeles flashes back to an image of Adam and Eve dreaming among the leaves, and the scattered leaves slowly resolve into a scene of bodies and rags in which Danton is crawling. The death of the figure in the dream is thus taken as a kind of ontological limit beyond which the penetration of other realities by the vision or dream cannot pass. Following a still more hallucinatory and temporally confused scene in London (among other things, Christ is being crucified there), Lucifer finally awakens Adam, hoping to have plunged his soul into despair, thus to claim it as his own. The film ends with an open question of whether God or Lucifer is the true "angel of history" and what role God plays within or beyond the human history that Adam is about to inaugurate. Hauntingly redoubling the question of who has the last word in history, God speaks to comfort Adam and Eve, admonishing them to "have faith and strive." Concluding the film, Lucifer mimics God's command word for word, letting its possible irony ring beyond the film. With an ambiguous smile and with the figure of death standing over Adam and Eve, he repeats, "Have faith and strive."

These films and the types I identify them as exemplifying invite reflection on four related critical and theoretical issues. First, by setting child characters against intense and difficult historical circumstances, they highlight the peculiar phenomenological capacities and limits of children's abilities to interpret, comprehend, and act in the world. Second, insofar as children exhibit in nascent form the capacities of adult subjects, and insofar as the unprecedented circumstances of twentieth-century history have raised serious issues of the comprehensibility of history by individuals, child characters offer a poignant metaphor for *adult* subjectivity faced with the baffling, inexplicable, and overwhelming contingencies of history. Third, simply because of their incompleteness, their immaturity, and their partial unformedness as social agents and actors, child characters may represent a utopian reserve of openness and hope within an otherwise closed historical horizon of adult experience. And finally, child characters and narrators offer filmmakers (and novelists) key narrative "devices" by which to approach artistically the intractable historical situation. In their acts of witnessing, their mimetic games, their imaginative transformations of themselves and others, and their travel across the divisions of time, they figuratively dramatize the individual's attempt to cope imaginatively and affectively with historical circumstances that often exceed his or her capacity to understand them rationally. Yet they also suggest alternative forms of historical witness, in which factual testimony yields its place of privilege to a wider range of subjectively inflected expressions of historical truth. These narrative figures adumbrate the basic building blocks of a new mode of historical testimony, a "figural realism" better able to represent the problematic nature of twentieth-century European historical experience.

Filmography

Germany Year Zero (Roberto Rossellini, Germany / Italy, 1947–48)
The Boy With Green Hair (Joseph Losey, USA, 1948)

Forbidden Games (René Clément, France, 1952)
The Spirit of the Beehive (Victor Erice, Spain, 1973)
Mirror (Andrei Tarkovsky, USSR, 1975)
The Tin Drum (Völker Schloendorff, Germany / France, 1979)
The Annunciation (András Jeles, Hungary, 1984)
Come and See (Elem Klimov, USSR, 1985)
The Navigator (Vincent Ward, Australia, 1988)
The Reflecting Skin (Phillip Ridley, U.K., 1990)
Tito and Me (Goran Markovic, Yugoslavia, 1992)
The Butcher Boy (Neil Jordan, Ireland, 1997)

CHAPTER 8

The Limits of Vision:
Hiroshima Mon Amour *and the*
Subversion of Representation

KYO MACLEAR

In 1957, following the international success of *Nuit et Brouillard* (*Night and Fog*, 1955), a fact-driven journey into the Nazi concentration camps, Director Alain Resnais was approached to make a documentary surveying Hiroshima twelve years after the atomic bombing. He agreed to take on the project and set off for the atomic city. After months spent filming on location, however, Resnais decided to abandon a documentary genre, opting instead for a fictional film which would devote its first fifteen minutes to footage from his aborted documentary. Acclaimed French writer Marguerite Duras was approached to write the revised dramatic screenplay and the film became a joint French-Japanese venture. Resnais' decision, motivated in large part by what he understood to be the limitations and inappropriateness of realist cinema in relation to the atomic bombings, has had a long-lasting impact.

Today, *Hiroshima Mon Amour* (1959) is one of the best known works of the French New Wave—an "avant-garde classic" that has continued to circulate in repertory theaters, film courses, and festivals. Variously remembered as a haunting love story, an antiwar picture, a tale of remembrance and forgetting, *Hiroshima Mon Amour* has persisted in evoking a range of interpretive responses. The paradox in all this might be that despite Resnais' conscious efforts to subvert assurances about docu-mimetic representation, the film has arguably become the source of many people's imagery of the city of Hiroshima and the experience.

Yet, the paradox manifested in viewer desires to "fill in" memory and meaning within the context of a film that so deliberately seems to "empty

234 • Witness and Memory

out" perceptual and epistemic certainties should not be lost or minimized. Indeed, it is precisely this tension between the desire to "know" something about the subject being represented (in this case, Hiroshima) and recognition of the limits of that knowing that, I submit, may comprise an ethical vision connected to a social practice of mourning trauma's *remains*. As a hybrid film, *Hiroshima Mon Amour* is comprised of many layers and forms of narrative. In the course of the first twenty minutes, for example, we move from an entwined lovemaking scene, to what appears to be a straightforward newsreel documentary, to a breezy onscreen conversation between two new lovers. Taken together, these contradictory plot lines—threading through fact and fiction—highlight the different ways memory inscriptions and film genres shape our understanding of historical trauma. As a "false" documentary, for example, the film calls forth our own atomic-image arsenal—unsealing any simple faith we might have in photo-realism so as to move us beyond evidentiary remembrance. But this deconstructionist move is always accompanied by another narrative gesture—a passionate, poetic reflection on memory which addresses the high stakes involved in forgetting and remembering loss. In this sense, Resnais offers what might be called a *parallax* approach to visual commemoration: he attends to the impossible task of representation and to the persistent struggle to express something about the subject, however incomplete and inadequate that "something" might be.[1]

Resnais' approach, in other words, recognizes the incommensurable gap between perception and reality, while encouraging us to explore the theme of what one sees and doesn't see in epistemological and ethical terms. *Hiroshima Mon Amour* thus introduces the possibility and necessity of elaborating a critical framework that might allow us to take up this gap (or aporia) as constitutive of the limits of knowledge. *How do we open a space in which to signal that which cannot be seen or shown? How might we encourage reflection about the relation of vision to knowledge and ethical action?*

These last questions resonate with concerns that have been recurrent in critiques of postmodern and deconstructionist approaches to historical representation. Cathy Caruth and other scholars have argued that deconstruction has been wrongly identified with the claim that historical reference is inherently fictive, and "accordingly been dismissed as denying memory, history, and all notions of truth" (Caruth and Esch 2). These misleading charges have led many scholars and critics to distance themselves from deconstruction as a philosophical discipline; to malign it as a destructive, nay-saying, even nihilist practice. What is generally missed, or willfully ignored, is the central contribution deconstruction can make in opening up fields of historical and ethical inquiry. In testing the criteria by which we compile and judge history, for example, deconstruction opens itself up to the unknown—inviting an awareness that historical reference and knowledge may not always occur, or present itself, in ways we immediately recognize. This recognition of indirect or unfamiliar reference is crucial to the study of historical trauma. Turning to such examples as the "gaps and breaks in survivor narratives," Caruth reminds us that trauma history and memory are seldom experienced in seamless or concrete ways.

Ultimately, the potential value of deconstruction rests in its application. Recognizing the limits of vision, to be sure, can either foreclose access to historical reality altogether or stress the provisional and fragile nature of its representation. Central to my view here is the point that a deconstructionist aesthetic requires a context that can foreground the underlying philosophical and ethical implications of problems of representation. The question of context is paramount—perhaps more so for works which openly play with cultural and historical references. Aestheticist approaches that broach the dismemberment of the past, the limits of trauma testimony, solely as a matter of formal interest invariably rationalize the violence.

Since the late 1960s, there has been a growing emphasis on conceptual minimalism in North American contemporary art practice, a bias toward postmodern abstraction and installation-based work. The gradual break from modernist representation—in a challenging of canonical notions of authorship, artistic value, realism, originality—has given rise to a range of contradictory practices. There is no unifying agenda tying these manifold expressions and artists together. While often sharing nonfigurative stylistic features (such as sparseness, simplicity, openness), each work demands a separate and situated response. In valorizing creative minimalism and aestheticizing memory "gaps," we may bypass the particular responsibilities involved in negotiating with the limits—the remains—of any given commemorative practice. To conclude, for example, that "less says more" is perhaps to skirt problems of representation and memory reconstruction entirely.

In what follows I will be looking at *Hiroshima Mon Amour* with an eye to elaborating what Drucilla Cornell has called a "philosophy of the limit" that can call forth the ethical aspirations of deconstruction. A philosophy of the limit, as suggested by Alain Resnais, might make us more humble about what we claim to have seen and allow us to move away from conflating seeing and understanding. But Cornell's philosophy of the limit pushes us further. Because *all* description and narrative constitute limits of remembrance, because the atomic bomb experience conjures an excess that cannot be fully incorporated, we are pressed to explore the ethical implications of partial memory. In a sense, "like the Angel of History," we are asked to witness trauma's ruins and remains while becoming "complicit in a process of making meanings and making history" (Rabinowitz 136).

Remembering at the limits is what I have chosen to call a practice of

*trans*memoration. It is a practice that ushers us to the borders of perception, thought, and possibility. When it comes to memory, the border is
more important than any temple, shrine, or monument. It is a place of remembering that a death, as unique as a life, is always in excess of any representational system, always more than a symbol or a slogan. Even as we
enlist artifacts and images to "name" and "picture" the dead, the limits bid
us keep our minds and hearts open to the people, losses, and sufferings
which cannot be captured. As Derrida suggests, these excesses, these remains, these "ghosts," call forth infinite responsibility and an aspiration to
live "more justly" (1994: xviii).

I. *Hiroshima Mon Amour*

Hiroshima Mon Amour follows a twenty-four-hour affair between a French
actress and a married Japanese architect. The one-night lovers are anonymous, unnamed through the film. *He*, the architect (Eiji Okada), is involved in a project of swift development, rebuilding over Hiroshima's
charred cityscape. *She*, a French film actress (Emmanuelle Riva), is finish-
ing up a peace film set in the atomic city. The two strangers meet in August
1957. *He*, originally from Hiroshima, has lost most of his family in the
bombing. *She*, originally from Nevers, France, where she was punished as a
collaborator following an affair with a German soldier, has a less obvious
relationship to the city of Hiroshima.

   The film begins with a sequence of grasping limbs and torsos. Cascading
into camera-dissolves, these sweat-soaked bodies can be seen moving into
the clutches of love or death. They enter into the visual ruins of a film
which will repeatedly intersperse images of sexuality and annihilation. The
off-screen voiceover is flat, formal, repetitive: a metronomic exchange
droned in counterpoint to the images of fluid passion that fill the screen.
The spectacle of their lovemaking in a hotel room slips into newsreel
footage of post-bomb Hiroshima. The dialogue continues. Set against a realist memoryscape, an "official parade of already well-known horrors from
Hiroshima" (Duras 9), the female voice claims a total vision. The male
voice refutes and inverts every statement.

   He: You saw nothing in Hiroshima. Nothing.
   She: I saw *everything. Everything.*

She continues to insist that she has seen *everything.*

   She: Four times at the museum in Hiroshima. I looked at the
   people. I myself looked thoughtfully at the iron. The burned iron.

The broken iron, the iron made vulnerable as flesh. I saw the bouquet of bottle caps: who would have suspected that? Human skin floating, surviving, still in the bloom of its agony. Stones. Burned stones. Shattered stones. Anonymous heads of hair that the women of Hiroshima, when they awoke in the morning, discovered had fallen out . . .

He: You saw nothing in Hiroshima. Nothing.

She: . . . I've always wept over the fate of Hiroshima. Always.

He: No. What would you have cried about?

She: I saw the newsreels. On the second day, History tells, I'm not making it up, on the second day certain species of animals rose again from the depths of the earth and from the ashes. Dogs were photographed. For all eternity. I saw them. I *saw* the newsreels. I *saw* them. On the first day. On the second day. On the third day.

He: (*interrupting her*) You saw nothing. Nothing.

As he repeats his incantation, his impersonal voice coldly denying her every claim, we see images of the Peace Park, the Survivors' Hospital, panoramic newsreels, the Hiroshima Peace Museum. What she describes, insists on having seen, is an archival history of Hiroshima. These well-ordered images, catalogued for museum-goers and memory-tourists, sweep by the screen. *He* suggests that what is being "seen" is a swift memorial that can offer little more than a design of the past: an architectonic view that pinches the vast horror between four walls for all to see. Arranged within the four walls are mementos, safeguarded memory-objects. Their presence offers a kind of solace, a sort of companionship. The four walls provide a center, a focal point, for envisioning meaning. Four walls so that we might know where to look to see *everything* (that counts, can be counted, accounted for); four walls so that we may be freed from looking *beyond* to bordering longings and miseries for which no records whatsoever exist.

As the narrative unfolds, we are forced to relinquish the provisional security of a single or unitary vision, the desire for omniscience, to see it all. The flickering film-frames accord with the experience of a glance: the random movement of a viewing process that cannot possibly ascertain everything. This is a way of seeing that highlights discontinuities. It is impossible to sustain a prolonged gaze. Resnais, thus, declines from projecting or asserting an absolute vision of Hiroshima. He offers no final moral ground, no steady harbor, from which to apprise the event of the atomic bombings. Instead, the film adopts a strategic mode of address, constantly subverting narrative authority, casting doubt on the reliability of perceptual claims. The film not only accentuates the limits of its own narrative construction, but also calls into question received sightings and knowledges. Always in excess of any name, image, or meaning, Hiroshima is never "given" as pure, uninterrupted memory. Instead of the reduction of memory to a site, Resnais invokes complex and even banal spaces of remembering where we confront the presence of loss through everyday living and chance encounters.

Hiroshima Mon Amour is, in this sense, a narrative that folds itself *into* and *away from* a commemoration of the bombings. It is a film of endless lamentation that is dramatically suspended between the acting out of a traumatic past and the difficult effort to work through it. The vexed impossibility of memory, the fleeting salve of amnesia, the unstitched terror of remembering and witnessing beyond bounded stories and sites: these are themes that reel through *Hiroshima Mon Amour*.

While Shoshana Felman suggests that *Hiroshima Mon Amour* instructs us "in the ways in which testimony has become a crucial mode of our relation to events of our times—our relation to traumas of contemporary history," it does so by consistently breaking with referential narration (1992: 5). The film evocatively gestures toward the unknowable, toward sites and sights that exceed our immediate frames of reference. These are events that dash efforts to gain hold, grasp, and enclose understanding. Unfathomable are the words: enemy, atrocity, destruction. They exist only in the larger perception of history's recording. "You have seen nothing" if you imagine this trauma self-transparent, or so the narrative seems to insist.[2]

II. Seeing Everything

For the French actress, history is obvious, undeniable. The burned iron, the human skin, the shattered stones: it is all there in the newsreel footage. As film viewers, we are positioned to share her unflinching faith in the camera's inclusive gaze. We are invited to share her point of view, the pathos of having seen it all, the *frisson* of sensual immersion. But, if we assume this surrogate perspective then we, too, are left open to the charge that we have seen nothing.

Unqualified and insistent, the repeated assertion of the actress that she has seen "everything" takes on the air of spectatorial conceit. Through rote remembrance, a recitation of visual evidence encountered in a once-infernal city, she has emotionally and cognitively incorporated the atomic bomb experience (Jackson 151).[3] The architect, by contrast, resists her desire to command total mastery over the meanings of Hiroshima. Her sense of sureness and certainty are disconcerting, he suggests, because they can only be spoken through a generic language, which too easily obliterates the particularities of this trauma. Rejecting an easy unity between seeing and knowing, defying immersed identification with the camera recording lens, his words stand in as a refutation of absolute memory.

By having his two central characters' stories cast doubt on each other, and by ensuring that their parallel narratives remain separate throughout the film, Resnais defies the principle of narrative resolution. The dimensions of power and authenticity invested in the French actress, as a witness, remain ambiguous and unresolved. More than simply presenting an optical paradox (*I see everything, I see nothing*), however, Resnais' filmic approach to the trauma of Hiroshima has carried a powerful reminder of its own ethical limits: no matter how much visual information he packed into the film, *Hiroshima Mon Amour* could not ultimately answer the enormous question of what the atomic bombs had meant to the world.

Instead, the film confronts assumptions that structure conventional films about Hiroshima—in particular, the view that there is an intact history out there waiting to be lured into vision and spoken as pure meaning. Resnais' "now you see it" and "now you don't" approach to the trauma of Hiroshima disperses the task of witnessing, openly deferring interpretation and response to viewers of his film. Foregrounding the limits of vision, Resnais turns attention to the violence implicit in our visualizing strategies, our own complicity in objectifying the visual field. If vision is a privileged sensory modality in Euro-American cultures, and if as Pierre Nora once remarked, "ours is an intensely retinal and powerfully televisual memory" (1989: 17), then *Hiroshima Mon Amour* might allow us to pose the question: What and how do we train our minds to picture, to know?

The question seems all the more apt when posed through the vehicle of film. The extraordinary vividness of film media, after all, encourages us to become quickly absorbed by its sensory field. Filmic sounds and images are frequently taken as perceptions rather than representations. We blush, become aroused, shiver with fear, turn away in revulsion. As if to jar us out of deep immersion from the outset, Resnais takes us on a voyeuristic trip through Hiroshima near the beginning of the film. This visual sweep through a city once-turned crematorium vacillates between curious indifference and pious fascination. Circus music plays as an atom molecule dangles like a disco globe from the Peace Museum ceiling. A cheerful young woman leads a Japanese tour bus through the downtown memory-topos. Hiroshima could be a theme park.

Resnais' attempt to capture the elusive relationship between vision and knowledge in *Hiroshima Mon Amour* is a way of indicting the hubris of the all-knowing eye—a fast tourist vision that might rein in the ruins. In questioning how our historical knowledge—our image of the past—got to be constructed from a given perception before the watchful gaze of a camera, he opens a space in which to consider the importance of perceiving anew. As such, *Hiroshima Mon Amour* provides a possible incentive for viewers to question the image repertoire that constitutes our sense of consciousness— or what we know. In gesturing toward the stubborn fissures that mushroom between images and meaning, the film registers how the perceptual experience of viewing recorded documentation of an event may not be commensurate with the intelligibility (the meanings) of that event.

III. Emptying Out

In many ways, *Hiroshima Mon Amour* exists as an anomaly within the context of witness art. In challenging precepts of historical realism, the film eludes a literalization of visual memory. In contrast to atomic bomb films that have been attached to notions of photographic transparency, that have attempted to reenact the experience "as it happened," *Hiroshima Mon Amour* yields the possibility of being read as a complete testimony. Promoted by Resnais as a "false documentary," *Hiroshima Mon Amour* resists becoming "just another film" about Hiroshima (that "other film" is there, represented as a peace film the actress has come to shoot). Instead, the dreamlike quality of film is mobilized in *Hiroshima Mon Amour* to evoke imaginative associations and memories that exceed any apparently literal codes.[4]

In her preface to the published manuscript of *Hiroshima Mon Amour*, Marguerite Duras writes, "Impossible to talk about Hiroshima. All one can do is talk about the impossibility of talking about Hiroshima." The refusal to represent events directly has been a constant feature of Duras' writing. In *Hiroshima Mon Amour*, we indirectly approach the trauma of nuclear annihilation through the recurring metaphor of fatal love. The French actress's tragic love affair with a German soldier in wartime France, her bittersweet fling with the Japanese architect, become provisional pathways into the immense trauma of Hiroshima. These trysts of passion and remembrance are given added historical valence because in each instance a national border has been crossed. Reproducing the terms of war in a disquieting way, the characters are forever identified with their respective cities. Otherwise nameless, each lover is given a toponym. Identified as *Hiroshima* and *Nevers*, they become ventriloquists for larger personal and social tragedies.

Both Duras and Resnais share the view that indirection is the only way to approach these events. The great majority of us were not direct witnesses to the atomic bombings. The fictive story of a love affair between a Japanese architect and a French actress is, thus, a necessary narrative replacement. It is necessary, if mundane, because we have missed the main event of Hiroshima being destroyed by the atomic bomb. We have been prevented from observing the event itself due to our belated arrival. The reduction is intended to give us a sense of the disproportionate scale of loss at Hiroshima. Whether this indirect appeal to a memory of the bombings has been sufficiently foregrounded in the film has been a central source of concern and dispute.

Some have argued that the love story comes to dominate the city's symbolic history. James Monaco, for example, states that it is too easy to read the film as "primarily a love story, one which uses Hiroshima and its history rather obscenely as background and filler to multiply the drama inherent in this supposedly intentionally banal story" (43). Others have suggested that through narrative placement and camera framing, the woman is too focally centered. The film revels masochistically in her sad story. Her death-tinged sadness, experienced as deeply personal, is thought to subsume the political matter of the atomic bombings within an arguably simplistic melancholia. Other writers have criticized Marguerite Duras for creating characters that are paralyzed, even destroyed, by the force of a theme-ridden allegory (Monaco 37).

While varying over time in tenor and pitch, the central issues addressed in criticisms of the film have related primarily to the risks involved in merging art and history, love and death, the personal and the public. For many critics, the strategy of postponed closure offered by *Hiroshima Mon Amour*—however aesthetically evocative it may be—is contentious, even immoral, given the weight of the disaster. Reviewing forty years of critical response, it becomes clear that something fundamental is at stake in witnessing at the limits. How we come to engage with the excesses and gaps activated by a representational practice largely depends on the viewing context surrounding that practice. *What facts of the film's narrative get foregrounded during its circulation? How do our interpretive frames allow us to engage* Hiroshima Mon Amour *toward a better understanding of the philosophical and ethical implications of attending to representational limits?*

Hiroshima Mon Amour reportedly received "thunderous acclaim" when first screened in 1959 at the Cannes Film Festival. It garnered an equally enthusiastic response from viewers and critics when it premiered in 1960 in the United States (Kreidl 55). The film's bittersweet, ambiguous ending was welcomed by American viewers. Its use of jump-cuts and layered narrative no doubt provided a contrast to Hollywood films, which were generally predisposed to melodrama and simple endings. French New Wave cinema, while eventually establishing its own customs, was a far cry from the conventions of American pop cinema.[5]

The overwhelmingly positive response to the film upon its initial release in North America raises the question of how it was marketed and billed by promoters and critics at the time. Glossing over contemporaneous reviews, it is immediately striking that critics—almost uniformly—failed to mention, let alone stress, that the film was about the "impossibility" of making a documentary about Hiroshima. Commenting on this elision, James Monaco concludes that *Hiroshima Mon Amour* did not draw praise because "it was a sophisticated 'false documentary' trying to deal with the question of memory and history of Hiroshima, but because it was a poignant love story with a remarkable—even shocking—setting. For most viewers of the film, the tale wags the dog" (44). In short, Duras and Resnais stand accused of creating a fiction that not only uses history, but to a great extent subsumes it.

Echoing this sentiment, Earl Jackson, Jr. has remarked on the dangers of presenting annihilation and obliteration through a strategy of "emptying out." Jackson questions to what extent Hiroshima, stripped of accessible historical and cultural associations, gets reduced in the film to an "ever absent-ed locus," a site of emptiness and nihilism, subsequently mortgaged to a psychosexual "metaphoric system" (150). *Hiroshima Mon Amour*, if read only as a narrative of love and loss, can thus be criticized for supplanting other dimensions of longing and mourning indirectly associated with the commemoration of mass atrocity. The allegorical doubling of the bombings with an autobiographical narrative of loss—namely the actress's loss of her German lover—means that atomic bomb survivors never enter the frame for longer than a few seconds. Displaced from direct characterization they are presented, at most, as incarnations of absence.

Robert Jay Lifton suggests that the bodily union of the lovers and the documentary footage of Hiroshima's grotesque encounter with mass death, present themes that despite their intensity, merely coexist. Lifton faults the film for having two parallel narratives that never confront each other, concluding that in the absence of a contextual referent, Hiroshima becomes a carte blanche: open to any story. As such, he argues that the film fails to address the distinctiveness of the atomic bombings. To quote Lifton:

> Indeed, many have asked . . . : "Why Hiroshima? Why not *Yokohama Mon Amour*?" The theoretical answer is that Hiroshima represents an ultimate in man's deadly destructiveness which Resnais wished to illuminate against the starkness of physical love. Yet the formulation remains abstract, apart, because the film has recorded but not grasped its environment. (1967: 468)

Lifton further notes that *Hiroshima Mon Amour* encountered virulent opposition and criticism in Hiroshima, even while it was being filmed.

Some *hibakusha* opposed the film's pervasive sensuality, claiming it was an insult to the dead (468). The fact that the film's title in Japanese was changed to *Twenty-Four Hour Love Affair* (*Nijuyo-jikan no Joji*) must have magnified these concerns—directing viewers towards a narrow interpretation of the narrative. In this context, the film's romantic story represents less a surrogate encounter with events too overbearing, too traumatic, to be faced head on, and more an evasion of history. In short, demons are banished from the bedroom.

These criticisms of *Hiroshima Mon Amour* serve as a reminder that the critical and ethical potential of the film cannot be secured in advance. Here, Resnais' refusal to allow cinematic vision to master the meaning of the atomic bombs, his strategy of "emptying out," are interpreted as idioms of escape evoking a flight from history. This contextual flight is seen to pave the way for an eroticization of death metaphors, the edification of narcissistic desire. Witnessing the impossibility of witnessing becomes an all-consuming process.[6] In postponing closure, the film has also been submitted to the charge that it integrates, even encourages, a dynamic of denial.

In light of these criticisms, the conceptual movement from a model of vision that "sees everything" to one that "sees nothing" is of ongoing concern to our practice of ethical deconstruction. As Derrida reminds us, confronting the lapses and gaps in our inability to imagine the ruins and remains need not shade over into refusal, incorporation, or the relegation of the trauma to the periphery of consciousness and concern:

> Needless to spell it out here, therefore, still less to insist on it too heavily: it is not a taste for the void or for destruction that leads anyone to recognize the right of the necessity to "empty out" increasingly and to deconstruct the philosophical response that consists in *totalizing*, in filling in the space of the question or in denying its possibility, in fleeing from the very thing it will have allowed one to glimpse. (1984: 30)

I cannot propose to offer insight into the true meaning or intent behind *Hiroshima Mon Amour*. I would, however, suggest that most of these criticisms engage the film solely at a descriptive or denotative level. That is, as a narrative about the atomic bombings. Bearing this emphasis in mind: What happens when we begin to see the film as about the production of memory, vision, and knowledge more generally? It is certainly true that the film does not readily reveal its meanings, that it retains a disturbing ambiguity. But it is, I would argue, precisely this underlying tension that makes the film so compelling. The film's deconstructive approach—which engenders a realization of its own limited vision—draws back into view the layered process by which memory is constructed, and our own role in this process. The need for historical inquiry and denotative knowledge is not diminished, but surpassed.

IV. Minding the Excess

At this point, readers might well ask whether or not *Hiroshima Mon Amour* is, in fact, actually engaged in representing the atomic bombings at all. Unlike *Night and Fog*, the film has moved away from verifiable facts and figures to register memory through evocation. *Hiroshima Mon Amour* deconstructs, leaving Hiroshima, as referent, in a ruin of representation. In so doing, the film challenges our desire to seek reconciliation with the past. It perplexes our efforts to establish closure so as to assuage the anxiety of that which eludes closure. But having acknowledged the impossibility of fully perceiving or comprehending what was experienced at Hiroshima, the question becomes: What are we left to commemorate: What is there to witness?

Flight is one of the organizing metaphors of *Hiroshima Mon Amour*, accentuated by a camera that seems at times literally to "fly" through the city. Foregrounding the false immediacy (or "thereness") of visual representation, and dispensing with the solidity of an "earthbound" rational perspective, Resnais encourages us to move into that space of perception and thought that might be found between "seeing everything" and "seeing nothing." Through recurrent flashbacks and afterimages, which defy linear chronology, he simulates the "irrational" experience of trauma survival—conveying both "the truth of an event and the truth of its incomprehensibility" (Caruth 1995: 153). Thus, oscillating between certainty and uncertainty, *Hiroshima Mon Amour* offers a model of witnessing that may be inherited by the viewer watching the film.

Again, Marguerite Duras' words re-echo: "Impossible to talk about Hiroshima. All one can do is talk about the impossibility of talking about Hiroshima." Duras directly addresses our inevitable infidelity to these events. The limits of vision inherent to the film connote a similar crisis of representation, or more specifically, a crisis of not having adequate frames to contain historical events. There are different positions from which to engage these limits of vision and knowledge—as reflected in the varied responses to the film. Our task is to consider the different responsibilities that come with each of these positions and not leave historical representations in an " 'unreconstructable' litter, thus undermining the possibility of determining precepts for moral action" (Drucilla Cornell 1992: 1).

Where are there gaps in our framings of the past? Is our lack of knowledge substantive or important? Why? Would our actions in the future be different if we could exceed our present understanding? *Hiroshima Mon Amour* enables such important witnessing questions by calling out beyond its own evidential frames of remembrance.

V. Transmemoration

In *Hiroshima Mon Amour* signs and images of trauma appear to be held in place through a viewing relation founded on absolute certainty and order. A standpoint that "sees everything," requires configuring and absorbing Hiroshima as a particular totality of memory and meaning. This memory is derived from a perspective that arrests and universalizes trauma artifacts—in museums, peace plazas, archives. Symbols of grisly death are, thus, embalmed through a positivist tradition, which in turn serves to limit possible memorializing positions for the viewer-witness.

In an effort to discern the limits of positivist and other incorporative orders of historical engagement, this final section turns to the possibility of elaborating *trans*memoration as a process of situated historical inquiry and ethical translation. My attempt to grapple with the possibilities of *trans*-memoration hinges on an understanding of experience, perception, and knowledge as historically contingent and located. Whereas the prefix "*com*" denotes togetherness, unity, and completeness, "*trans*" derives its associations from words such as "across," "over," "beyond." According to the *Oxford Dictionary of English Etymology* (1986), "commemorate" means to "relate to memory together" or "recollect in unity." *Trans*memoration, by contrast, signals a coming to terms (to language) with the ways in which our identities and understandings are unevenly implicated in wider social and symbolic formations structured on power and inequality. *Trans*memoration conveys the *trans*-it between disparate experiences, knowings, languages, cultures, times, and geographies.

The work of Cornell and Derrida is extremely helpful to any discussion of *trans*memoration. Both have suggested that "heeding the call of otherness" cannot be achieved through narcissistic or universalizing modes of identification. Calling attention to the limits of every historical translation, they seek to register yet-unspoken claims of otherness, which cannot be encompassed by any given narrative, and thus point to the narrative's contradictions and exclusions.

In this sense, they suggest, ethics is not about establishing a common ideal (in the name of such "universals" as humanity or national history). Nor is it about establishing a moral blueprint for how we should behave. Herein defined, ethics focuses rather "on the kind of person one must become in order to develop a nonviolative relationship to the Other" (Cornell

1992: 13). An ethical relation, in other words, assumes a commitment to guard otherness "against the appropriation that would deny her difference and singularity" (62).

Derrida employs a metaphoric trinity of ghosts, hauntings, and specters to introduce us to a different politics of memory and inheritance. Breaking with a metaphysics of presence and absence, Derrida discusses the possibility of forging an ethical connection to those others who are "not present, nor presently living, either to us, in us, or outside us" (1994: xix). While the "ghost" cannot be named in any fixed manner, while the "haunt" has no concrete referent, they are still liminal members of our contemporary ethical community. As Derrida writes: "The ghost, *le re-venant*, the survivor appears only by means of figure or fiction, but its appearance is not nothing, nor is it mere semblance" (1986b: 64).

The "not nothing" invoked by Derrida introduces the ghost as an excess, the unnamable remainder, which nonetheless makes ingresses into the lives and psychic unconscious of those surviving terror. The "not nothing" invokes also the importance of revisiting distinctions between the real and the imaginary, where hard-line fact-and-fiction distinctions collapse in the face of trauma. For many the task of overcoming the hauntings of trauma memory, the struggle to lay the ghosts to rest, are impossibilities. The challenge invoked by both Cornell and Derrida is two-pronged. On the one hand, it involves addressing the excessive and untranslatable dimensions of loss; on the other hand, we are asked to probe the normative limits of language and narrative which act to bar certain memories of violence, trauma, and injustice. The fear that the excess remains of collective mourning may destabilize normal language and life has resulted in efforts to isolate and assimilate the surplus significance of these events. How these traumas and testimonies get marginalized at the same time as they are written into the mythic and metaphoric structures of national commemoration and public memory is a matter that warrants ongoing scrutiny. The collective representation of death, through commemoration, may contribute to its very idealization.

*Trans*memoration, in the sense being proposed, may allow us to move the task of remembering beyond the triumphalist phase of mourning and beyond the "assimilationist's dream" of a full absorption of difference (Bhabha 224). In order to guard against the assimilation of difference, both Walter Benjamin and Homi Bhabha have introduced the importance of recognizing the "foreignness" or "newness" of testimonies. Surpassing our present orders of language and knowledge, this "newness" precludes the possibility of a total transfer of memory and meaning. These yet-unknown memories and experiences may, nonetheless, through a process of *trans*memoration, revisit or haunt the orders that have made their testimony *impossible*. In welcoming the ghosts of other histories and collective memories, *trans*memoration challenges the authority of progressive modern time and the foundations of national communities.

As Benjamin notes, translation marks the "stage of continued life" for a testimonial form, restoring new energy to the past (1969: 71). It is the realization that every act of translation involves a gesture of re-cre⁻tion which makes it an ethical practice. Never *given*, *trans*memoration is always an aspiration, a life-filled task. It exposes ethics to be a fraught process of understanding our complicity and responsibility to witness, to interpret, to act, toward the cessation of violence and oppression. Bidding us continually to test the limits of vision and remembrance, enjoining us to mind the aporia between seeing and knowing "everything" or "nothing," an ethical community might herein be defined as a space where contradictions can be maintained without a hastened rush for conclusions or harmony. It is a space that yields a common field of possibility and hope through the friction of questioning and reflection.

CHAPTER **9**

Ex/propriating Survivor Experience, or Auschwitz "after" Lyotard

KARYN BALL

J'ai analysé des milliers de documents. J'ai inlaslablement poursuivi de mes questions spécialistes et historiens. J'ai cherché, mais en vain, un seul ancien déporté capable de me prouver qu'il avait réellement vu, de des propres yeuxs, une chambre à gaz.[1]

—Robert Faurisson

When Robert Faurisson invoked a scientistic bias toward "hard evidence" to deny the existence of the gas chambers in 1978, he exploited the silence of the murdered who could not repudiate his claims. His denial deployed disciplinary reason to denigrate the reality of the victims' deaths and thereby cast doubt on the historical authority of survivor testimony about the death camps. Despite his intentions, Faurisson's remarks did not touch off a crisis surrounding the historical authority of survivor testimony.[2] Nevertheless, his views resonated somewhat uncomfortably with a post-war Nietzschean skepticism that became increasingly influential among left-leaning philosophers following World War II, the Algerian struggle, and in the wake of 1968. This skepticism responded to a perceived "will to power" imbedded in discourse, including the discourse of witnesses. What needed to be defended, therefore, was not the historical reality of the gas chambers, but rather the moral authority of the Holocaust survivors as witnesses.

One means of defending this authority might be to emphasize the "authenticity" of testimony as a measure of a witness's proximity to the events in question. Yet from a Derridean perspective, this criterion is itself suspect. So construed, authenticity conflates "truth" with the immediacy of an allegedly "originary" presence. This mimetic logic assumes that presence can be reactivated through language, which is to say, through an appropriate definition that treats the object concerned as if it were a stable referent.

The historical referent is a mimetic effect of the disciplinary *proper* as a nexus of epistemological, hermeneutical, moral, and aesthetic constraints that guide the process of historical interpretation. The object *proper* is, in effect, an idealized interpretation of an event that anchors and regulates the writing of history. This understanding of the referent is consonant with Jacques Derrida's formulation of the *proper* as an enframing device that serves to arrest *différance* as a movement of temporalization and displacement within language. *Différance* affects the sign as a substitution for the thing itself, a substitution that is at once secondary, provisional, differential, and arbitrary. The sign is, thus, a problematic "detour" for an idealist conception of historical reality that identifies empirical truth with unmediated presence (1982a: 9).

Derrida's essay on *différance* was first published in 1968, a year whose events further politicized the French *Tel Quel* group's literary and philosophical engagement with the power and productivity of textual praxis. The critical intervention of Jean-François Lyotard into the Faurisson controversy should be read in relation to this post-World War II, post-1968 juncture that informed the philosophical turn toward the sign. Lyotard's intervention is significant for its attempt to weigh the consequences of an anti-foundationalist approach to the problem of historical judgment. It is an intervention that is conspicuously marked by his dialogue with Derrida as a leading philosopher in the French critique of humanism. To counter the negationist threat, Lyotard does not suggest that scholars defend the authenticity of testimonial narratives. Nor does he encourage historians to abandon their attempts to evaluate the facticity of different narratives and modes of representation altogether. Instead, he stresses the asymmetries among epistemological, moral, and aesthetic judgments that pressure their legitimacy as consensus-based speech-acts. For Lyotard, the epistemological problem of judging history is, in the end, a practical issue: it involves the task of deciding which and whose aims will govern the judgment of a given claim. In principle, this question of aim entails a question of *genre* as a category that provides the rules for linking heterogeneous phrases. Genres hold the power to synthesize knowledge, to determine criteria of validity, and, thus, to define the *proper* as a referential norm.

In *Le Différend*, published in 1983, Lyotard considers the philosophical consequences of Faurisson's negationism for the ontological and historical integrity of Holocaust testimony. In that context, Lyotard directly addresses the problem of reference as it bears on Faurisson's denial of the gas chambers. Lyotard reads this denial as an indication of the disbelief that the exteriority of mass death precipitates. For Lyotard, this disbelief is a sign that the event of anonymous mass death cannot be understood or validated on the basis of empirical and ontological concepts of experience. He consequently reflects on the conditions for defending the validity of testimony about mass death in the gas chambers when the language of experience is inadequate to represent it. This defense stresses the fragility of the gas chambers as a historical referent that is vulnerable to contestation. In this respect, *The Differend* continues the critique of experience launched in "Discussions, or Phrasing 'after Auschwitz'" (1980) as a means of reflecting on the limits of knowledge about the gas chambers. In both "Discussions" and *The Differend*, Lyotard explores the limits of ontological, phenomenological, and empiricist discourses through which one comes to know the "unknowability" of mass death.

"Discussions" brings Derrida's critique of humanism to bear on Theodor W. Adorno's reflections on "Metaphysics after Auschwitz" in *Negative Dialectics*. In *The Differend*, this critique is taken up from the vantage point of Lyotard's analysis of reference and, specifically, *designation* as the affiliation between names and referents. "The Referent, the Name" is a chapter of *The Differend* that is devoted to the problematic character of designation as it bears on the authority of survivor testimony. My discussion of that chapter will focus on how Lyotard's analysis of designation both undermines and reinforces the authority of survivor testimony. His investment in Kant's critique of aesthetic judgment inclines Lyotard to seek the answer to this question in the subject rather than the object of testimony, in the reception rather than the experiential referent of accounts about mass death. Following my consideration of Lyotard's discussion of reference, I will therefore consider the question of how Lyotard "disciplines" the Holocaust by formalizing the conditions of its philosophical, moral, and aesthetic reception. For if the referent of the death camps is "unrepresentable" as an experience, then Lyotard must assume the existence of an "audience" who is able and willing to attest to this limit.

I. The Referent, the Name

Before I present my reading of *The Differend*, it will be helpful to introduce the terms of paramount importance in Lyotard's reflections on language and judgment. This vocabulary bears the signs of Lyotard's reaction against the rationalist tradition of philosophies of language which assume that an ideal ground for communication must be established through recourse to a transcendental consensus or intersubjectivity. For Lyotard, in contrast, "There is no 'language' in general [i.e., in the structuralists' sense], except as the object of an Idea [in the Kantian sense]" (xii). Language is thus a *Ding-an-sich* that orients and regulates linguistics.

To separate himself from the rationalist tradition, Lyotard adopts a Wittgensteinian perspective to stress the agonistic and rhetorical aspects of discourse as a series of *language games*. Wittgenstein employed this term in his analysis of contingent relations among various categories of utterance. Following Wittgenstein, Lyotard defines these categories "in terms of rules specifying their properties and the uses to which they can be put—in exactly the same way as the game of chess is defined by a set of rules determining the properties of each of the pieces, in other words, the proper way to move them." Modifying the rules changes the game while utterances which do not abide by the rules are said not to belong to the game that is based on them. By implication, then, "every utterance should be thought of as a 'move' in the game" wherein "to speak is to fight, in the sense of playing" (1984b: 10).

Lyotard's reading of this "play" stresses the way in which the social bond "is composed," in Anne Barron's words, "not of the exchanges of free-standing, self-possessed individuals, but of the 'moves' of multiple language games, which, because innumerable, unstable and interlocking, produce a plurality of identities. . . ." (32). Within this framework, Lyotard's use of the term *linkage* or, specifically, *phrase linkage*, is an attempt to purge his discourse of all traces of a unified subject or agent who might be understood as playing language games as well as being played by them. Instead, he opts in favor of the absolute spontaneity of the *phrase* as a purely contingent occurrence, a neutral "happening" or "arrival" in language that "expresses" no necessary content. Indeed, the contingency of phrasing constitutes the practical condition of a thought that at once defines and is defined by the situating of its addressee, addressor, referent, and sense "instances" in a phrase "universe."[3]

His emphasis on the neutrality and rhetoricity of the phrase will subsequently allow Lyotard to focus on the provisional modes in which different phrases are connected and to foreground the role of rules that determine the possible connections between various phrases. Accordingly, phrases are subject to the rules of their respective *phrase regimens* or *regimes*, including reasoning, knowing, describing, showing, and prescribing. By distinguishing among phrases in terms of their regime, Lyotard emphasizes the disciplinary power of the aims that govern phrases and determine their relations. Lyotard also stresses that phrase regimes are not translatable into each other. They can, however, be linked "in accordance with an end fixed by a genre of discourse" where a *genre* should be understood as the rubric that "supplies the rules for linking together heterogeneous phrases, rules that are proper for attaining certain goals. . . ." (1988: xii).

Although linkage between heterogeneous phrases is sometimes difficult, linkage "happens," and is, in fact, unavoidable. For this reason, there is no "last phrase" in Lyotard's universe since even the silence that would follow the so-called last phrase is itself a phrase, and since a phrase would then be required to affirm that the penultimate phrase was the last.[4] But if, for Lyotard, linkage between phrases is necessary in the logical sense, the mode of their linkage is not. Hence, the constant conflict among genres of discourse does not merely reflect the contestation over the value of a phrase and its orientation. As I have already suggested, it also enacts a crisis of legitimation whereby no proper mode of presentation can be determined without first presupposing the primacy of one genre and one intention over others, that is, without presupposing a synthesis of the multiple as a one.

In "Discussions, or Phrasing 'after Auschwitz,' " Lyotard reads Adorno's critique of this presupposition as a critical intervention into the history of metaphysics. In this reading, such a synthesis represents the method and end of a totalizing speculative logic that is improper "after Auschwitz." Auschwitz is thus Adorno's model for a thought that derails positive reason. In comparison with *The Differend*, however, the problem of reference receives comparatively cursory attention in "Discussions" where it arises in the context of Lyotard's elaboration on the anonymous erasure of proper names in the death camps. In that context, Lyotard highlights the ways in which the proper name *Auschwitz* defies Hegel's view of names as place-markers that anchor memories. In opposition to this view, Lyotard constructs "Auschwitz" in the era of its "after" thought as an impossibly negative concept for the anonymous, bureaucratic, and instrumental erasure of proper names that took place in the camps. This construction respects Adorno's sensitivity about protecting the particular against a thematizing usurpation. Figured negatively as an "anonym," "Auschwitz" cannot be incorporated into the unity of a speculative universal. It must, therefore, remain unintelligible for an aggrandizing positive reason.

In *The Differend*, Lyotard dwells on the problems that the experiential referent of testimony poses for historical verification in pragmatist terms. In that context, he stresses the rhetoricity of judgment as a function of the competition among different aims and their respective genres. This competition suggests that the judgment of testimony cannot be reduced to a quest for a "proper" approach to the true, and, accordingly, not in terms of the "correct" mimesis of the historical referent as such. Rather, if the stakes of judging Holocaust testimony are to become clear, then the ontological and empirical status of survivor experiences must be problematized in relation to their rhetorical and aesthetic power.

To a certain extent, Lyotard's general preference for aporias of judgment reflects a modernist recalcitrance to adopt the rhetoric of clarity and its positivistic tendencies. This is a recalcitrance that also surfaces in Adorno's *Aesthetic Theory* and consistently throughout Derrida's *oeuvre*. One might say that Derrida has made it his particular *forte* to disarticulate intelligibility as a function of the referent's presumed conceptual unity and stasis. In this vein, his formulation of *différance* to stress the historicity of meaning is a corrective to the metaphysical view that designation is stable and ontologically based. Relevant here is Hegel's provision in the *Science of Logic* that the conceptual stability produced by positive reason is the condition of understanding. This provision points in the direction of a theory of fixation whereby a conceptual nexus assumes its status as a determinate referent. The *proper* is a rhetorical and disciplinary instrument of this process that curtails the production of referential variations.

Earlier I remarked that Faurisson capitulates to disciplinary reason when he disavows, on positivistic grounds, the validity of survivor testimony as evidence for the existence of the death camps. On the other hand, it is worth considering how negationist views such as Faurisson's may compel Holocaust scholars to shore up their object of inquiry against the contingencies of morally inappropriate revisions. In this instance, the Holocaust *proper* is an idealized concept that orients and regulates interpretation. In addition, it is important to note that configurations of the object *proper* are, broadly speaking, composite memories insofar as they entail imaginary reconstructions of prior ideas. In this respect, the Holocaust *proper* is an idealized memory that establishes the imaginary locus of a discipline. This is not to imply that interpretive "reactivations" of traumatic history are repetitions of the same. In keeping with Derrida's formulation of *différance*, I would stress that repetitions affect differentiations in the nexus of concepts and images that "belong to" an object's semantic field. Of course, these differentiations do not merely transpire *within* fields insofar as the "field" itself must be "cut out" from the flux of possible, virtual, and intersecting fields. For this reason, the delimitation of objects of inquiry as ideal concepts is inseparable from their circumscription as disciplinary *topoi*.

The so-called fixation of the referent is an important issue for analytic philosophers who relate it to the proper name's *rigidity* in describing its invariability across multiple contexts. Derrida's work frequently draws on analytic discussions of rigidity in order to deconstruct the *proper* as a figure that "enframes" and thus fixes the essential "properties" "belonging to" referents. Lyotard shares Derrida's interest in the relation between intelligibility and reference. It is an interest that is profoundly influenced by Wittgenstein and Saul Kripke who both resist the idealist tendency to ontologize meaning. Indeed, Lyotard's attention to designation is explicitly informed by their respective considerations of the practical and intuitive status of proper names. These considerations suggest that the relation between names and referents is not necessary in the philosophical sense; it therefore cannot establish a stable foundation of truth and understanding.

I have already mentioned Lyotard's recourse to Wittgenstein's language games to emphasize the rhetorical parameters of knowledge production. In this measure, Kripke's contribution to Lyotard's thinking also deserves a brief elaboration.[5] Among his significant contributions to twentieth-century philosophy, and French poststructuralism in particular, is Kripke's nominalist critique of essentialism as a view of identity that posits the properties of objects as essential, that is, as substantial and/or necessary predicates. For Kripke, in contrast, "a property cannot meaningfully be held to be essential or accidental to an object independently of its description" (41). In this respect, proper names are not the markers of referents understood as stable, invariable contents; they are, intuitively, *rigid designators* that designate the object wherever it exists (49).

Exploring the implications of this observation in relation to survivor testimony, Lyotard's analysis of reference extends the analytic critique of essentialism to the idealist and ontological views of reference. These views tend to associate the rigidity of proper names with the stability of their referents and, in the process, they posit the "truth" of an object as a stable and extractable "substance." Reciprocally, "truth" is figured as a "property" that "belongs to" objects rather than a provisionally attributed meaning. In this view, the property of truth would not be affected by resituating the referent in an alternate universe of phrases.

In keeping with this view, granting the reality of the gas chambers would be a matter of recognizing the "property rights" of Holocaust survivors as eyewitnesses of the "truth." However, Lyotard's Marxist leanings compel him to criticize proprietary notions of historical memory that inform the human and linguistic sciences. Proprietary constructions of memory presume that the sentences of survivors contain a "value" that is exchangeable. Hence, the "information" that the survivor-witness "holds" is comparable to a private possession that "belongs to" that survivor (12).

The analysis carried out in "The Referent, the Name" dissembles this proprietary figure by interrogating the conditions of possibility for perceiving a necessary filiation between referents and names. It is an interrogation that stresses the formal and rhetorical contingencies of historical denomination. For Lyotard, there is no necessary ontological or logical link between the various phrases at play in designation. Instead, it must be assumed that these phrases (ostensive, descriptive, and nominative) are heterogeneous and that the rules for their association are subject to the context and goals by which they are contingently framed.

Kripke speaks of clusters of descriptions that comprise the content of a referent associated with a given name. This content is, by implication, variable insofar as descriptions are representations that foreground certain aspects of objects above and against others. It is interesting to consider this malleable and arbitrary aspect of description in relation to Hegel's formulation of understanding, which suggests that positive or synthetic reason is required for the purpose of producing a stable image of an object as an intelligible, determinate content. The *proper* regulates and anchors disciplinary discourse by means of this fixed image.

On the basis of this formulation, I have defined the disciplinary object *proper* as a delimited and idealized nexus of concepts posited as a referent. My definition entails that the desire for this object is beholden to rationalist conceptions of language that presuppose the stability of referents as the condition of understanding and communication. Lyotard repudiates correspondence theories of truth that adopt the verisimilitude between the referent and its respective description as the determining criterion of the referent's reality. According to Lyotard, designation "is not, nor can it be, the adequation of the *logos* to the being of the existent" (37). The "properness" of a name does not derive from any ontological basis in its referent. Indeed, the ontological argument is false, according to Lyotard, since "nothing can be said about reality that does not presuppose it" (32).

Lyotard's disavowal of the ontological argument echoes Pierre Vidal-Naquet's "A Paper Eichmann" wherein the historian critically responds to Faurisson's denial. Vidal-Naquet has observed that Holocaust revisionists such as Faurisson, "use a 'non-ontological' proof in their inquiry into the question of the gas chambers" (32). Their arguments are, in contrast, manifestly empiricist in assuming that seeing is a sufficient condition for verification. This belief is shared by those who value survivor testimony as an authoritative source of "eyewitness" evidence. For Lyotard, neither empiricist nor ontological perspectives offer viable approaches to the problem of verifying history.

His dialogue with Vidal-Naquet provides Lyotard with an occasion to propose a thesis that is pivotal to this argument. He suggests that the negationist repudiation of the gas chambers' reality "conforms to the annihilation of the referent's reality during verification procedures" (32). By this account, Faurisson's denial of the gas chambers presumes that death is a reality that can be seen and named. Citing Kripke, Lyotard emphasizes that this stance supposes that reality has a proper name, an assumption that undermines the authority of eyewitness verification insofar as proper names cannot, themselves, be "seen." The name is not, itself, an object of cognition (that is, a sensory event to be described). What is more, a cognitive phrase that describes an object would not be sufficient to establish the "properness" of a name as a measure of its referent's reality. Descriptions cannot be validated in the absence of ostensive phrases that show or display the object at stake. Rather, if the "properness" of designation is intelligible as such, then it is so by virtue of the name's exclusivity and invariability in marking itself from one phrase to the next.

Extrapolating from Kripke, Lyotard speaks of the proper name's *quasi-deictic rigidity* across a variety of signifying chains. In this connection, it is helpful to recall that a *deictic* is a marker for an ostensive phrase that shows or points out the object at stake. In Lyotard's words, deictics relate "the instances of the universe presented by the phrase in which they are placed back to a 'current' spatio-temporal origin so named 'I-here-now.' " So defined, deictics serve to designate reality inasmuch as they "designate their object as an extra-linguistic permanence, as a 'given.' " However, they cannot attest to the permanence of this object conceived as an origin of a phrase universe. This "origin" would be tied to a particular phrase whose universe deictics serve to mark, a universe appearing and disappearing with the phrase to which it belongs (33).

By extension, a name functions *like* a deictic in that it situates the referent, the addressor, and the addressee of any phrase in relation to an "as-if-here." However, insofar as the name "remains fixed throughout a sequence of phrases," it is to be distinguished from "full" deictics that change from phrase to phrase (41). Hence if description cannot "free itself from denomination" and "reference cannot be reduced to sense," this is because the name is "a linchpin between an ostensive phrase with its deictics and any given phrase with its sense or senses" (41, 43).

Lyotard remarks the name's twin capacity to designate and be signified; however, he is also careful to note the implications of its function as a rigid designator. This function suggests an independence from the variety of ostensives and other phrases that situate its referent in various phrases. Ultimately, however, the name's capacity to endow its referent with reality remains contingent insofar as "phrases belonging to heterogeneous families can affect the referent of a single proper name by situating it upon different instances in the universes they present" (49). This is to suggest that the referent of a name changes from phrase to phrase; in other words, a name's rigidity belies the alterity of its referent:

> There is no question of validating the truth of name: a name is not a property attributed to a referent by means of a description (a cognitive phrase). It is merely an index which, in the case of the anthroponym, for example, designates one and only one human being. The properties attributed to the human being designated by this name could be validated, but not his or her name. The name adds

no property to him or her. Even if initially many names have a signification they lose it, and they must lose it. (35)

The name's status as a rigid designator suggests that it cannot be determined by its sense; but neither is this sense furnished by the name. Instead,
designation, as Lyotard understands it, is the effect of a learned association
between a name and various phrases comprising its contents. He contends
that learning names involves situating or perceiving them "in relation to
other names by means of phrases" (44). However, because learning involves
perception, this claim raises the question of how to theorize denomination
without resorting to the idea of experience.

As I have already indicated, Lyotard views experience as problematic insofar as it "can only be described by means of a phenomenological dialectic" (45). A phenomenological dialectic regulates the indeterminacy of
experience by sublating that which it negates. In the negationists' eyes, it is
precisely these negated aspects that controvert the truth of survivor testimony as a narrative of experience. For if the witness cannot present a complete account, this is because her testimony is partial and may even be
contradicted by those aspects that the finitude of her perspective prevented
her from perceiving. Her testimony's authority will therefore depend on
the rigidity of the proper names that anchor her account and that situate it
in relation to other testimonies.

Lyotard observes that the referent of a proper name is strongly determined "in terms of its location among networks of names and of relations
between names (worlds)." At the same time, the sense of a name is weakly
determined because the name appears in multiple, heterogeneous contexts
(50). This paradox follows from two distinctions that inform Lyotard's approach to the problem of historical verification. Following Frege, Lyotard
distinguishes between sense (*Sinn*) and reference (*Bedeutung*) in order to
stress the difference between logic and cognition. In the logical genre, sense
is presented by well-formed expressions (propositions) that occupy places
in "logical space." These places are determined by means of truth tables that
map possible relations between elementary propositions. By virtue of their
formal necessity, Lyotard observes that logical propositions delimit what is
possible, but they cannot determine what is real. Only the cognitive genre
has a bearing on whether a knowable reality corresponds to a given propo-
sition that is a logical expression. This is to assert that sense is merely a formally necessary possibility which is not to be conflated with reality.
Ultimately, a referent can only be verified through a cognition that presupposes the referent's logical possibility (51).

The distinction between sense and reference informs the relation between objects of history and objects of perception that organizes Lyotard's

understanding of historical denomination. The object of history is the referent of the proper name arising from a world "which is a fairly stable complex of nominatives." The object of perception, on the other hand, is determined by "a field of loose complexes of ostensives and deictics" (50). Stated differently, the perceptual object is the referent of an ostensive phrase while the historical object is the referent of a nominative phrase. Yet this distinction is not absolute: to learn an historical name is to situate it in relation to other names by means of phrases which constitute a system of cross-references. It is this system of interrelated references that presents a "world" wherein other names have senses attached to them that can be fixed and verified through ostensive phrases. In this respect, ostensives and their respective perceptual objects also ground the networks of names that make up history.

This "insight" is, perhaps, merely a formal elaboration on the commonplace that perception conditions history. It is, nevertheless, crucial to Lyotard's argument about the problem of validating the experience of a witness as an historical referent. In dialogue with Wittgenstein, Lyotard emphasizes that the ostensive is the "showing of the case" that also alludes to what is not the case. The negative dimension of ostensives is, thus, a feature of the partiality and finitude of perception that prevents a witness from seeing and attesting to "everything." The reality to which she bears witness is, instead, "shadowed" by those negated aspects, those senses, which s/he cannot show, but which, nevertheless, remain (logically) possible. Lyotard observes that the perceptive field and the historical world are both "hollowed out" by the negation that "is entailed respectively (and differently) by the shown and the named" (51).

Wittgenstein figures this modality of logical possibility as a *Spielraum* bordered by tautology on the one side and contradiction on the other. In this manner, he establishes a metaphoric space for the "swarm" of possible senses of indeterminate quantity and quality that inhabit the "hollow" between the named and shown referent. Insofar as the modality of possibility is "axed on the future," Wittgenstein's hollow also becomes Lyotard's figure for "time considered as the condition of modalizations." In the sensible field, changes of meaning "happen" over time insofar as different aspects of an object are alternately and differentially manifested, recognized, and negated in successive moments of perception.

Wittgenstein's *Spielraum* and *hollow* provide spatial figures for the flux of simultaneous and successive interpretations that affect the contours of a referent. In this manner, he "half-opens the door of logic onto phenomenology" insofar as he transfers "into the logical order the 'hollow' which, in the (sensible) field, envelops the referents of ostensives" (55). Both history and perception are negatively determined by this hollow that also affects the integrity of the witnessing "I." Language, space, and time displace and attenuate the variable content of this "I" as a marker of positionality.

Lyotard's reflections on the "I" owe their impetus to his critical reading of Hegel's *Phenomenology of Spirit* wherein the idealist split between substance and appearance is dialectically absolved. The resulting synthesis is determined as much by what it negates as by what it posits. Indeed, if "Dialectical logic maintains the experience and the subject of the experience within the relative," as Lyotard claims, then it is in light of this structural negation (46). This relativity yields a potential basis for critical reflection; however, it is a potential that is undermined by the aggrandizing speculative logic with which Hegel's phenomenological dialectic is inextricably bound. In this respect, then, the phenomenological concept of experience "presupposes that of an I which forms itself (*Bildung*) by gathering in the properties of things that come up (events) and which constitutes reality by effectuating their temporal synthesis." It consequently endows experiences "with the property of accumulation (*Resultat, Erinnerung*) and places them in a continuity with the final absolute" (45–46).

Lyotard's perspective on Hegel rehearses the principal tenets of the symptomatic amalgam of phenomenology, existentialism, and humanism that Derrida identifies with a post-Hegelian critique of the transcendental subject.[6] Although Hegel was himself a critic of Kantian idealism, his evolutionary narrative about perception, consciousness, and absolute spirit in the *Phenomenology* nevertheless reproduces the ideal of a sovereign subject who reigns over a coherent unity of perceptions. By limiting the perceptual agency of the witness, Lyotard attests to his desire to distance himself from Hegel's model of absolute consciousness. For Lyotard, there is no "absolute witness" in the sense that the witness is not a sovereign consciousness who can represent his/her perceptions as a unified totality. He therefore objects to the implication that events would be (mere) phenomena in relation to the witness conceived as a coherent "I" of phenomenological experience. In his view, the privilege of this "I" in the discourse of experience presupposes its self-identity as an absolute presence. This alleged presence is, then, the condition permitting "the subordination of truth to the doctrine of evidence" which requires that an object first be verified before it can exist; in other words, seeing is believing (45–46).

To counteract this fallacy, Lyotard asserts that the "I" and the idea of experience attached to it are not philosophically "necessary for the description of reality." Indeed, even in Hegel's *Phenomenology of Spirit* it becomes clear that the "I" at the center of experience is, itself, merely "a deictic which has no import outside the phrase universe that it currently designates" (46).[7] From one moment or phrase to the next, there is thus "no guarantee that I am the same" because the contingency of phrasing enjoins that a subject is "not the unity of 'his' or 'her' experience." (46). In other words, experience is not a stable referent that can be agreed upon or verified and "reality does not result from an experience" (46).

This last point extends a line of argument introduced in "Discussions" where Lyotard objected to the totalizing and synthetic character of the speculative formulation of experience. In keeping with his prejudice against the category of experience so defined, Lyotard claims that an experience-based description does not have "a *philosophical value* because it does not question its presuppositions (the I or the self, the rules of speculative logic)" (46, emphasis added). The implication is that the category of experience is insufficiently critical to fulfill Lyotard's standards of philosophical rigor. Such an argument raises the question as to whether Lyotard also holds witnesses accountable to his philosophical and disciplinary standards that would require them to acknowledge the finitude of their descriptions.

Lyotard has already demonstrated that descriptions "are not necessary for the assertion that a referent is real" (46). Moreover, attempts to represent an experience are necessarily partial and inconsistent (i.e., subject to the ephemerality of deictic markers and the relativity of the possible). The survivor as a witness is consequently caught in a double bind that enjoins her to admit this partiality and at the same time attest to the credibility of her account. The only option left to the witness is to establish credibility by associating the various, transitional deictics of her experience with the quasi-deictic rigidity of the name in accordance with the rules of denomination. But insofar as perception is the condition of such associations, her experiences as an eyewitness are always already subject to the contingency of future perceptions, associations, and interpretations.

To the extent that the witness anticipates this future, she confronts the negation inherent in the modality of the possible. Nevertheless, Lyotard cautions that "we" must not metaphorize the negation "at the heart of testimony" "into the experience of a subject, but rather as a linking of phrases" (55). To reiterate, the activity of connecting phrases is regulated by genres that provide the rules for linkage in keeping with particular aims. However, the evaluation of testimony presents particular problems insofar as the rules of verification are incommensurable with the rules of justice. This constitutive incommensurability underscores the status of testimony as an empirical derivation that, paradoxically, cannot be empirically verified by others. Testimony narrates an experience that cannot be fixed as a referent nor validated as such. Moreover, it would be impossible to validate survivor experience on moral grounds that require consensus about its status as a referent in relation to the law.

The referent of testimony is empirical experience; yet the implication of

Lyotard's analysis of designation is that this referent cannot be presupposed by any paradigm of justice or validity. Neither is "truth" an ontologically predicated "property" of the witness who testifies since her identity is subject to the flux of interpretations and the heterogeneity of phrasing. As a result of this flux, there is no way of verifying or judging her testimony inasmuch as there is no way of confirming the experience from which it derives. By demonstrating the impossibility of judging experience, Lyotard reveals the sociopolitical indeterminacy of historical testimony.

Ultimately, then, Lyotard disarticulates ontological and empirical views of experience in order to stress that the interpretation of testimony is subject to a shifting horizon of recognition and negation. He consequently opens an aporia not only for historical verification, but also for judgments of reality in general. This aporia troubles the litigation of crimes whose representation is fraught with "disputed phrases." Lyotard refers to this dispute as a case of *differend* that expropriates the authority of a victim's testimony and holds justice in abeyance:

> I would like to call a differend [*différend*] the case where the plaintiff is divested of the means to argue and becomes for that reason a victim. If the addressor, addressee, and the sense of the testimony are neutralized, everything takes place as if there were no damages. A case of differend between two parties takes place when the "regulation" of the conflict that opposes them is done in the idiom of one of the parties while the wrong suffered by the other is not signified in that idiom. (9)

A differend is affected by a plaintiff's inability to prove a wrong; yet this inability is itself the product of an asymmetrical power-relation whereby the empowered party disavows or fails to recognize the intelligibility of the plaintiff's claim. By failing to understand and subsequently validate the plaintiff's testimony, the judge silences her complaint and thereby reduces her to a victim. Her silence is the sign of this injustice that results from a failure of judgment.

Lyotard's analysis of designation links the negativity and indeterminacy of experience with the finitude of the witness as a subject of knowledge. This linkage suggests that the silence of the witness is affected by her withdrawal from the demand of speech. It is a demand that requires her to find an appropriate expression for an indeterminate and perhaps disavowed knowledge. His argument focuses on testimony about the gas chambers whose reality Faurisson negates. His response is to enumerate the silences of survivors who feel prevented, unable, or incompetent to speak. In these cases,

Silence does not indicate which instance is denied, it signals the denial of one or more of the instances. The survivors remain silent,
and it can be understood 1) that the situation in question (the case)
is not the addressee's business (he or she lacks the competence, or he
or she is not worthy of being spoken to about it, etc.); or 2) that it
never took place (this is what Faurisson understands); or 3) that
there is nothing to say about it (the situation is senseless, inexpress-
ible); or 4) that it is not the survivors' business to be talking about it
(they are not worthy, etc.). Or, several of these negations together.
(14)

For Lyotard, silence is an index that one or more of the addressor, addressee, signification, and referent instances of a phrase has/have been neu-
tralized or denied. Yet it does not necessarily negate the referent as
Faurisson has supposed. It can, instead, point to the ineptitude of the audience to hear and to respond to testimony and to the inadequacy of language as its mode of production. It may also indicate a survivor's guilt
about living in the aftermath of mass death.

In general, Lyotard defines the differend as "the unstable state and instant of language wherein something which must be able to be put into
phrases cannot yet be. This state includes silence, which is a negative
phrase, but it also calls upon phrases which are in principle possible" (13).
The sign of the differend is a feeling, one that arises from the negativity or
"indetermination of meanings left in abeyance [*en souffrance*]." This feeling
is the index of "our" recognition "that what remains to be phrased exceeds
what [existing idioms] can presently phrase." It subsequently becomes
"our" task by way of literature, philosophy, and politics "to bear witness to
differends by finding idioms for them" (13).

Lyotard asserts that a differend is disclosed by "what one ordinarily calls
a feeling," yet this feeling "does not arise from an experience felt by a subject. It can moreover not be felt" (13, 57). Instead, it must be witnessed as a
sign that "something 'asks' to be put into phrases, and suffers from the
wrong of not being able to be put into phrases right away" (13). It is significant that Lyotard employs scare quotation marks here to indicate a certain
distance from his own choice of verbs. These verbs are notable because they
endow the silence that results from injustice with the ability to ask and to
suffer. This personification is symptomatic of the paradox that Lyotard's
philosophical position entails. For if the sign of a differend is a feeling, then
the question becomes how one comes to know this feeling in the absence of
empirical experience. Indeed, as Lyotard himself poses the question, "how
can it be established that [this feeling] is or is not felt?" (57).

His answer to this question is circular: the feeling arises from a silence and this silence is "not a state of mind," but a sign. This explanation does not, of course, rule out the possibility that signs themselves might be perceived and thus experienced. It would therefore seem that Lyotard's segregation of feeling from experience is somehow arbitrary, perhaps even ideological insofar as it attests to a differend put into play by Lyotard's own discourse. This differend evolves from his investment in an overdetermined post-Hegelian and post-humanist perspective that is an historical product of a late twentieth-century skeptical distaste for acritical formulations of agency that presuppose a voluntaristic, sovereign, and/or bourgeois-humanist subject. It is this perspective that leads Lyotard to reduce experience to a speculative, synthetic logic and that consequently propels him to reject the category of experience *tout court*.

It is worth contemplating whether Lyotard's post-humanist position leads him to disallow the possibility of agency altogether. In the case of survivors, for example, Lyotard argues that what "is subject *to* threats is not an identifiable individual, but the ability to speak or to keep quiet" (46). However, it is unclear what this abstract "ability" to speak or not to speak signifies apart from some minimal notion of agency as a subject's potential to become or avoid becoming a victim. Here I am assuming that threats to communication are only intelligible for speakers who must face them. In this respect, I find Lyotard's post-humanist stance too extreme when it strikes at the very agency of the witness as a narrator of memories. From a critical philosophical standpoint, the witness is not a voluntaristic transcendental subject who retains complete control over the contents of her memory, but this understanding need not jettison experience as a basis of survivor testimony.

Despite his conspicuous investment in Wittgensteinian notions of language, Lyotard's response to Faurisson paradoxically betrays a hint of the noumenal *Ding-an-sich* that cannot, by definition, be empirically verified. The gas chambers presumably fall into this category along with the experience of surviving the death camps. Lyotard has proclaimed his desire to bear witness to all differends and not only those attached to the proper name *Auschwitz*. In view of this assertion, it is difficult to understand how he can maintain that death in the gas chambers remains "unrepresentable" above and beyond any other non-traumatic historical events that do not necessarily leave behind ostensible traces of themselves. Lyotard's insistence on the manifold senses that attach to historical names and that cannot be represented as a totality is relevant here. Such an argument suggests that events always exceed their subsequent representations. However, in stressing the "inadequacy" of language to represent the gas chambers, is Lyotard not, in effect, claiming that the gas chambers in particular transcend signification?

Lyotard observes that the only way one "could make a 'beautiful death' out of 'Auschwitz' death . . . is by means of a rhetoric" (109). Yet it is by virtue of his recourse to a sacralizing rhetoric that his negative representation of the gas chambers redeems this possibility. In this vein, Lyotard's translation of Kant into Wittgenstein provides a means of converting the moral shock aroused by the gas chambers into a semiotic and aesthetic phenomenon that preserves the traumatic aura of the death camps as a philosophical-historical sign. Within this economy, Auschwitz is a figure for the anonymous effacement of those gassed, shot, buried, and cremated millions who cannot be brought back. This figuration does not merely expose the limits of representation and judgment. It also sacralizes the victims' suffering by veiling their experiences in a negative aura of "unrepresentability." In addition, to remove the Holocaust from the possibility of representation implies an attendant desire to freeze the traumatic meaning of the Final Solution as a transcendent moral crisis. The silent suffering of the persecuted subsequently assumes a memorial centrality as the determinate negation that organizes and thereby disciplines collective memory of the Holocaust.

In sum, Lyotard appears to replay the repressive arguments for the Holocaust's uniqueness when he constitutes the survivors' silences as signs of its historical and moral magnitude. In this economy, the "unrepresentability" thesis performs two rhetorical functions: first, it enables Lyotard to protect the traumatic specificity of the gas chambers against a positivistic and empiricist will toward presence; second, it provides him with an opportunity to theorize the aesthetic conditions of the Holocaust's reception as a trauma to and of language. In the final analysis, it remains obscure how theorizing this aesthetic as a "para-experience" does not ultimately concede a negative ontological dimension to the silence surrounding "Auschwitz." This dimension is implicit in Lyotard's citation of Plato's *Republic* wherein silence obtains an ontological status. In Lyotard's words, "Language is the sign that one does not know the being of the existent. When one knows it, one is the existent, and that's silence."[8] The Platonic opposition between language and being compels mimesis as a "compromise." Plato finds that mimesis is deceitful when it takes the form of idolatry; yet as simulacrum it "is also a signpost on the path to the true, to the 'proper.' " For this reason, mimesis as verisimilitude should be regulated according to Plato for whom "There needs to be good *typoi*, good print keys that give appropriate simulacra" (22).

I have been suggesting that Lyotard attempts to provide these *typoi* in the course of modeling an appropriate philosophical response to Faurisson's positivistic denial of the gas chambers. These *typoi* regulate (and thus discipline) historical mimesis through a negative aesthetic that urges historians in particular to acknowledge the silences undermining their ability to judge and/or verify events. Yet it is doubtful that such an aesthetic could effectively mitigate the injustice that failures in language bring to pass. For if, as Lyotard states, silence "does not indicate which instance is denied, it signals the denial of one or more of the instances," then it will be difficult if not impossible to determine which instance to reinstate in the interests of reversing the differend in question.

Ultimately, then, Lyotard has suggested that the negativity of Auschwitz produces a "non-experiential feeling" which does not fall into the category of experience. This feeling announces the wrong committed against the victims (both the survivors and the dead) that silences their knowledge of the gas chambers. Silence is, consequently, a measure of an anticipated failure—the failure to satisfy "cognitive rules for the establishment of historical reality and for the validation of its sense" (54). It is a failure proper to a historical situation that literalizes the poststructuralist figure of a "lost" or "missing" referent:

> . . . with Auschwitz, something new has happened in history (which can only be a sign and not a fact), which is that the facts, the testimonies which bore the traces of *here*'s and *now*'s, the documents which indicated the sense or senses of the facts, and the names, finally the possibility of various kinds of phrases whose conjunction makes reality, all this has been destroyed as much as possible. (57)

The Nazis' destruction of the evidence of their crimes imposes still another silence on knowledge. Lyotard cautions that this silence is not the same as a forgetting, but reflects the pain of responding to the magnitude of the Final Solution. This pain should therefore be read as a sign that language is not "our" instrument and that "our" understanding founders over an "indetermination of meanings left in abeyance" (56–57).

Lyotard evokes an image of the shades of the exterminated who "continue to wander" in this "indetermination of meanings" after their right to express the wrongs against them was extinguished with their lives (56–57). He hears their silence as a summons to recognize and to ameliorate the injustice of inadequate communication—to right the wrong committed against the murdered by instituting new addressees, new addressors, new significations, and new referents. Paradoxically, despite the fact that "we" do not employ language, according to Lyotard, "we" must nevertheless attempt to answer his summons by reversing differends.[9] Lost is the sense in which the name *Auschwitz* forbids a synthesis of a *we* as its result.

In some measure, this contradiction might be read as a reflection of the fraught synthesis of Kant and Wittgenstein that organizes Lyotard's aporetics of judgment. As Richard Beardsworth has noted, Lyotard repudiates the humanist subject presumed by Kant's division among the domains of cognition, description, and prescription because it anticipates the analogical finalization of the differences figured in this division. Hence, while Lyotard wants to retain the implications of Kant's critical philosophy, he presumably also hopes to avoid falling prey to a Kantian nostalgia for a subject whose faculties (reason, understanding, and imagination) could be reunified in aesthetic experience.

To this end, Lyotard translates the Kantian faculties and their respective domains into a Wittgensteinian vocabulary of incommensurable phrase regimens. This pragmatist turn allows Lyotard to problematize the splitting of the subject by and in language. It is also a strategy that permits him to sidestep the danger of a resurrected transcendental subject; however, by reinscribing these faculties as phrase categories, he surreptitiously occupies the empty place of the judging subject who defines and "navigates" their respective domains. Ultimately, then, his efforts to expunge the traces of Kantian subjectivism from his own discourse finalizes the very splits in knowledge that Derrida, in contrast, might tend to blur.

Further contradictions emerge in his presentation of *The Differend*. In that context, Lyotard ostensibly circumvents the danger of resurrecting a unified author-subject by minimizing style. His recourse to an epigrammatic format of numbered paragraphs is a citation of Wittgenstein as well as a means of offsetting the appearance of a fluid argument. At the same time, this stylistic choice may be critically aimed at a form of discourse prevalent among social scientists keen on neutralizing the subjectivity of their analyses. Ironically, however, it is precisely through this a-stylistic device that the absent, judging, and navigating subject comes to resonate in the echo among formally similar instances of chiasmic paradox spiraling toward their culmination in "The Sign of History." Regarding this final chapter of *The Differend*, my suspicion is that Lyotard's return to Kant by way of the indeterminacy of the sublime historical sign might somehow permit a veiled return of the Hegelian result as the philosophical *we* of authorship. This *we* tacitly "realizes" and absolves the evacuated seat of philosophical judgment that is the regulatory ideal and guiding thread of the book.

The encroachment of this *we* throughout "Discussions" and *The Differend* suggests that Lyotard's semiotics of reception ultimately sidesteps the issue of its normative power to formalize particular moral feelings for a virtual community of respondents. The implicit *sensus communis* presupposed here indicates that Lyotard's anti-ontological repudiation of experience cannot elude the specter of consensus as a speculative result. For if the emphasis must now be displaced from the ontological and empirical "substance" of "Auschwitz" as a historical experience to its rhetorical and affective function as a sign, then it will be difficult to account for a shared recognition of this sign without reproducing a *we* of judgment.

By converting a moral sensibility into an aesthetic para-experience, Lyotard falls into the trap of normalizing certain moral reactions to traumatic events as the properly aporetic effects of failed communication. It is in this respect that his framework contradicts itself. For in postulating a literacy based on the "witnessing" of historical-moral silences, Lyotard seems to take the intelligibility of these silences for granted. This presupposition finesses the legitimation crisis that is Lyotard's principal trope by converting "Auschwitz" into a paradigmatic case for the fraught future of justice. He consequently fails to avoid the very tendency that he criticizes in the work of his nemesis, Jürgen Habermas, who also reads "Auschwitz" as a moral-historical sign.[10]

Specifically, Lyotard finds fault with what he perceives as Habermas' naïve resolution of the crisis of legitimacy through recourse to an ideal of democratically achieved consensus.[11] Lyotard views Habermas' faith in consensus as naïve insofar as it assumes that "it is possible for all speakers to come to agreement on which rules or metaprescriptions are universally valid for language games, when it is clear that language games are heteromorphous, subject to heterogeneous sets of pragmatic rules." In the second place, Habermas' perspective presupposes that "the goal of dialogue is consensus," which Lyotard perceives as a "particular state of discussion, not its end" (1984b: 65).

Habermas intervenes in the 1986 West German Historians' Debate (*der Historikerstreit*) about the centrality of the Holocaust in German history by arguing in favor of moral rather than strictly scientific criteria. This strategy leads him to institute the Jewish victims' perspective as the horizon of German historical-moral judgment and consensus. In this manner, the victims' suffering becomes a moral ideal of Nazi period historical consciousness *proper* and the measuring rod against which subsequent judgments of propriety are to be gauged. I agree with Habermas that a morally desirable consensus would establish the victim's perspective as a critical basis for judging historical responsibility. Yet such a framework should not presume that because a victim-centered moral consensus is desirable that it is also inevitable.

Despite his desire to distance himself from Habermas, it remains questionable whether Lyotard manages to avoid reproducing Habermas' normative foundation of communication when he dwells on the exteriority of "Auschwitz." Like Habermas, Lyotard's response to historical revisionism constructs "Auschwitz" as a moral-historical sign. In contrast to Habermas,

Lyotard radicalizes the philosophical implications of Adorno's prohibition of redemptive meaning in relation to the Holocaust by emphasizing its skeptical and negative aspect. This radicalization leads him to a paradox. For if he rejects the ontological presuppositions of experience, then Lyotard must find another way to fulfill his "postmodern" agenda to "save the honor of the name" from the totalitarian fantasy to "seize reality" (1984a: 82).

In this connection, his consideration of the Holocaust illuminates an important contradiction that affects a postwar anti-foundationalist philosophy haunted by the specters of European fascism, Stalinism, and capitalist hegemony. On the one hand, there is a Marxist-attenuated philosophical praxis that repudiates humanist-bourgeois notions of self; on the other hand, there is an axiological impetus to protect this self lest philosophy capitulate to the banality of an evil that propelled the Nazis to dehumanize the Jews and to efface the evidence of their murders. A sense of moral propriety demands that outsiders to the event refuse to capitulate to this banality by remaining sensitive to the survivors' traumatic suffering and by remembering the fates of those who did not survive; yet it is still not clear from the foregoing discussion how anti-foundationalist critiques of the humanist subject understand the materiality of this suffering. My final remarks will therefore be devoted to a theoretical consideration of moral propriety defined as respect for the specificity of survivor memory in the context of discourse about the Holocaust. How might an anti-foundationalist perspective on language and identity establish a framework for attending to this specificity? How does a post-humanist disarticulation of the subject illuminate the dynamics of traumatic memory as an experience of the vicissitudes of the sign?

II. Survivor Memory: The Same that Does Not Return

Respect for the authority of survivor memory sometimes leads Holocaust scholars to conflate the authenticity of testimony with the "first-handedness" of its experiential referent. For Lyotard, in contrast, the name *Auschwitz* enjoins this very distinction. Lyotard's writings about Auschwitz assume that the gas chambers permanently scarred Western faith in an intuitive moral consensus. Auschwitz is, thus, the name of a wound that exposed the duplicity of humanist universalism. It is, for Lyotard, a sign of history as a failure of community; yet it is not, in the end, the only such sign of historical-moral transition. Western history is punctuated by these signs and the silences that attend them. Thought must therefore bear witness to these silences as the signs of injustice.

In responding to Adorno and Derrida's critiques of metaphysics, Lyotard repudiates the possibility of metaphysical experience as a "return to the same" and as an anticipation of a beautiful death that affects the redemptive closure for an individual's life. This reading anticipates his rejection of experience as a basis for the historical authority of victim testimony in *The Differend*. Unfortunately, this rejection also belies a theoretical violence to the extent that it expropriates a survivor's ontological investment in the empirical validity of her own experiences. This expropriation is not what Derrida has in mind. He does not contest the empirical validity of the experiences from which survivor testimonies derive; indeed, he defends this validity, in some measure, against the implications of his own philosophy.[12] It is more precise to say that he abides with Emmanuel Levinas in objecting to a metaphysical figuration of experience that writes it as the self-propriation of a subject whose encounter with the world is nothing more than a solipsistic return to the same.[13]

It is important to acknowledge that the survivor may, in moments, actively or unconsciously desire the very return movement which, for Derrida and Levinas, generally represents an objectionable will to self-sameness and sovereignty, albeit with very different implications. For the survivor, such a return would mean a reversal of the losses and suffering that the Holocaust inflicted; yet this reversal is not only impossible as a form of idealist subjectivism. There cannot be a "return to the same" for Holocaust survivors because their losses are material and implacable. The bereaved and persecuted memory remains elsewhere with respect to the daily rituals of post-Holocaust existence. A mode of relating with absent parents, siblings, spouses, and children is made heavy by their murders along with the possibility of a complacency that was irremediably violated by hunger, hopelessness, and the constant threat of death.[14]

In *Holocaust Testimonies: The Ruins of Memory*, Lawrence Langer identifies an "unheroic" memory as an attribute of the survivor's loss of an impromptu sense of self. The self that persists is damaged and diminished by the desperation and humiliation of victimization. Langer has observed that the survivor's tainted memory bears witness to lost possibilities of intention and self-narration. At the same time, she yearns for a complacency that can never be regained. A ruined memory circles around the ideal of a unified self that was destroyed by the Nazi persecution and murder of the Jews, and was thereafter cut off from the present. An irreparably scarred dignity haunts her memories of the events that preceded the catastrophe while the traumatic irrevocability of bereavement preempts her ability to be fully invested in the present. Drawing on Langer's analysis of survivor testimony, I want to suggest that Holocaust memory is distinguished by an affective economy that operates at a loss; it is the economy of a grieving sensibility that is shot through with vigilant despair.

Lyotard explores this sensibility in an essay dedicated to Hannah Arendt entitled "The Survivor." In this essay, he softens his prior repudiation of phenomenological and ontological notions of experience in the course of addressing the philosophical specificity of survivor life after the death camps. Lyotard notes that the very meaning of the word *survivor* "implies that an entity that is dead or ought to be is still alive" (144). For Lyotard, survival is thus defined by the "desolate contingency" of living after probable death. The survivor subsists in the hollow of a past that is simultaneously lost and betrayed—she hovers between memories of a life that the Third Reich destroyed and memories of the death camps that have faded with time and distance:

> One question, however, is whether something is not forgotten in this turning back on the no longer, something that therefore does not survive, a remainder which does not remain. What seems as though it must necessarily be lost is the presence then of what is now past.... There is a moral sadness of the very thing that is retained and transmitted; the sadness of Minerva's owl, of what is bound. The tradition of what was then experienced in the present is its betrayal. The past is betrayed by the simple fact that the present it was is made absent. It lacks a certain mode, the one of the quick, the lively, even as it is recalled. (145)

Once again, Lyotard's writings on Auschwitz dismantle the subject of experience in the name of a negative aesthetic. His figuration of the survivor is both contradictory and consistent with this aesthetic which reflects his aporetic inclinations. The survivor's memory is hereby constructed as an uncrossable impasse that does not allow her to resuscitate the presence of the past. Unfortunately, Lyotard poeticizes this impasse when he writes that "every entity is a survivor" insofar as an "authentic mode of presence" is unimaginable (149). In this respect, the survivor's inability to "return to the same," that is, to reconstitute a coherent image of self, models the fate of a decentered identity that dwells in the "house of language" as it were. By the same token, survivor memory loses its specificity in becoming still another illustration of the sign under siege.

This criticism is not to suggest that the traumatic memory of survivors lies somehow beyond the errancy of the signifier. Certainly, memory as a sign will simultaneously reflect and go beyond an anti-foundationalist view of reference and designation. Indeed, to the extent that memories are comprised of emblematic images that stand in for experiences and events, they perform a function similar to proper names in marking the travels of their historical referents. Lyotard's analysis of designation in *The Differend* demonstrates that the proper name is a quasi-deictic marker whose power to fix the contents of its referent is situational and therefore provisional.

A disciplinary attempt to fix the referent finds its tropological corollary in my own heuristic of the way in which traumatic memory may become fixed as an idealized image of the event that occasioned it. This heuristic adopts Freudian psychoanalysis in order to propose a psycho-semiotic theory of working-through as a process of desublimation. Derrida's critique of the metaphysical subject is crucial to this examination which focuses on compulsive repetition as a symptom of a mimetic drive to reproduce the affective plenitude of a traumatic experience. To reiterate, Derrida foregrounds the *différance* of identity as a contingent effect of interpretation. He also recognizes that the vicissitudes of desire and identity are indissociable from the slippage of signifiers and signifieds. This slippage endlessly rewrites the meanings that it simultaneously (de) constitutes. It therefore illuminates the historicity of referents as signs whose intelligibility is at once provisional and constructed.

This is to suggest that analysis can aim to desublimate a subject's affective investment in the ontological substance of her trauma *proper* by exposing the provisionality of experience and memory as signs of identity. Extrapolating from Derrida, I understand the compulsive narration of a traumatic event as a mimetic process that is structurally geared to perform the very act of dispossession that the subject feels driven to guard against. This process is also disciplinary to the extent that it is governed by an idealized memory that has been endowed with the status of an epistemological key to an imaginary loss of subjective unity. Compulsive repetition gradually loosens a subject's cathexis with this affectively charged memory-image. The trauma *proper* thereafter loses its status as the origin and referent of post-traumatic identity. Analysis enacts a "linguistic turn" for the traumatized subject by *turning* this investment into language.[15] Ultimately, then, the aim of working-through would be to defuse the power of particular traumatic images to paralyze and thereby regulate interpretations of the past.

In the interests of respecting the specificity of trauma as a historical and affective experience, I also want to foreground the psychic reality of a *desire* for unified identity beyond the phenomenological category of experience.[16] This desire is informed by the structure of narrative as a poetic mode of communicating transpired experiences.[17] Such a figuration acknowledges the power of wounding events to constitute various narratives of identity as well as to be (re) constituted in their turn. This does not mean that I wish to redefine traumatic experience as an ideal or originary "substance" that consciousness "masters" through a totalizing and cathartic representation. Instead, I see experience and memory as related narrative tenses of a corporeal sensibility that is always partial, always fractured, and never in possession of itself.[18]

In extending Derrida's critique of the *proper*, this heuristic of traumatic memory treats it as a sign that is vulnerable to appropriation, expropriation, and dehiscence. While this construction explicitly assumes the differentiation of traumatic repetitions as a function of the aphanisis of collective and individual identity, it also implies a view of traumatic fixation as an identity-formative reaction against *différance*. Derrida's reflections on the alterity of identity and meaning suggest that any self-concept cannot stand up to the dispossession that the passage of time enacts. Yet to the extent that identity is experienced as provisional, this dispossession also feeds a subject's desire for wholeness, unity, and consistency. The ubiquitous narrations of this desire in Western philosophy, ego psychology, and popular culture are an index that these ideals are not merely illusions, but strongly held beliefs: they reflect a deeply entrenched ideology of self-interpretation that constructs identity as an enduring "substance" or continuous meaning. A critique of this ideology calls for an attendant attempt to theorize the subject of belief as one who is, perhaps, naïvely invested in the socially-mediated ideal of a coherent and determinate self. A theory of traumatic memory should seek to account for this desire along with the materiality of the actions, behaviors, and symptoms affected by it, rather than simply to decry it as the veil of an ontological illusion. It is precisely in this respect that the psychoanalytic view of the subject is less idealistic than many poststructuralist perspectives.

CHAPTER 10

Between History and Memory: The Voice of the Eyewitness

JAMES E. YOUNG

"For all of us there is a twilight zone between history and memory," Saul Friedlander has written, quoting Eric Hobsbawm, "between the past as a generalized record which is open to relatively dispassionate inspection and the past as part of, or background to, one's own life . . ." (1993: vii). But in a gentle departure from Hobsbawm and others, Friedlander has concluded that the opposition between memory and history is far from clear-cut. On the one hand, he concedes we must continue distinguishing between public memory and historiography, and that "the process involved in the molding of memory is, theoretically at least, antithetical to that involved in the writing of history. No poetic representation of a recent and relevant past has to be imagined as a continuum: the constructs of public-collective memory find their place at one pole, and the 'dispassionate' historical inquiries at the opposite pole. The closer one moves to the middle ground, that is, to an attempt at general interpretations of the group's past, the more the two areas—distinct in their extreme forms—become intertwined and interrelated" (vii). Given his own personal history as so exquisitely wrought in *When Memory Comes*, this kind of historiographical positioning cannot come as a complete surprise. But until the first volume of his *Nazi Germany and the Jews* appeared, Friedlander had also kept the projects of personal memory and Holocaust history separate.

Now, however, in the Introduction to what is clearly his "life's work," Friedlander opens his history of the Holocaust with these words: "Most historians of my generation, born on the eve of the Nazi era, recognize either explicitly or implicitly that plowing through the events of those years entails not only excavating and interpreting a collective past like any other, but also recovering and confronting decisive elements of our own lives" (1997: 1). As a hidden child survivor whose parents were murdered at Auschwitz, Friedlander could have distinguished between those historians whose lives were directly affected by events and those shaped only indirectly by events. But he does not. Indeed, he seems also to be speaking for a generation of historians born after the Holocaust, as well, whose lives have been shaped not by the history of this time, but by the memory of others, as passed down to them. "For the next generation of historians—and by now also for the one after that—as for most of humanity, Hitler's Reich, World War II, and the fate of the Jews of Europe do not represent any shared memory," he writes.

> And yet, paradoxically, the centrality of these events in present-day historical consciousness seems much greater than it was some decades ago. The ongoing debates tend to unfold with unremitting bitterness as facts are questioned and evidence denied, as interpretations and commemorative endeavors confront one another. . . . In these debates, the historian's role is central. For my generation, to partake at one and the same time in the memory and the present perceptions of this past may create an unsettling dissonance; it may, however, also nurture insights that would otherwise be inaccessible. (1)

Here he recognizes the unique role of the historian whose personal memory was forged in the historical events he now writes. Moreover, as Friedlander also makes explicit in the introductions to his reflections on Holocaust historiography and his brilliant history of the Holocaust itself, the altogether disruptive voices of the historian and the victims must be heard if this past is to be understood at all.

In this essay, I would like to reflect narrowly on the ways Saul Friedlander's integration of both the historian's and the survivor's voices into Holocaust historiography suggests the basis for an uncanny kind of history-telling in its own right: an anti-redemptory narrative that works through, yet never actually bridges, the gap between a survivor's "deep memory" and historical narrative.[1] For like Friedlander, I find that it may be the very idea of "deep memory" and its incompatibility with narrative that constitutes one of the central challenges to Holocaust historiography. Like Friedlander, I am also troubled by the near-blanket exclusion of the survivor's memory from normative histories of the Holocaust. This is why I ask here what can be done with what Friedlander has termed the "deep memory" of survivors, that which remains essentially unrepresentable. Is it possible to write a history that includes some oblique reference to such deep memory, but which leaves it essentially intact, untouched, and thereby deep? By extension, what role, if any, might the survivor's deep memory play in writing the history of the *Shoah*?

Here I suggest, after Patrick Hutton, that "What is at issue here is not how history can recover memory, but, rather, what memory will bequeath to history" (72). That is, how will the memory of survivors enter (or not enter) the historical record? Or to paraphrase Hutton: How will the past be remembered as it passes from living memory to history? Will it always be regarded as so overly laden with pathos as to make it unreliable as documentary evidence? Or is there a place for the understanding of the witness, as subjective and skewed as it may be, for our larger historical understanding of events?

As an example of deep memory, Friedlander refers to the last frame of Art Spiegelman's so-called "comic-book" of the Holocaust, *Maus: A Survivor's Tale*, in which the dying father addresses his son, Artie, with the name of Richieu, Artie's brother who died in the Holocaust before Artie was even born. The still apparently unassimilated trauma of his first son's death remains inarticulable—and thereby deep—and so is represented here only indirectly as a kind of manifest behavior. But this example is significant for Friedlander in other ways as well, coming as it does at the end of the survivor's life. For Friedlander wonders, profoundly I think, what will become of this deep memory after the survivors are gone. "The question remains," he says, "whether at the collective level . . . an event such as the *Shoah* may, after all the survivors have disappeared, leave traces of a deep memory beyond individual recall, which will defy any attempts to give it meaning" (1992b: 41). The implication is that, beyond the second generation's artistic and literary representations of it, such deep memory may be lost to history altogether.

To date, in fact, the survivor's memory has played little if any role in Holocaust historiography, due primarily to the somewhat forced distinction historians have maintained between memory and history: history as that which happened, memory as that which is remembered of what happened. Not only does such an ironclad distinction impose an artificial distance between the two categories, in Friedlander's eyes, but it also leaves no room for the survivor's voice, much less room for the survivor's memory of events, whose value is thereby lost to the historian. The problem, according to Friedlander, is that "most historians approaching the subject have dealt either with descriptions of the background or with narrations of the *Shoah*, never, to my knowledge, with an *integrated* approach to both" (50). What seems to be missing is history-telling that includes both the voice of the historian and the memory of survivors, commentary and overt interpretation of events that deepen the historical record *and* resist "hasty ideological closure." In response to this perceived void in Holocaust historiography, Friedlander proposes an historiography whose narrative skein is disrupted by the sound of the historian's own, self-conscious voice, the introduction of what he calls "commentary" into the narrative. "Whether this commentary is built into the narrative structure of a history or developed as a separate, superimposed text is a matter of choice," he says, "but the voice of the commentator must be clearly heard" (53). In most cases, this commentary will probably be that of the self-aware historian, and it will serve to "disrupt the facile linear progression of the narration, introduce alternative interpretations, question any partial conclusion, withstand the need for closure" (53). Unlike other historians, who grow restive at the sound of their own voices, anxious that their implied subjectivity seems to undercut any sense of disinterested authority, Friedlander aims to mark just this interestedness. In so doing, he would restore the historian's reasons for writing such history to the historical record.

Not only does the absence of the historian's voice betray the essential opaqueness at the heart of these events, but as Friedlander makes clear in his Introduction to *Nazi Germany and the Jews*, historical understanding of this time remains altogether impossible without taking into account the voices of the victims as well. "For it is their voices that reveal what was known and what *could* be known," he writes. "Theirs were the only voices that conveyed both the clarity of insight and the total blindness of human beings confronted with an entirely new and utterly horrifying reality" (2). Throughout *Nazi Germany and the Jews*, Friedlander thus interlayers the historian's narrative with that of both victims and survivors. He recognizes what too many others have ignored: that once we take into account the eyewitnesses' voices, their apprehension or misapprehension of events, their reflexive interpretations of experience, we understand more deeply why and how the victims responded to unfolding events as they did.

By recognizing the role their own narratives may have played in their lives, we acknowledge that their ongoing narrative grasp of events was very much a part of the historical reality itself. By returning the victims' voices and subjectivity to the historical record, Friedlander restores a measure of contingency to history as it unfolds, opening up the possibility of historical causes and effects otherwise lost in our projection of a hindsight logic onto events. If Maurice Halbwachs' main aim as historian was to show how unreliable memory was as a guide to realities of the past, Friedlander shows in his integrated history that the realities themselves, as they actually unfolded, owe an essential debt to those who lived and remembered them.

For Friedlander, this has meant confronting two of the traditional taboos of rational historiography: the sound of the historian's voice and the memory of the eyewitness, neither of which has been permitted by historians anxious to suppress all signs of their own writing hands in a particular history (i.e., their subjectivity) and altogether intolerant of the tricks memory plays on survivors as they recall events. In Friedlander's case, however, his incorporation of these voices into history has not led to an abandonment of historical standards but a deepening of them. Instead of denying the historian's role as necessarily interested narrator of events, Friedlander merely acknowledges this role as part of the historical reality itself. And then, owing perhaps to both his sensitivity for the survivor's plight and to his needs as historian, Friedlander incorporates the living memory of survivors into historical narrative, not to privilege it but to show better how events were apprehended (or misapprehended) as they unfolded.

As Amos Funkenstein has made abundantly clear in *Perceptions of Jewish History*, the very notion of historical facts evolved from that which was perceived first as self-evident to that which became meaningful only in its context, whether delivered by an eyewitness or subsequent historian. Ironically, we have moved from a time in which facts seemed to declare their own importance, thus making the eyewitness to events the best historian, to a time when fact is regarded as completely dependent for both meaning and factuality on its context, making the authority of the eyewitness somewhat negligible. The irony comes when historians continue to discount the significance accorded facts by eyewitnesses because of their subjective proximity to events, even as they declare the historical fact once again to be self-evident. This is why we need to find a middle road by which the living memory of the eyewitness might be assimilated to the historical record without using it only rhetorically to authenticate any given narrative, without allowing it to endow the surrounding narrative with the seeming naturalness of the survivor's voice.

What then does such history-writing look like? Despite (or perhaps because of) their sophistication, even when historians and philosophers of history like Hayden White, Amos Funkenstein, or Saul Friedlander look for models of such history, the best they can come up with are often kinds of fiction, imaginative memoirs, and hybrid forms like the comix. In a parallel vein, Michael Andre Bernstein has also found that the best examples of what he calls "sideshadowed" and "anti-apocalyptic history" are similarly the fiction of Robert Musil or poetry of Yehuda Amichai. What might such sideshadowed history look like? Very much, according to Bernstein, like the end of Yehuda Amichai's poem "The Tourist":

> Once I was sitting on the steps near the gate at David's Citadel and I put down my two heavy baskets beside me. A group of tourists

stood there around their guide, and I became their point of reference. "You see that man over there with the baskets? A little to the
right of his head there's an arch from the Roman period. A little to
the right of his head." "But he's moving, he's moving!" I said to myself: Redemption will come only when they are told, "Do you see
that arch over there from the Roman period? It doesn't matter, but
near it, a little to the left and then down a bit, there's a man who has
just bought fruit and vegetables for his family." (137–38)

Like Friedlander's, this is the uncanny middle voice of one who is in history
and who tells it simultaneously, one who lives *in* history as well as *through*
its telling.

Simply put, such history "will incorporate the different ways individuals
evaluated their circumstances at the time, and do so without flaunting a
foreknowledge of the impending catastrophe" (Michael Bernstein 25). That
is, it will do what only those works written before or during the catastrophe
can do: remain oblivious to their end. Even though it is easy to agree completely with this aim, one also wonders whether it is actually possible to
write history pretending to be blind to the present moment, when it is
probably that present moment that makes a particular history worth writing about in the first place. Bernstein would argue, rightly, that this is the
kind of thinking we must escape. He believes, again rightly, that these lives
in and of themselves make such history worth writing, that if we permit
them to acquire significance only in light of their terrible end, then we have
handed the Nazis a posthumous victory. But the impossible question remains: Can we forget what we already know in order to write a past that is
properly blind to its later stages?

I would say no. But then this is where the survivor's memory comes in.
On the one hand, it is clear that not even the survivor can forget what transpired after the Holocaust in telling us what happened then: that is, even
the survivor's story is necessarily organized retrospectively. At the same
time, however, *how* the survivor has organized this story still reveals a kind
of understanding unique to someone who has known events both directly
and at some remove. The survivor's memory includes both experiences of
history and of memory, the ways memory has already become part of personal history, the ways misapprehension of events and the silences that
come with incomprehension were part of events as they unfolded then *and*
part of memory as it unfolds now.

Can the silences of a witness be part of the essential historical truth of
the events here? They can if historians come to hear these silences and to
grasp their role as part of the empirical data they are collecting. Can mistakes become part of this data as well? Yes, when they tell us about how and

why a victim responded to events at the time. Moreover, when these errors of fact in the survivor's story are known to be mistakes even after the fact by the victims, it becomes less likely that they will reveal them at all—thus suppressing a significant kind of evidence, that is, evidence of a kind of knowledge (however mistaken) they had at the time.

At one point in his and Shoshana Felman's book on *Testimony*, Dori Laub relates an all-too-representative response of historians to a survivor's video testimony. The survivor, a woman now in her 60s, was recalling details of the short-lived *Sonderkommando* uprising at Auschwitz, which she had witnessed in 1943. "All of a sudden," she said, "we saw four chimneys going up in flames, exploding. The flames shot into the sky, people were running. It was unbelievable" (59). Unbelievable, indeed, retorted the historians who watched this tape, since only one chimney had been blown up. To their minds, such "flawed" testimony was as worthless to their inquiry into events as it was dangerous to historical truth.

But here conventional historians blind themselves to the actual, empirical value of such mistaken testimony. After all, like all eyewitnesses, this woman was not testifying to "what happened," but to what she *saw*. The historians' job is to deduce what happened from what she and many other witnesses saw. And since part of what she saw necessarily includes what she has understood (as in "Yes, I see now"), part of the historians' job is also to take into account what this witness has understood of the events she witnessed. None of which seems to have crossed the minds of the historians who watched these video testimonies.

The interviewer and therapist, Dori Laub, is disconcerted, even shocked by the disregard these historians seem to have shown for what he regards as the actual subject of her testimony: not the historical events themselves but the extraordinary impact they had on her. That is, even though she had seen these events, her testimony had abstracted from them only the generic act of resistance itself, heretofore unimaginable to this woman. This breaking of a framework (a world in which Jewish revolts did not occur) was, for Laub, also an empirical historical truth. That such an integral change in this woman's world-view should be disregarded by the historians is inconceivable to the psychoanalyst, for whom internal changes in the psychic landscape are as "real" and verifiable as those in the external, physical landscape.

But this still doesn't quite pinpoint the crucial data historians miss when they ignore or devalue the patently subjective and mistaken testimony to be found in so much video testimony. For by discounting the understanding an eyewitness had of events at the time they unfolded, historians also ignore the very reasons the witness and other survivors, as well as victims, responded to events as they did. Ultimately, this is to ignore the highly contingent reasons events actually unfolded. Moreover, by discounting the actual, if quotidian contingencies of the moment, historians succumb further to the hindsight knowledge that blinds them to many of the actual causes and effects of events as they occurred. This is why conventional historians may make such ineffective interviewers: they are so convinced of their hindsight logic, that they constantly lead witnesses into confirming what they already know. By leading witnesses away from making historically inaccurate statements, such historians ignore the value of these mistaken perceptions for understanding how this knowledge—as fallible as it was—may have woven itself into the very course of events as they unfolded.

For the same reasons historians find oral or video testimony so unreliable as a source for actual names, dates, and places (as the victims' very reality was often choreographed for them by the Nazis, so too have the survivors' memories of this time been screened retrospectively through the stories of others and their own subjective experiences since the war), they tend to discount the historical value of the diaries and memoirs. But in so doing, these historians may be ignoring the value of these works' subjectivity for further understanding of the historical facts themselves and why they unfolded as they did. That is, once we take into account the eyewitnesses' voices, their literary construal or misconstrual of events, and their reflexive interpretations of experience, we understand more deeply why and how the victims responded to unfolding events as they did. Attempting to disentangle them after the fact, as if we could separate the fact of the victims' experiences from their own apprehension of these experiences, is to negate part of the historical reality itself. By returning their voices and subjectivity to the historical record, however, we restore a measure of contingency to history as it unfolds, opening up the possibility of historical causes and effects otherwise lost in our projection of a hindsight logic onto events.

Instead of disqualifying competing accounts, therefore, we can accept that every Holocaust writer has a different story to tell, not because what happened to so many others was intrinsically "different," but because *how* victims and survivors have grasped and related their experiences comprises the core of their story. While historians may still attempt to sort through such narratives for the most accurate and historically verifiable accounts available, they need not discard the remaining accounts as so much archival chaff. Instead, they might now begin to examine the historical agency in these eyewitnesses' narratives. For in the final analysis, no document can be more historically authentic than that embodying the victims' grasp of events at the time. Nothing can be more authentic than the ways in which the diarists' interpretations of experiences gathered the weight and force of agency in their lives. Nothing is more "true" than the consequences for a life that issue from the manner in which this life may have been narrated the previous day. In this sense, the diaries assume an historical importance far beyond whatever facts they could possibly deliver. In the diaries of Chaim Kaplan, Emmanuel Ringelblum, Zelig Kalmanovitsh, and others, we have incontrovertible truth of the ways in which their narratives of events may have constituted the basis for action within these same events. Thus, the narrative grasp of events might be said to have woven itself back into the unfolding course of events.[2]

Some, like Michel Foucault, have suggested that since every record of history is also a representation and therefore subject to all of a culture's mediating forces, including the political, the study of history can be only the study of commemorative forms. But here I would like to return to the somewhat more quaint notion of history conceived always as a combination of events and their representations. To date, in fact, I have also made commemorative forms—such as monuments, museums, and days of remembrance—part of my historical inquiry.[3] Unlike Foucault, however, I would not displace more traditional notions of history with this hypermediated version of history, but only add the study of commemorative forms to the study of history, making historical inquiry the combined study of both *what happened* and *how it is passed down* to us.

The historian has long demanded the impossible feat: to ignore the present moment as we tell of past ones. In effect, historians have asked themselves to forget the present as they recount the past. Rather than pretending to forget why something is worth remembering and telling in the first place, we need to acknowledge that the history we write is worth writing at least partly because of where we stand now. In this way, historical inquiry might remain a search for certainties about substantive realities, even as it is broadened to encompass the realities of history's eventual transmission. Extended backward into the notion of history "as it happened," such a conception includes as part of its search for verifiable fact the search for verifiable, yet highly contingent representations of these facts as they unfolded. Instead of enforcing an absolute breach between what happened and how it is remembered, we might also ask what happens when the players of history remember their past to subsequent generations. For as Saul Friedlander's extraordinary work makes absolutely clear, this is not memory only, but also another, invaluable kind of history-telling.

Notes on Contributors

Karyn Ball teaches critical and literary theory in the Department of English at the University of Alberta in Edmonton. She has published and presented conference papers on Freudian psychoanalysis and the impact of the Holocaust on continental theory and cultural studies. In 2000, she edited a special issue of *Cultural Critique* on the topic of "Trauma and its Cultural Aftereffects" (#46). Her article, "Wanted, Dead, or Distracted: On Ressentiment in History, Philosophy, and Everyday Life," was published in *Cultural Critique* (fall 2002).

Harriet Davidson is a Professor of English at Rutgers University, and serves as Director of Women's Studies. She is the author of *T. S. Eliot and Hermeneutics: Absence and Interpretation in the Waste Land*, and editor of the Longman Critical Reader, *T.S. Eliot* (1999). She is currently working on a book on Adrienne Rich's poetry.

Ana Douglass writes and teaches in Reno, Nevada. She is the author of *"Transcendental Homelessness": Modernism, the Culture Concept, and the Novel*, a study of the intersection between the anthropological and the literary in modernism. Her most recent publication, "Catechizing without Shelter," appeared in *The European Legacy: Toward New Paradigms*.

William A. Douglass founded the Basque Studies Program and is an Emeritus Professor of Anthropology at the University of Nevada, Reno. He most recently edited two volumes, *The Basque Diaspora=La Diaspora Vasca* and *Basque Cultural Studies*.

Kyo Maclear is an independent writer and editor based in Toronto. Her first book, *Beclouded Visions: Hiroshima-Nagasaki and the Art of Witness* (State University of New York, 1999), addresses questions of historical memory and witnessing in twentieth-century art. Her work has been published in several art and culture magazines, including *Toronto Life, Brick, Mix, Fuse* and *This Magazine*.

Tyrus Miller is Associate Professor of Literature at the University of California, Santa Cruz. He is author of *Late Modernism: Politics, Fiction, and the Arts Between the World Wars*, and is completing a manuscript entitled *Afterlives of the Readymade: Perspective and Delay in Avant-Garde Aesthetics*. In 2001–2004, he is director of the University of California Study Center in Budapest, Hungary.

Cindy Patton is Director of Graduate Studies at the Graduate Institute of the Liberal Arts, Emory University. She is the author of *Sex and Germs: The Politics of AIDS, Fatal Advice: How Safe Sex Went Wrong, Inventing AIDS, Last Served?: Gendering the HIV Pandemic*, and has recently co-edited *Queer Diasporas*.

Thomas A. Vogler is Professor of English and Comparative Literature at the University of California, Santa Cruz. He has published on a wide range of authors and topics, from the seventeenth through the twentieth centuries. Among his current projects is a book on "writing *writing*."

James E. Young is Professor of English and Chair of Judaic and Near Eastern Studies at the University of Massachusetts, Amherst. His publications include *The Texture of Memory: Holocaust Memorials and Meaning in Europe, Israel, and America*, and *At Memory's Edge: After-Images of the Holocaust in Contemporary Art and Architecture*. In 1997, Professor Young was appointed by the Berlin Senate to the five-member *Findungskommission* for Germany's national "Memorial to Europe's Murdered Jews," now under construction in Berlin.

Joseba Zulaika is Professor of Anthropology and Director of the Basque Studies Program at the University of Nevada, Reno. He is the author of *Basque Violence: Metaphor and Sacrament, Chivos y soldados: la mili como ritual de inciación*, and has recently co-authored *Terror and Taboo: The Follies, Fables, and Faces of Terrorism*.

Notes

Introduction

1. For recent examples see Peter Novick, *The Holocaust in American Life*, Tim Cole, *Selling the Holocaust*, Norman Finkelstein, *The Holocaust Industry*.

2. John Treat, *Writing Ground Zero*, and Lisa Yoneyama, *Hiroshima Traces*, are good general introductions to the Hiroshima/Nagasaki discourse.

3. See Benjamin's "The Author as Producer": "I spoke of the procedure of a certain modish photography whereby poverty is made an object of consumption. In turning to New Matter-of-factness [*die neue Sachlichkeit*] as a literary movement, I must take a step further and say that it has made the struggle against poverty an object of consumption" (1979: 231). See Michael Davidson, "Not Sappho, Sacco" for an excellent discussion of 1930s U.S. "realist" poetics. In 1935 the Historical Division of the Farm Security Administration (FSA) instituted a project to document in photographs the shocking poverty of rural communities in the U.S. producing a total of 70,000 negatives on file in the Library of Congress. Walker Evans, Dorothea Lange, Gordon Parks, and Marion Post Wolcott were among the many distinguished artists who contributed to this effort. Agee's *Let Us Now Praise Famous Men*, with photographs by Walker Evans, is one of the better known examples from this period.

4. The Japanese term "*hibakusha*" is more precise than "victim" or "survivor." It means "one who was subjected/exposed to the bomb and/or to radiation."

5. See Michael Schudson, *Watergate in American Memory: How We Remember, Forget, and Reconstruct the Past*. He uses the example of Watergate to show the degree to which personal memory is social, acquired at second hand rather than from immediate experience. Schudson points out that it is common to consider memory as "a property of individual minds," but he argues that memory is "essentially social," that it is located in "rules, laws, standardized procedures, and records . . .

books, holidays, statues, souvenirs." As Kerwin Klein observes, in this view "Memory is not a property of individual minds, but a diverse and shifting collection of material artifacts and social practices" (130), and this jibes with the growing interest in monuments, memorials, and museums during this period.

6. Binjamin Wilkomirski's *Fragments* claims to be an authentic memoir of a three- or four-year-old child's experience in death camps, and the result of a successful "recovered memory therapy." He claims to have been born in Latvia around 1939, and that after seeing his father murdered he was transported to a series of camps beginning with Majdanek. The work is narrated as from the perspective of a confused and frightened child, in a series of disjointed flashbacks that describe horrible details of life in the camps with great vividness. *Fragments* quickly became an international bestseller, and won a number of important awards. Now it is generally accepted that the work is a fraud. Daniel Ganzfried, himself the son of a Holocaust survivor, and author of a "fictional" account of Holocaust experience, *The Dispatcher*, was the first to point out that public records show Wilkomirski was born in Switzerland in 1941 to an unmarried Protestant woman, and adopted by a Swiss couple (now deceased) who named him Bruno Doessekker. Wilkomirski claims the papers were part of an identity cover-up, like others done to protect children during the war. Ganzfried has documents that show Wilkomirski/Doessekker started school in Switzerland in 1947, a year before he says he arrived in the country. He told Ganzfried he was circumcised, but his ex-wife and a former girlfriend say he is not. Elena Lappin's "The Man With Two Heads" has a detailed account of the whole affair. See also Philip Gourevitch, "The Memory Thief." For Araki Yasusada see Vogler, in this volume. 173–74.

7. Cornell's work was inspired by the Surrealists. He is best known for his "boxes," in which he arranged various items he picked up from junk shops and dime stores— a doll's arm, a piece of broken mirror, a page from a Latin primer, a cheap toy, a bottle label. . . . His term for the tracking down of such materials was the "metaphysics of ephemera." For reproductions of Cornell's work and commentary on it, see *Joseph Cornell*, edited by Kynaston McShine, with commentaries by Dawn Ades, Carter Ratcliff, P. Adams Sitney, and Lynda Roscoe Hartigan. For his own writing, see Mary Ann Caws' *Theater of the Mind*.

8. See Philip Winslow's book *Sowing the Dragon's Teeth*. Human rights groups estimate the total number of live landmines at over 100 million, spread over sixty-eight of the world's poorest countries. Twenty million of these are buried in South Africa. Angola and Cambodia have the highest number of amputees in the world thanks to their rich endowment of landmines. The weapon was first invented for use by the U.S. Army in the Seminole War of 1840. The delayed but continuous random violence of landmines works in slow motion to kill or maim a new victim every few minutes at some place in the world.

9. And it is still growing, according to Allen Young in *The Harmony of Illusions: Inventing Post-Traumatic Stress Disorder*. Post-traumatic stress disorder (PTSD) was formulated by U.S. psychiatrists largely in response to the conspicuous symptoms of Vietnam veterans, its widespread use as a legal defense for veterans in criminal

cases, and demands by veterans' groups that it be officially recognized. It was listed in 1980 in the *Diagnostic and Statistical Manual of Mental Disorders*, published by the American Psychiatric Association. For an overview of the writing on post-traumatic stress since the late 1970s, see Blake, Albano, and Keane, "Twenty years of Trauma." For a detailed discussion of PTSD see Nancy C. Andreasen, "Post-traumatic Stress Disorder" in Kaplan and Sadock's *The Comprehensive Textbook of Psychiatry*. Jonathan Shay scrutinizes the traumatic reactions of U.S. troops in *Achilles in Vietnam*. In *Worlds of Hurt*, Kali Tal traces ways in which the emergence of PTSD in the wake of the Vietnam War shifted attention from the U.S. soldiers as agents of genocidal violence perpetrated against the North Vietnamese to the veterans as victims of trauma, even if that is the trauma of having inflicted trauma on others. Now a recognized medical specialty, "psychotraumatology" has come a long way from the battlefields and includes almost every possible kind of psychologically stressful experience. For a useful overview see Ruth Leys, *Trauma: A Genealogy*. Judith Lewis Herman's *Trauma and Recovery* explores familial sexual and emotional traumatization, and traces the ideological roots of trauma to the anti-Vietnam War movement and to feminism. Kirby Farrell's *Post-traumatic Culture: Injury and Interpretation in the Nineties* investigates trauma as a cultural trope serving a variety of ideological interests in literary and cinematic narratives. For specific relationships between the more general discussion of PTSD and Holocaust survivors, see Ghislaine Boulanger's review of Judith Herman's *Trauma and Recovery*. For some interesting views on "the politics of trauma" and the equation of "pain" with "truth" in the context of contemporary identity politics, see Lauren Berlant, "The Subject of True Feeling: Pain, Privacy, and Politics." The collection of essays edited by Paul Antze and Michael Lambek, *Tense Past: Cultural Essays in Trauma and Memory*, includes a wide variety of disciplinary and interdisciplinary examples of the ways past events and experiences are mediated by cultural frameworks, systems of narrativization, and the present context of recollection. Daniel Goleman has a less technical overview of the field of trauma research in Chapter 13 of *Emotional Intelligence*. In *The Politics of Victimization: Victims, Victimology, and Human Rights*, Robert Elias explores the potential for ambivalence in the cultural valorization of trauma. The status of "victim" implies passivity and can lead to pity and even to contempt for weaklings and losers. For studies that focus on trauma and memory, see Cathy Caruth's collection of essays, *Trauma: Explorations in Memory*, and her *Unclaimed Experience: Trauma, Narrative, and History*. For a study of the role issues of trauma and memory play in the medical and legal arenas, see Paul Applebaum, Lisa Uyehara, and Mark Elin, *Trauma and Memory: Clinical and Legal Controversies*.

10. Daniel Schacter's *Searching for Memory* provides a detailed and useful study of the debate and its history.

11. See notes 36 and 38 for these similarities.

12. Unlike the Vietnam War, which saw almost unlimited access to reporters, the operations in the Gulf were severely controlled to limit the potential for witness. The Afghan incursion has continued this repressive regime, reminiscent of the information ban on the atomic bomb effects.

13. For a survey of the recent attraction to the corpse as a subject for photographic art, see Annie Proulx's "Dead Stuff." Peter Schwenger's "Corpsing the Image" is a relevant study of the work of Joel-Peter Witkin.

14. Issues surrounding the concept of memory have become significant in a number of disciplines and discourses in the last 20 years. See Kerwin Klein's "On the Emergence of Memory in Historical Discourse" for a useful overview of what he calls "memory talk" as it is institutionalized in contemporary "memory industry."

15. Marita Sturken's study of cultural memory in the U.S. shows the interrelatedness of personal memory and collective remembering and the distinction between history as public discourse distinct from private memory. See *Tangled Memories: The Vietnam War, the AIDS Epidemic, and the Politics of Remembering* for detailed studies of specific examples.

16. See Ong's *Orality and Literacy* for the general picture.

17. A notable exception is the interesting work on institutional or systematic forgetting, and especially on the rhetorical organization of remembering and forgetting to be found in David Middleton and Derek Edwards, *Collective Remembering*.

18. In his incomplete fragment, *Toward a Philosophy of the Act*, Bakhtin takes a quite different view, but he is clearly contemplating an "event" on a smaller scale, where individual agency can still be imagined: "The ongoing event can be clear and distinct, in all its constituent moments, to a participant in the act or deed he himself performs. . . . And he understands the ought of his performed act, that is, *not* the abstract law of his act, but the actual, concrete ought conditioned by his unique place in the given context of the ongoing event" (30). At the opposite end of the spectrum are notions of *durée* in which even the Holocaust or Hiroshima/Nagasaki would not constitute an event. For Heidegger, Hiroshima is only a journalistic footnote to something that started centuries ago. Fernand Braudel, who introduced the notion of the "long event" or "*durée*," argues that the significant "events" of history are trends and tendencies that extend over centuries in relation to stable geographic features of a terrain and to longstanding mental frameworks.

19. The first documented instance of biological warfare can be attributed to Lord Jeffrey Amherst, eponym for the town and university. In 1763 he issued a written order to "extirpate this execrable race" (the Atlantic Seaboard indigenes already reduced at that time by 99 percent) by distributing as gifts items taken from a smallpox infirmary. This was done during a peace parley with Pontiac's Confederacy, and the ensuing epidemic killed almost 100,000. See Stearn and Stearn, *The Effects of Smallpox on the Destiny of the Amerindian* (44–45).

20. Western demographers estimate that 30,000,000 died in this famine. Dissident former officials, basing their claims on documentary evidence, have claimed a toll as high as forty-six million, but these figures include total deaths, the millions who would have died in any case. The Deng Ziaoping regime acknowledged twenty million deaths. Becker calls it a "secret famine" because of the success (until late 1970s) of the Chinese official policy of denial and secrecy. The consequent horrors included family decisions about which members were most expendable (hence young girls died first). People were reduced to eating a mixture

of weeds and earth, and often died from the constipation it produced. Flesh was cut from human corpses to be eaten, and intra-family cannibalism was common. Those who dissented from the official version of events, or who stole grain to survive, were labeled "right opportunists" and Becker records their treatment: they were beaten, kicked, dragged behind trucks, nailed to walls, ears were cut off, or iron wires threaded through them. People were buried with only the head exposed, then the skull was smashed to expose the brains. See Jasper Becker, *Hungry Ghosts: China's Secret Famine.*

21. As reported in the *Washington Post* on September 17, 1997 (article by Timothy Guinnane, Associate Professor of Economics, Yale University), several states had at that time mandated that the Famine be taught in schools as an example of genocide, as a part of courses originally intended for the study of the Holocaust. More states are considering enacting similar measures, in response to The Irish Famine Curriculum Committee that has pushed this "lesson of history" for ideological reasons.

22. At the outer reaches of discourse are the theological visions of those like Marilyn McCord Adams, who assures her readers that those who suffer "horrendous evils" such as the Nazi genocide, will have a "postmortem" state in which God will heal and restore the victims who will then somehow be able to find a positive aspect in their suffering. She does not tell us what this is or how it works, because only God has the "superlative imagination needed to make sense of horrors that stump us"(82). Emil Fackenheim regards the Holocaust as a unique "blessing" in which "philosophers and Christians today and tomorrow . . . are reached by a blessing across the abyss, coming to them from the darkest Jewish night. It is a blessing the like of which the world has never seen" (303). Emmanuel Levinas finds the archetype of gratuitous human suffering in the Holocaust, which provides a message of hope in which the suffering of another person, even though absolutely useless, meaningless, and inexorably evil to the person who suffers, can take on a meaning through the "inter-human claim" that it makes upon us as witnesses and be transformed into a *meaningful* suffering in the subject who responds to the *meaningless* suffering of the victim" (1988a: 157–62).

23. Better choices are offered by David E. Stannard, in *American Holocaust: Columbus and the Conquest of the New World.* He argues that the European and white American destruction of the native peoples of the Americas was the most massive act of genocide in the history of the world. Also, the institution of slavery in North America lasted 20 times as long as the Nazi genocide and killed at least ten times as many people.

24. Plus a maze of other unanswerable issues raised by complex problems relating to how Jewish identity is constituted. Surely not by the Nazis, who had neither right nor ability to make the determination, and who could make mistakes even by their own criteria. There were Jews who did not consider themselves Jews but were killed anyway. The Catholic Church, which canonized her in 1998, maintains that Sister Teresa Benedicta of the Cross was killed in Auschwitz because she was a Catholic. But before converting she was Edith Stein, born a Jew in Silesia,

and others claim she was murdered because she was a Jew. See Harry James Cargas, *The Unnecessary Problem of Edith Stein*, for more details and arguments. The general issue is still a very important one in the U.S., where the federal government claims the right to employ a system of identifying Native Americans according to a formal eugenics code called "blood quantum." See M. A. Jaimes, "Federal Indian Identification Policy," for more details. The consequences of such identity criteria include very important legal and economic decisions as well as those of dignity and cultural autonomy.

25. We could also quibble with particular claims for failed imagination, as when White claims "a growth in world population hitherto unimaginable" for our era, forgetting about Malthus, who in his *Essay on the Principle of Population* (1798) imagined *more* growth in world population than has happened, or than is now expected to happen in the next millennium. This is by no means the only example where we can find an *excess* of imagination of the future by a prior age rather than a deficiency.

26. There is increasing evidence that the war could have been ended months before the Hiroshima/Nagasaki horror if Roosevelt had abandoned his insistence on unconditional surrender and let the Emperor keep his position (a condition agreed to immediately after the bombings). Japanese envoys had been making overtures for a year in many different places (Sweden, Switzerland, Portugal, the Vatican, etc.) indicating the war could be ended if the Emperor were retained. On July 18, 1945, the Emperor himself wrote a letter "looking for peace" (President Truman's words) and followed it with a telegram to the same effect. General Eisenhower had told Secretary of War Henry L. Stimson of his "grave misgivings" about using a weapon that would shock world opinion and was "no longer mandatory as a measure to save American lives." As if in agreement, President Truman announced the event to the American public and identified Hiroshima as "an important Japanese Army base" (Bernstein and Matusow 39). Gar Alperovitz's *The Decision to Use the Atomic Bomb* includes more evidence along these lines. Martin Sherwin's *A World Destroyed* and Barton Bernstein's "Atomic Diplomacy and the Cold War" (and other essays in that volume) also challenge the official justification for using the bomb. In the 1991 Gulf War different justifications were used for the slaughter of retreating Iraqi troops after the cease-fire, with successful suppression of information by the military and the government at the time and for many years after. See Seymour Hersh, "Overwhelming Force," for a thorough report of this and related events.

27. Other examples of the range of approaches can be found in Irving Horowitz: *Taking Lives: Genocide and State Power*, Richard Rubenstein: *The Age of Triage*, Israel Charny: *Toward the Understanding and Prevention of Genocide*, Isidor Walliman's and Michael Doblowski's edited collection of essays: *Genocide and the Modern Age*, Ervin Staub: *The Roots of Evil: The Origins of Genocide and other Group Violence*, Florence Mazian: *Why Genocide?*, and Frank Chalk's and Kurt Jonassohn's edition of essays on *The History and Sociology of Genocide*. Barbara Harff and Ted Gurr provide a useful overview in "Toward Empirical Theory of Genocides and Politicides."

28. The work is currently owned by Charles Saatchi, an active collector of contemporary "cutting edge" and extremist art. The prints were part of an exhibition ("Disasters of War: Francisco de Goya, Henry Darger, Jake and Dinos Chapman") at P.S. 1 Contemporary Art Center, Long Island City, Queens, in January and February of 2001. Kyo Maclear, in *Beclouded Visions*, discusses a number of artists' responses to the atomic bombing of Japan.

29. See Kyo Maclear (58–60, 200). Frenkel's work can be followed on the *Body Missing* Web site, http://www.yorku.ca/BodyMissing/intro.html, which consists of an elaborate web of traces relating to the Holocaust, offering a number of ways to connect images of contemporary testimony with death camp lists and art confiscated by the Nazis for Hitler's museum. As Maclear points out, "Frenkel makes our role as witnesses explicit" (200).

30. The first report was recorded by the journalist George L. Steer of *The Times* (London), who was covering the Republican side of the Basque campaign in the Spanish Civil War. The attack happened on Monday, April 26. His report appeared in *The Times* of London and *The New York Times* on April 28, 1937. Steer's account was disputed from the beginning by Nationalists and their sympathizers. See Nicholas Rankin, "Bombs, What bombs?" for an account of the controversy.

31. An increasing number of witness studies show that the passage of time is not the primary problem for accuracy of perception and recall. In 1997 *The Journal of Credibility Assessment and Witness Psychology* (*JCAAWP*) was begun to specialize in witness issues and phenomena. It exists primarily on the Web (http://truth.boisestate.edu/jcaawp/default.html), and deals with a number of topics, including eyewitness memory, traumatic memory, child witness, confession phenomena, and interrogation. A recent example of the unreliability of eyewitnesses can be found in the June Report of the National Transportation Safety Board, which announced that it had gathered 349 eyewitness accounts of the crash of American Airlines Flight 587 near Kennedy International Airport in New York. In the 93 seconds it took for the plane to hit the ground, witnesses reported hundreds of different perceptions. A spokesman for the Board, Ted Lopatkiewicz, said "I don't think I'm making any news by saying that eyewitness testimony at a plane crash and probably at many traumatic events is unreliable" (*The New York Times*, June 22, 2002).

32. Pezzetti is the director of the audio-visual department of the Centro Documentazione Ebraica Contemporanea in Milan. A historian, he has specialized on Auschwitz and served as consultant on films, including Benigni's *La vita é bella* (Life Is Beautiful). In Ruggiero Gabbai's documentary film *Memoria* (1997), he is featured interviewing Italian Auschwitz survivors. His CD-ROM, *Destinazione Auschwitz*, has been distributed through the Italian school system and will soon be translated into English. It is "the culmination of Pezzetti's work as an archivist and historian," organized as a virtual tour of the camp with re-creations based on original architectural blueprints, maps, and survivor testimony. The CD's most startling innovation is a form of virtual time travel, using a "camera matching" technique, in which black-and-white archival photos, including a number taken

by the Nazis, can be compared with color photos of the same locations in the present-day camp. See Carlo Celli, "Interview with Marcello Pezzetti."

33.   The Spielberg Survivors of the Shoah Foundation is currently spending a hundred million dollars to videotape aging survivors' testimony, to be housed in the new east wing of the Museum of Jewish Heritage in New York, a three-year $60 million addition to the existing facilities. Peter Novick predicts that the results will be "a meretricious, Hollywood-to-the-max sort of evocation" (1999: 351). Elena Lappin records Spielberg's boast: "We have collected more than 50,000 testimonies in thirty-one languages across fifty-seven countries. That's more than fourteen years of material [in playing time], enough videotape to circumnavigate the globe" (9).

34.   In *The Myth of Repressed Memory*, Elizabeth Loftus and Katherine Ketcham critique the 1980s enthusiasm for traumatic amnesia, challenging the reality of repressed memories, arguing that patients can learn to demonstrate symptoms that conform to their therapists' expectations. They are part of a large-scale reaction to the PTSD craze and share a psychological perspective that does not think memory works in the simplistic mechanical fashion so often assumed in cases of "recovered" memory. Daniel Schacter's *Searching for Memory* provides a detailed and useful study of this debate and its history.

35.   See Felman 2001: 232, for a useful short bibliography of works on the law relating to victims, on the victims' rights movement in criminal law, and on victim impact statements.

36.   The *testimonio* is a form of collective autobiographical witnessing that gives voice to oppressed peoples. As defined by John Beverley, it is "a novel or novella-length narrative in book or pamphlet (that is, printed as opposed to acoustic) form, told in the first person by a narrator who is also the real protagonist or witness of the events he or she recounts, and whose unit of narration is usually a 'life' or a significant life experience" (1996a: 24). It is always linked to a group or class situation marked by trauma in the form of marginalization, oppression and struggle. See the discussion by Ana Douglass in this volume.

37.   Smith's main argument is more complex. We also imagine how someone at a distance from us might view our actions. We create this imaginary witness, named the "impartial spectator" by Smith, in our own minds.

38.   The similarities can be seen clearly in John Treat's description of the Japanese genre of testimonial literature: "By 'recording' is meant testimony: the chronological narration of recalled experience from a single and unified first-person point of view wholly identifiable with the author, which is to say the testifying survivor. . . . 'I' (*watakushi*) so often commences these memoirs because both the genre and the experience converge upon that singular pronoun, charging it with both narrative and historical 'authority'. . . . The eye-witness subject is itself a rhetorical position insofar as it argues for an inarguable right to experience that is constituted as 'remembered' " (49). This reads like a description of *I, Rigoberta Menchú*.

39.   "Each visitor to the U.S. Holocaust Memorial Museum will have a very special

companion. Upon entering the Museum, everyone receives a passport-sized 'Identity Card' bearing the name and family history of an individual victim of the Holocaust. As the visitor proceeds through the Museum's permanent exhibit, he or she will learn how the Holocaust affected the fate of his or her companion. Whatever the outcome—death or new life—each visitor will have been given the opportunity to feel the impact of the Holocaust on someone very much like him—or herself" (Museum membership solicitation brochure).

40. The self-consciously designed inaugural event of "nuclear theory" was a conference organized and hosted by the Department of Romance Studies at Cornell in the spring of 1984. This was followed by a collection of papers from the conference published in *Diacritics*, with a Preface that outlined an agenda. The movement is discussed at length in Solomon's *Discourse and Reference in the Nuclear Age.*

41. See *www.midastours.com.* "The Holocaust. Great Guides, Great Company. Full Colour Brochure from Midas Tours."

42. According to James Tatum, the Vietnamese term for the conflict is literally "the war against the Americans" (639). His essay describes Chris Burden's conceptual project for *The Other Vietnam Memorial* and includes photographs of Vietnamese monuments, including the desolate ARVN National Cemetery where goats graze on the abandoned graves and markers.

43. Martin Harwit's *An Exhibit Denied* details the long struggle to make a responsible full-coverage exhibition on the bombing, rather than a chauvinistic celebration. The efforts were finally silenced when the Republicans, led by Newt Gingrich—a professor of history—won control of Congress in 1994. They appointed newly critical members to the Smithsonian Board of Regents who saw that the new secretary, I. Michael Heyman, canceled the project and substituted a celebratory display on the airplane and its crew. Harwit, who had been recruited in 1987 from a professorship in astronomy at Cornell, specifically to increase the museum's scholarship and create exhibits with more historical depth, was fired. The "silencing" of Hiroshima had already started in 1945, immediately after the U.S. used on a civilian population a weapon whose killing power and tortuous effects far exceed those of poison gas and biological weapons, both banned by the major powers and the U.N. On September 19, 1945, the Allied Occupation GHQ issued a press code restricting reference to A-bomb matters in speech, reporting, and publication. The GHQ's Economic and Scientific Bureau later announced that surveys and studies of A-bomb matters by the Japanese would require permission from GHQ, and publication of A-bomb data was prohibited. Almost all of the Japanese publications related to the atomic bomb casualties were censored and suppressed by the authority of the Special Press Code, which lasted for six years and eight months. The banned manuscripts, books, and photographs were secretly sent to a United States Government agency. They have recently been released from the Library of Congress and other U.S. Library archives by the Freedom of Information Act (Nakano xix). In *Hiroshima Notes*, Oe describes specific instances of this suppression of witness by the occupation forces, "because it

depicted too vividly the A-bomb realities, and it was anti-American as well" (173). The Atomic Bomb Casualty Commission initially suppressed publication of the connection between atomic radiation and leukemia, although it later contributed to research that established a statistical connection (Oe 135–36). More recently we have seen in the Persian Gulf War a refusal by the Allied Powers to conduct an enemy body count, or to identify and bury the dead, accompanied by restricting press access to, information about, and representation of the enemy dead. Margot Norris has discussed how this "pre-censorship" (as Walter Cronkite called it) "inaugurated the creation of something like an originary silence—a partially blank space of discourse and representation whose absence can only be inferred, rather than an effacement whose occlusions may be lifted or an erasure whose traces may be restored" (225). The Allies used more explosive power there in six weeks than in all of World War II, producing at least two, perhaps three times the fifty-eight thousand casualties suffered by the U.S. during nine years in Vietnam, for a kill ratio of more than one hundred Iraqis to one Allied. This was a victory over a "Third World" country, reminiscent of the Italians bombing the Ethiopians in 1937 or of the battle of Omdurman in 1898, where the British art of killing from a distance allowed them to slaughter 11,000 African Muslims in five hours, while suffering only 48 casualties. After the battle they killed 16,000 wounded to bring the kill ratio to 562 to 1. As Churchill put it in *The River War* (1899), "The strongest and best-armed savage army yet arrayed against a modern European power had been destroyed and dispersed, with hardly any difficulty, comparatively small risk and insignificant loss to the victors" (quoted in Lindqvist 67). Norris identifies this massive destructiveness and indifference towards the dead, identified as a triumph of civilization and enlightenment over a primitive amoral inhumane culture, as a form of American Orientalism.

44. See Jan T. Gross's book *Neighbors: The Destruction of the Jewish Community in Jedwabne* for a horrifying account of the slaughter by Polish residents of almost all of the town's 1,600 Jewish residents in a single day, July 10, 1941. Plans are under way to replace a small monument attributing the massacre to the Germans that has stood in Jedwabne for many years.

45. "The West as America" exhibition included 164 paintings, sculptures, and engravings covering a hundred years of creative activity, all focused on the period of expansion and conquest of the West. The effect was an unmasking of a geographical fantasy and projection, linked in the formation of a mythical space that has been of the utmost ideological importance in the construction of a collective U.S. national identity. "As Seen by Both Sides" was put together by a number of organizations and individuals (including both Vietnamese and North American) as a gathering of a representative selection of the work of artists from both countries. See *As Seen by Both Sides: American and Vietnamese Artists Look at the War*. Ed. C. David Thomas (exhibition catalogue, Boston University Art Gallery, Boston, 14 Jan.–24 Feb. 1991).

46. The closest thing may be a $110-million National Underground Railroad Freedom Center, scheduled to open in 2004 on the Cincinnati waterfront. One idea,

according to the president and CEO Edwin J. Rigaud, is to convert visitors into "present-day freedom conductors" who, leaving the museum, will follow in the metaphorical footsteps of heroes like Harriet Tubman and Levi Coffin. Exhibitions and programs will link the history of slavery and the Underground Railroad with more contemporary and global freedom movements, including apartheid in South Africa, the U.S. civil rights movement, the protests in Tiananmen Square, the suffrage movement, and the international women's movement. With a strong ideological commitment to finding a redemptive promise in the Underground Railroad's example of interracial cooperation and courage, the project risks watering down history in the interest of attracting visitors. See Julia M. Klein, "One More River to Cross."

The Menchú Effect: Ana Douglass

1. The title in the English edition is *I, Rigoberta Menchú: An Indian Woman in Guatemala.*

2. Stoll's text has initiated a heated debate within both academic and political circles. The majority of responses have polarized the debate along the political extremes that defined the Guatemalan conflict for the last thirty years. The response from conservatives in the United States is best reflected in the campus newspaper campaign accusing Menchú of being a "fraud," initiated by David Horowitz's Center for the Study of Popular Culture. Horowitz suggested in these articles that professors who taught Menchú in their classes were intellectually dishonest and should be challenged by their students for including her now that Stoll had exposed the "lies" in her account. From the academic left, the response has been heavily, although certainly not exclusively anti-Stoll, and at times shockingly personal in tone. A recent collection, *The Rigoberta Menchú Controversy,* reflects the tone of the debate within the academy. In many ways Arturo Arias, the editor of the collection, should have considered naming it *The Stoll Controversy,* since most of the authors included in the collection dedicate more space and thought to discrediting Stoll than to rethinking Menchú and her text.

3. For selections from the international media coverage that followed upon Larry Rohter's "Tarnished Laureate" (*New York Times,* December 15, 1998), the first major article in the press reflecting Stoll's research, see Arias 2001b: 58–129.

4. I am taking this term, "the hermeneutics of solidarity," from Alberto Moreiras. For a fuller discussion of the term, see his "The Aura of *Testimonio.*"

5. I situate myself among these early critics. In 1993, I gave a paper, "Catechizing without Shelter," at the ISSEI Conference, "The European Legacy: Towards New Paradigms," in Graz, Austria, in which I clearly developed a line of argument intended to underscore my political solidarity with Menchú and her cause. This paper was later published as part of the conference in *The European Legacy: Toward New Paradigms: Fourth International Conference of the International Society for the Study of European Ideas* Vol. 1, No. 1.

6. Since the original writing of this piece, Mary Louise Pratt published "*I, Rigoberta*

Menchú and the 'Culture Wars.' " Pratt documents in detail the historical forces at work during the 1980s and, as a player in the push for a more inclusive curriculum at Stanford, provides a valuable account of the battle over Stanford's Western culture course. While I find her text especially helpful in outlining the historical context from which the current debate about Menchú and Stoll emerged, I find her argument less convincing in terms of her understanding of the consequences of the Menchú debate and her somewhat tendentious dismissal of Stoll's work.

7. John Beverley stands out among those literary critics concerned with defining the phenomena of witness within Latin American literatures. It is important to note, however, that while literary critics took the lead in defending texts of witness during the turbulent culture debates of the 1980s, the concept of culture as represented in anthropology also played a critical role in these debates. Whereas literary critics like Beverley, and to a lesser extent, George Yúdice, addressed the generic boundaries and origins of testimonial literatures, anthropologists tended to see the value in texts of witness for their tendency to chronicle the rituals and community lives of indigenous cultures. The distinction is significant because in many ways the anthropological reading of testimonials necessarily brought to bear greater pressures and critical scrutiny of the narrative of the "native informer." That David Stoll, an anthropologist, should be the vehicle by which Menchú's "truth value" was brought into question seems highly appropriate given the different approaches of the two disciplines to texts of witness in general.

8. For a discussion of the concept of "Latinamericanism" as analogous to Said's concept of "Orientalism," see Enrico M. Santí's "Latinamericanism and Restitution."

9. Pratt discusses how the "culture wars" were "the result of a fatal collision between two historical processes: on the one hand, the arrival on university faculties of the 'children of the 60s,' and on the other, the arrival at the White House of Ronald Reagan along with a dogmatic political right hungry for power" (2001: 30). Her discussion of the power struggle between those affiliated with the Hoover Institute of War, Revolution, and Peace at Stanford and the faculty in favor of a more diversified curriculum is particularly useful for understanding the motivations and the passions driving the "culture wars."

10. At least D'Souza's assertion that Menchú's rhetoric reflects a socialist agenda can be supported with evidence from the text; his charge that Menchú articulates a Western feminist agenda, on the other hand, is highly suspect. To ascribe a feminist agenda to Menchú's text is to misread a basic recurring theme of her testimonial—her consistent *dismissal* of feminism as an important component of her personal philosophy or politics. Her renunciation of marriage and motherhood, a chapter heading that D'Souza sees as evidence of her feminism, is actually motivated more by practical demands placed upon her as a voice for her community on a world-wide stage than out of what D'Souza clearly construes as a "militant" feminist rejection of traditional roles for women. In keeping with the experiences of women involved in liberation movements throughout the world, Menchú actually reflects in great detail on the need for Guatemalan women to table any discussion of feminist concerns until the greater struggle, fought side by side with

their male counterparts, is resolved. Menchú is quite comfortable making an argument for why women "have [a] job to do just like any other *compañero*"; she also argues, however, that "it would be feeding *machismo* to set up an organization for women only, since it would mean separating women's work from men's work" and that "by creating an organization for women [they] would be presenting the system which oppresses [them] with another weapon" (1984: 221, 222). In other places in the text, Menchú expresses at minimum ambivalence, at times open disregard for the Western feminist ideas she encountered in her increasingly international activism.

11. John Beverley has written extensively over the years on the subject of *testimonio*, and what I find most compelling about his work is the incremental rethinking with each piece, building upon what is clearly his sense that texts of witness have a particularly complicated place in history, in literature, but most importantly, in the "real" world, and his honest engagement with the complex theoretical questions that arise with each rethinking of the genre. While in his contribution to the Arias collection, "What Happens When the Subaltern Speaks: Rigoberta Menchú, Multiculturalism, and the Presumption of Equal Worth," he ultimately rejects Stoll's work, seeing it as yet another Western attempt to silence the subaltern by structuring an argument where "the subaltern can, of course, speak, but only through *us*, through our institutionally sanctioned authority," he also critiques some of the arguments used in support of Menchú, suggesting that the notion that Menchú deploys "Mayan forms of storytelling [that] merge the individual experience in the collective" is not an "entirely convincing" explanation for the discrepancies in her text (2001: 233, 221).

12. Two texts stand out in the Arias collection for including a discussion of the genre of *testimonio* and the ethnographic exchange embedded within these texts. W. George Lovell and Christopher H. Lutz, in "The Primacy of Larger Truths: Rigoberta Menchú and the Tradition of Native Testimony in Guatemala," situate Menchú's text in a tradition extending back to the sixteenth century. In contrast, Ileana Rodríguez focuses on Stoll, rather than Menchú, asserting that Stoll's text replicates the questionable Western reading of the indigenous subject common to early ethnographic texts. She notes that Stoll "repeats a thematics that is five hundred years old and in which he is unable to discern between misunderstandings (that which translations are unable to account for), silences (that which informants are not ready to tell), and lies (that which informants believe the interrogator wants to hear)" (335).

13. See Douglass: *"Transcendental Homelessness": Modernism, the Culture Concept, and the Novel* for a discussion of anthropology's attempts to consolidate its own rhetoric.

14. See Emery for a more detailed consideration of the history of proto-ethnographic testimonials in Latin America.

15. A recurrent theme in the Arias collection is whether or not Stoll's research is appropriately rigorous. Arias, Pratt, Taracena, and others suggest his work is "journalistic," in their attempts to undermine his credibility. The anthropologists in the

collection are less inclined to follow this line of argument. In "Telling Truths: Taking David Stoll and the Rigoberta Menchú Exposé Seriously," Kay B. Warren suggests that we might think of Stoll's text as an experimental text. She argues, "rather than dismissing Stoll as an ideologically motivated outlaw, as some have, it makes more sense to understand him as someone who reveals telling dilemmas that have propelled [anthropology] into the new millennium. This shift in anthropology's scope makes it all the more essential to ask why his work generates such heated criticism" (199).

16. By offering this extremely brief section on the political and social history of Guatemala, I am attempting to provide a minimal context from which we can consider the emergence of Menchú's text. In no way am I attempting to be either comprehensive or definitive. I am simply setting forth the circumstances behind the torture and disappearance of literal bodies in Guatemala—the trajectory of consideration in Menchú's text. The sources for this brief discussion of the demographics, land distribution, and human rights violations in Guatemala are primarily human rights groups and texts sympathetic to these same groups. Certainly, a more comprehensive discussion of the history and politics of Guatemala would apply some pressure to the numbers cited here and the "interpretation" of controversial events such as the massacre at Panzós. This level of consideration exceeds the intended goal of this section, which is simply to acknowledge that, in effect, the level of atrocities and human rights abuses committed in Guatemala over the past 40 years (regardless of contested numbers and charges of responsibility) warranted a witness. While until quite recently Menchú served as the most visible witness to these events, the formation of the United Nations-supported Guatemalan Truth Commission Accord, entered jointly by both sides in the Guatemalan conflict, suggests that, even though the events of the past forty years are still contested, the effort to arrive at a sustainable, agreed upon narrative of those events is at minimum going forward. Among the charges of the Truth Commission Accord is to establish "the commission for the historical clarification of human rights violations and acts of violence" and to attend to "the Guatemalan people's right to be fully aware of the truth with regard to these events, whose clarification will contribute to keeping these sorrowful, pain filled pages of our history from repeating, and will strengthen the democratization process in the country" (Guatemalan Truth Commission Accord, English translation). The jury is still out on the success of these efforts.

17. During the 1980s, the indigenous peoples of Guatemala actually constituted the majority of the population. Maya Indians made up fifty-five percent of the population. The indigenous population included some twenty-two languages and ethnic groups. These communities continue to live predominantly in the rural highlands, also known as the altiplano. See Simon's *Eternal Spring, Eternal Tyranny* for a discussion of the demographics and social history of Guatemala.

18. That many of Menchú's family and neighbors worked in the coffee *fincas* is indisputable, but Stoll argues that "judging from Uspantán sources . . . Rigoberta never worked on plantations" (1999: 25). Stoll also charges that the land disputes

were not solely motivated by tensions between the indigenous population and the landowning Ladinos. This claim is central to the controversy that surfaced with the publication of his work.

19. President Arbenz attempted to assuage the United Fruit Company by offering the company compensation based upon the company's own tax records. Arbenz offered the company U.S. $1.2 million; however, the company demanded U.S. $1.6 million (Simon 20). For greater detail on the Arbenz reforms and the CIA-supported coup of 1954, see Michael McClintock's *The American Connection: Volume Two: State Terror and Popular Resistance in Guatemala* and Richard H. Immerman's *The CIA in Guatemala: The Foreign Policy of Intervention.*

20. One of the great ironies of United States involvement in Guatemala is that the United States government's line on who was the source of instability in the region almost always rested with a charge that Fidel Castro and the Cuban military were behind any unrest. In a speech delivered on March 13, 1967, Castro suggests that "there is not a single event of all that takes place in this uneasy continent that does not lead to an immediate and trite accusation blaming Cuba. . . . Anything that happens anywhere: If it takes place in Colombia, Cuba is immediately to blame; if it is in Guatemala, Cuba is immediately to blame; if a military uprising occurs in Santo Domingo which leads to intervention by Yankee troops—an intervention that still continues—the inevitable reason for it is Cuba" (quoted in Duncan and Goodsell 481).

21. The number of acts of political repression during this period is staggering. Simon notes,

> Amnesty International recorded over 300 cases of "disappeared" Guatemalans between July 1977 and June 1978, most of them murdered shortly after their abductions, including 61 government-directed death squad killings in August 1977 alone. Specific urban sectors were targeted. Dr. Mario Lopez Larrave, ex-Dean of the San Carlos Law School and a prominent labor lawyer, was machine-gunned by army soldiers in the town of Panzós, after the peasants had publicly announced that they would travel there to protest the expropriation of their land in the province of Alta Verapaz. One day before the massacre, bulldozers had excavated two mass graves on the outskirts of town. (29)

The number of protests in response to these atrocities grew with each event. The funerals of Robin García and Mario Mujia were attended by 200,000 mourners. In response to the Panzós massacre, some 100,000 Guatemalans protested in the streets of Guatemala City. The occupation of the Spanish Embassy, the most central of events in Menchú's testimony, is another example of the kinds of protest generated within peasant movements in response to the political repression of the government, the military, and the paramilitary forces circulating during this time. For a further discussion of the specific acts of political repression during the late 1970s and early 1980s, see Amnesty International Report 1978; Amnesty International: Guatemala: The Human Rights Record; Guatemala 1978: The Massacre at Panzós (IWGIA Document No. 33, translation by Kjeld K. Lings); Witness to Political Violence in Guatemala: The Suppression of a Rural Movement (Shelton Davis and Julie Hodson).

22. A less contentious, but no less relevant critique of Menchú is that her position in the CUC and as a catechist made her an outsider to the Maya experience and that if we look more closely at the rituals discussed in her text, we can find mistakes in her representation of Maya culture. In "Menchú Tales and Maya Social Landscapes: The Silencing of Words and Worlds," Duncan Earle points out that some of the religious representation—"the divining system and the calendar"—were inaccurate (291). The significance of these inaccuracies goes more to complicating our notion of the unity of Maya culture than to undermining Menchú's credibility.

23. Menchú's statements appear in *"La conciencia de Rigoberta," El Periódico* (Guatemala City), December 14, 1997. According to Stoll, a brief exchange between Menchú and revolutionary leaders occurred around this time in the press, and Menchú affirmed more than once that Burgos-Debray had edited the text to such an extent Menchú felt that she was not its primary author.

24. Stoll uses the Spanish version of Menchú's second text, *Rigoberta: La nieta de los Mayas*, and provides this English translation. The published English version of Menchú's text is titled *Crossing Borders* and is different in several instances. For reasons of simplicity, I use the English title when referring to this text.

25. In an interview with Luis Aceituno in *El Periódico de Guatemala*, January 3, 1999, Taracena "breaks his silence" and asserts that he played a vital role in the formation of the text. He notes that the reason his name did not appear with the publication of the text was that his political affiliation at the time with the EGP (Guerilla Army of the Poor) would have influenced the way that the text was received. Therefore, he and Burgos-Debray agreed to "eliminate any mention of [him] in the text so that there would remain no trace of [his] participation" (Aceituno 84). As far as the controversy over Menchú's role in the text goes Taracena argues that "the book is a narration only by Rigoberta, with her own rhythm, with her own inventions, if there are any, with her own emotions, with her own truths. What we did afterward was the work of editing" (Aceituno 85).

26. Stoll chronicles some of the subtler editorial issues, like the inclusion of chapter epigraphs, that were a point of contention between Menchú, members of the Guatemalan Solidarity group, and Burgos-Debray. For a more detailed consideration of these issues, see Stoll 1999: 177–88.

27. Despite his much publicized criticism of Menchú, Stoll has been consistent in asserting the importance of her role in bringing world attention to the Guatemalan conflict and has been equally insistent that in no way does he deny that Rigoberta, her family, her community, and all of Guatemala suffered terrible atrocities and losses over the past four decades. As recently as the Arias collection, he reaffirms these sentiments, stating that although he "felt obliged to point out gaps between

Rigoberta's story and that of her neighbors," he also believes that "It is not important if her relatives died a bit differently than she says they did. . . . it is not hard to
defend her narrative strategy because her most important claim is true—the
Guatemalan army was indeed slaughtering defenseless villagers" (2001: 393, 395).
Despite these statements, Stoll has been the consistent target of very personal attacks on his credibility as an anthropologist and his political motivations.

28.   While Stoll documents at length the land ownership issues facing Vicente
      Menchú and other residents of Uspantán, he does, however, contradict Menchú's
      account for the reason behind the land disputes. According to Menchú, the
      Ladino landlords backed by the Guatemalan army were behind the move to strip
      the residents, including her father, of lands that they had farmed for generations.
      She also documents her father's attempts to work within the established system of
      land distribution. Vicente Menchú, according to his daughter, traveled to the cap-
      ital to talk to representatives at the National Institute for Agraian Transformation
      (INTA), and was turned away in his request for a title to his land, discovering that
      "the Government had made a deal to take the peasants' land away from them"
      (Menchú 1984: 103). While even Stoll admits that land disputes were heavily me-
      diated by the powers of the INTA and the Guatemalan Government, most often
      falling on the side of the Ladino land-owning minority, he also documents,
      through personal interviews with other residents of Menchú's village, that Vi-
      cente Menchú's land dispute was a result of an internal dispute between him and
      members of his wife's family. For a fuller consideration of the issue of land dis-
      putes in Menchú's text, see Stoll 1999: 1–42.

29.   Menchú's first response to Stoll's attacks was to attribute his findings to Western
      racism. When asked about the controversy that has circulated since the publica-
      tion of Stoll's work, she says, "I hate to speculate unless I have evidence. We are
      not going to say it was the CIA, but we cannot believe that someone wasn't behind
      this either" (Aznárez 111, 115). Her responses have changed somewhat over time,
      but they consistently reflect her awareness of the kind of rhetoric necessary to
      succeed on the international stage of public opinion.

30.   Nearly every text included in the Arias collection addresses the question of au-
      thenticity in texts of witness. See Beverley's "What Happens When the Subaltern
      Speaks: Rigoberta Menchú, Multiculturalism, and the Presumption of Equal
      Worth," Elzbieta Sklodowska's "The Poetics of Remembering, the Politics of For-
      getting: Rereading *I, Rigoberta Menchú*," Mario Roberto Morales' "Menchú after
      Stoll and the Truth Commission," and Victor D. Montejo's "Truth, Human Rights,
      and Representation: The Case of Rigoberta Menchú" for the most comprehensive
      discussions of authenticity in texts of witness. Of the fourteen academic essays in-
      cluded in the Arias collection, these four texts balance critical inquiry, theoretical
      models, political importance, historical significance, and legitimate critique of
      both Menchú and Stoll.

31.   For a complete discussion of the "impossibility of mimesis" in texts of witness, see
      Alberto Moreiras' "The Aura of *Testimonio*."

32.   See Mario Roberto Morales for a reading of the Menchú controversy using Lacan's theory of subject formation and the mirror stage.

33.   National Public Radio ("All Things Considered," May 10, 1999) included a copy of a transcript of Abner Louima's testimony during his civil rights case. In this testimony, Louima is questioned about a claim he made early on that the police chanted "It's Giuliani time" while beating him in a car and sodomizing him later with a stick. Louima admitted to the lie. The exchange is part of official court transcripts.

34.   The recent case of Amadou Diallo underscores the problem of bearing witness to acts of police violence in America. In many respects, the only witness to the death of Diallo (outside of the police who shot him) was his bullet-riddled body; in the absence of a victim to bear witness to his own victimization, the police were exonerated from all charges against them, even excessive force.

35.   Stoll is very critical of what he sees as the "postmodern" influences altering the way that anthropologists can talk about different cultures. This area of his text receives very little criticism, but is one of the weaker parts of his argument, even as it is certainly representative of a significant debate within his discipline. For a defense of Stoll and a critique of postmodernism, see Patai 270–87.

36.   For a discussion of the performative nature of language in Menchú's text using Lyotard's theory of language games, see Sommer 237–51. Also, see Patton in this volume for a use of Lyotard's theory in a discussion of witnessing in the O.J. Simpson trial.

37.   For a discussion of the social biographical nature of *testimonio* literatures, see John Beverley's "The Margin at the Center: On *Testimonio*," and George Yúdice's "*Testimonio* and Postmodernism."

38.   In *Bodies That Matter: On the Discursive Limits of 'Sex,'* Judith Butler argues that "the abject designates . . . those 'unlivable' and 'uninhabitable' zones of social life which are nevertheless densely populated by those who do not enjoy the status of the subject, but whose living under the sign of the 'unlivable' is required to circumscribe the domain of the subject" (3).

Excessive Witnessing: Joseba Zulaika

1.   See Clements' *Witness to War: An American Doctor in El Salvador.*

2.   I use "truth game" in the sense of the art of truth-telling or *parrhesia* practiced by Socrates and the Cynics. In order to communicate their approach to the truth, they elaborated peculiar "games of truth," such as critical preaching, scandalous behavior, or provocative dialogue. See James Miller, *The Passion of Michel Foucault*, Chapter 11.

3.   See Genet, *Prisoner of Love.*

4.   See Zulaika, "The Anthropologist as Terrorist" and Zulaika and Douglass, *Terror and Taboo.*

5.   See Rappaport, "The Obvious Aspects of Ritual."

6. For a viable characterization of "abyss," see Lyotard in *The Differend*: "We see no reason to grant a 'mystical' profundity to the abyss that separates cognitives and prescriptives. (Kant is sometimes drawn into this, as is Wittgenstein. Pascal, because he is the closest to the sophists, is in the last analysis more 'reasonable,' even with tears of joy.) Incommensurability, in the sense of the heterogeneity of phrase regimens and of the impossibility of subjecting them to a single law (except by neutralizing them), also marks the relation between either cognitives or prescriptives and interrogatives, performatives, exclamatives. . . . For each of these regimens, there corresponds a mode of presenting a universe, and one mode is not translatable into another" (128).

7. See Gerstein, "Do Terrorists Have Rights?" for an argument in which he justifies torture.

8. See Zulaika, *Chivos y soldados: la mili como ritual de inciación*.

Witness in the Wilderness: William A. Douglass

1. See James Clifford, *The Predicament of Culture: Twentieth-Century Ethnography, Literature, and Art* and *Routes: Travel and Translation in the Late Twentieth Century*; Mary Helms, *Ulysses' Sail*. Alun Kenwood, *Travellers' Tales, Real and Imaginary*; Mary Louise Pratt, *Imperial Eyes: Travel Writing and Transculturation* and George Robertson, et al., *Travellers' Tales: Narratives of Home and Displacement*.

2. Someone said to Socrates that a certain man had grown no better by his travels. "I should think not," he said; "he took himself along with him." And Horace: "Why should we move to find Countries and climates of another kind?/What exile leaves himself behind?" (quoted in Montaigne 176).

3. Lévi-Strauss had worked closely with Georges Monnet, a socialist deputy. In 1936 the party was victorious in the French elections. "I was already in Brazil, and he became minister in the government in the Popular Front. I was expecting him to call me. It was obvious that in their victory my former comrades had forgotten me" (Lévi-Strauss and Eribon 54). Marxist anthropologist Stanley Diamond upbraids Lévi-Strauss' "inauthenticity," stemming from his apostasy as both an indifferent Jew and questionable political activist (322–31).

4. "Every morning I went to the New York Public Library. What I know of anthropology I learned during those years" (Lévi-Strauss and Eribon 43).

5. He considered various offers from Kurt Lewin, Alfred Kroeber, and Talcott Parsons to teach in the United States, "But I had no desire to start life as an exile again" (55). Nor would this be his last rejection or close call. In 1973, Lévi-Strauss was elected to the *Académie française* as the sole candidate (another had withdrawn). In characterizing the election (with his standard siege mentality) he notes, "It was hardly a triumph! I was elected on the first vote, with a majority of exactly one" (83).

6. This sentence, which in the original reads "Je hais les voyages et les explorateurs" (1955: 13), has been treated differently by English translators. John Russell ren-

ders it "Travel and travellers [British spelling] are the two things I loathe" (Lévi-Strauss 1964: 17), whereas the John and Doreen Weightman version reads "I hate travelling and explorers" (Lévi-Strauss 1973: 3). I believe the latter is more precise in its opting for "explorers" over "travelers" and better serves the purposes of the present comparison with Roosevelt's expeditionary "explorations."

7. The complexity of Roosevelt's career and the surfeit of published information about him make it difficult to sum him up. The following description will concentrate mainly upon those features in his background and personality relevant to understanding the South American explorer.

8. His first publication, a co-authored catalogue self-published when he was nineteen, was *The Summer Birds of the Adirondacks in Franklin County N.Y.* (Roosevelt and Minot 1877). A mutual interest in natural history is one point of convergence between Roosevelt and Lévi-Strauss. The latter noted that in writing *Totemism*, *The Savage Mind*, and his series of books on mythology, "... I lived surrounded by books on botany and zoology. Moreover, my curiosity about such matters dates back to my childhood" (Lévi-Strauss and Eribon 111–12).

9. Beginning in his Harvard days, Roosevelt was a serious student of scientific racism (Dyer 1–20). Even while in the White House he remained fully conversant with the literature, giving it a critical reading. Despite his background and (mild) Germanophilia, TR rejected Aryanism and the notion of Anglo-Saxon and Teutonic racial superiority (26–27). As a neo-Lamarckian, Roosevelt wrote that human progress was "due mainly to the transmission of acquired characters, a process which in every civilized state operates so strongly as to counterbalance the operation of that baleful law of natural selection which tells against the survival of some of the most desirable classes" (39).

10. The nation's plutocrats were delighted to see their popular nemesis leave office and the country. J.P. Morgan reputedly hailed the departure by raising his glass and saying, "America expects that every lion will do his duty" (Brands 646).

11. Of course, Lévi-Strauss is not unique in this regard since there is longstanding anthropological ambivalence towards the explorer as well as the missionary ("we are not missionaries, colonial officers, or travel writers"—Clifford 1997: 64). Yet anthropologists, missionaries, and explorers are all seekers of the primitive at the edges of "civilization"—each for his own purposes. However, while the anthropologist is at pains to distinguish himself from the voyeuristic adventurer and zealous proselytizer, given the paucity of any sources regarding primitive peoples, the anthropological monograph often incorporates the accounts of explorers and missionaries into its text. Nor are the roles mutually exclusive. There have been many anthropologist/missionaries, and one suspects that there is a bit of the explorer in most anthropologists. (As an adolescent my favorite author was Richard Halliburton.) Elsewhere, Lévi-Strauss admits to as much when discussing his vocation: "I was envisaging a way of reconciling my professional education with my taste for adventure. For as a child and adolescent how many expeditions had I launched in the French countryside and even the Paris suburbs!" (Lévi-Strauss and Eribon 16).

12. In an early chapter the reader is taken on a "magic carpet" ride to India where Lévi-Strauss experienced a similar tropical malaise.

13. Ultimately he is forced to admit that most of the tribes had been "shattered by the development of European civilization, that phenomenon which, for a widespread and innocent section of humanity, has amounted to a monstrous and incomprehensible cataclysm" (*Tristes Tropiques* 367).

14. Asked whether he would have liked to have penned a literary work, Lévi-Strauss notes that he attempted (and quickly abandoned) writing a play that was to be called *Tristes Tropiques*. He characterized it as "vaguely Conradian" and stated, "I would have liked to have written his books" (Lévi-Strauss and Eribon 1988: 91). In a late listing of his favorite novels he mentions Conrad first (166).

15. Elsewhere, however, Lévi-Strauss states that he had no particular interest in Brazil or America and that his involvement there was more a matter of circumstance and convenience (Lévi-Strauss and Eribon 56).

16. In their seminal work Clifford and Marcus note that, by the sixties, anthropologists were beginning to question the discipline's "expository conventions." They cite three texts as constituting "earlier disturbances": Michel Leiris' "aberrant" *L'Afrique fantôme* (1934), *Tristes Tropiques*, and Laura Bohannan's *Return to Laughter* (Bowen, 1954) (1986: 13). The linkage between Leiris and Lévi-Strauss is far from casual. Lévi-Strauss reports meeting Leiris for the first time in the early 1950s, after assuming his post at the Musée de l'Homme. He remarks, "I didn't know his work and read it with delight" (Lévi-Strauss and Eribon 53). They became close friends. *L'Afrique fantôme* is, in many respects, a precursor of *Tristes Tropiques*. See Chapter 6, "Tell about Your Trip: Michel Leiris" in Clifford 1988.

17. At times this preoccupation assumes ironic form: "[W]hen I arrived in Brazil to take part in the founding of the university, I regarded the lowly status of my Brazilian colleagues with a mixture of pity and condescension. Watching these poorly-paid professors, who were obliged to undertake odd jobs on the side in order to make a living, I felt proud to belong to a country of long-established culture, where a member of the professional classes could feel secure and respected. Little did I imagine that, twenty years later, my hard-working pupils would occupy university chairs, in some fields more numerous and better equipped than their French equivalents, and provided with libraries such as we would be delighted to possess" (*Tristes Tropiques* 101).

18. Of Rio de Janeiro, Roosevelt had noted earlier, "The intellectual stimulus comes chiefly from France; more French than Portuguese books are read" (*The Outlook*, December 20, 1913: 839).

19. In point of fact, TR would generate discrete texts of his South American travels. The first, which details his tourist and diplomatic mission to several South American countries, was published in installments in *The Outlook* (for which he was a contributing editor). They were posted to the publisher from South America and printed within a few weeks of having been written. When his articles in *The Outlook* were issued together as *Through the Brazilian Wilderness*, Roosevelt added a wonderful appendix which breaks travelers down into three types. First, there is

the superficial "steamer" tourist who travels from one great seaport to another with the occasional shoreside excursion. Less superficial is the traveler who visits the long-settled interior districts of a particular country and thereby experiences its infrastructure and inhabitants first hand. This type of venture does not, in itself, have "scientific" merit. However, such journeys may be framed in such terms (Roosevelt 1919: 355). Finally, there is "the work of the true wilderness explorers who add to our sum of geographical knowledge" (357). Roosevelt was not simply laying claim to the true-explorer's mantle. Rather, he was categorizing his entire South American tour, since, during its course, he had been cast in all three roles of "tourist," "serious traveler," and "wilderness explorer." The point may only be appreciated fully if his *Scribner's* articles are taken into account along with *The Outlook* ones.

20. Recently, Lévi-Strauss published *Saudades do Brasil*, a photographic memoir (his belated lantern show?) that provides a frozen frame of his youthful adventures in Brazil. In his captioning of the many photographs of naked indigenous women, the anthropologist, too, renders aesthetic judgment. Regarding two adolescent girls, we are told, "The attractiveness of the Nambikwara, notwithstanding their wicked reputation, is largely explained by the presence in their midst of very young women who were graceful despite their sometimes rather thick waists" (142). Other young women are described as "dreamy when the mood struck them . . ." (143) and ". . . mocking, provocative. . ." (144).

21. *The Outlook* noted, "Those who came to Mr. Roosevelt's lecture with the idea that they were to hear a list of hairbreadth escapes and blood-curdling adventures were surely disappointed, for Mr. Roosevelt was much more concerned with the presentation of the scientific questions aroused by his explorations in South America than with any desire to present a striking and picturesque narrative" (284).

22. In England he had a lively debate when the "scientific merits" of his expedition were challenged (Brands 744).

23. In this regard, and whether or not one agrees with his conclusions, in terms of professional and personal experience, not to mention previous literary output, President Roosevelt's credentials for opining regarding this subject are far more impressive than those of Citizen Lévi-Strauss. There is also a beguiling quality to Roosevelt's optimism versus Lévi-Strauss' unrelenting pessimism. Contemplating his Brazilian expedition Roosevelt remarked, "I have to go. It's my last chance to be a boy!" (Nathan Miller 535); relieved to have put his Brazilian sojourn behind him, in the last paragraph of *Tristes Tropiques*, Lévi-Strauss comments, "Oh! Fond farewell to savages and explorations" (473).

24. It might be noted, however, that history was on Roosevelt's side in this regard. In the introduction to *Saudades*, Lévi-Strauss notes, ". . . the Nambikwara today lead a precarious existence close by the religious mission and government posts that watch over the Indians; or else camp by the side of a road traveled by heavy trucks; or again on the outskirts of the city of 60,000 inhabitants (that was ten years ago; the figure must be higher now) that is rising in the heart of their territory, where in my day the only signs of civilization left after an abortive at-

tempt at penetration were a dozen shanties made of mud-plastered wattle in which a few mixed-blood families languished dying of hunger and disease" (10).

25. Lévi-Strauss devotes a chapter entitled "The Apotheosis of Augustus" to his retreat from daily reality while with the Nambikwara. During such withdrawal he pens a drama set in the classical world. Roosevelt, while supposedly stripping down to the bare essentials for the descent of the River of Doubt, takes along the last two volumes of Gibbon, the plays of Sophocles, More's *Utopia*, Marcus Aurelius, and Epictetus (247).

26. Hayden White's (1978) seminal essay on the occidental perceptions of wildness could have been written with *Tristes Tropiques* and *Through the Brazilian Wilderness* foremost in mind.

27. The scholarly trappings of *Tristes Tropiques* are sloppy even by continental European standards. The original Plon French edition contains a bibliography of 21 items, including Roosevelt's work. None is ever cited in the text itself, and the works in the bibliography are neither alphabetized nor arranged chronologically. In the 1962 Union Generale d'Éditions edition, the bibliography is excluded altogether. Russell's English translation retains the bibliography while Weightman's does not.

28. Geertz suggests that in eschewing the traveler's tale, Lévi-Strauss is rejecting its *haute vulgarisation* during the Third Republic, as reflected in certain works by Gide, Loti, and Malraux (1988: 35). In my view the Roosevelt text was far more pertinent.

29. In *Conversations with Claude Lévi-Strauss*, he remarks, "Finally, why not admit it? I realized early on that I was a library man, not a fieldworker. I don't mean this disparagingly, quite the contrary, but fieldwork is a kind of 'women's work' (which is probably why women are so successful at it). Myself, I had neither the interest nor the patience for it" (Lévi-Strauss and Eribon 44).

30. In the sense that he evokes his visit to this institute prior to embarking on his speaking tour of other South American countries before joining Rondon for the "real" expeditions considerably later.

31. During his eventual descent of the River of Doubt, Roosevelt has his own encounters with a venomous serpent: "One of the men almost stepped on a poisonous coral-snake, which would have been a serious thing, as his feet were bare. But I had on stout shoes, and the fangs of these serpents—unlike those of the pit-vipers—are too short to penetrate good leather. I promptly put my foot on him, and he bit my shoe with harmless venom" (255). Lévi-Strauss was not immune to the temptation of invoking snakes as the metaphor for the danger of tropical exploration. In *Saudades* there is a graphic photograph of a dead disemboweled "7-meter female water boa" and her deceased progeny (87).

32. Nor was Lévi-Strauss always able to resist the adventurous trope. After citing a passage from *Tristes Tropics*, Geertz notes, " 'My Life Among the Headhunter,' or 'Two Years in Darkest Africa' could hardly be better, or worse, than this Richard Burton / T.E. Lawrence sort of tone" (1988: 35).

33. In their Brazilian ventures both were collectors of evidence for prestigious scientific institutions. His Brazilian missions and experiences prompted Lévi-Strauss, the anthropologist, to speculate on the commonalities and development of Amerindian cultures of both South and North America (279–89), whereas Roosevelt, the naturalist, pondered the Darwinian issues of the purpose of animal coloration (enigmatically in some species camouflaging while in others garishly revelatory) and the parallel evolution of large mammals in South America, North America, and Africa (37, 70–77).

34. Later changed to Rio Teodoro since "Roosevelt" was difficult to pronounce in Portuguese.

35. Lévi-Strauss sums up his Brazilian expedition by stating, "Perhaps, then, this is what travelling was, an exploration of the deserts of my mind rather than those surrounding me?" (430).

An All White Jury: Cindy Patton

1. This chapter was begun immediately after the criminal trial verdict. I have tried, through my revisions, to sustain my own "feeling" for the event and its coverage. I have, therefore, chosen to defer attention to the civil trial to others. There are substantive reasons for this decision. Mindful of Lyotard's care in separating "genres" of discourse, it seems important to me to recognize that a criminal trial and a civil trial, even concerning the same action, are, literally, different. The rules of evidence and the construction and use of juries, to mention only two technical areas of importance to the present argument, are different in the two types of trial. Thus, the interplay of race, gender, and citizenship are different. I will suggest here that the criminal trial became merged with ideas of civil rights trials, and with issues of representation (in the political sense) of racial minorities, hate crimes, and the history of violence against African Americans. The issues in the civil trial link up with somewhat different, no less raced, discourses and institutions in America. Regina Austin has very interestingly addressed issues of race in commercial law, work that would raise interesting questions about the ways in which a monetary penalty might inflect racism in different ways than criminal penalties (or even criminal penalties for economic crimes, the primary focus of her work). Second, in my unsystematic observation as a consumer of the media reportage of the civil verdict, I did not detect the rhetoric of "new possibilities" for discussion of race that was so prominent in the immediate post-criminal verdict coverage. It seems likely that the rhetorical frame of the civil trial responds to the frame of the criminal trial, including the continuing explicit or oblique references to the need for "dialogue about race."

2. The judicial review process is supposed to deal with miscarriages of justice, and this usually happens by freeing those improperly convicted or paying civil penalties to individuals whose rights have been violated. But as even a cursory review of the media coverage of such cases shows, the plaintiffs—though making their case as a member of a class—do not represent the class as a group: this is why mone-

tary damages awarded in civil rights cases always seem strange. Apparently, an individual or smaller fraction of a class get the compensation for wrongs committed against the group as a whole. To really come to grips with the racism in the judicial system, the law would need to take itself to task, an act that would have to also occur on behalf of the offended class. This would happen via an individual plaintiff who would then bear the weight of all the wrongs against her or his class: an impossible burden, even if the court had the will to undertake such a self-criticism.

3. The John Singleton film *Higher Learning* has one of the most palpable scenes of Black men trying to cope with white women's impulsive fear of them. A young white woman who reflexively grabs her purse when a young Black man—whom she knows from one of her classes—enters the elevator. He recognizes her move and looks weary—though he attempts to look "safe"—as she catches herself in her racist gesture.

4. The incompleteness of this switch in semiotic register is why I cannot abide liberals repeating racist, or sexist, or homophobic jokes in an effort to contest them. Whatever the surface lesson in recognizing these jokes as problematic, retelling under almost any circumstances gives teller and hearer an opportunity indirectly to consume nasty bits of hatred they cannot "enjoy" directly.

5. In real life, we know that bruises and broken bones heal more quickly than criminals are arraigned, but the use of fictional photos to represent fictional battering destabilizes the referent events by distancing what happened from the possibilities of redress. A CNN special report, aired at the time of the trial, on training police to work with female victims of violence sealed the fate of photographic representation and battering. In emphasizing the value of photographic documents of victims' conditions, the report undermined the very evidence they were trying to explain. In the training, policewomen make themselves up to look like "realistic" battered women: this inadvertently raised a possibility that O.J. would mobilize after the trial was over: that Nicole was in costume.

6. Readers who are interested in issues of sampling may be interested to learn that on June 20, 1996, a simple hit, "O.J. Simpson," in the Wilson database, netted 977 entries. Of these, I initially examined roughly 95, culling from these about 25 which most closely related to the issues I have outlined here. I excluded Los Angeles newspapers because I was interested in media that imagined their audience not to be local to the trial. I also excluded the many trial round-up articles and those covering the multitude of issues concerning the technical and scientific problems with evidence. I also excluded law media and periodicals that do not have a general, national circulation. I included two major neo-conservative periodicals: *American Spectator* and *National Review*, in part because of their national audience and in part because I am most familiar with their past coverage of the kinds of political issues raised in this case. Wilson does not index many Black periodicals, but does include *Jet*, *Essence*, and *Ebony*, as well as *Black Scholar*, which I reviewed in order to better understand the differences from the "mainstream" media. Because this essay is in the mode of critical analysis and theoretical elabo-

ration, I have chosen to cite only a few examples epigraphically. Thus, my immersion in the texts is evident mainly in my "reading" rather than in a more conventional display of particular content.

7. I signal the problem with the term "domestic violence" because it simultaneously feminizes violence and erases women from its purview. One of the problems in the legal arguments in this case, I will suggest, had to do with the question of whether and how to differentiate between similar acts of criminal violence by men against known versus unknown women. The term "violence against women" is no less problematic, in part because of its ideological roots in a feminist analysis that has had difficulty agreeing to a figure for race. But more significantly: the construct of women as a victim class abstracts from Nicole Brown Simpson in a way that did not make it easier to hold an individual perpetrator responsible for an individual crime, either the murder alleged in the trial, or the beatings which seemed to be less in dispute. Indeed, while the issue of violence against women and domestic violence was present in the trial coverage, the issue of how to treat wife killing was still insecure.

8. Here I wish to elaborate on Benedict Anderson's concept of "imagined community," as a partial replacement for the Habermasian concept of "public sphere." First, in my view, Anderson is more satisfying in his historical documentation of how print capitalism and a wide variety of colonial regimes together engender a general concept of "nationness" or imagined community, which nevertheless have among them important differences. If nothing else, this opens up space for considering the ways in which a "national public" in Europe, or in Germany, differs from that in the U.S. We should not dilute Anderson's powerful concept with creeping pluralism. For Anderson, it is the capacity to imagine oneself as a people, as a nation, with people you've never met. This is an affective relationship—"political love"—that may find a variety of particular modes for organizing disparate languages and institutional organization of literacy and citizenship. (Anderson takes the cultural and policing weight of linguistic differences very seriously, especially as means to distribute government jobs in increasingly geographically dispersed colonial states.) This emphasis on political love, on the affective relation to nation, opens up an interesting way of examining the organization of belonging in the U.S. For example, at least from W. E. B. Du Bois, we see a codification of a "duality" of affect, which throughout the nineteenth and twentieth centuries reflects not only a real condition of Black habitation but, by the 1950s, is incorporated as a paradigm of citizenship which reconciles American's dematerialization of geographical origin (retained as the prefatory element to American) and materialization of national affiliation in the present. This suturing of two differently manifest structures of affective relation is inherently rough, but perhaps infinitely recoupable, allowing a wide swath in how an imagined "Black community" can be contained within the "other country" of (demographically, and partially culturally, white) America. The historical insight of Anderson's general framework could be more intensively mined here—late capitalist U.S. with its "democratization" of the media has, in some regards, internally repeated what occurred when

the European states competed in the colonization process. I have elsewhere described this as the "geo-phagia" of nation—the tendency within the idea of imagined communities to take up all possible space, as opposed to the early-modern spatialization of kingdoms with various forms of non-space or contended space in between. Now the entire world is mapped—only the specific locations of the lines of demarcation can change. A few places—the landless Palestinian nation, the unrecognized nation of Taiwan, and Tibet, whose religious diaspora is described by some as intentional, even while the "religious" leader, the Dalai Lama, is interpreted by China as a threat to sovereignty and to the cultural contiguity of Chineseness—sit as complications to the general map which persists as a European vision of the world. Even China is drawn in relation to what was or was not occupied during Europe's colonial heyday.

9. I may use this term with uncomfortable certainty for some readers. How can I possibly redraw the lines of white and Black so easily? Even opinion polls distinguished a plurality of positions, based on race and gender, and to some extent region. What I mean by my easy use of these terms is that despite what individual, complexly situated people believed or said to pollsters, the mainstream media nevertheless kept "slipping" into the correlation of opinion/knowledge and the broad categories of Black and white. I am not suggesting that the media hailed viewers by these specific subjectivities. Far from it. Instead, I am proposing, we were enticed into procedures of citizenship which were already racially divided by an explicit history, but were also structured by a differential system of victim iconographies. There was no performativity here: whites enacted a racial position that is, in the case of dispensing judgment, completely secure. On the other hand, the insecure connection between Black men and white women was very clearly "performatively" iterated through the rules for representing a "victim's" body. This disjuncture between a secured difference and an insecure one cannot, in my view, be adequately handled within either the Habermasian or the Althusserian frameworks, although each may be interestingly addressed by one alone. It is this dislinkage between two systems of oppressive demarcation that I am trying to address here in a concrete and historicized place.

10. Toni Morrison offered this term in her volume on the Hill-Thomas hearings.

11. Hate crime statutes were attached to civil rights laws and to the sentencing phase in criminal cases. Thus, systematic hatred writ small could be invoked for enhanced sentencing: "hate" provides a particularly despicable motive for crimes which could be committed for more casual or pragmatic reasons.

12. Since the 1960s, scholars and media pundits have debated whether violent acts of protest and outrageous speech are a form of communication or a symptom of a breakdown in communication. Either circumscription of Black speech practice still admits Black rage as an audible collective—and public—reaction. Just compare the idea of Black rage to the idea of women's rage: even with the burst of coverage about wife abuse, a collective reaction by women is only representable as maternal or sororal concern. Women's magazine coverage of the trial was dominated by discussion of Denise Brown's campaign (ventriloquizing Nicole's now

silenced "I told you so!") to keep Nicole's memory and plight alive and through discussion of what would happen to the Simpson-Brown children. The latter, along with the several photos of the Brown and Simpson women comforting each other during the trial, suggested that within the extended bi-racial family, concern for children could overcome racism. Women as a vengeful class was unthinkable.

13. I have been a reporter, and have spent many years writing about news reportage. Thus, I want to make clear once again that while I am critical of the coverage, I understand reportage as a collaborative project between the many professionals who gather and produce news. All these people are constrained by both professional norms and ideals and by the fact that they inherit and reestablish ways of seeing the world. Readers may be interested to read Pierre Bourdieu's analysis of the problem of journalism, with its ties to commercial and to educational "fields" that influence—sometimes in the extreme—what it is possible to say in the media. Bourdieu cautions intellectuals to understand the structuring processes of news production; critical voices cannot easily circumvent the systems—especially of "fast thinking"—that are required of the television guest or news interviewee. I have been influenced by Bourdieu's reading of journalism here: this is why the images and commentary, however anti-racist they sometimes sounded, and perhaps were, fell prey nevertheless to sinister uses.

14. Although it is now several years since the Simpson trial, it seems important to note, again, that racism can—and does—find many objects, not only Black Americans, but also, as we saw in the wake of 9/11, Arab Americans, not to mention the many people of color both in the U.S. and around the world who do not carry U.S. citizenship. The challenge of the new discourse of terrorism is to maintain vigilance against our suturing to judging audiences, and to recognize the nuance of the many forms of racism, without ever forgetting the two crimes against humanity committed first and foremost by Americans: against slaves and their descendants and against the First Nations who resided on the lands that now define "our" border. As I suggest in the last section of this paper, such vigilance means not assuming that biases are structured in the same way; rather, we must undertake ongoing analysis of the modes and reproduction of multiple systems and affects that result in wrongs. *And do something about them.*

Poetry, Witness, Feminism: Harriet Davidson

1. See my "I Say I Am There: Siting/Citing the Subject of Feminism and Poststructuralism."

2. The place of performance in the women's movement is also crucial and has been brilliantly analyzed by Elin Diamond in *Unmaking Mimesis: Essays on Feminism and Theater.* I will return to this work later. Several books have recently grappled with the social role of poetry. Cary Nelson's *Repression and Recovery: Modern American Poetry and the Politics of Cultural Memory 1910–1945* opens up a whole

new literary history for American poetry, as well as clarifying theoretical problems around political poetry. Nelson's current project is to continue to find material evidence of poetry in social movements—such as a card he found with a
union poem on it, small enough to be passed around the factory palm to palm
without being seen. Maria Damon's *The Dark End of the Street: Margins in American Vanguard Poetry* also contains great insight into the social use of poetry, particularly in the third chapter, where she discusses poetry written by a group of
high school students.

3. See Elaine Scarry's *The Body in Pain: The Making and Unmaking of the World* on
the inverse relations between structures of rational authority and the body. This
extraordinary book has been extremely influential on my thinking about witness.

4. In the academic world of poetry, the shift toward the personal "confessional"
voice generally gets subsumed under a tradition of lyric subjectivity tied to Romanticism. Even with a greater and greater acceptance of this kind of poetry, it is
viewed by most poetry critics as strictly personal, cut off from either a social or
political text, resulting in a complete misreading of the power and impact of the
poetry. For other critics dealing with the social text of this poetry see Walter
Kalaidjian, *Languages of Liberation: The Social Text in Contemporary American Poetry* and Jacqueline Rose's extraordinary book, *The Haunting of Sylvia Plath.*

5. See Robin Morgan's introduction to *Sisterhood is Powerful: An Anthology of Writings from the Women's Liberation Movement* for a description of the consciousness-raising technique, step by step, beginning with personal testimony.

6. See Leonard Lawlor for a critique of the imagination by poststructuralism.

7. See Scarry on the inaccessibility of pain to the other.

8. See Beverley, especially chapters four and five.

9. See especially the first chapter. I am obviously greatly influenced by Felman,
though I would like to critique problems in her work on witness. She is not historical enough in thinking about the witness, though she wants some link to history. For her form tends to universalize itself. The main problem in her work can
be seen in her chapter devoted to Paul de Man, when she interprets his silence
about his wartime collaboration with the Nazis as a silent witness to his guilt. Her
attachment to silence as formally indicative of witness, apart from any contextual
impact, hurts her argument, and I want to pull witness into an arena where silence must always be in relation to speech.

10. See Scarry on the way pain is non-identical with the subject of pain.

11. If modernism is obsessed with the knowledge that it can't know, then the postmodern emphasizes that it doesn't know how much it knows.

12. One problem of witness is to say what is urgent—what seems worth witnessing
to? Feminist poetry is often seen as not important enough to warrant a witness;
but we do not want to get into what Paul Gilroy, comparing slavery with the
Holocaust, calls a "bidding process" that he is "revolted by" (upublished interview, October 26, 1994). Rather than the "revolting" argument of whether an oppressed woman can be equated with a Holocaust survivor or whether the violence

against women can hold its own in any litany of outrage, witness reminds us to remain tied to specific contexts of rhetoric and politics in which the issue and audience are created.

13. Diamond's groundbreaking work on temporality in performance in the last chapter of *Unmaking Mimesis: Essays on Feminism and Theater* opens up this difficult problem in nuanced and moving ways. My discussion is indebted to her work. I hope eventually to be able to elaborate my discussion about poetry as powerfully as she does in theater. The discussion that I have not yet tackled is the differences between performance on a stage and on the page.

14. This essay is in *Blood, Bread and Poetry: Selected Prose 1979–85*.

15. This is especially effective in her selected poems *The Fact of a Doorframe* where the last line of this poem is the last line of the whole book. In this volume the poem is printed with a period at the end. When the poem is reprinted in *Your Native Land Your Life,* the poem is near the beginning of the book and is printed with no period at the end.

Poetic Witness: Thomas A. Vogler

1. Weinberger claimed that "Yasusada is the pseudonym of an anonymous American poet who has brilliantly written all the work, complete with slightly awkward bits of translationese." Emily Nussbaum suggested that Yasusada was in fact Kent Johnson, a 41-year-old professor at Highland Community College in Illinois. Mikhail Epstein offered an alternative construction that rivals Nabokov at his most elaborate, maintaining that the work was originally composed in Russian by the famous writer Andrei Bitov and then translated by Kent Johnson and a Russian-speaking informant into English. Marjorie Perloff has written an extremely useful article that locates the Yasusada invention in the context of postwar Japanese poetry and theory. She points out that it's "absurd" to call the affair a hoax, because for centuries "writers have invented fictional personae and passed them off as the real thing" (1997: 32). The "complete" poems were published in 1997 by Roof Books under the title *Doubled Flowering: From the Notebooks of Araki Yasusada.* The case is similar to that of Rahila Khan, whose fictional accounts of generational conflicts in the Asian community in Britain earned her a publishing contract with Virago Press in 1989. When it was revealed that the reclusive Asian woman was in fact a man named Toby Forward (a "left-wing, feminist, anti-racist Anglican vicar"), Virago canceled the contract charging that Forward "pretended to occupy a space that isn't his." For details see Karl Miller, 148–49.

2. The shift can go the other way. Elie Wiesel did not like Jerzy Kosinski's *The Painted Bird* (published as fiction by Houghton Mifflin after much debate on its proper category) but changed his mind when Kosinski reassured him that it was fact, and he wrote an enthusiastic and favorable review for the *New York Times.* As Elizabeth Pochoda puts it, the difference is that between a sado-masochistic fairy tale and the "true story of a victimized child" (30).

3. Harrison's *A Cold Coming: Gulf War Poems* had been published the year before,

with a cover photograph by Kenneth Jarecke from *The Observer* (February 28) in which the charred head of an Iraqi soldier leans through the windscreen on his burned-out vehicle. He died when a convoy of Iraqi vehicles retreating from Kuwait City was attacked by Allied Forces in what they called a "turkey shoot." See Seymour Hersh, "Overwhelming Force," for the first sustained attempt to bring the details of this sorry episode to light.

4. "From what we have said it will be seen that the poet's function is to describe, not the thing that has happened, but a kind of thing that might happen, i.e., what is possible as being probable or necessary. . . . Hence poetry is something more philosophic and of graver import than history, since its statements are of the nature rather of universals, whereas those of history are singulars. By a universal statement I mean one as to what such or such a kind of man will probably or necessarily say or do—which is the aim of poetry, though it affixes proper names to the characters. . ." (*Poetics* 9). In his lecture *The Philosophy of Fine Art* (delivered in 1829, pub. 1835) Hegel continued and refined the view of poetry and prose as "two distinct spheres of consciousness" (1975: 26). Poetry (Hegel's name for whatever reaches beyond the mundane in any of the arts) can particularly do so in its medium of language, which should "relatively speaking at any rate, exclude the external world of natural fact" (20) so that it might most fully be "free of all subordination to the material of sense" (13), reaching towards universality by "negating its sensuous medium" (16) and working through the "ideal world of the imagination" (16). When it does touch on historical occasions, events, "poetry has nothing to do with the accidental or incidental fact as such," but strives "to clothe the ideal notion of its material in its genuine manifestation as truth, and to bring the world of external fact into reconciled accord with its own most ideal substance" (51). In the twentieth century, T. S. Eliot continued the traditional opposition: "Bad verse may have a transient vogue when the poet is reflecting a popular attitude of the moment; but real poetry survives not only a change of popular opinion but the complete extinction of interest in the issues with which the poet was passionately concerned" (4).

5. Even critics practicing poststructuralist theoretical modes tend to continue the isolation of lyric discourse. A typical example is the collection of essays in *Lyric Poetry: Beyond the New Criticism* in which, as Jonathan Arac notes in his afterword, "it emerges clearly that the new new criticism shares with the old New Criticism an emphasis that is textual and technical, more concerned with method than with scholarship, and fundamentally unhistorical, especially in its confidence about the extensive applicability of its operative terms" (346). Critics like Victor Li and Próspero Saíz, with something of a deconstructionist bent, combine a definition of lyric poetry as a late-Romantic quest for presence and assertion of the self, with a warning against writing ahistorically about it.

6. A typically conflicted performance by Bloom, in which "we hold the heights, the realm of the aesthetic," in a culture war battle of Thermopylae. "That 1996 anthology is one of the provocations for this introduction, since it seems to me a monumental representation of the enemies of the aesthetic who are in the act of

overwhelming us. It is of a badness not to be believed" (1998: 15, 16). But Bloom has to believe passionately in such badness, such depths, in order to identify a vertical hierarchy of merit in which his aestheticism is a mirror image of that which he condemns. Even while the "enemies of the aesthetic" are overwhelming "us," they are "a rabblement of lemmings leaping off the cliffs into the waters of oblivion" (1998: 16). In her Introduction to the 1996 selection of "the best" American poetry of 1995, Rich had specifically stated that her selections were not all "the best" by the prevailing "universal" standards. She made a point of selecting a range of poems that included unfamiliar names from small presses, poems by prisoners, poems in Spanglish, as well as mainstream poems by poets like Kunitz, Merrill, Merwin, Kleinzahler. But for Bloom, only part of a volume that represents only a tenth of David Lehman's "The Best of" series is too much contamination of "our elitist art" (1998: 19). Is the rabblement of lemmings leaping, or being pushed? For an example of how political diatribes against the political like Bloom's can be, see William J. Bennett's "Why We Fight: Moral Clarity and the War on Terrorism." Bennett evokes a universal standard of "good" and "evil" and proceeds with the same rhetoric employed by Bloom, including the persistent use of "we" and other first-person pronouns.

7.   *The Real Thing: Testimonial Discourse and Latin America*, ed. Georg M. Gugelberger.

8.   Forché's first attempt to define "a poetry of witness" was in "El Salvador: An Aide Memoire" (1981).

9.   Judith Butler caricatures the lack of precision typical of such discussions: ". . . discourse is all there is, as if discourse were some kind of monistic stuff out of which all things are composed; the subject is dead, I can never say 'I' again; there is no reality, only representations. These characterizations are variously imputed to postmodernism or poststructuralism, which are conflated with each other and sometimes conflated with deconstruction, and sometimes understood as an indiscriminate assemblage of French feminism, deconstruction, Lacanian psychoanalysis, Foucauldian analysis, Rorty's conversationalism and cultural studies" (214).

10.   A few years after the war the literary editor of a Hiroshima newspaper invited its readers to submit tanka related to their experience of the bombing. Of the more than 6,500 tanka submitted, Seishi Toyota selected 1,000 for the anthology *Kashù Hiroshima*. Nakano's volume contains 103 of those tanka. The authors range from the well-known and respected to the amateur *hibakusha*, but there is no biographical information provided in the book. Bradley's collection is 352 pages of extremely varied kinds and quality of writing, including Native Americans and Japanese Americans as well as poets from Japan, Germany, Norway, and Russia in translation. Tony Harrison's volume is an attempt to represent his 1995 film/poem broadcast on BBC on the fiftieth anniversary of the bombing. Schull spent two and a half years fighting the Japanese in the Pacific during World War II, and became a member of the Atomic Bomb Casualty Commission immediately after. In this book he tells the story of how the ABCC proceeded and the re-

sults of its findings. First, an historical account of the 1945 bombings and the earliest attempts to cope with the disaster. Then a discussion of the full range of Commission findings, including the late effects of radiation exposure (chiefly cancer and leukemia), the developmental abnormalities of infants exposed in utero (chiefly microcephaly and mental retardation). The text is supported by photographs, graphs, and tables providing information in great detail. Hogan's book is a collection of essays that survey the topic from the decision to drop the bomb to the 1995 controversy over the Enola Gay exhibition. Another impressive survey is the work of the Committee for the Compilation of Materials on Damages Caused by the Atomic Bombs in Hiroshima and Nagasaki, available in translation.

11. For critiques of Celan, see Felstiner, 225–26. Adorno's famous statement, "After Auschwitz, to write a poem is barbaric" (*"Nach Auschwitz, ein Gedicht zu schreiben, ist barbarisch."*) is often taken to refer to Celan's "Todesfuge," but Adorno probably did not know the poem at that time. The comment was in *"Kulturkritik und Gesellschaft,"* originally written in 1949 in the United States, first published in 1951, then collected in *Prismen* and published in Berlin, 1955. It was republished in 1965 ("Engagement," in *Noten zur Literatur* III, 125–27) and in *Gesellschaftstheorie und Kulturkritik* in 1975.

12. See the "Introduction" (this volume, 13–14) for examples of changing styles in fashion photography and contemporary art.

13. The editors (Lew Daly, Alan Gilbert, Kristin Prevallet, Pam Rehm) published six issues in 1994–1997. My quotations are taken *passim* from the various introductions to them. The conceit of a "radical transparency of language" is the editors' favorite and most often repeated phrase, suggesting a naïve epistemology in which an unambiguous intention can shine through the text without interference. This reverses the pathology of what Kristeva calls the "True-Real" (*Le Vréel*), a mode of hysterical discourse where the speaking subject in search of the "true-real" no longer distinguishes between the sign and its referent, taking the signifier for the real in a way that leaves no room for the signified. Since the signifier is the material part of the linguistic sign, to make it transparent seems a form of inverse hysteria; perhaps we should call it the Real-True (*Le RéeVer*)?

14. This is a small sample from a large and growing field, a selection I made on grounds of exemplarity and manageability. It includes an interdisciplinary scholar of comparative literature, a scholar of the literature of the Nazi genocide, and a poet. Unless noted otherwise, quotations from Felman are from *Testimony: Crises of Witnessing in Literature*; from Langer: *Art from the Ashes: A Holocaust Anthology*; from Forché: *Against Forgetting: Twentieth-Century Poetry of Witness*.

15. The Resnais/Duras film, *Hiroshima Mon Amour*, begins with this issue of witness, as the unnamed French actress, who has come to Hiroshima to play in a film on peace, tells her Japanese lover that she has seen everything in Hiroshima. She names the horrors and the exhibits, and we see what she saw; but the Japanese man insists: "You saw nothing. Nothing. . . . You know nothing" (*Hiroshima* 18, 29). The Synopsis in the published version spells it out: "Impossible to talk about

Hiroshima. All one can do is talk about the impossibility of talking about Hiroshima. . . . This beginning, this official parade of already well-known horrors
from Hiroshima, recalled in a hotel bed, this *sacrilegious* recollection is voluntary.
One can talk about Hiroshima anywhere, even in a hotel bed, during a chance, an
adulterous love affair" (9). Lyotard begins his meditation on the Nazi genocide in
a similar mode: "You are informed that human beings endowed with language
were placed in a situation such that none of them is now able to tell about it. Most
of them disappeared then, and the survivors rarely speak about it. When they do
speak about it, their testimony bears only upon a minute part of this situation.
How can you know that the situation itself existed?" (*Differend* 3).

16.   I use "Nazi genocide" instead of "the Holocaust" in part because of the frequent
      narrowing of the term to the Nazi attempt to exterminate the Jews. I am influ-
      enced in this by Henry Friedlander who, in his *The Origins of Nazi Genocide*,
      chooses the term to refer to the mass murder of human beings because of racial
      or biological status, including all victim groups.

17.   *The American Heritage Dictionary* notes that, "When referring to the massive de-
      struction of human beings by other human beings, *holocaust* has a secure place in
      the language. Fully 99 percent of the Usage Panel accepts the use of *holocaust* in
      the phrase *nuclear holocaust.* Sixty percent accepts the sentence *As many as two
      million people may have died in the holocaust that followed the Khmer Rouge
      takeover in Cambodia.* But because of its associations with genocide, extended ap-
      plications of *holocaust* may not always be received with equanimity. When the
      word is used to refer to death brought about by natural causes, the percentage of
      the Panel's acceptance drops sharply. Only 31 percent of the Panel accepts the sen-
      tence *In East Africa five years of drought have brought about a holocaust in which
      millions have died.* Just 11 percent approved the use of *holocaust* to summarize the
      effects of the AIDS epidemic. This suggests that other figurative usages such as *the
      huge losses in the Savings and Loan holocaust* may be viewed as overblown or in
      poor taste." The term "genocide" was coined in 1944 by the Polish jurist Raphael
      Lemkin (combining Greek *genos* for "race" or "tribe" and Latin-*cide* "killing"). Ac-
      cording to Lemkin, "Generally speaking, genocide does not necessarily mean the
      immediate destruction of a nation except when accomplished by mass killing of
      all the members of a nation. It is intended rather to signify a coordinated plan of
      different actions aimed at destruction of the essential foundations of the life of
      national groups, with the aim of annihilating the groups themselves. The objec-
      tive of such a plan would be disintegration of the political and social institutions,
      of culture, language, national feelings, religion, and the economic existence of na-
      tional groups, and the destruction of personal security, liberty, health, dignity,
      and the lives of individuals belonging to such groups. Genocide is the destruction
      of the national group as an entity, and the actions involved are directed against in-
      dividuals, not in their individual capacity but as members of the national group"
      (79). Article II of the U.N.'s 1948 Convention on Punishment and Prevention of
      the Crime of Genocide (UN GOAR Res. 260A (III) 9 December 1948: effective 21
      January 1951) specifies five categories of activity as genocidal when directed

against an identified "national, ethnical, racial, or religious group," and therefore criminal under international law. Article III specifies five acts punishable under the law: "a) Genocide; b) Conspiracy to commit genocide; c) Direct and public incitement to commit genocide; d) Attempt to commit genocide; e) Complicity in genocide." Article IV states that all persons shall be held accountable for acts committed under Article III "whether they are constitutionally responsible rulers, public officials, or private individuals." Most nations rapidly ratified the Genocide Convention, but the U.S. declined for forty years, finally doing so under "The Proxmire Act" (Genocide Convention Implementation Act of 1988, Title 18, Part I, U.S.C.) which narrowed significantly application to the United States. The applicability was further narrowed by a "Resolution of Ratification" adopted on February 19, 1986 ("The Lugar-Helms-Hatch Sovereignty Package") which in effect exempted the U.S. from any interpretation of the Genocide Convention except those it chose to make. The now notorious refusal of U.S. public officials to employ or sanction the term for the Rwandan masssacres can be interpreted as a conscious attempt to avoid category E of the Conventions. See Christopher Tayler's *Sacrifice as Terror: The Rwandan Genocide of 1994* for a vivid account of the slaughter of a million Tutsis, one-seventh of the total population.

18. In an equally strange manner the Hungarian editors print the phrase "without diacritics" *with* diacritics (*Ékezetek nélkül*), missing the point altogether. I am indebted to Rita Kerestezi for generous assistance with Radnóti's Hungarian.

19. A fairly recent development in the law bears some striking resemblances to the kind of witness literature I am concerned with here. See the Introduction for a brief description of the Victims' Rights Movement, 37–38.

20. I don't mean to suggest that there cannot be indexical signs in poetic texts. But even if there are such signs, we can't know their semiotic status without other evidence. A good example is Dan Pagis, who was born in Czernowitz, Bukovina, and grew up in a Jewish family speaking German and, probably, Rumanian. After three years in a Lager, he emigrated to Israel where he became a Hebrew poet and scholar. As Forché observes, "His Hebrew was the result of history, of displacement—it was the very mark of his exile" (43). But the Hebrew of another poet, for whom it is the mother tongue, would be an indexical sign of nativity; for a poet like Richard Sherwin, who chose to emigrate from the U.S. to Israel, of an affirmation of Jewishness, and so on.

21. John Dower makes a comparable list of what he calls "the familiar iconography" of the Hiroshima bombing: "The stunning flash (*pika*) of the bomb, followed by a colossal blast (*don*) that shattered buildings kilometers away. Nakedness or semi-nakedness, from the blast stripping clothing away. Eerie silence. People walking in lines with their hands outstretched and skin peeling off—like automatons, dream-walkers, scarecrows, a line of ants. Corpses 'frozen by death while in the full action of flight.' A dead man on a bicycle. A burned and blinded horse. Survivors in crowded ruined buildings, lying in vomit, urine, and feces" (viii).

22. None of the sequence of "mad papers," written in a "fit," has a signature, none is mailed, and all survive only in mutilated form ("torn in half" and "scratched

through"). Her "eloquent nonsense" (Lovelace's description) is presented in its "affectingly incoherent" (Richardson's note) form, telling us that it can tell us nothing: "O what dreadful things have I to tell you! But yet I cannot tell you. . . . I cannot tell what . . . so I can write nothing at all" (V, 327).

23. Kant had written that "we express ourselves incorrectly if we call any object of nature sublime, although we can quite correctly call many objects of nature beautiful. . . . All that we can say is that the object is fit for the presentation of a sublimity which can be found in the mind, for no sensible form can contain the sublime properly so-called" (83–84). A considerable portion of the force of his verbal discrimination is to be found in the sublime as a species of experience that explicitly does not ground itself in objects. For the sublime, insofar as it finds fit objects, involves those that are "great beyond all measure," objects, that is, that specifically elude the apprehension we think ourselves to have of the objects of our perceptions. The elusiveness of the sublime—the way it is specifically a counter to our cognition of natural objects—becomes even clearer when Kant remarks that "we must seek a ground external to ourselves for the beautiful of nature, but seek it for the sublime merely in ourselves and in our attitude of thought, which introduces sublimity into the representation of nature" (84).

24. The European tradition or genre of the sublime began when Longinus' *Peri Hupsous* was rediscovered in the seventeenth century. It grew to overwhelming popularity in the eighteenth century, largely as a reaction to a dissatisfaction with the "beautiful" as the height of aesthetic perception. The pendulum swing then is a lot like the one we seem to be going through in recent years. The sublime is not limited to "literary" rhetoricians, and seems almost a natural response to certain kinds of events. Sent over to investigate the recent famine in Ireland in the mid-nineteenth century, a Society of Friends correspondent wrote from Ireland that "We have no language to convey to you any adequate idea of the amount of misery to be found on every side" (*Transactions* 188). Another contemporary made the same point more effusively: "No language is adequate to give the true, the real picture; one look of the eye into the daily scenes there witnessed would overpower what any pen, however graphic, any tongue, however eloquent, could portray" (Nicholson 9).

25. Dominick LaCapra describes this aspect of Felman's text as a "routinization of hyperbole or excess, and uncontrolled transference and acting-out—often justified through a restricted theory of performativity or enactment" (1997: 246).

26. The Romantic poets developed their own versions, like Keats' stout Cortez, "Silent, upon a peak in Darien" at the first sight of the Pacific, or Wordsworth's fascination with tropes of inarticulation that figure a meaning beyond words. Cole and Swartz have an interesting discussion of the frequent situation in Wordsworth, "in which another's silence marks, by a kind of transfer, the poet's access to a sublime beyond language" (147) hinting at truths that cannot be spoken.

27. For recent coverage of the event see the two volumes edited by Ara Sarafian.

28. I am indebted to Lindqvist for directing me to Ratzel. He also points out the strik-

ing difference between Ratzel's *Politische Geographie* of 1897 and his *Anthropogeographie* of 1891, which denied that the dying out of inferior races is predestined, noting that Ratzel became a founding member of the Pan-Germanic League (a radical right-wing organization that advocated the creation of a German colonial empire) in 1891. Lindqvist discusses the Herero extermination as a deliberate imitation by the Germans of the art that Americans, British, and other Europeans had exercised throughout the nineteenth century—the art of hastening the extermination of a people of 'inferior culture' " (149–72). Rubenstein, in *Genocide and Civilization* (1987), develops a more elaborate argument to the same effect.

29. This "poetic witness" was written by Oberleutnant Graf Schweinitz, in *Die Kämpfe der deutschen Truppen in Südwestafrika. Auf Grund amtlichen Materials bearbeitet von der kriegsgeschichtlichen Abteilung I des grossen Generalstabes. Erster Band. Der Feldzug gegen die Hereros* (Berlin, 1906), quoted in Lindqvist 149. There is at least one example of literary witness of the Hereros in English. In Thomas Pynchon's novel *V*, chapter 9 is devoted to "Foppl's Siege Party," which takes place in 1922 and stages a recreation of the 1904–07 Herero uprising. In *Gravity's Rainbow* the uprising is recounted from the Herero point of view by Oberst Enzian. For a truly obscene silence on this atrocity, it is hard to match the flurry of recent travel literature extolling the virtues of luxurious vacations in Namibia, while bemoaning the endangered wild life and ignoring the extinction of the Herero. See Andrew Powell, "Mombo King."

30. Such a history could start with the demographic catastrophe that followed Columbus' arrival in America. In the next three hundred years a population of over seventy million was reduced to five percent of that number, as the population of Europe increased by 400–500 percent. When the Europeans arrived in Mexico in 1519 there were around 25 million people. Fifty years later there were 2.7 million; a hundred years later there were 1.5 million. Most died from disease, hunger, and slave labor conditions. In 1500 there were about five million indigenous American natives in the area now the United States; by 1900 only half a million remained. (See Lindqvist, Crosby, Borah, Thornton, Churchill, Stannard, Rosenbaum, Denevan, Kuper, Dobyns, Todorov, Mooney.) And it would have to include three centuries of African atrocities and the slave trade: "No human disaster, with the exception of the Flood (if that biblical legend is true) can equal in dimension of destructiveness the cataclysm that shook Africa. We are all familiar with the slave trade and the traumatic effect of this on the transplanted black but few of us realize what horrors were wrought on Africa itself. Vast populations were uprooted and displaced, whole generations disappeared, European diseases descended like the plague, decimating both cattle and people, cities and towns were abandoned, family networks disintegrated, kingdoms crumbled, the threads of cultural and historical continuity were so savagely torn asunder that henceforward one would have to think of two Africas: the one before and the one after the Holocaust" (Ivan Van Sertima, quoted in Ngugi 86). Robin Blackburn's recent study provides an exhaustive account of the slave trade, showing how it resulted in the largest forced migration in human history, and how in order to supply the

European traders, African slavers devastated whole areas, and effectively exterminated entire peoples, in the African hinterland. In *Kapital* Marx links both these
massive atrocities to the beginnings of the capitalist world system in the sixteenth
century, when Europeans began to seize the land and labor of peasants at home
and of natives in other lands. For Marx the discovery of gold and silver in America, the extirpation, enslavement, and entombment in mines of the aboriginal
population, the beginning of the conquest and the looting of the East Indies, the
turning of Africa into a warren for the commercial hunting of black-skins, signal-
ized the rosy dawn of the era of capitalist production. He ironically identifies
these "idyllic proceedings" as the chief moments of primitive capitalist accumulation.

The Burning Babe: Tyrus Miller

1. Klimov is also making a claim to witness and testimony with respect to the audi-
    ence of his film. His title refers to the words of the angel who greets Mary and
    Mary Magdalene at the empty tomb of Christ in *Matthew* 28: 6–7: "He is not here;
    for he is risen, as he said. Come, see the place where the Lord lay. And go quickly,
    and tell his disciples that he is risen from the dead." *Come and See* was intended to
    memorialize the heroic struggle on the fortieth anniversary of the Liberation
    from Nazism; it won the Grand Prize at the film festival that was connected with
    the anniversary. Yet as a statement by Sergei Gerasimov in a roundtable discussion
    at that event suggests, the problem of bearing witness and keeping alive the his-
    torical memory of the period was particularly urgent as it had fallen into increas-
    ing oblivion and as a new threat of neo-fascism in Russia began to emerge: "Let's
    be honest. Even our young people are far from dedicated to the tragic events of
    the military past. There are even those among them who, not wanting to think
    about the tragic pages of history, would rather watch films of the most inane
    kind" (quoted in Troncale 194).
2. The films I specifically treat here can be found in the filmography following the
    text. A more extensive list of films pertinent to this topic and helpful to me in for-
    mulating the argument of this essay would include: *Afraid of the Dark, Alice in the
    Cities, Au Revoir Les Enfants, The Bad Seed, Being Two Isn't Easy, Bicycle Thieves,
    The Blue Kite, Burnt By the Sun, The Children Are Watching Us, China My Sorrow,
    Down to the Cellar, Empire of the Sun, Fanny and Alexander, The 400 Blows, Free-
    dom is Paradise, Freeze Die Come to Life, Hate, Hope and Glory, The Innocents,
    Journey of Hope, Léolo, Lessons at the End of Spring, Lord of the Flies, MacArthur's
    Children, Ma Vie en Rose, The Member of the Wedding, Pixote, Radio Flyer, Rhap-
    sody in August, The Road to Life, Scarecrow, Shoeshine, The Sixth Sense, Small
    Change, The Thief, Time Bandits, To Kill a Mockingbird, Vigil, Village of the
    Damned, Walkabout, When Father Was Away on Business, Where Is the Friend's
    Home?, Whistle Down the Wind,* and *Zero for Conduct.*
3. This displacement of attention from the crucial event is typical of what Peter

Brunette has nicely termed "dedramatization" in Rossellini. See his *Roberto Rossellini*, 84.

4. See Rossellini's discussion of *Germany Year Zero* in "Ten Years of Cinema": "The Germans were human beings like all the rest. What was it that could have carried them to this disaster? A false philosophy, the essence of Nazism; the abandoning of humility for a cult of heroics; the exaltation of strength over weakness, vaingloriousness over simplicity? That is why I chose to tell the story of a child, an innocent, who through the distortion of a utopian education was brought to the point of committing a crime while believing he was accomplishing something heroic" (65).

5. I have been influenced in my formulation of this category by Vivian Sobchack's phenomenological concept of the "marked body" and more generally by her rich discussion of the "lived body," which she develops out of the philosophy of Maurice Merleau-Ponty. My use of the concept of the marked body differs somewhat from her discussion, although in what I believe is a fundamentally complementary way. She raises it primarily in the context of issues of social oppression and the way corporeal features such as sex-specific traits and skin color may be coded in reductive, pejorative ways. In contrast, my emphasis here falls on seeing corporeal signs as a site of hermeneutic conflict, with marked bodies being the basis of interpretative resistance and self-assertive counternarratives as well the material of discriminatory and reductive social codings. See Sobchack, *The Address of the Eye*, 143–63.

6. It is worth noting that Losey himself saw these allegorical senses as distinct, with his screenplay writer's pacifist slant winning out over his own directorial intention to present an anti-racist message: "Well, I quarrel very much with Dore Schary's concept of the basic subject. It was not an anti-war picture as a concept, as a device, it was anti-racist. The best scene in the film for me is the one in which the schoolteacher, after a certain amount of persecution of the boy by the children, asks how many of the children have black hair, how many have blond hair, how many have red hair—two hands—how many have green—one hand. This is the essence of the idea, this is what should have been done primarily, and it wasn't. The important thing to speak about then was peace. It's even more important now—hence, perhaps, the quite unrealistically good reviews in France where it is being seen for the first time" (Losey 72–73).

7. As Annette Insdorf points out in *Indelible Shadows: Film and the Holocaust*, 168.

8. Deleuze describes the different sorts of time-image in idiosyncratic terms. The main types include crystals of time, which involve "faceted" conjunctions of actual and virtual elements and an order of "rotation" from facet to facet; "sheets of past," as distinct zones or fields of time between which a narrative may shift; and "peaks of present" contracting temporal relations into singular, atomic events indiscernibly fusing the elements of perception, memory, and anticipation. Although Deleuze's metaphysical categories are fascinating and suggestive in their speculative reach, my use of his notion of time-image is more modestly pragmatic and descriptive, seeking only to reveal certain commonalities between particular instances of modernist film narration.

The Limits of Vision: Kyo Maclear

1. Alain Resnais, commenting on his self-reflexive film approach, once stated, "Just as with Brecht you knew you were at the theatre, so I want you never to forget in my work that you are at the cinema. What I show on the screen is filmed images which announce themselves as such" (quoted in Heath 105).

2. "You have seen nothing" has multiple possible meanings. It may refer to those rendered invisible by national narratives of history (for example, the Korean *hibakusha*). It may evoke experiences that cannot be encompassed by visual framings of knowledge. It may address epistemic and affective distinctions between insiders/outsiders and spectators/witnesses.

3. Earl Jackson, Jr. explores the film's visual economy with a view towards understanding its gender-inverted scopophilia. He further discusses the film's gendered East/West trope, focusing on how *Hiroshima Mon Amour* engages (without subverting) hierarchical binarisms of gender and racial difference. It would be productive to read Jackson's thoughtful textual critique of the film alongside this essay, with an eye to questioning how Orientalist assumptions founded on notions of immutable difference may serve to essentialize the speaking subjects, fixing insider/outsider denominations—thus precluding the possibility of ethical commemoration.

4. Both Robert Jay Lifton and Claude Lanzmann have remarked on the ethical responsibility that filmmakers have to attempt to ensure that the "dream-langue" of film does not erupt into a perpetual nightmare, producing an indiscriminate and sensationalist image of historical calamity and death that precludes any contemplated encounter with trauma (Lifton 1967: 458).

5. Art and cinema have been used both intentionally and unwittingly as catharsis from disturbing memories embedded in the psyches of post-trauma nations. For example, Francis Ford Coppola, in seeking assistance from the U.S. Department of Defense for *Apocalypse Now*, attempted to convince President Jimmy Carter that the film would be therapeutically valuable, helping to "put Vietnam behind us, which we must do so we can go to a positive future" (quoted in Suid 314).

6. The theme of trauma beyond imagination, trauma that resists location, is prevalent in nuclear literature and art. In some cases, Hiroshima functions as a transcendental signifier of loss. The annihilation of Hiroshima as place acts as a metaphor for the annihilation of (transhistoric) memory. In the Jungian work of Michael Perlman, for example, Hiroshima takes on archetypal significance. Perlman writes: "*Hiroshima is the place of no place*, revealing a deep lacuna, a placelessness, at the heart of postindustrial culture" (91).

Ex/propriating Survivor Experience: Karyn Ball

1. "I have analyzed thousands of documents. I have tirelessly pursued specialists and historians with my questions. I have tried in vain to find a single former deportee capable of proving to me that he had really seen, with his own eyes, a gas chamber" in "The Problem of the Gas Chambers or the Rumor of Auschwitz," (*Le*

Monde, December 29, 1978). The article is also included in Faurisson's *Mémoire en défense: contre ceux qui m'accusent de falsifier l'histoire* (73–75).

2. On Faurisson and the French negationists see Pierre Vidal-Naquet's *Les Assassins de la mémoire: Un Eichmann de papier et autres essais sur le révissionisme.*

3. Accordingly, "Rather than defining a grammatical or semantic unit, a *phrase* designates a particular constellation of instances, which is as contextual as it is textual—if it is not indeed precisely what renders the 'opposition' between text and context impertinent" (1988: 194). Unless otherwise noted, all quotations from Lyotard are from *The Differend* (1988) and are identified by page number.

4. Since phrasing entails an endless series, "For a phrase to be the last one, another one is needed to declare it, and it is then not the last one" (11).

5. It might seem arbitrary to focus on Kripke at the expense of other names not necessarily limited to the analytic camp, and notably those of Louis Hjelmslev, Roman Jakobson, and Charles Sanders Peirce among others; however, in order to prevent my discussion from exploding into a potentially infinite regression of names and influences, I have limited my discussion to those proper names which Lyotard regularly cites. Kripke's *Naming and Necessity* is the transcription of a series of three lectures delivered at Princeton in January, 1970. In that context, Kripke's principal argument is that "we have a direct intuition of the rigidity of names, exhibited in our understanding of the truth conditions of particular sentences" (14). In his preface, he lists three theses which ground the premise that names function as rigid designators: 1) "that identical objects are necessarily identical"; 2) "that true identity statements between rigid designators are necessary"; 3) "that identity statements between what we call 'names' in actual language are necessary" (4). Notably, this is a premise in which Kripke is not himself invested insofar as he is not logically committed to any thesis about names. I cite these theses because they offer a useful shorthand for the philosophical assumptions underpinning the "necessity" of stable designation as a condition of truth. Although Lyotard's position on reference tends to be more intimately bound up with Wittgenstein than Kripke, it may be helpful to keep this shorthand in mind while considering the complex ways in which Lyotard's analysis of designation in *The Differend* confronts and repudiates the necessity and ontological idealism of the concept of an invariable referent.

6. See Derrida, "The Ends of Man," in *Margins of Philosophy*, 109–36.

7. In Hegel's terms, the apparent continuity of the "I" that affects its determinacy and substance is merely an appearance that accrues from the consolidation of its various instances into what he calls a "mediated simplicity or universality." See the chapter on "Sense-Certainty: or the 'This' and 'Meaning' [*Meinen*]" in *The Phenomenology of Spirit*, 58–66.

8. Lyotard, *The Differend*, 22, *Plato Notice* (citing Plato *Letter* VII, 342 a–d).

9. Lyotard writes that the "addressor must be understood as a situated instance in a phrase universe, on a par with the referent, the addressee, and the sense. 'We' do not employ language" (55).

10. See Habermas' interventions in the 1986 West German Historians' Debate, in "A

Kind of Settlement of Damages (Apologetic Tendencies) Concerning the Public Use of History."

11. In Lyotard's words, "it seems neither possible, nor even prudent, to follow Habermas in orienting our treatment of the problem of legitimation in the direction of a search for universal consensus" (1984b: 65).

12. Derrida defended the veracity of Holocaust testimony in his lecture on "The History of the Lie" at the Staatsbibliothek West in Berlin, 1996.

13. In this respect, Derrida's views are consonant with Emmanuel Levinas' critique of the narcissistic subject of metaphysics. See *Totality and Infinity* and *Otherwise Than Being or Beyond Essence*. See also the selected writings collected in *The Levinas Reader*.

14. In Cordelia Edvardson's *Burned Child Seeks the Fire: A Memoir,* the narrator describes her recalcitrance in the face of a foster family whose happiness on Christmas Eve cannot relieve her from the recent traumatic experience of surviving Auschwitz.

15. This is to suggest that analysis aim to desublimate a subject's affective investment in the ontological substance of her trauma *proper* by exposing the provisionality of experience and memory as signs of identity.

16. Derrida insists that the metaphysics of presence is the name of violence and disavows the hermeneutics of identity as a foundation of meaning. Yet this disavowal leads to another disavowal and a violence staged as a vigilance. For disavowing the hegemony of meaning need not produce an expropriation of the experience of identity. This experience is also a sensibility that is not always geared toward the mastery of difference and a redemptive "identity-in-meaning" (or *Sinnstiftung*) as such.

17. In this connection, it is interesting to contemplate how Aristotle's criteria of unity and wholeness might poetically figure for an *a priori,* hence transcendental "need" for narrative as Paul Ricoeur has suggested. The question that this thesis raises is whether the ubiquity of narrative representations creates the desire for unified identity or whether the desire for unified identity creates a need for narrative. I agree with Ricoeur that they reciprocally reproduce each other insofar as narratives reflect and reproduce a desire for unity and wholeness in staging their possibility. See Ricoeur's *Time and Narrative.*

18. My perspective is indebted to Maurice Merleau-Ponty's and Emmanuel Levinas' respective reflections on sentience. Their work has led me to consider the corporeal dimensions of personal memory, a memory situated in a senescent body whose movements subject it to successive temporal, spatial, and social displacements. Sentience, so conceived, affects the historicity of memories as signs that stand in for transpired experiences.

Between History and Memory: James E. Young

1. An earlier version of this essay appeared as "Between History and Memory: The Uncanny Voices of Historian and Survivor," *History and Memory* 9:1/2 (Fall 1997). Although this essay focuses narrowly on the voices of the historian and

survivor in Holocaust historiography, much of this material is also drawn from James E. Young, "Toward a Received History of the Holocaust," *History and Theory* 36:4 (December 1997): 21–43.

2. For a much more elaborate discussion of the agency Holocaust diaries played in the unfolding of events, see James E. Young, *Writing and Rewriting the Holocaust: Narrative and the Consequences of Interpretation*, 1–39.

3. See James E. Young, *The Texture of Memory: Holocaust Memorials and Meaning*.

Works Cited

Aaron, Frieda W. 1990. *Bearing the Unbearable: Yiddish and Polish Poetry in the Ghettos and Concentration Camps*. Albany: State University of New York Press.

Aceituno, Luis. 2001. "Arturo Taracena Breaks His Silence: Interview by Luis Aceituno." *The Rigoberta Menchú Controversy*, ed. Arturo Arias. Minneapolis and London: University of Minnesota Press, 82–94.

Acocella, Joan. 2000. "The Third Way: Kazuo Ishiguro Mixes Method and Madness." *The New Yorker* (September 11), 95–96.

Adams, Marilyn McCord. 1999. *Horrendous Evils and the Goodness of God*. Ithaca, NY: Cornell University Press.

Adorno, Theodor W. 1967. "The Valery Proust Museum." *Prisms*, trans. Samuel and Shierry Weber. London: Spearman.

———. 1973. *Negative Dialectics*, trans. E.B. Ashton. New York: Continuum.

———. 1975. *Gesellschaftstheorie und Kulturkritik*. Frankfurt am Main: Suhrkamp Verlag.

———. 1977. "Commitment." *Aesthetics and Politics*. London: Verso.

———. 1983. "Cultural Criticism and Society." *Prisms*, trans. Samuel and Shierry Weber. Cambridge, MA: MIT Press.

———. 1985. "Commitment." *The Essential Frankfurt School Reader*, ed. Andrew Arato and Eike Gebhardt. New York: Continuum.

Agee, James and Walker Evans. 1960. *Let Us Now Praise Famous Men: Three Tenant Families*. Boston: Houghton Mifflin.

Alperovitz, Gar. 1965. *Atomic Diplomacy: Hiroshima and Potsdam*. New York: Simon and Schuster.

———. 1995. *The Decision to Use the Bomb and the Architecture of an American Myth*. New York: Alfred A. Knopf.

Alphen, Ernst van. 1997. *Caught by History: Holocaust Effects in Contemporary Art, Literature, and Theory*. Stanford, CA: Stanford University Press.

American Heritage Dictionary of the English Language. 1992. 3d. ed. New York: Houghton Mifflin. Electronic version 1994. INSO Corp.

Améry, Jean. 1966. *Jenseits von Schuld und Sühne.* Munich: Szczesny.

———. 1980. *At the Mind's Limits: Contemplations by a Survivor on Auschwitz and its Realities,* trans. Sidney Rosenfeld and Stella P. Rosenfeld. Bloomington: Indiana University Press.

Amichai, Yehuda. 1986. "Tourists." *Selected Poetry of Yehuda Amichai,* ed. and trans. Chana Bloch and Stephen Mitchell. New York: Harper and Row, 137–138.

Amnesty International. 1978, 1979. *Amnesty International Report.* London: Amnesty International Publications.

———. 1987. *Amnesty International: Guatemala: The Human Rights Record.* London: Amnesty International Publications.

Anderegg, Michael, ed. 1991. *Inventing Vietnam: The War in Film and Television.* Philadelphia: Temple University Press.

Anderson, Benedict. 1983. *Imagined Communities: Reflections on the Origin and Spread of Nationalism.* London: Verso.

Andreasen, Nancy C. 1985. "Post-traumatic Stress Disorder." *The Comprehensive Textbook of Psychiatry/iv,* 4th ed., ed. H. I. Kaplan and B. J. Sadock. Baltimore: Williams & Wilkins.

Antze, Paul and Michael Lambek, eds. 1996. *Tense Past: Cultural Essays in Trauma and Memory.* New York: Routledge.

Appadurai, Arjun. 1993. "Disjuncture and Difference in the Global Cultural Economy." *The Phantom Public Sphere,* ed. Bruce Robbins. Minneapolis: University of Minnesota Press.

Arac, Jonathan. 1985. "Afterword: Lyric Poetry and the Bounds of New Criticism." *Lyric Poetry: Beyond New Criticism,* ed. Chaviva Hošek and Patricia Parker. Ithaca and London: Cornell University Press, 345–356.

Arendt, Hannah. 1958a. *The Human Condition.* Chicago: University of Chicago Press.

———. 1958b. *The Origins of Totalitarianism,* rev. ed. Cleveland and New York: World Publishing Co.

———. 1963. *Eichmann in Jerusalem: A Report on the Banality of Evil.* New York: Viking.

———. 1968. *Men in Dark Times.* London and New York: Harcourt, Brace, & World.

Arias, Arturo. 2001a. "Rigoberta Menchú's History within the Guatemalan Context." *The Rigoberta Menchú Controversy,* ed. Arturo Arias. Minneapolis and London: University of Minnesota Press, 3–28.

———, ed. 2001b. *The Rigoberta Menchú Controversy.* Minneapolis and London: University of Minnesota Press.

Aristotle. 1941. *De Poetica,* ed. Richard McKeon. New York: Random House.

Arnold, Matthew. 1961. "The Function of Criticism at the Present Time." *The Poetry and Criticism of Matthew Arnold,* ed. A. Dwight Culler. Boston: Houghton Mifflin, 237–258.

Arshi, Sunpreet, Carmen Kirstein, Riaz Naqvi and Falk Pankow. 1994. "Why Travel? Tropics, En-tropics and Apo-tropaics." *Travellers' Tales: Narratives of Home and*

Displacement, ed. George Robertson, Melinda Mash, Lisa Tickner, Jon Bird, Barry Curtis and Tim Putnam. London and New York: Routledge.

Ashbery, John. 1992. *Flow Chart*. New York: Alfred A. Knopf.

Aznaréz, Jesús. 2001. "Rigoberta Menchú: Those Who Attack Me Humiliate the Victims" (Interview). *The Rigoberta Menchú Controversy*, ed. Arturo Arias. Minneapolis and London: University of Minnesota Press, 109–117.

Bakhtin, M. M. 1993. *Toward a Philosophy of the Act*, trans. Vadim Liapunov. Austen: University of Texas Press.

Barnet, Miguel. 1973. *Esteban Montejo: The Autobiography of a Runaway Slave*. New York: Random House.

Barron, Anne. 1992. "Lyotard and the Problem of Justice." *Judging Lyotard*, ed. Andrew Benjamin. New York: Routledge.

Barthes, Roland. 1972. "Jeunes Chercheurs." *Communications* 19.

———. 1975. *The Pleasure of the Text*, trans. Richard Miller. New York: Hill and Wang.

———. 1981. *Camera Lucida: Reflections on Photography*, trans. Richard Howard. New York: Hill and Wang.

Bartov, Omer. 1996. *Murder in Our Midst: The Holocaust, Industrial Killing, and Representation*. New York: Oxford University Press.

———. 1998. "Our Hell on Earth." *Times Literary Supplement* (September 18).

Bass, Ellen and Laura Davis. 1988. *The Courage to Heal: A Guide for Women Survivors of Child Sexual Abuse*. New York: Perennial Library.

Bateson, Gregory and Mary Catherine Bateson. 1987. *Angels Fear: An Investigation into the Nature and Meaning of the Sacred*. London: Rider.

Baudrillard. Jean. 1981. *Simulacres et simulation*. Paris: Galilée.

———. 1983. *Simulations*, trans. Paul Foss, Paul Patton, and Philip Beitchman. New York: Semiotext(e), Inc.

———. 1990. *La transparence du mal: essai sur les phénomènes extrêmes*. Paris: Gallimard.

Bauman, Zygmunt. 2000. *Liquid Modernity*. Cambridge, U.K.: Polity Press; Malden, MA: Blackwell.

Beardsworth, Richard. 1992. "Lyotard's Agitated Judgment." *Judging Lyotard*, ed. Andrew Benjamin. London: Routledge.

Becker, Jasper. 1996. *Hungry Ghosts: China's Secret Famine*. London: Murray.

Ben Gurion, David. 1971. *Israel: A Personal History*, trans. Nechemia Meyers and Uzy Nystar. New York: Funk & Wagnalls.

Benda, Julien. 1928. *The Betrayal of the Intellectuals*. New York: William Morrow & Co.

Benjamin, Walter. 1969. *Illuminations*, ed. Hannah Arendt. Trans. Harry Zohn. New York: Schocken Books.

———. 1979. *Reflections*, trans. Edmund Jephcott. New York and London: Harcourt Brace Jovanovich.

Bennett, William J. 2002. *Why We Fight: Moral Clarity and the War on Terrorism*. New York: Doubleday.

Berenbaum, Michael. 1990. *A Mosaic of Victims: Non-Jews Persecuted and Murdered by the Nazis*. New York: New York University Press.

————. 1993. *The World Must Know: The History of the Holocaust as Told in the United States Holocaust Memorial Museum*. Boston: Little, Brown.

Berger, Alan L. 1997. *Children of Job: American Second-Generation Witnesses to the Holocaust*. Albany: State University of New York Press.

Berger, John. 1993. *The Sense of Sight*. New York: Vintage International.

Berlant, Lauren. 1999. "The Subject of True Feeling: Pain, Privacy, and Politics." *Cultural Pluralism, Identity Politics, and the Law*, ed. Austin Sarat and Thomas R. Kearns. Ann Arbor: University of Michigan Press.

Bernstein, Barton J. 1976. "Atomic Diplomacy and the Cold War." *The Atomic Bomb: The Critical Issues*, ed. Barton Bernstein. Boston: Little, Brown.

Bernstein, Barton J. and Allen J. Matusow, eds. 1966. *The Truman Administration: A Documentary History*. New York: Harper & Row.

Bernstein, Michael Andre. 1994. *Foregone Conclusions: Against Apocalyptic History*. Berkeley, Los Angeles, and London: University of California Press.

Beverley, John. 1993. *Against Literature*. Minneapolis: University of Minnesota Press.

————. 1996a. "The Margin at the Center: On *Testimonio*." *The Real Thing: Testimonial Discourse and Latin America*, ed. Georg M. Gugelberger. Durham, NC: Duke University Press, 23–41.

————. 1996b. "The Real Thing." *The Real Thing: Testimonial Discourse and Latin America, ed*. Georg M. Gugelberger. Durham, NC: Duke University Press, 266–286.

————. 2001. "What Happens When the Subaltern Speaks: Rigoberta Menchú, Multiculturalism, and the Presumption of Equal Worth." *The Rigoberta Menchú Controversy*, ed. Arturo Arias. Minneapolis and London: University of Minnesota Press, 219–236.

Bhabha, Homi K. 1994. "How Newness Enters the World: Postmodern Space, Postcolonial Times and the Trials of Cultural Translation." *The Location of Culture*. New York and London: Routledge.

Blackburn, Robin. 1997. *The Making of New World Slavery: From the Baroque to the Modern, 1492–1800*. London: Verso.

Blake, Dudley David, Anne Marie Albano, Terence Keane. 1992. "Twenty Years of Trauma: Psychological Abstracts 1970 through 1989." *Journal of Traumatic Stress* 5.

Blanchot, Maurice. 1986. *The Writing of the Disaster*, trans. Ann Smock. Lincoln and London: University of Nebraska Press.

Bloom, Harold. 1982. *Agon: Toward a Theory of Revisionism*. New York and London: Oxford University Press.

————. 1995. *The Western Canon: The Books and School of the Ages*. New York: Harcourt Brace.

————, ed. 1998. *The Best of the Best American Poetry: 1988–1997*. New York: Scribner Poetry.

Böhm-Duchen, Monica, ed. 1995. *After Auschwitz: Responses to the Holocaust in Contemporary Art*. London: Humphries.

Borah, Woodrow. 1951. *New Spain's Century of Depression*. Berkeley: University of California Press.

Borowski, Tadeusz. 1976. *This Way for the Gas, Ladies and Gentlemen*, trans. Barbara Vedder. New York: Penguin.

Bouchard, Larry D. 1989. *Tragic Method and Tragic Theology: Evil in Contemporary Drama and Religious Thought.* University Park: Pennsylvania State University Press.

———. 2000. "Postmodern Tragedy, Contingency, and Culpability. *The Hedgehog Review* 2:2 (Summer), 18–28.

Boulanger, Ghislaine. 1994. Review of Judith Herman's *Trauma and Recovery. Tikkun* (March–April).

Bourgois, Philippe. 1990. "Confronting Anthropological Ethics: Ethnographic Lessons from Central America." *Journal of Peace Research* 27:1.

Bowen, Elizabeth Smith. [Laura Bohannan]. 1954. *Return to Laughter.* New York: Harper and Row.

Boyarin, Jonathan. 1992. *Storm from Paradise: The Politics of Jewish Memory.* Minneapolis: University of Minnesota Press.

Bradley, John, ed. 1995. *Atomic Ghost: Poets Respond to the Nuclear Age.* Minneapolis: Coffee House Press.

Brands, H.W. 1997. *T.R.: The Last Romantic.* New York: Basic Books.

Braudel, Fernand. 1972, 1973. *The Mediterranean and the Mediterranean World.* 2 vols, trans. Siâ Reynolds. New York: Harper and Row.

———. 1977. *Écrits sur l'histoire.* Paris: Flammarion.

Braw, Monica. 1991. *The Atomic Bomb Suppressed: American Censorship in Occupied Japan.* London: M. E. Sharpe, Inc.

Brecht, Berthold. 1979. *Poems, 1913–1956*, ed. John Willet and Ralph Mannheim. New York: Methuen.

Brittin, Alice, and Kenya Dworkin. 1993. "Rigoberta Menchú: 'Hemos sido protagonistas de la historia,' " trans. Alice Brittin. *Nuevo Texto Crítico* 6.11, 207–222.

———. 1995. "Close Encounters of the Third World Kind: Rigoberta Menchú and Elisabeth Burgos's *Me llamo Rigoberta Menchú." Latin American Perspectives* 22.4.

Brooks, Peter. 1995. "Illicit Stories." *diacritics* 25:3 (Fall) 41–51.

Brooks, Peter and Paul Gewirtz, eds. 1996. *Law's Stories: Narrative and Rhetoric in the Law.* New Haven: Yale University Press.

Brown, Daniel P., Alan W. Scheflin and D. Corydon Hammond, eds. 1998. *Memory, Trauma Treatment, and the Law: An Essential Reference on Memory for Clinicians, Researchers, Attorneys and Judges.* New York: Norton.

Brown, Peter. 1998. *The Body and Society: Men, Women and Sexual Renunciation in Early Christianity.* New York: Columbia University Press.

Brunette, Peter. 1987. *Roberto Rossellini.* New York and Oxford: Oxford University Press.

Bryant, Charles S. and Abel Much. 1864. *A History of the Great Massacre, by the Sioux Indians in Minnesota.* Cincinnati, OH: Rickey and Carroll.

Buell, Lawrence E. 1999. "In Pursuit of Ethics." *PMLA* 114.1 (January), 7–19.

Burgos-Debray, Elisabeth. 1984. Introduction. *I, Rigoberta Menchú: An Indian Woman in Guatemala*, ed. Elisabeth Burgos-Debray. London: Verso.

Burleigh, Michael. 1998. *Ethics and Extermination: Reflections on Nazi Genocide.* Cambridge: Cambridge University Press.

Butler, Judith. 1993. *Bodies that Matter: On the Discursive Limits of "Sex."* New York: Routledge.

———. 1995. "Contingent Foundations: Feminism and the Question of 'Postmodernism.' " *Critical Encounters: Reference and Responsibility in Deconstructive Writing*, ed. Cathy Caruth and Deborah Esch. New Brunswick, NJ: Rutgers University Press, 213–232.

Callinicos, Alex. 1995. *Theories and Narratives: Reflections on the Philosophy of History.* Durham, NC: Duke University Press.

Canetti, Elias. 1978. *The Human Province.* New York: Seabury Press.

Capote, Truman. 1965. *In Cold Blood.* New York: Random House.

Cargas, Harry James, ed. 1994. *The Unnecessary Problem of Edith Stein.* Blue Ridge Summit, PA: University Press of America.

Caruth, Cathy. 1964. *Unclaimed Experience: Trauma, Narrative, and History.* Baltimore: Johns Hopkins University Press.

———, ed. 1995. *Trauma: Explorations in Memory.* Baltimore: Johns Hopkins University Press.

Caruth, Cathy and Deborah Esch, eds. 1995. *Critical Encounters: Reference and Responsibility in Deconstructive Writing.* New Brunswick, NJ: Rutgers University Press.

Celan, Paul and Nelly Sachs. 1993. *Paul Celan/Nelly Sachs: Briefwechsel*, hrsg. von Barbara Wiedemann. Frankfurt am Main: Suhrkamp.

Celli, Carlo. 2000. "Interview with Marcello Pezzetti." *Critical Inquiry* 27.1 (Autumn), 149–157.

Cervantes, Miguel de Saavedra. 1963. *The Adventures of Don Quixote*, trans. J. M. Cohen. Baltimore: Penguin Books.

Césaire, Aimé. 1972. *Discourse on Colonialism.* New York: Monthly Review Press.

Chalk, Frank and Kurt Jonassohn, eds. 1990. *The History and Sociology of Genocide.* New Haven: Yale University Press.

Charlton, James, ed. 1986. *The Writer's Quotation Book: A Literary Companion.* New York: Penguin.

Charny, Israel W. 1984. *Toward the Understanding and Prevention of Genocide.* Boulder, CO, and London: Westview Press.

Churchill, Ward. 1994. *Indians Are Us? Culture and Genocide in Native North America.* Monroe, ME: Common Courage Press.

Clark, Ian. 1985. *Nuclear Past, Nuclear Present: Hiroshima, Nagasaki, and Contemporary Strategy.* Boulder, CO: Westview Press.

Clauson, Christopher. 1982. *The Place of Poetry: Two Centuries of an Art in Crisis.* Lexington: University Press of Kentucky.

Clements, Charles. 1984. *Witness to War: An American Doctor in El Salvador.* Toronto and New York: Bantam Books.

Clifford, James. 1988. *The Predicament of Culture: Twentieth-Century Ethnography, Literature, and Art.* Cambridge, MA: Harvard University Press.

———. 1997. *Routes: Travel and Translation in the Late Twentieth Century.* Cambridge and London: Harvard University Press.

Clifford, James and George E. Marcus. 1986. *Writing Culture: The Poetics and Politics of Ethnography*. Berkeley, Los Angeles, London: University of California Press.

Cocker, Mark. 1998. *Rivers of Blood, Rivers of Gold: Europe's Conquest of Indigenous Peoples*. New York: Grove Press.

Codrington, Andrea. 1996. "Revolution in Cliché-land." *The Baffler* 8, 101.

Cohen, Arthur. 1988. *The Tremendum*. New York: Crossroad Publishing.

Cole, Lucinda and Richard G. Swartz. 1994. " 'Why Should I Wish for Words?': Literacy, Articulation, and the Borders of Literary Culture." *At The Limits of Romanticism: Essays in Cultural, Feminist, and Materialist Criticism*, ed. Mary A. Favret and Nicola J. Watson. Bloomington: Indiana University Press, 143–69.

Cole, Tim. 1999. *Selling the Holocaust: From Auschwitz to Schindler: How History is Bought, Packaged, and Sold*. New York: Routledge.

Comay, Rebecca. 1990. "Redeeming Revenge: Nietzsche, Benjamin, Heidegger, and the Politics of Memory." *Nietzsche as Postmodernist: Essays Pro and Contra*, ed. Clayton Koelb. Albany: State University of New York Press, 21–38.

Committee for the Compilation of Materials on Damages Caused by the Atomic Bombs in Hiroshima and Nagasaki, ed. Soichi Iijima, Seiji Imahori, Kanesaburo Gushima. 1981. *Hiroshima and Nagasaki: The Physical, Medical, and Social Effects of the Atomic Bombings*. New York: Basic Books; Tokyo: Iwanami Shoten.

Conquest, Robert. 1986. *The Harvest of Sorrow: Soviet Collectivization and the Terror-Famine*. New York: Oxford University Press.

Cornell, Drucilla. 1992. *The Philosophy of the Limit*. New York and London: Routledge.

———. 1995. "What Is Ethical Feminism?" *Feminist Contentions: A Philosophical Exchange*, ed. Seyla Benhabib, Judith Butler, Drucilla Cornell, and Nancy Fraser. New York and London: Routledge.

Cornell, Joseph. 1993. *Joseph Cornell's Theater of the Mind: Selected Diaries, Letters, and Files*, ed. Mary Ann Caws. New York and London: Thames and Hudson.

Crosby, Alfred W. 1972. *The Columbian Exchange: Biological and Cultural Consequences of 1492*. Westport, CT: Greenwood Press.

Damon, Maria. 1993. *The Dark End of the Street: Margins in American Vanguard Poetry*. Minneapolis: University of Minnesota Press.

Darwin, Charles. 1962. *The Origin of Species*. London: Macmillan.

Das, Veena. 1990. "Introduction: Communities, Riots and Survivors." *Mirrors of Violence: Communities, Riots and Survivors in South Asia*, ed. Veena Das. Oxford: Oxford University Press.

Davidson, Harriet. 1995. "I Say I Am There: Siting/Citing the Subject of Feminism and Poststructuralism." *Critical Encounters: Reference and Responsibility in Deconstructive Writing*, ed. Cathy Caruth and Deborah Esch. New Brunswick, NJ: Rutgers University Press, 241–261.

Davidson, Michael. 1997. *Ghostlier Demarcations: Modern Poetry and the Material Word*. Berkeley, Los Angeles, London: University of California Press.

Davis, Shelton, and Julie Hodson. 1982. *Witness to Political Violence in Guatemala: The Suppression of a Rural Movement*. Boston: Oxfam America.

Deleuze, Gilles. 1989. *Cinema 2: The Time-Image*, trans. Hugh Tomlinson and Robert Galeta. Minneapolis: University of Minnesota Press.

de Man, Paul. 1979. *Allegories of Reading*. New Haven: Yale University Press.

Denevan, William, ed. 1976. *The Native Population of the Americas in 1492*. Madison: University of Wisconsin Press.

Derrida, Jacques. 1978. *La vérité en peinture*. Paris: Flammarion.

———. 1982a. "Différance." *Margins of Philosophy*, trans. Alan Bass. Chicago: University of Chicago Press, 1–27.

———. 1982b. "The Ends of Man." *Margins of Philosophy*, trans. Alan Bass. Chicago: University of Chicago Press, 109–136.

———. 1984. "No Apocalypse, Not Now: Full Speed Ahead, Seven Missiles, Seven Missives." *diacritics* 14.

———. 1986a. *Glas*, trans. John P. Leavey, Jr. and Richard Rand. Lincoln and London: University of Nebraska Press.

———. 1986b. *Memoires: For Paul de Man*, trans. Cecile Lindsay, Jonathan Culler, and Eduardo Cadava. New York: Columbia University Press.

———. 1987. *The Truth in Painting*, trans. Geoff Bennington and Ian McLeod. Chicago and London: University of Chicago Press.

———. 1991. *Cinders*, ed. and trans Ned Lukacher. Lincoln: University of Nebraska Press.

———. 1994. *Specters of Marx: The State of the Debt, the Work of Mourning, and the New International*, trans. Peggy Kamuf. New York and London: Routledge.

———. 1999. *The Gift of Death*, trans. David Wills. Chicago: University of Chicago Press.

Des Forges, Alison. 1999. *"Leave None to Tell the Story": Genocide in Rwanda*. New York: Human Rights Watch.

DeShazer, Mary K. 1994. *A Poetics of Resistance: Women Writing in El Salvador, South Africa, and the United States*. Ann Arbor: University of Michigan Press.

Des Pres, Terrence. 1976. *The Survivor: An Anatomy of Life in the Death Camps*. New York: Oxford University Press.

Dews, Peter. 1987. *Logics of Disintegration: Post-Structuralist Thought and the Claims of Critical Theory*. London: Verso.

Diamond, Elin. 1997. *Unmaking Mimesis: Essays on Feminism and Theater*. New York and London: Routledge.

Diamond, Stanley. 1993. *In Search of the Primitive: A Critique of Civilization*. New Brunswick, NJ, and London: Transaction Books.

Diner, Dan. 2000. *Beyond the Conceivable: Studies on Germany, Nazism, and the Holocaust*. Berkeley, Los Angeles, London: University of California Press.

Dionysus Longinus on the Sublime. 1770. Trans. William Smith, 4th ed., corrected and improved. London.

Dobyns, Henry F. 1966. "Estimating American Aboriginal Population: An Appraisal of Techniques with a New Hemispheric Estimate." *Current Anthropology* VII, 395–416.

Douglass, Ana. 1996. "Catechizing without Shelter." *The European Legacy: Toward New Paradigms: Special Issue Fourth International Conference of the International Society for the Study of European Ideas* 1:1, ed. Ezra Talmor and Sascha Talmor. Cambridge, MA: MIT Press.

———. 1997. *"Transcendental Homelessness": Modernism, the Culture Concept, and the Novel*. Ann Arbor: UMI.9814065.

Dower, John W. 1986. *War Without Mercy: Race and Power in the Pacific War*. New York: Pantheon.

D'Souza, Dinesh. 1992. *Illiberal Education: The Politics of Race and Sex on Campus*. New York: Vintage.

Duncan, W. Raymond and James Nelson Goodsell. 1970. *The Quest for Change in Latin America: Sources for a Twentieth-Century Analysis*. Oxford: Oxford University Press.

Duras, Marguerite. 1961. *Hiroshima Mon Amour: Text by Marguerite Duras for the film by Alain Resnais*, trans. Richard Seaver. New York: Grove Weidenfeld.

Düttmann, Alexander Garcia. 1993. "What Will Have Been Said About AIDS." *Public* 7.

Dyer, Thomas G. 1980. *Theodore Roosevelt and the Idea of Race*. Baton Rouge and London: Louisiana State University Press.

Dyson, Michael Eric. 1996. *Between God and Gangsta Rap: Bearing Witness to Black Culture*. New York: Oxford University Press.

Earle, Duncan. 2001. "Menchú Tales and Maya Social Landscapes: The Silencing of Words and Worlds." *The Rigoberta Menchú Controversy*, ed. Arturo Arias. Minneapolis and London: University of Minnesota Press, 288–308.

Easthope, Antony. 1983. *Poetry as Discourse*. London: Routledge.

Edvardson, Cordelia. 1997. *Burned Child Seeks the Fire: A Memoir*, trans. Joel Agee. Boston: Beacon Press.

Elias, Robert. 1986. *The Politics of Victimization: Victims, Victimology, and Human Rights*. New York: Oxford University Press.

Eliot, T. S. 1967. "The Social Function of Poetry." *On Poetry and Poets*. New York: Farrar, Straus & Giroux.

Emery, Amy Fass. 1996. *The Anthropological Imagination in Latin American Literature*. Columbia: University of Missouri Press.

Epstein, Mikhail. 1997. "Some Speculations on the Mystery of Araki Yasusada." *Witz* 5:2 (Summer).

Erbach, Karen. 1995. "Schindler's List Finds Heroism Amidst Holocaust." *Oskar Schindler and His List*, ed. Thomas Fensch. Forest Dale, VT: Paul Eriksson, 99–109.

Erikson, Kai. 1996. "Notes on Trauma and Community." *Trauma: Explorations in Memory*, ed. Cathy Caruth. Baltimore: Johns Hopkins University Press.

Eshleman, Clayton. 1995. "Complexities of Witness." *Sulfur* 37.

Espada, Martin. 1995. *Poetry Like Bread: Poets of the Political Imagination*. Willimantic, CT: Curbstone Press.

Ezrahi, Sidra Dekoven. 1980. *By Words Alone: The Holocaust in Literature*. Chicago: University of Chicago Press.

———. 1989. "The Holocaust and the Shifting Boundaries of Art and History." *History and Memory* 1:2.

Fackenheim, Emil. 1982. *To Mend the World*. New York: Shocken Books.

Farrell, Kirby. 1998. *Post-traumatic Culture: Injury and Interpretation in the Nineties*. Baltimore and London: Johns Hopkins University Press.

Faurisson, Robert. 1980. *Mémoire en défense: contre ceux qui m'accusent de falsifier l'histoire*. Paris: La Vielle Taupe.

Feinstein, Stephen C., ed. 1995. *Witness and Legacy: Contemporary Art About the Holocaust*. Minneapolis, MN: Lerner.

Felman, Shoshana, ed. 1980. *Literature and Psychoanalysis: The Question of Reading: Otherwise*. Baltimore and London: Johns Hopkins University Press.

———. 1985. *Writing and Madness*, trans. Martha Noel Evans, Shoshana Felman, and Brian Massumi. Ithaca, NY: Cornell University Press.

———. 1997. "Forms of Judicial Blindness." *Critical Inquiry* 23 (Summer).

———. 2001. "Theaters of Justice: Arendt in Jerusalem, the Eichmann Trial, and the Redefinition of Legal Meaning in the Wake of the Holocaust." *Critical Inquiry* 27 (Winter).

Felman, Shoshana and Dori Laub. 1992. *Testimony: Crises of Witnessing in Literature, Psychoanalysis and History*. New York and London: Routledge.

Felstiner, John. 1995. *Paul Celan: Poet, Survivor, Jew*. New Haven and London: Yale University Press.

Ferman, Claudia. 2001. "Textual Truth, Historical Truth, and Media Truth: Everybody Speaks about the Menchús." *The Rigoberta Menchú Controversy*, ed Arturo Arias. Minneapolis and London: University of Minnesota Press, 156–170.

Finkelstein, Norman. 2000a. *The Holocaust Industry: Reflections on the Exploitation of Jewish Suffering*. New York: Verso.

———. 2000b. "How the Arab-Israeli War of 1967 Gave Birth to a Memorial Industry." *London Review of Books* (6 January).

Finkielkraut, Alain. 1989. "Interview with Emmanuel Levinas and Alain Finkielkraut on Radio Communauté, 28 September." Shlomo Malka. *The Levinas Reader*, ed. Seán Hand. Cambridge, U.K.: Basil Blackwell.

Fisch, Harold. 1990. *Poetry With a Purpose: Biblical Poetics and Interpretation*. Bloomington: Indiana University Press.

Flanzbaum, Hilene, ed. 1999. *The Americanization of the Holocaust*. Baltimore and London: Johns Hopkins University Press.

Forché, Carolyn. 1981. "El Salvador: An Aide Memoire." *American Poetry Review* 10 (July/Aug.).

———, ed. 1993. *Against Forgetting: Twentieth-Century Poetry of Witness*. New York and London: W. W. Norton.

Foster, Hal. 1996a. "Obscene, Abject, Traumatic." *October* 78 (Fall).

———. 1996b. *The Return of the Real: The Avant-Garde at the End of the Century*. Cambridge, MA and London: MIT Press.

Foucault, Michel. 1961. *Folie et déraison: Histoire de la folie á l'age classique*. Paris: Plon.

———. 1970. *The Order of Things: An Archaeology of the Human Sciences*. New York: Vintage.

———. 1972. *The Archaeology of Knowledge*, trans. A. M. Sheridan Smith. New York: Pantheon.

———. 1973. *Madness and Civilization: A History of Insanity in the Age of Reason*, trans. Richard Howard. New York: Random House.

———. 1977. *Discipline and Punish: The Birth of the Prison*. New York: Pantheon Books.

———. 1978a. *The History of Sexuality: Vol. 1: An Introduction*, trans. Robert Hurley. New York: Vintage.

———. 1978b. *The History of Sexuality*. New York: Pantheon Books.

———. 1980. "Truth and Power." *Power/Knowledge: Selected Interviews and Other Writings 1972–1977*, ed. Colin Gordon. Trans. Colin Gordon, Leo Marshall, John Mepham, Kate Soper. New York: Pantheon Books.

Frankl, Viktor. 1984. *Man's Search for Meaning*, rev. ed. New York: Pocket Books.

Freud, Sigmund. 1953–1957a. "The Aetiology of Hysteria." *The Standard Edition of the Complete Psychological Works of Sigmund Freud*, ed. James Strachey, Vol. 3. London: Hogarth.

———. 1953–1957b. "Remembering, Repeating, and Working-Through." *The Standard Edition of the Complete Psychological Works of Sigmund Freud*, ed. James Strachey, Vol. 12. London: Hogarth.

———. 1953–1957c. "Group Psychology and the Analysis of the Ego." *The Standard Edition of the Complete Psychological Works of Sigmund Freud*, ed. James Strachey, Vol. 18. London: Hogarth.

Fridman, Lea Wernick. 2000. *Words and Witness: Narrative and Aesthetic Strategies in the Representation of the Holocaust*. Albany: State University of New York Press.

Friedlander, Henry. 1996. *The Origins of Nazi Genocide: From Euthanasia to the Final Solution*. Chapel Hill: University of North Carolina Press.

Friedlander, Saul. 1979. *When Memory Comes*. New York: Farrar, Straus, Giroux.

———, ed. 1992a. *Probing the Limits of Representation: Nazism and the "Final Solution."* Cambridge, MA: Harvard University Press.

———. 1992b. "Trauma, Transference, and 'Working Through' in Writing the History of the Shoah." *History and Memory* 4 (Spring-Summer).

———. 1993. *Memory, History and the Extermination of the Jews of Europe*. Bloomington and Indianapolis: University of Indiana Press.

———. 1997. *Nazi Germany and the Jews*, Vol. I. New York: HarperCollins.

Funkenstein, Amos. 1993. *Perceptions of Jewish History*. Berkeley, Los Angeles, Oxford: University of California Press.

Fussell, Paul. 1975. *The Great War and Modern Memory*. New York: Oxford University Press.

Geddes, Jennifer. 2000. "On Evil, Pain, and Beauty: A Conversation with Elaine Scarry." *Hedgehog Review* 2:2 (Summer), 78–87.

Geertz, Clifford. 1973. *The Interpretation of Cultures*. New York: Basic Books.

———. 1984. "Anti-relativism." *American Anthropologist* 86.

———. 1988. *Works and Lives: The Anthropologist as Author*. Stanford, CA: Stanford University Press.

———. 1992. "Genet's Last Stand." *The New York Review of Books* (November 19).

Gelles, Paul. 1998. "*Testimonio*, Ethnography, and Processes of Authorship." *Anthropology Newsletter* 39:3, 16–17.

Genet, Jean. 1992. *Prisoner of Love*, trans. Barbara Bray. Hanover, NH and London: Wesleyan University Press.

Gerstein, Robert. 1989. "Do Terrorists Have Rights?" *The Morality of Terrorism: Religious and Secular Justifications*, 2d ed. Ed. Rapoport, David C. and Yonah Alexander. New York: Columbia University Press.

Gewirtz, Paul. 1996. "Victims and Voyeurs: Two Narrative Problems at the Criminal Trial." *Law's Stories: Narrative and Rhetoric in the Law*, ed. Peter Brooks and Paul Gewirtz. New Haven: Yale University Press.

Gibson, William. 1987. *Count Zero*. New York: ACE Books.

Gilbert, Martin. 1996. " 'The Most Horrible Crime': Churchill's Prophetic, Passionate and Persistent Response to the Holocaust." *Times Literary Supplement* (June 7), 3–5.

Gioia, Dana. 1992. *Can Poetry Matter? Essays on Poetry and American Culture*. Saint Paul, MN: Graywolf Press.

Goffman, Erving. 1974. *Frame Analysis: An Essay on the Organization of Experience*. New York: Harper.

Goldberg, Vicki. 1992. "Images of Catastrophe as Corporate Ballyhoo." *New York Times* (May 10).

Goleman, Daniel. 1995. *Emotional Intelligence*. New York: Bantam Books.

Gottlieb, Roger S., ed. 1990. *Thinking the Unthinkable: Meanings of the Holocaust*. New York/Mahwah: Paulist Press.

Gourevitch, Philip. 1993. "Behold Now Behemoth. The Holocaust Memorial Museum: One More American Theme Park." *Harper's Magazine* (July).

———. 1995. "Letter from Rwanda: After the Genocide." *The New Yorker* (December 18).

———. 1999. "The Memory Thief." *The New Yorker* (June 14), 48–68.

Graham, Colin. 1994. " 'Liminal Spaces': Post-Colonial Theories and Irish Culture." *The Irish Review* 16 (Autumn/Winter), 29–48.

Grandin, Greg. 2000. *The Blood of Guatemala: A History of Race and Nation*. Durham, NC: Duke University Press.

Greenspan, Hank. 1996. "On Being a 'Real Survivor.' " *Sh'ma* (March 29).

Greenspan, Henry. 1999. "Imagining Survivors: Testimony and the Rise of Holocaust Consciousness." *The Americanization of the Holocaust*, ed. Hilene Flanzbaum. Baltimore and London: Johns Hopkins University Press, 45–67.

Gross, Jan T. 2001. *Neighbors: The Destruction of the Jewish Community in Jedwabne*. Princeton: Princeton University Press.

Guatemalan Truth Commission Accord (Translated in English). 9 April 1999. *http://www.stile.lut.ac.uk/~gyedb/STILE/Email 000s048/* 18 March 2001.

Guevara, Che. 1996. *Reminiscences of the Cuban Revolutionary War*. Translated from *Pasajes de la guerra revolucionaria*. New York: Pathfinder.

Gugelberger, Georg M., ed. 1996a. *The Real Thing: Testimonial Discourse and Latin America*. Durham, NC: Duke University Press.

———. 1996b. Introduction: "Institutionalization of Transgression: Testimonial Discourse and Beyond." Gugelberger, Georg M., ed. *The Real Thing: Testimonial Discourse and Latin America*. Durham, NC: Duke University Press, 1–19.

Habermas, Jürgen. 1988. "A Kind of Settlement of Damages (Apologetic Tendencies)

Concerning the Public Use of History," trans. Jeremy Leaman. *New German Critique* 44.

Halbwachs, Maurice. 1952. *Les cadres sociaux de la mémoire* (1925, reprint Paris, 1952).

———. 1968. *La mémoire collective*. Paris: Presses Universitaires de France.

———. 1992. *On Collective Memory*, ed. and trans. Lewis Coser. Chicago: University of Chicago Press.

Hand, Seán, ed. 1989. *The Levinas Reader*. Cambridge, U.K.: Basil Blackwell.

Harff, Barbara and Ted Robert Gurr. 1988. "Toward Empirical Theory of Genocides and Politicides. Identification and Measurement of Cases since 1945." *International Studies Quarterly* 32, 359–71.

Harpham, Geoffrey. 1995. "Ethics." *Critical Terms for Literary Study*. 2nd ed. Ed. Frank Lentricchia and Thomas McLaughlin. Chicago: University of Chicago Press, 387–405.

Harrison, Tony. 1992. *The Gaze of the Gorgon*. Newcastle on Tyne: Bloodaxe Books. (Text of film/poem first shown on BBC 2 Television 3 October 1992).

Hartman, Geoffrey H. 1994. "Introduction: Darkness Visible." *Holocaust Remembrance: The Shapes of Memory*, ed. Geoffrey H. Hartman. Oxford, U.K.; Cambridge, MA: Blackwell.

———. 1996. *The Longest Shadow*. Bloomington and Indianapolis: Indiana University Press.

Heath, Stephen. 1974. "Lessons from Brecht." *Screen* 15, no. 2 (summer): 103–27.

Hegel, Georg Wilhelm Friedrich. 1975. *Aesthetics*, trans. T. M. Knox. Oxford: Oxford University Press.

———. 1977. *The Phenomenology of Spirit*, trans. A.V. Miller. New York: Oxford University Press.

———. 1980. *Lectures on the Philosophy of World History: Introduction, Reason in History*. Cambridge: Cambridge University Press.

Helms, Mary. 1988. *Ulysses' Sail*. Princeton: Princeton University Press.

Henderson, Brian. 1980. *A Critique of Film Theory*. New York: Dutton.

Herman, Judith Lewis. 1992. *Trauma and Recovery: The Aftermath of Violence—From Domestic Abuse to Political Terror*. New York: Basic Books.

Hernandez, Raymond. 1996. "New Curriculum from Albany." *New York Times* (Dec. 1), 52.

Hersh, Seymour. 2000. "Overwhelming Force." *The New Yorker* (May 22).

Hertz, Neil. 1992. "Dr. Johnson's Forgetfulness, Descartes' Piece of Wax." *Eighteenth-Century Life* 16:3 (November) 167–181.

Hilberg, Raul. 1985. *The Destruction of the European Jews*, 3 vols., rev. and definitive ed. New York: Holmes & Meier.

———. 1988a. "Developments in the Historiography of the Holocaust." *Comprehending the Holocaust: Historical and Literary Research*, ed. Asher Cohen, Joav Gelber, Charlotte Ward. Frankfurt am Main and New York: P. Lang.

———. 1988b. "I Was Not There." *Writing and the Holocaust*, ed. Berel Lang. New York: Holmes & Meier.

———. 1996. *The Politics of Memory: The Journey of a Holocaust Historian*. Chicago: Ivan R. Dee.

Hillesum, Etty. 1983. *An Interrupted Life: The Diaries of Etty Hillesum, 1941–1943*, trans. Arnold J. Pomerans. New York: Pantheon.

———. 1986. *Letters from Westerbrook*, trans. Arnold J. Pomerans. New York: Pantheon.

Himmler, Heinrich. 1946. *Nazi Conspiracy and Aggression*. International Military Tribunal at Nuremberg, vol. 4, Document 1919-PS (Speech in April, 1943). Washington, D.C.: Government Printing Office.

Hochschild, Adam. 1998. *King Leopold's Ghost: A Story of Greed, Terror, and Heroism in Colonial Africa*. New York: Houghton Mifflin.

Hogan, Michael J., ed. 1996. *Hiroshima in History and Memory*. Cambridge: Cambridge University Press.

Holman, Bob. 1994. "Congratulations. You Have Found the Hidden Book: Invocation." *Aloud: Voices from the Nyorican Poets Café*, ed. Miguel Algarin and Bob Holman. New York: Henry Holt and Co.

Holtzman, Karen, ed. 1994. *Burnt Whole: Contemporary Artists Reflect on the Holocaust*. Washington, D.C.: Washington Project for the Arts.

Horne, Donald. 1984. *The Great Museum: The Re-Presentation of History*. London: Pluto.

Horowitz, Irving Louis. 1982. *Taking Lives: Genocide and State Power*. New Brunswick, NJ and London: Transaction Books.

Hošek, Chaviva and Patricia Parker, eds. 1985. *Lyric Poetry: Beyond New Criticism*. Ithaca and London: Cornell University Press.

Hough, Richard et al. 1982. *Land and Labor in Guatemala: An Assessment*. Washington, D.C.: Agency for International Development.

Hutcheon, Linda. 1988. *A Poetics of Postmodernism: History, Theory, Fiction*. New York: Routledge.

Hutton, Patrick H. 1993. *History as an Art of Memory*. Hanover, NH and London: University Press of New England.

Huyssen, Andreas. 1994. "Monument and Memory in a Postmodern Age." *The Art of Memory: Holocaust Memorials in History*, ed. James E. Young. New York: Prestel.

———. 1995. *Twilight Memories: Marking Time in a Culture of Amnesia*. New York: Routledge.

Immerman, Richard. 1982. *The CIA in Guatemala: The Foreign Policy of Intervention*. Austin: University of Texas Press.

Insdorf, Annette. 1989. *Indelible Shadows: Film and the Holocaust*. 2nd ed. Cambridge: Cambridge University Press.

International Military Tribunal. 1949. *Trial of the Major War Criminals before the International Military Tribunal* (Blue Series). Nuremberg.

International Work Group for Indigenous Affairs (IWGIA). *Guatemala 1978: The Massacre at Panzós*. IWGIA Document No. 33. Trans. Kjeld K. Lings. Copenhagen: IWGIA.

Jabès, Edmond. 1988. "Repondre à repondre pour." Unpublished.

Jackson, Earl, Jr. 1994. "Desire at Cross-Cultural Purposes: *Hiroshima Mon Amour* and *Merry Christmas, Mr. Lawrence*." *positions east asia cultures critique* 2:1 (Spring), 133–174.

Jaimes, M. Annette. 1992. "Federal Indian Identification Policy: A Usurpation of Indigenous Sovereignty in North America." *The State of Native America: Genocide, Colonization, and Resistance.* Boston: South End Press, 123–138.

James, William. 1950. *Principles of Psychology.* 2 vols. New York: Dover.

Jameson, Fredric. 1982. *The Political Unconscious: Narrative as a Socially Symbolic Act.* Ithaca, NY: Cornell University Press.

———. 1988a. "Beyond the Cave: Demystifying the Ideology of Modernism." *The Ideologies of Theory: Essays 1971–1986, Volume 2: The Syntax of History.* Minneapolis: University of Minnesota Press, 115–132.

———. 1988b. "Regarding Postmodernism—A Conversation with Fredric Jameson. *Universal Abandon? The Politics of Postmodernism,* ed. Andrew Ross. Minneapolis: University of Minneapolis Press.

———. 1992. *Signatures of the Visible.* New York and London: Routledge.

———. 1995. "Marx's Purloined Letter." *New Left Review* (January/February).

Jeffreys, Mark. 1995. "Ideologies of Lyric: A Problem of Genre in Contemporary Anglophone Poetics." *PMLA* 110:2 (March).

Kalaidjian, Walter. 1989. *Languages of Liberation: The Social Text in Contemporary American Poetry.* New York: Columbia University Press.

Kant, Immanuel. 1966. *Critique of Judgment,* trans. J. H. Bernard. New York: Hafner.

Kaplan, Harold. 1994. *Conscience and Memory: Meditations in a Museum of the Holocaust.* Chicago: University of Chicago Press.

Katz, Jacob. 1981. "Was the Holocaust Predictable?" *The Holocaust as Historical Experience,* ed. Yehuda Bauer and Nathan Rotenstreich. New York: Holmes and Meier.

Kenwood, Alun, ed. 1992. *Travellers' Tales, Real and Imaginary, in the Hispanic World and its Literature.* Madrid: Voz Hispánica.

Kershaw, Ian. 2000. *Hitler, 1936–45: Nemesis.* New York: Norton.

Ketchum, Richard M. 1949. "Memory as history." *American Heritage* 42 (November).

Kierkegaard, Søren. 1941. *Fear and Trembling,* trans. Walter Lowrie. Princeton: Princeton University Press.

Kimmelman, Michael. 1997. "In the Faces of the Living, Honor for the Dead." *The New York Times* (September 12).

Kinsella, John. 1996. *The Radnóti Poems.* Cambridge, U.K.: Equipage.

Kirmayer, Laurence. 1996. "Landscapes of Memory: Trauma, Narrative, and Dissociation." *Tense Past: Cultural Essays in Trauma and Memory,* ed. Paul Antze and Michael Lambek. New York: Routledge.

Kleber, Rolf J. and Charles R. Figley, Berthold P. R. Gersons, eds. 1995. *Beyond Trauma: Cultural and Societal Dynamics.* New York: Plenum Press.

Klein, Julia M. 2001. "One More River to Cross." *The American Prospect* (June 4).

Klein, Kerwin Lee. 2000. "On the Emergence of Memory in Historical Discourse." *Representations* 69 (Winter), 127–150.

Kleinman, Arthur, Veena Das and Margaret Lock, eds. 1997. *Social Suffering.* Berkeley: University of California Press.

Kodolányi, Gyula. 1996. "Commentary" (on the translations of Miklós Radnóti). *Poems for the Millenium,* ed. Jerome Rothenberg and Pierre Joris. Berkeley, Los Angeles, London: University of California Press, 717–718.

Kosinski, Jerzy. 1976. *The Painted Bird*. 2nd ed. Boston: Houghton Mifflin.

Kramer, Jane. 1995. "The Politics of Memory." *The New Yorker* (August 14).

Kreidl, John Francis. 1977. *Alain Resnais*. Boston: Twayne Publishers.

Kren, George M., and Leon Rappaport. 1980. *The Holocaust and the Crisis of Human Behavior*. New York: Holmes and Meier Publishers, Inc.

Kripke, Saul A. 1980. *Naming and Necessity*. Cambridge, MA: Harvard University Press.

Kristeva, Julia. 1982. *Powers of Horror: An Essay on Abjection*, trans. Leon S. Roudiez. New York: Columbia University Press.

———. 1986. "The True-Real." *The Kristeva Reader*, ed. Toril Moi. New York: Columbia University Press.

Kuper, Leo. 1981. *Genocide: Its Political Use in the Twentieth Century*. New Haven: Yale University Press.

LaCapra, Dominick. 1994. *Representing the Holocaust: History, Theory, Trauma*. Ithaca, NY: Cornell University Press.

———. 1997. "Lanzmann's *Shoah*: 'Here There Is No Why.' " *Critical Inquiry* 23:2 (Winter), 231–269.

———. 1999. *History and Memory after Auschwitz*. Ithaca, NY: Cornell University Press.

Lacoue-Labarthe, Phillippe. 1990. *Heidegger, Art and Politics*. Oxford and Cambridge, MA: Basil Blackwell.

Lamb, Jonathan. 1995. *The Rhetoric of Suffering: Reading the Book of Job in the Eighteenth Century*. Oxford: Clarendon Press; New York: Oxford University Press.

Lang, Berel, ed. 1988. *Writing and the Holocaust*. New York and London: Holmes and Meier.

———. 1990. *Act and Idea in the Nazi Genocide*. Chicago: University of Chicago Press.

———. 1999. *The Future of the Holocaust: Between History and Memory*. Ithaca, NY: Cornell University Press.

———. 2000a. "The History of Evil, the Holocaust, and Postmodernity." *The Hedgehog Review* 2:2 (Summer), 57–66.

———. 2000b. *Holocaust Representation: Art Within the Limits of History and Ethics*. Baltimore: Johns Hopkins University Press.

Langer, Lawrence L. 1978. *The Age of Atrocity: Death in Modern Literature*. Boston: Beacon Press.

———. 1992. *Holocaust Testimonies: The Ruins of Memory*. New Haven: Yale University Press.

———. 1995a. *Admitting the Holocaust*. New York: Oxford University Press.

———, ed. 1995b. *Art from the Ashes: A Holocaust Anthology*. New York: Oxford University Press.

———. 1999. *Preempting the Holocaust*. New Haven: Yale University Press.

Lanzmann, Claude. 1985. *Shoah*. Paris: Éditions Fayard.

———. 1991. "Seminar on Shoah." *Yale French Studies* 79.

———. 1995. "Ihr sollt nicht weinen." *"Der gute Deutsche": Dokumente zur Diskussion um Steven Spielbergs "Schindler's Liste" in Deutschland*. Ausgew. und mit einem Nachw. hrsg. von Christoph Weiss. St Ingbert: Röhrig, 173–78.

Lappin, Elena. 1999. "The Man With Two Heads." *Granta* 66 (Summer), 7–66.

Laub, Dori. 1992. "Bearing Witness." Shoshana Felman and Dori Laub. *Testimony: Crises of Witnessing in Literature, Psychoanalysis, and History.* New York and London: Routledge.

Lawlor, Leonard. 1992. *Imagination and Chance: The Difference Between the Thought of Ricoeur and Derrida.* Albany: State University of New York Press.

Leach, Edmund. 1970. *Claude Lévi-Strauss.* New York: Viking Press.

Leak, Andrew and George Paizis. 2000. *The Holocaust and the Text: Speaking the Unspeakable.* New York: Macmillan.

Leiris, Michel. 1934. *L'Afrique fantôme.* Paris: Gallimard.

Lemann, Nicholas. 1992. "The Vogue of Childhood Misery." *Atlantic* (March).

Lemkin, Raphael. 1944. *Axis Rule in Occupied Europe.* Washington, D.C.: Carnegie Endowment for International Peace/Rumford Press.

Levi, Primo. 1986. *Survival in Auschwitz: The Nazi Assault on Humanity.* (Original title *Se questa é un uomo*; English title: *If This Is a Man*), trans. Stuart Woolf. New York: Collier Books.

———. 1989. *The Drowned and the Saved*, trans. Raymond Rosenthal. New York: Vintage International.

———. 1995. "Shame." *Art from the Ashes: A Holocaust Anthology*, ed. Lawrence Langer. New York: Oxford University Press, 108–120.

———. 1996. "Afterward: the author answers his reader's questions" to *If this Is A Man* and *The Truce.* London: Vintage.

Levinas, Emmanuel. 1969. *Totality and Infinity*, trans. Alphonso Lingis. Pittsburgh: Duquesne University Press.

———. 1988a. "Useless Suffering," trans. Richard Cohen. *The Provocation of Levinas: Rethinking the Other*, ed. Robert Bernasconi and David Wood. London and New York: Routledge.

———. 1988b. *The Provocation of Levinas: Rethinking the Other*, ed. Robert Bernasconi and David Wood. London and New York: Routledge.

———. 1989a. *The Levinas Reader*, ed. Seán Hand. Oxford and Cambridge, MA: Basil Blackwell.

———. 1989b. "Interview with Emmanuel Levinas and Alain Finkielkraut on Radio Communauté, 28 September, 1982," Shlomo Malka. *The Levinas Reader*, ed. Seán Hand. Oxford and Cambridge, MA: Basil Blackwell.

———. 1991. *Otherwise Than Being or Beyond Essence*, trans. Alphonso Lingis. Boston: Kluwer Academic Publishers.

Lévi-Strauss, Claude. 1955. *Tristes tropiques.* Paris: Plon.

———. 1964. *Tristes Tropiques*, trans. John Russell. New York: Atheneum.

———. 1965. *Tristes tropiques.* Paris: Union Generale d'Éditions.

———. 1973. *Tristes Tropiques*, trans. John Weightman and Doreen Weightman. New York: Washington Square Press.

———. 1995. *Saudades do Brasil: A Photographic Memoir*, trans. Sylvia Modelski. Seattle and London: University of Washington Press.

Lévi-Strauss, Claude and Didier Eribon. 1988. *Conversations with Claude Lévi-Strauss*, trans. Paula Wissing. Chicago and London: University of Chicago Press.

Leys, Ruth. 2000. *Trauma: A Genealogy*. Chicago: University of Chicago Press.

Li, Victor P. H. 1984. "Narcissism and the Limits of the Lyric Self." *Tropic Crucible: Self and Theory in Language and Literature*, ed. Ranjit Chatterjee and Colin Nicholson. Singapore: Singapore University Press.

Lifton, Robert Jay. 1961. *History and Human Survival*. New York: Random House.

———. 1967. *Death in Life: Survivors of Hiroshima*. New York: Basic Books.

———. 1976. *The Life of the Self: Toward a New Psychology*. New York: Simon and Schuster.

———. 1979. *The Broken Connection: On Death and the Continuity of Life*. New York: Simon and Schuster.

Lifton, Robert Jay and Eric Markusen. 1991. *The Genocidal Mentality: Nazi Holocaust and Nuclear Threat*. London: Macmillan.

Lifton, Robert Jay and Greg Mitchell. 1995. *Hiroshima in America: Fifty Years of Denial*. New York: Putnam's Sons.

Lindqvist, Sven. 1996. *"Exterminate All the Brutes,"* trans. Joan Tate. New York: The New Press.

Linenthal, Edward T. 1994. "The Boundaries of Memory: The United States Holocaust Memorial Museum." *American Quarterly* 46.

Lipstadt, Deborah E. 1993. *Denying the Holocaust: The Growing Assault on Truth and Memory*. New York: Macmillan, Inc.

Loftus, Elizabeth and Katherine Ketcham. 1994. *The Myth of Repressed Memory: False Memories and Allegations of Sexual Abuse*. New York: St. Martin's Press.

Longinus. See Dionysus Longinus.

Lopate, Phillip. 1989. "Resistance to the Holocaust." *Tikkun* 4 (May–June).

Lorde, Audre. 1994. "Who said it was simple." *Feminism in Our Time: The Essential Writings, World War II to the Present*, ed. Miriam Schneir. New York: Vintage Books.

Losey, Joseph. 1968. *Losey on Losey*, ed. Tom Milne. Garden City, New York: Doubleday & Company.

Lovell, W. George, and Christopher H. Lutz. 2001. "The Primacy of Larger Truths: Rigoberta Menchú and the Tradition of Native Testimony in Guatemala." *The Rigoberta Menchú Controversy*, ed Arturo Arias. Minneapolis and London: University of Minnesota Press, 171–197.

Lowe, David M. 1995. *The Body in Late-Capitalist USA*. Durham, NC: Duke University Press.

Lyotard, Jean-François. 1984a. *The Postmodern Condition: A Report on Knowledge*, trans. Geoff Bennington and Brian Massumi. Minneapolis: University of Minnesota Press.

———. 1984b. "Answering the Question: What Is Postmodernism?" trans. Régis Durand. *The Postmodern Condition: A Report on Knowledge*, trans. Geoff Bennington and Brian Massumi. Minneapolis: University of Minnesota Press, 71–84.

———. 1988. *The Differend: Phrases in Dispute*, trans. Georges Van den Abbeele. Minneapolis: University of Minnesota Press.

———. 1990. *Heidegger and "The Jews,"* trans. Andreas Michel and Mark S. Roberts. Minneapolis: University of Minnesota Press.

———. 1993. "The Survivor," trans. Robert Harvey and Mark S. Roberts, *Toward the Postmodern*. Atlantic Highlands, NJ: Humanities Press.

MacIntyre, Alasdair. 1984. *After Virtue: A Study in Moral Theory.* 2d ed. Notre Dame: University of Notre Dame Press.

Maclear, Kyo. 1999. *Beclouded Visions: Hiroshima, Nagasaki and the Art of Witness.* Albany: State University of New York Press.

Macmillan, Malcom. 1997. *Freud Evaluated: The Complete Arc.* Cambridge, MA: MIT Press.

Madison, James. 1961. *The Federalist,* No. 37, ed. Jacob E. Cooke. Middletown, CT: Wesleyan University Press.

Maier, Charles S. 1993. "A Surfeit of Memory? Reflections on History, Melancholy and Denial." *History & Memory* 5 (Fall-Winter).

Malka, Shlomo. 1989. "Interview with Emmanuel Levinas and Alain Finkielkraut on Radio Communauté, 28 September, 1982." *The Levinas Reader,* ed. Seán Hand. Cambridge, MA: Basil Blackwell.

Malthus, Edward. 1798. *Essay on the Principle of Population.* London.

Mann, Thomas. 1956. *Der Tod in Venedig.* Frankfurt and Hamburg: Fischer Bücherei.

———. 1970. *Death in Venice,* trans. Kenneth Burke. New York: Modern Library.

Marcus, George E. and Michael M.J. Fischer. 1986. *Anthropology as Cultural Critique: An Experimental Moment in the Human Sciences.* Chicago: University of Chicago Press.

Marx, Karl. 1906–1909. *Capital: A Critique of Political Economy,* 3 vols., ed. Frederic Engels. Chicago: C. H. Kerr.

Mazian, Florence. 1990. *Why Genocide?* Ames: Iowa State University Press.

McCabe, Patrick. 1992. *The Butcher Boy.* New York: Fromm International Publishing.

McClintock, Michael. 1985. *The American Connection: Volume Two: State Terror and Popular Resistance in Guatemala.* London: Zed Books.

McShine, Kynaston, ed. 1980. *Joseph Cornell.* New York: Museum of Modern Art.

Melson, Robert. 1992. *Revolution and Genocide: On the Origins of the Armenian Genocide and the Holocaust.* Chicago and London: University of Chicago Press.

Menchú, Rigoberta. 1983. *Me llamo Rigoberta Menchú y asi me nació la conciencia.* Barcelona: Editorial Argos Vergara.

———. 1984. *I, Rigoberta Menchú: An Indian Woman in Guatemala,* ed. Elizabeth Burgos-Debray. Trans. Ann Wright. London: Verso.

———. 1998a. With Dante Liano and Gianni Miná. *Rigoberta: La nieta de los Mayas.* Madrid: Aguilar [English ed. *Crossing Borders*].

———. 1998b. *Crossing Borders,* trans. and ed. by Ann Wright. London: Verso.

Micale, Mark S. 1995. *Approaching Hysteria: Disease and its Interpretations.* Princeton: Princeton University Press.

———. 2000. "We cannot stress enough." *Times Literary Supplement* (October 27), 6–7.

Michaels, Walter Benn. 1999. " 'You Who Never Was There': Slavery and the New Historicism—Deconstruction and the Holocaust." *The Americanization of the Holocaust,* ed. Hilene Flanzbaum. Baltimore and London: Johns Hopkins University Press, 181–197.

Middleton, David and Derek Edwards, eds. 1990. *Collective Remembering.* London: Sage.

Miller, James. 1993. *The Passion of Michel Foucault.* New York: Simon and Schuster.

Miller, Karl. 1990. *Authors.* New York: Oxford University Press.

Miller, Nathan. 1992. *Theodore Roosevelt: A Life.* New York: William Morrow and Company, Inc.

Milosz, Czeslaw. 1983. *The Witness of Poetry.* Cambridge, MA.: Harvard University Press.

Moll, Michael. 1988. *Lyrik in einer entmenschlichten Welt: Interpretationsversuche zu deutschsprachigen Gedichten aus nationalsozialistischen Gefängnissen, Ghettos und KZ's.* Frankfurt: R.G. Fischer.

Monaco, James. 1979. *Alain Resnais.* New York: Oxford University Press.

Monk, Ray. 1990. *Ludwig Wittgenstein: The Duty of Genius.* New York: Free Press.

Monk, Samuel H. 1960. *The Sublime.* Ann Arbor: University of Michigan Press.

Montaigne. 1948. *The Complete Works of Montaigne: Essays, Travel Journal, Letters,* trans. Donald M. Frame. Stanford, CA: Stanford University Press.

Montejo, Victor D. 2001. "Truth, Human Rights, and Representation: The Case of Rigoberta Menchú." *The Rigoberta Menchú Controversy,* ed. Arturo Arias. Minneapolis and London: University of Minnesota Press, 372–391.

Mooney, James M. 1928. *The Aboriginal Population of America North of Mexico.* Washington, D.C.: Smithsonian Miscellaneous Collections LXXX, No. 7.

Moore, Richard. 1967. *Historical Dictionary of Guatemala.* Metuchen, NJ: Scarecrow Press.

Morales, Mario Roberto. 2001. "Menchú after Stoll and the Truth Commission." *The Rigoberta Menchú Controversy,* ed. Arturo Arias. Minneapolis and London: University of Minnesota Press, 351–371.

Mordekhai, Thomas Laurence. 1993. *Vessels of Evil: American Slavery and the Holocaust.* Philadelphia: Temple University Press.

Moreiras, Alberto. 1996. "The Aura of Testimonio." *The Real Thing: Testimonial Discourse and Latin America,* ed. Georg M. Gugelberger. Durham, NC: Duke University Press, 192–224.

Morgan, Robin. 1970. *Sisterhood is Powerful: An Anthology of Writings from the Women's Liberation Movement.* New York: Vintage Books.

Morris, David B. 1991. *The Culture of Pain.* Berkeley: University of California Press.

Morrison, Toni, ed. 1992. *Race-ing Justice, En-gendering Power: Essays on Anita Hill, Clarence Thomas, and the Construction of Social Reality.* New York: Pantheon Books.

Mulvey, Laura. 1989. *Visual and Other Pleasures.* Basingstoke, U.K.: Macmillan.

Nakano, Jiro, ed. and trans. 1995. *Outcry from the Inferno: Atomic Bomb Tanka Anthology.* Honolulu: Bamboo Ridge Press.

National Public Radio. 1999. "All Things Considered." (May 10).

Nelson, Cary. 1989. *Repression and Recovery: Modern American Poetry and the Politics of Cultural Memory 1910–1945.* Madison: University of Wisconsin Press.

Neusner, Jacob, ed. 1993. *In the Aftermath of the Holocaust.* New York: Garland.

Ngugi wa Thiong'o. 1986. *Decolonising the Mind. The Politics of Language in African Literature.* London: James Currey; Nairobi: Heinemann Kenya; Portsmouth, NH: Heinemann.

Nichols, Bill. 1991. *Representing Reality: Issues and Concepts in Documentary*. Bloomington and Indianapolis: Indiana University Press.

Nicholson, Asenath. 1850. *Lights and Shades of Ireland in Three Parts*. London: Houlston
and Stoneman.

Nietzsche, Friedrich Wilhelm. 1966. *Beyond Good and Evil: Prelude to a Philosophy of the
Future*, trans. Walter Kaufman. New York.

Nora, Pierre. 1974. "Le retour de l'événement." *Faire de l'histoire: Nouveaux problèmes*,
ed. Jacques Le Goff and Pierre Nora. Paris: Gallimard.

———. 1984. *Les lieux de mémoire*, sous la direction de Pierre Nora. Paris: Gallimard.

———. 1989. "Between Memory and History: Les lieux de mémoire." *Representations*
26 (Spring).

Norris, Margot. 1991. "Military Censorship and the Body Count in the Persian Gulf
War." *Cultural Critique* 19.

———. 2000. *Writing War in the Twentieth Century*. Charlottesville and London: University Press of Virginia.

Novick, Peter. 1995. "Holocaust Memory in America". *The Art of Memory: Holocaust
Memorials in History*, ed. James E. Young. New York: Prestel.

———. 1999a. "Atrocity's Yardstick." *University of Chicago Magazine* (June/August).

———. 1999b. *The Holocaust in American Life*. Boston and New York: Houghton Mifflin.

Nussbaum, Emily. 1996. "Turning Japanese: The Hiroshima Poetry Hoax." *Lingua
Franca* 6:7 (November).

Oda, Makoto. 1990. *The Bomb*, ed. D. H. Whittaker. Tokyo and New York: Kodansha International.

Oe, Kensaburo. 1996. *Hiroshima Notes*, trans. David L. Swain and Toshi Yonezawa. New
York: Grove Press.

Ondaatje, Michael. 1992. *The English Patient*. New York: Random House.

Ong, Walter. 1982. *Orality and Literacy: The Technologizing of the Word*. London:
Methuen.

Ophir, Adi. 1987. "On Sanctifying the Holocaust: An Anti-Theological Treatise." *Tikkun*
2: 1.

Oppen, George. 1972. Interview in *The Contemporary Writer: Interviews with Sixteen
Novelists and Poets*, ed. L. S. Dembo and Cyrena N. Pondrom. Madison: University of Wisconsin Press.

Orwell, George (Eric Blair). 1983. *1984*. New York: New American Library.

Osiel, Mark. 1995. "Ever Again: Legal Remembrance of Administrative Massacre." University of Pennsylvania Law Review 144 (December).

Ostriker, Alicia. 1987. "Dancing at the Devil's Party: Some Notes on Politics and Poetry."
Politics and Poetic Value, ed. Robert Von Hallberg. Chicago and London: University of Chicago Press.

Ōta, Yōko. 1990. *City of Corpses*. In *Hiroshima: Three Witnesses*, ed. and trans. Richard
H. Minear. Princeton: Princeton University Press.

Pagis, Dan. 1981. *Dan Pagis: Points of Departure*, trans. Stephen Mitchell. Philadelphia:
Jewish Publication Society.

Paine, Robert. 1981. "When Saying is Doing." *Politically Speaking: Cross-Cultural Studies of Rhetoric*, ed. Robert Paine. Philadelphia: Institute for the Study of Human Issues.

Patai, Daphne. 2001. "Whose Truth? Iconicity and Accuracy in the World of Testimonial Literature." *The Rigoberta Menchú Controversy*, ed. Arturo Arias. Minneapolis and London: University of Minnesota Press, 270–287.

Patton, Cindy. 1995. "Censoring Race." Journal of Communication (Spring).

Pearse, Andrew. 1975. *The Latin American Peasant*. London: Frank Cass and Company.

Peirce, Charles S. 1966. *Collected Papers of Charles Sanders Peirce*. 2 vols., ed. Charles Hartshorne, Paul Weiss and Arthur W. Burks. Cambridge, MA: Harvard University Press.

Perlman, Michael. 1988. *Imaginal Memory and the Place of Hiroshima*. New York: State University of New York Press.

Perloff, Marjorie. 1987. *The Dance of the Intellect: Studies in the Poetry of the Pound Tradition*. Cambridge, U.K.: Cambridge University Press.

———. 1993. "Empiricism Once More." *Modern Language Quarterly* 54:1 (March), 121–132.

———. 1997. "In Search of the Authentic Other." *Boston Review* XXII:2 (April/May), 26–33.

Pezzetti, Marcello. 2001. *Destinazione Auschwitz*. CD-ROM. Milan: Centro Documentazione Ebraica Contemporanea.

Pick, Daniel. 1993. *War Machine: The Rationalisation of Slaughter in the Modern Age*. New Haven: Yale University Press.

Pierssens, Michel. 1980. *The Power of Babel: A Study of Logophilia*. London: Routledge & Kegan Paul.

Pinsky, Robert. 1987. "Responsibilities of the Poet." *Politics and Poetic Value*, ed. Robert Von Hallberg. Chicago and London: University of Chicago Press.

Plath, Sylvia. 1981. *The Collected Poems*, ed. Ted Hughes. New York: Harper & Row.

Pochoda, Elizabeth. 1996. Review of *Jerzy Kosinski: A Biography*, by James Park Sloan. *The Nation* (March 11).

Pomian, Krzysztof. 1984. *L'orde du temps*. Paris: Gallimard.

Popper, Karl. 1979. *Objective Knowledge: An Evolutionary Approach*, rev. ed. Oxford: Clarendon Press; New York: Oxford University Press.

Powell, Andrew. 2001. "Mombo King." *Expedia Travels* (January/February).

Power, Samantha. 2002. *"A Problem from Hell": America and the Age of Genocide*. New York: Basic Books.

Pratt, Mary Louise. 1992. *Imperial Eyes: Travel Writing and Transculturation*. London and New York: Routledge.

———. 2001. "I, Rigoberta Menchú and the 'Culture Wars.'" *The Rigoberta Menchú Controversy*, ed. Arturo Arias. Minneapolis and London: University of Minnesota Press, 29–48.

Proulx, Annie. 1997. "Dead Stuff." *Aperture* 149 (Fall).

Prunier, Gérard. 1995. *The Rwanda Crisis: History of a Genocide*. New York: Columbia University Press.

Pulsifer, Harold Trowbridge. 1914. "An Explorer Reports." *The Outlook* 107:6 (June 6), 282–284.

Rabaté, Jean-Michel. 1996. *The Ghosts of Modernity*. Gainesville: University Press of Florida.

Rabinowitz, Paula. 1993. "Wreckage on Wreckage: History, Documentary, and the Ruins of Memory." *History and Theory* 32:2.

Radnóti, Miklós. 1966. *Összes Versei És Müfordításai*. Budapest: Magyar Helikon.

———. 1979. *Eclogák*. [Budapest]: Magyar Helikon: Szépirodalmi.

———. 1980. *The Complete Poetry*, ed. and trans. Emery George. Ann Arbor, MI: Ardis.

———. 1992. *Foamy Sky: The Major Poems of Miklós Radnóti*, trans. Zsuzsanna Ozsváth and Frederick Turner. Princeton: Princeton University Press.

———. 1993. "Seventh Eclogue," trans. Emery George. *Against Forgetting: Twentieth-Century Poetry of Witness*, ed. Carolyn Forché. New York and London: W. W. Norton.

———. 1994. "Seventh Eclogue," trans. Steven Polgar, Stephen Berg, and S. J. Marks. *Truth and Lamentation: Stories and Poems on the Holocaust*, ed. Milton Teichman and Sharon Leder. Urbana and Chicago: University of Illinois Press.

———. 1996. "Seventh Eclogue," trans. Clayton Eshleman and Gyula Kodolányi. *Poems for the Millennium*, ed. Jerome Rothenberg and Pierre Joris. Berkeley, Los Angeles, London: University of California Press.

Rajchman, John. 1983. "Foucault, or the Ends of Modernism." OCTOBER 24 (Spring) 37–62.

Rankin, Nicholas. 1997. "Bombs, What bombs?" *Times Literary Supplement* (May 2), 7–8.

Rappaport, Roy. 1979. "The Obvious Aspects of Ritual." *Ecology, Meaning, and Religion*. Richmond, VA: North Atlantic Books.

Rauschning, Hermann. 1940. *The Voice of Destruction*. New York: G. P. Putnam's Sons.

Reiter, Andrea. 2000. *Narrating the Holocaust*, trans. Patrick Camiller. London and New York: Continuum.

Rhees, Rush. 1984. *Recollections of Wittgenstein*. Oxford: Oxford University Press.

Rich, Adrienne. 1984. *The Fact of a Doorframe*. New York: Norton.

———. 1986a. *Blood, Bread and Poetry: Selected Prose 1979–1985*. New York: Norton.

———. 1986b. *Your Native Land, Your Life: Poems*. New York: Norton.

Richardson, Samuel. 1943. *Claríssa*. Shakespeare Head Press ed. Oxford: Blackwell.

Richer, Jean, ed. 1975. *Paul Verlaine*. Paris: Éditions Pierre Seghers.

Ricoeur, Paul. 1984, 1985, 1988. *Time and Narrative*. Vols 1 & 2. Trans. Kathleen McLaughlin and David Pellauer, Vol. 3, trans. Kathleen Blamey and David Pellauer. Chicago: University of Chicago Press.

———. 1995. "Evil, a Challenge to Philosophy and Theology." *Figuring the Sacred: Religion, Narrative and Imagination*. Indianapolis: Fortress Press.

Ringelblum, Emmanuel. 1959. *Notes from the Warsaw Ghetto*. New York: McGraw Hill.

Robertson, George, Melinda Mash, Lisa Tickner, Jon Bird, Barry Curtis and Tim Putnam, eds. 1994. *Travellers' Tales: Narratives of Home and Displacement*. London and New York: Routledge.

Rodríguez, Ileana. 2001. "Between Silence and Lies: Rigoberta Va." The Rigoberta Menchú Controversy, ed. Arturo Arias. Minneapolis and London: University of Minnesota Press, 332–350.

Rohter, Larry. 1998. "Tarnished Laureate." *The Rigoberta Menchú Controversy*, ed. Arturo Arias. Minneapolis and London: University of Minnesota Press, 58–65.

Ronell, Avital. 1994. *Finitude's Score: Essays for the End of the Millennium*. Lincoln: University of Nebraska Press.

Roosevelt, Theodore. 1913a. "An Ancient Brazilian City." *The Outlook* 105:15 (December 13), 800-802.

———. 1913b. "Rio de Janeiro." *The Outlook* 105:16 (December 20), 837–841.

———. 1914. "Glimpse of Paraguay." *The Outlook* 107:6 (June 6), 306–309.

———. 1919. *Through the Brazilian Wilderness*. [1914]. New York: Scribner and Sons. First published in eight monthly installments in *Scribner's Magazine* April-November.

Rose, Gillian. 1992. *The Broken Middle: Out of Our Ancient Society*. Cambridge, MA: Blackwell.

———. 1993. "Walter Benjamin: Out of the Sources of Modern Judaism." *Judaism and Modernity: Philosophical Essays*. Oxford: Blackwell.

———. 1994. *Judaism and Modernity: Philosophical Essays*. Oxford: Blackwell.

———. 1995. *Love's Work*. London: Chato & Windus.

———. 1996. "Beginnings of the day: Fascism and representation." *Mourning Becomes the Law*. Cambridge: Cambridge University Press.

Rose, Jacqueline. 1991. *The Haunting of Sylvia Plath*. Cambridge, MA: Harvard University Press.

Rosenbaum, Alan S. 1996. *Is the Holocaust Unique? Perspectives on Comparative Genocide*. Boulder City, CO: Westview Press/HarperCollins.

Rosenblatt, Roger. 1995. "A Nation of Fained Hearts," in *Special Report: The Simpson Verdict, Time* (October 16), 40–45.

Rosenfeld, Alvin H. 1980. *A Double Dying: Reflections on Holocaust Literature*. Bloomington: Indiana University Press.

———. 1997a. "Americanization of the Holocaust. *Commentary* (June).

———, ed. 1997b. *Thinking About the Holocaust: After Half a Century*. Bloomington: Indiana University Press.

Rossellini, Roberto. 1992. "Ten Years of Cinema." *My Method: Writings and Interviews*, ed. Adriano Aprà. Trans. Annapaola Cancogni. New York: Marsilio Publishers.

Rothenberg, Jerome and Pierre Joris. 1995. *Poems for the Millennium*. Vol. 1. Berkeley, Los Angeles, London: University of California Press.

Rowbotham, Sheila. 1983. *Dreams and Dilemmas*. London: Virago.

Rubenstein, Richard L. 1983. *The Age of Triage*. Boston: Beacon Press.

Ryback, Timothy W. 2000. *The Last Survivor: In Search of Martin Zaidenstadt*. London: Picador.

Said, Edward. 1978. *Orientalism*. New York: Random House.

Saíz, Próspero. 1989. "Deconstruction and the Lyric." *From Ode to Anthem: Problems of*

Lyric Poetry, ed. Reinhold Grimm and Jost Hermand. Madison: University of Wisconsin Press.

Santi, Enrico M. 1992. "Latinamericanism and Restitution." *Latin American Literary Review.* 20:40, 88–96.

Sarafian, Ara, ed. 1995. *United States Official Documents on the Armenian Genocide.* 2 vols. Watertown, MA.: *Armenian Review.*

Scarry, Elaine. 1985. *The Body in Pain: The Making and Unmaking of the World.* New York: Oxford University Press.

———. 2000. "On Evil, Pain, and Beauty: A Conversation with Elaine Scarry." *Hedgehog Review* 2:2 (Summer) 78–87.

Schacter, Daniel. 1996. *Searching for Memory: The Brain, the Mind, and the Past.* New York: Basic Books.

Scheper-Hughes, Nancy. 1992. *Death Without Weeping: The Violence of Everyday Life in Brazil.* Berkeley: University of California Press.

———. 1995. "The Primacy of the Ethical: Propositions for a Militant Anthropology." *Current Anthropology* 36 (June).

Schneir, Miriam. 1994. *Feminism in Our Time: The Essential Writings, World War II to the Present.* New York: Vintage Books.

Schudson, Michael. 1992. *Watergate in American Memory: How We Remember, Forget, and Reconstruct the Past.* New York: Basic Books.

Schull, William J. 1995. *Effects of Atomic Radiation: A Half-Century of Studies from Hiroshima and Nagasaki.* New York: Wiley-Liss.

Schwenger, Peter. 2000. "Corpsing the Image." *Critical Inquiry* 26 (Spring).

Scott, Joan W. 1991. "The Evidence of Experience." *Critical Inquiry* 17:4 (Summer).

Segev, Tom. 1994. *The Seventh Million. The Israelis and the Holocaust.* New York: Hill and Wang.

Selden, Koko and Mark Selden, eds. 1989. *The Atomic Bomb: Voices from Hiroshima and Nagasaki.* Armonk, NY: M. E. Sharpe.

Shay, Jonathan. 1995. *Achilles in Vietnam: Combat Trauma and the Undoing of Character.* New York: Simon & Schuster.

Shelley, Percy Bysshe. 1977. *Shelley's Poetry and Prose*, ed Donald R. Reiman and Sharon B. Powers. New York: Norton.

Sherwin, Martin J. 1975. *A World Destroyed: The Atomic Bomb and the Grand Alliance.* New York: Alfred A. Knopf.

Simon, Jean-Marie. 1987. *Guatemala: Eternal Spring, Eternal Tyranny.* New York: Norton.

Sklodowska, Elzbieta. 2001. "The Poetics of Remembering, the Politics of Forgetting: Rereading *I, Rigoberta Menchú.*" *The Rigoberta Menchú Controversy,* ed. Arturo Arias. Minneapolis and London: University of Minnesota Press, 251–269.

Smith, Adam. 1976. *The Theory of Moral Sentiments.* Oxford: Oxford University Press.

Snyder, Jill, ed. 1994. *Impossible Evidence: Contemporary Artists View the Holocaust.* Reading, PA: Freedman Gallery/Albright College.

Sobchack, Vivian. 1992. *The Address of the Eye: A Phenomenology of Film Experience.* Princeton: Princeton University Press.

————. 1999. "Toward a Phenomenology of Nonfictional Film Experience." *Collecting Visible Evidence*, ed. Jane M. Gaines and Michael Renov. Minneapolis: University of Minnesota Press.

Solomon, J. Fisher. 1988. *Discourse and Reference in the Nuclear Age*. Norman and London: University of Oklahoma Press.

Sommer, Doris. 2001. "Las Casas's Lies and Other Language Games." *The Rigoberta Menchú Controversy*, ed. Arturo Arias. Minneapolis and London: University of Minnesota Press, 237–251.

Sontag, Susan. 1977. *On Photography*. New York: Farrar, Strauss and Giroux.

————. 1978. *Against Interpretation and Other Essays*. New York: Octagon Books.

Soper, Kate. 1983. "Contemplating a Nuclear Future." *Over Our Dead Bodies: Women Against the Bomb*. London: Virago Press.

Spiegelman, Art. 1986. *Maus I, A Survivor's Tale, Part I: My Father Bleeds History*. New York: Pantheon Books.

————. 1991. *Maus II: A Survivor's Tale: And Here My Troubles Began*. New York: Pantheon Books.

————. 1994. *The Complete Maus*. CD-ROM. New York: the Voyager Company.

————. 1996. "Mein Kampf, My Struggle." *New York Times Magazine*, May 11: 36–37.

Spivak, Gayatri. 1997. "In a Word: Interview" with Ellen Rooney. *The Second Wave: A Reader in Feminist Theory*, ed. Linda Nicholson. New York and London: Routledge.

Stafford, Barbara Maria. 1991. *Body Criticism: Imaging the Unseen in Enlightenment Art and Medicine*. Cambridge, MA and London: MIT Press.

Stannard, David E. 1992. *American Holocaust: Columbus and the Conquest of the New World*. New York: Oxford University Press.

Staub, Ervin. 1989. *The Roots of Evil: The Origins of Genocide and Other Group Violence*. Cambridge: Cambridge University Press.

Stearn, Walter and Allen E. Stearn. 1945. *The Effects of Smallpox on the Destiny of the Amerindian*. Boston: Bruce Humphries.

Stein, Eric. 1986. "History Against Free Speech: The New German Law Against the 'Auschwitz'—and Other—'Lies.' " *Michigan Law Review* 85.

Stendhal [Marie-Henri Beyle]. 1962. *The Charterhouse of Parma*, trans. C. K. Scott-Moncrieff. New York: New American Library.

Stephanson, Anders. 1988. "Regarding Postmodernism—A Conversation with Fredric Jameson." *Universal Abandon? The Politics of Postmodernism*, ed. Andrew Ross. Minneapolis: University of Minneapolis Press.

Stewart, Susan. 1984. *On Longing: Narratives of the Miniature, the Gigantic, the Souvenir, the Collection*. Baltimore: Johns Hopkins University Press.

Stoll, David. 1998. "Life Story as Mythopoesis." *Anthropology Newsletter* 39:4, 9–11.

————. 1999. *Rigoberta Menchú and the Story of All Poor Guatemalans*. Boulder, CO: Westview.

————. 2001. "The Battle of Rigoberta." *The Rigoberta Menchú Controversy*, ed. Arturo Arias. Minneapolis and London: University of Minnesota Press, 392–410.

Sturken, Marita. 1997. *Tangled Memories: The Vietnam War, the AIDS Epidemic, and the Politics of Remembering*. Berkeley: University of California Press.

Suid, Lawrence H. 1978. *Guts and Glory*. Reading, MA: Addison-Wesley.

Sukenick, Ron. 1968. *Up*. New York: Dial.

Sutzkever, Abraham. 1981. *Burnt Pearls: Ghetto Poems of Abraham Sutzkever*, trans. Seymour Mayne. Oakville, Ontario: Mosaic Press.

Swanson, Guy E. 1965. "On Explanations of Social Interaction." *Sociometry* XXVIII.

Szymborska, Wislawa. 1995. *View with a Grain of Sand: Selected Poems*, trans. Stanislaw Barańczak and Clare Cavanagh. New York: Harvest/Harcourt Brace.

Tal, Kali. 1996. *Worlds of Hurt: Reading the Literatures of Trauma*. New York: Cambridge University Press.

Tatum, James. 1996. "Memorials of the America War in Vietnam." *Critical Inquiry* 22:4 (Summer), 634–678.

Taylor, Christopher C. 1999. *Sacrifice as Terror: The Rwandan Genocide of 1994*. New York: Berg.

Teichman, Milton and Sharon Leder. 1994. *Truth and Lamentation: Stories and Poems on the Holocaust*. Urbana and Chicago: University of Illinois Press.

Thomas, E. David, ed. 1991. *As Seen by Both Sides: American and Vietnamese Artists Look at the War*. Boston: Boston University Art Gallery.

Thompson, E. P. 1966. *The Making of the English Working Class*. New York: Random House.

———. 1982. "Notes on Extremism, the Last Phase of Civilization." *Zero Option*. London: Merlin Press.

Thornton, Russell. 1987. *American Indian Holocaust and Survival: A Population History Since 1492*. Norman: Oklahoma University Press.

Thucydides. 1962. *The Peloponnesian War*, trans. Rex Warner. London: Cassell and Company, Ltd.

Todorov, Tzvetan. 1984. *The Conquest of America: The Question of the Other*, trans. Richard Howard. New York: Harper and Row.

Tóibín, Colm. 1998. "Erasures." *London Review of Books* (July 30), 17–23.

Townsend, Chris. 1999. *Vile Bodies: Photography and the Crisis of Looking*. New York: Prestel-Verlag.

Transactions of the Central Relief Committee of the Society of Friends During the Famine in Ireland in 1846 and 1847. Dublin: 1852.

Treat, John Whittier. 1995. *Writing Ground Zero: Japanese Literature and the Atomic Bomb*. Chicago: University of Chicago Press.

Troncale, Joseph. 1992. "The War and Kozintsev's Films *Hamlet* and *King Lear*." *The Red Screen: Politics, Society, Art in Soviet Cinema*, ed. Anna Lawton. London: Routledge.

Tylor, Edward B. 1958. *Primitive Culture*. New York: Harper.

Ugresic, Dubravka. 1996. "The Confiscation of Memory." *New Left Review* 218.

United States Strategic Bombing Survey. 1946. *The Effects of Atomic Bombs on Hiroshima and Nagasaki*. Washington, D.C.: United States Government Printing Office.

United States. U.S. Department of State. 1980. *Country Reports on Human Rights Practices*. Washington D.C.: State Department.

Valesio, Paolo. 1980. *Novantiqua: Rhetorics as a Contemporary Theory*. Bloomington: University of Indiana Press.

Vendler, Helen. 1988. *The Music of What Happens: Poems, Poets, Critics*. Cambridge, MA: Harvard University Press.

———. 1995a. "A Nobel for the North." *The New Yorker* (October 23), 84–89.

———. 1995b. *The Breaking of Style: Hopkins, Heaney, Graham*. Cambridge, MA: Harvard University Press.

Venuti, Lawrence. 1992. Introduction. *Rethinking Translation: Discourse, Subjectivity, Ideology*, ed. Lawrence Venuti. New York: Routledge.

Verlaine, Paul. 1975. *Paul Verlaine*, ed. Jean Richer. Paris: Éditions Pierre Seghers.

Vidal-Naquet, Pierre. 1987. *Les assassins de la mémoire: Un Eichmann de papier et autres essais sur le révisionisme*. Paris: Éditions La Découverte.

———. 1992. *Assassins of Memory: Essays on the Denial of the Holocaust*, trans. Jeffrey Mehlman. New York: Columbia University Press.

Virgil. 1987. *The Aeneid of Virgil*, trans. Rolfe Humphries. New York: Macmillan.

Vogler, Thomas A. 1986. "Romanticism and Literary Periods: The Future of the Past." *New German Critique*, No. 38 (Spring/Summer).

———. 1989. "Rhetoric and Imagination." *Stanford Literature Review*, 6:1 (Spring), special issue on "History and Memory in European Romanticism," ed. Carolyn Springer.

———. 1994. "Shaking the Memory." Introduction to catalogue for *The Packwood Diaries: Artists' Books and Graphic Works*. Portland, OR: Comus Gallery.

———. 1997. "The Rhetoric of Suffering." *Religion and Literature* 29:1 (Spring).

Volkogonov, Dmitri. 1996. *Trotsky: The Eternal Revolutionary*, trans. Harold Shukman. New York: The Free Press.

Von Hallberg, Robert, ed. 1987. *Politics and Poetic Value*. Chicago and London: University of Chicago Press.

Waldrop, Rosmarie. 1990. "Alarms & Excursions." *The Politics of Poetic Form: Poetry and Public Policy*, ed. Charles Bernstein. New York: Roof, 45–72.

Walliman, Isidor and Michael N. Doblowski, eds. 1987. *Genocide and the Modern Age*. New York: Greenwood Press.

Warren, Kay B. 2001. "Telling Truths: Taking David Stoll and the Rigoberta Menchú Exposé Seriously." *The Rigoberta Menchú Controversy*, ed. Arturo Arias. Minneapolis and London: University of Minnesota Press, 198–218.

Weber, Ronald. 1980. *The Literature of Fact: Literary Nonfiction in American Writing*. Athens: Ohio University Press.

Weinberger, Eliot. 1996. "Can I Get a Witness?" *Village Voice Literary Supplement* (July), 8.

Weiskel, Thomas. 1976. *The Romantic Sublime: Studies in the Structure and Psychology of Transcendence*. Baltimore: Johns Hopkins University Press.

Wheatcroft, Geoffrey. 2000. "Horrors Beyond Tragedy." *Times Literary Supplement* (June 9), 9–10.

White, Hayden. 1978. "The Forms of Wildness: Archaeology of an Idea." *Tropics of Discourse: Essays in Cultural Criticism*. Baltimore: Johns Hopkins University Press.

———. 1999. *Figural Realism: Studies in the Mimesis Effect.* Baltimore & London: Johns Hopkins University Press.

Whitman, Bill. 2000. "Desert Safari." *National Geographic Traveler* (September).

Wiesel, Elie. 1978. "Trivializing the Holocaust." *New York Times* (April 16).

———. 1989. "Forward." Annette Insdorf. *Indelible Shadows: Film and the Holocaust.* 2nd ed. Cambridge: Cambridge University Press.

———. 1997. "The Holocaust as a Literary Inspiration." *Dimensions of the Holocaust.* Evanston, IL: Northwestern University Press.

———. 2000. *Night.* 2d ed., trans. Stella Rodway. New York: Bantom.

Wiesel, Elie and Philippe-Michaël de Saint-Cheron. 1990. *Evil and Exile,* trans. Jon Rothschild. Notre Dame, IN: University of Notre Dame Press.

Wilkomirski, Binjamin. 1995. *Bruchstücke.* Frankfurt: Suhrkamp Verlag.

———. 1996. *Fragments.* New York: Schocken Books.

Williams, Raymond. 1976. *Keywords: A Vocabulary of Culture and Society.* New York: Oxford University Press.

———. 1980. "The Writer: Commitment and Alignment." *Marxism Today* 24 (June), 22–25.

———. 1983. *The Year 2000.* New York: Pantheon Books.

Wilshire, Bruce. 1982. *Role Playing and Identity: The Limits of Theatre as Metaphor.* Bloomington: Indiana University Press.

Winslow, Philip C. 1998. *Sowing the Dragon's Teeth: Land Mines and the Global Legacy of War.* Boston: Beacon.

Witek, Joseph. 1989. "History and Talking Animals: Art Spiegelman's *Maus.*" *Comic Books as History.* Mississippi: University of Mississippi Press.

Wordsworth, William. 1966. *Literary Criticism of William Wordsworth,* ed. Paul M. Zall. Lincoln: University of Nebraska Press.

———. 1979. *The Prelude: 1799, 1805, 1850,* ed. Jonathan Wordsworth, M. H. Abrams, Stephen Gill. New York and London: Norton.

Wyschogrod, Edith. 1998. *An Ethics of Remembering: History, Heterology, and the Nameless Other.* Chicago and London: University of Chicago Press.

Yasusada, Araki. 1997. *Doubled Flowering: From the Notebooks of Araki Yasusada,* ed. and trans. Tosa Motokiyu, Ojiu Norinaga, and Okura Kyojin. New York: Roof.

Yerushalmi, Yosef Hayiim. 1986. *Zakhor: Jewish History and Jewish Memory.* Seattle: University of Washington Press.

Yoneyama, Lisa. 1999. *Hiroshima Traces: Time, Space, and the Dialectics of Memory.* Berkeley, Los Angeles, London: University of California Press.

Young, Allan. 1995. *The Harmony of Illusions: Inventing Post-Traumatic Stress Disorder.* Princeton: Princeton University Press.

Young, James E. 1987. "Interpreting Literary Testimony: A Preface to Rereading Holocaust Diaries and Memoirs." *New Literary History* 18:2 (Winter).

———. 1990. *Writing and Rewriting the Holocaust. Narrative and the Consequences of Interpretation.* Bloomington: Indiana University Press.

———. 1993. *The Texture of Memory: Holocaust Memorials and Meaning.* New Haven: Yale University Press.

————, ed. 1994. *The Art of Memory. Holocaust Memorials in History*. New York: Prestel.

————. 1997a. "Between History and Memory: The Uncanny Voices of Historian and Survivor." *History and Memory* 9:1/2. (Fall), 47–58.

————. 1997b. "Toward a Received History of the Holocaust." *History and Theory* 36:4 (December).

————. 1998. "The Holocaust as Vicarious Past: Art Spiegelman's *Maus* and the After-images of History." *Critical Inquiry* 24.3 (Spring).

————. 1999. "America's Holocaust: Memory and the Politics of Identity." *The Americanization of the Holocaust*, ed. Hilene Flanzbaum. Baltimore and London: Johns Hopkins University Press, 68–82.

————. 2000. *At Memory's Edge: After-Images of the Holocaust in Contemporary Art and Architecture*. New Haven: Yale University Press.

Yúdice, George. 1996. "*Testimonio* and Postmodernism." *The Real Thing: Testimonial Discourse and Latin America*, ed. Georg M. Gugelberger. Durham, NC: Duke University Press, 42–57.

Zelizer, Barbie. 1998. *Remembering to Forget: Holocaust Memory Through The Camera's Eye*. Chicago and London: University of Chicago Press.

Zimmerman, Marc. 1996. "Testimonio in Guatemala: Payeras, Rigoberta, and Beyond." *The Real Thing: Testimonial Discourse and Latin America*, ed. Georg M. Gugelberger. Durham, NC: Duke University Press, 101–129.

Zulaika, Joseba. 1988. *Basque Violence: Metaphor and Sacrament*. Reno: University of Nevada Press.

————. 1989. *Chivos y soldados: la mili como ritual de inciación*. San Sebastián: Baroja.

————. 1996. "The Anthropologist as Terrorist." *Fieldwork under Fire: Contemporary Studies of Violence and Survival*, ed. Carolyn Nordstrom, Antonius C.G.M. Robben. Berkeley: University of California Press.

Zulaika, Joseba and William A. Douglass. 1996. *Terror and Taboo: The Follies, Fables, and Faces of Terrorism*. New York: Routledge.

Index

Moore, Richard, 65
Moreiras, Alberto, 58, 61, 82, 84, 85, 86,
    297(n), 303(n)
Morgan, Robin, 160
Morrison, Toni, 313(n)
Morrow, Bradford, 174
Moses (Book of Deuteronomy), 43
Mulvey, Laura, 139
Mundé, 117, 120
*Murder One,*138, 139
Musée de l'Homme, 111, 307(n)
Muselmann, 21
Museum of Jewish Heritage, 21–22, 35,
    40, 49, 294(n)
Museum of Tolerance (Beit Hashoah),
    35, 49
Musil, Robert, 279

Nabokov, Vladimir, 173
Nagasaki, 6, 9, 22, 30, 32, 40, 47, 50, 53,
    204, 287(n), 290(n), 292(n)
Nakano, Jiro, 180, 183, 295(n)
Nambikwara (Nhambiquara), 116, 120,
    123, 126, 128, 308–309(n)
National Air and Space Museum, 50
National Gallery, 99
National Geographic Society, 122
Nationalists (Spanish Civil War), 293(n)
National Museum of American Art, 53
National Underground Railroad Freedom
    Center, 296(n)
The Navigator: A Time Travel Adventure
    (Ward), 228–29
Nazi Darwinism, 211–12
Nazi genocide, 184, 189, 190, 193, 194,
    195, 196, 198, 200, 201, 202, 203,
    204, 205, 291(n), 320(n); *see also*
    Holocaust
Nazi Germany and the Jews (Friedlander),
    275, 278
Negative Dialectics (Adorno), 251
Nelson, Cary, 157, 179, 314(n)
Neuromancer Trilogy (Gibson), 8–9
Neusner, Jacob, 24
New Criticism, 157
New York Police Department, 76
New York Times, 75, 76, 77, 156, 293(n)

Ngugi wa Thiong'o,
Nicaragua, 65, 78
Nicholson, Asenath, 31–32
Nietzsche, Friedrich Wilhelm, 37, 90, 98,
    100, 175, 249
Night and Fog (Nuit et Brouillard,
    Resnais*)*, 233, 244
Nijuyo-jikan no Joji, 152; *see also Hi-*
    roshima Mon Amour
9/11 (September 11), 9, 36, 48, 202,
    314(n)
1984, 16, 19, 43
1968, 249, 250
Niven, David, 33
Nobel Peace Prize, 87
Nobel Prize for Literature, 51
Nora, Pierre, 5–6, 17, 239
Norris, Margot, 296(n)
"North American Time" (Rich), 154–55,
    169–71
Novick, Peter, 18, 24, 29–30, 34, 287(n),
    294(n), 316(n)
Nuclear theory, 295(n)
Nullification in O. J. Simpson Criminal
    Trial, 147–48
Nussbaum, Emily, 174
N-word, 136

Odyssey (Homer), 203
Oe, Kensaburo, 181, 295(n), 296(n)
O. J. Simpson Criminal Trial; *see The*
    People of California vs., Orenthal
    James Simpson
Omdurman, the battle of, 296
Ondaatje, Michael, *The English Patient*, 50
Orientalism, 3, 59, 296(n), 298(n)
Orwell, George, 16, 19, 43
Osiel, Mark, 17
Ostriker, Alicia, 179
Ōta, Yōko, 40–41
Outcry from the Inferno (Nakano),
    180–81, 183
The Outlook, 114, 119, 120, 122, 307(n),
    308(n)
Oxford Dictionary of English Etymology,
    245
Oxford English Dictionary, 154

About the Cover Image

The image that appears on the cover is Paul Klee's "Angelus Novus," a 1920 watercolor now in the Israel Museum, Jerusalem. It belonged to Walter Benjamin, who identified it as "the Angel of History" in his *Theses on the Philosophy of History*, IX. His memorable description there makes it also an apt image of the Angel of Witness:

"There is a Klee painting named 'Angelus Novus.' It shows an angel looking as though he is about to move away from something he is fixedly contemplating. His eyes are staring, his mouth is open, his wings are spread. This is how one pictures the Angel of History. His face is turned toward the past. Where a chain of events appears to us, *he* sees one single catastrophe which keeps piling wreckage and hurls it in front of his feet. He would like to stay, to awaken the dead and make whole what has been smashed. But a storm is blowing in from Paradise that has got caught in his wings with such a violence that he can no longer close them. The storm irresistibly propels him into the future, to which his back is turned, while the pile of debris before him grows skyward. What we call progress is *this* storm."